Reading the New Testament

Reading the New Testament

MARK KEOWN

MORPHE PUBLISHERS
AUCKLAND

Copyright © 2022 Mark J. Keown. All rights reserved. Except for brief quotations in critical publications and reviews, no part of this book may be reduced in any manner without prior permission from the publisher. Write: Permissions, Morphe Publishers, 58 Schnapper Rock Road, Schnapper Rock, Auckland 0632, New Zealand. All translations the authors unless specified.

Cover Image, James Kovin: https://unsplash.com/photos/ITiJrBI3XnE

Contents

Acknowledgments	1
Abbreviations	2
Introduction	v

Part I. Main Body

1.	The Formation, Content, and Structure of the New Testament	7
2.	Principles of New Testament Study	38
3.	Setting, Then and Now, and the Synoptic Problem	100
4.	The Synoptic Gospels—Mark and Matthew	118
5.	Luke and Synoptic Gospel Themes	127
6.	More Synoptic Gospel Themes	160
7.	John's Gospel	189
8.	The Acts of the Apostles	200
9.	Paul's Life, Mission, and Letters	216
10.	Paul's Early Letters	242
11.	The Prison Letters of Paul	309
12.	Hebrews	398
13.	The General or Catholic Epistles	434
14.	Revelation	501
	Works Referenced	519

I want to acknowledge God, Father, Son, and Spirit for his constant goodness and for calling me to this work. I thank Laidlaw College and its people for their support and encouragement over the years. I also thank the enthusiastic students who continue to come to my classes, challenging me with great questions. Thanks also to Jeremy Tattersall, who read through the material and made many helpful suggestions. I also thank my phenomenal wife and co-worker, the Rev Dr Emma Keown, for her love and support in all I do. I must also mention my lovely daughters, Gracie, Annie, Esther, and my recently deceased mum, Nolarae–I love you all. I am truly blessed.

Abbreviations

1 Cor	1 Corinthians
1 En.	1 Enoch
1 Kgs	1 Kings
1QM	War Scroll (DSS)
1 Pet	1 Peter
1 Sam	1 Samuel
1 Thess	1 Thessalonians
1 Tim	1 Timothy
2 Cor	2 Corinthians
2 En.	2 Enoch
2 Kgs	2 Kings
2 Macc	2 Maccabees
2 Pet	2 Peter
2 Sam	2 Samuel
2 Thess	2 Thessalonians
2 Tim	2 Timothy
Ant.	Josephus, *Antiquities of the Jews*
AD	anno domini ("in the year of our Lord")
Asc. Isa.	Ascension of Isaiah
AYBD	*The Anchor Yale Bible Dictionary.*
BC	Before Christ
1 Sanh.	Babylonian Talmud Sanhedrin
BDAG	*A Greek-English Lexicon of the New Testament and Other Early Christian Literature.*
BrillDag	*The Brill Dictionary of Ancient Greek.*
CD	Damascus Document (DSS)
Dan	Daniel
DPL	*Dictionary of Paul and His Letters.*
DSS	Dead Sea Scrolls
Eph	Ephesians
Exod	Exodus

Ezek	Ezekiel
Gen	Genesis
Gal	Galatians
Deut	Deuteronomy
DNTB	Dictionary of New Testament Background.
DJG	Dictionary of New Testament Background.
Heb	Hebrews
Hos	Hosea
Isa	Isaiah
Jas	James
Jer	Jeremiah
J.W.	Josephus, The Wars of the Jews
Jub.	Jubilees
LBD	The Lexham Bible Dictionary.
LEB	Lexham English Bible
Lev	Leviticus
Life	Josephus, The Life of Flavius Josephus
LXX	The Septuagint
Matt	The Gospel of Matthew
mss	Manuscripts
Neh	Nehemiah
NET	New English Translation
NT	New Testament
Num	Numbers
NZRFU	New Zealand Rugby Football Union
PDBS	Pocket Dictionary of Biblical Studies.
PDSNT	Pocket Dictionary for the Study of New Testament Greek.
Phil	Philippians
Phlm	Philemon
Prov	Proverbs
Ps	Psalm (s)
Pss. Sol.	Psalms of Solomon
OT	Old Testament
Q	Quelle ("source")
Rev	Revelation

Rom	Romans
RWC	Rugby World Cup
s.a.	see also
Sib. Or.	Sibylline Oracles
Tit	Titus
T, Reu.	Testament of Reuben
Zech	Zechariah
Zeph	Zephaniah

Introduction

A few years ago, I authored a book designed as a basic introduction to the New Testament for students at Laidlaw College entering biblical study. This work is a revised version of the book *The New Testament A Taster* (Morphe, 2020), rebranded as *Reading the New Testament*. The material is rebranded, reorganized, revised, and supplemented to fit with the revised course I now teach at Laidlaw on the NT. I have also added indices to aid students in finding Scripture references and themes.

For fuller material on the same subjects, please consult my three-volume work, *Discovering the New Testament* (Lexham, 2018-22), which gives much more detail. This material is introductory but ensures students can consider the underlying ideas that inform contemporary biblical scholarship. Each chapter has suggested biblical passages and questions for consideration.

1. The Formation, Content, and Structure of the New Testament

Part 1: The Formation of the New Testament

Introduction

The first Scriptures used by early Christians were the Hebrew Scriptures (Old Testament [OT]) and the LXX or Septuagint—a Greek translation of the Hebrew from several hundred years before Christ.[1] These include the Old Testament and Apocrypha, included today in some Bibles.[2] The influence of OT writings, both in Hebrew and Greek, is seen in the many citations, allusions, and echoes of the OT Scriptures through the NT. Over time, the teachings of Christ and the apostles were shared orally and eventually written down for transmission. Then, over time, the individual documents were

---

1. This is a rewrite of my earlier work, Mark J. Keown, *Discovering the New Testament: An Introduction to Its Background, Theology, and Themes: The Gospels & Acts*, Vol. I (Bellingham, WA: Lexham Press, 2018), 1:5–9.
2. E.g., my Logos NRSV includes Tobit, Judith, Greek Esther, Wisdom of Solomon, Sirach, Baruch, Letter of Jeremiah, Azariah and the Three Jews, Susanna, Bel and the Dragon, 1–4 Maccabees, 1 and 2 Esdras, the Prayer of Manasseh, and Psalm 151.

formed into collections near or after the death of luminaries like Peter, Paul, and John. Eventually, after debate over what should be included, the NT was formed into the twenty-seven-volume work we have today. What follows is a summary of this process.

Oral and Fragmented Written Transmission

Some scholars date James as early as AD 46–48. However, most scholars see James as a later document, agreeing that Paul's letters are the first writings of the NT written between AD 48 and 66 (there are disagreements over the dating of these documents, however). Some scholars consider Galatians the first (AD 48), while others see 1 Thessalonians as Paul's first letter (AD 50). Mark is generally agreed to be the first Gospel. It was written in AD 55–75, probably in the mid to late 60s. Assuming Jesus died in AD 30 or 33, the first Gospel was written twenty to thirty-five years after his resurrection. Matthew and Luke based their Gospels on Mark, and the material common to these two later Gospels indicates the existence of another set of the teaching of Jesus (Q).

Before the writing down of the traditions, the stories about Jesus and the early church were passed on orally. There may have been some earlier documents in Aramaic or Greek; however, this is difficult to prove. One possibility is that there existed an earlier Aramaic version of Mark, evidenced by the Aramaic words and phrases that remain in the Gospel (e.g., Mark 7:34; 14:36; 15:34). The document Q, if it existed, may also have been a collection of early Aramaic or Greek snippets of the Jesus tradition.

Recognizing this period of oral and fragmented written transmission has caused some scholars to question the authenticity of the accounts. Form Critics have argued that the stories grew from some small event and were supplemented and mythologized in the early church (Christian Chinese Whispers).[3] However, other studies have shown that oral and fragmented transmission does not mean the accounts are historically unreliable. As a rabbinic teacher, Jesus undoubtedly taught the same things across Israel and expected his followers to memorize them and pass them on. Cultures in the ANE that transmit their traditions orally do so with remarkable accuracy. Richard Bauckham has shown that eyewitnesses were essential sources for the Gospels, and the Gospels and Acts read as eyewitness accounts. We can be confident of the accurate transmission of their eyewitness testimony.[4]

The Writing of the Original Documents

The stories of Jesus were gathered together by the Gospel writers and formed into the Gospel we have. Each Gospel is shaped in a particular way due to the context in which they were written. Acts is the second part of Luke's Gospel, filling out the story of the expansion of the Christian movement to Rome. These Gospels were collections of the teachings about Jesus attributed to key Apostles: Peter (Mark's Gospel), Matthew, Paul (Luke-Acts), and John. The NT letters were part of ongoing conversations between the writer and recipients, e.g., Paul and the Philippians. They are snapshots

---

3. See later in Chapter Three on Form Criticism.
4. See R. J. Bauckham, *Jesus and the Eyewitnesses. The Gospels as Eyewitness Testimony* (Grand Rapids: Eerdmans, 2006). See also Luke 1:2, where we see that Luke drew on eyewitness accounts for his Gospel. The "we passages" in Acts indicate he was also a traveling companion of Paul. These also indicate Luke was also with Paul in Jerusalem, and several NT letters place Luke and Mark in Rome with Paul and Mark with Peter (Col 4:10, 14; Phlm 24; 1 Pet 5:13).

in which the writer responds to particular situations and concerns. They are all to be read in context, and insights from them applied carefully to today's world.

The Grouping of the Documents

The documents were then gathered together, and this likely began early. The four Gospels became a collection in the mid-second century. The development of heretical movements such as Marcionism, Gnosticism, and false Gospels caused the church to acknowledge the authority of the four works in our Bibles. The Muratorian Canon (AD 170–200)[5] includes, alongside these four Gospels, Acts, Paul's letters, Jude, 1–2 John, and Revelation. Only Hebrews, James, 3 John, and 1 and 2 Peter are excluded. Also included are the Wisdom of Solomon and the Apocalypse of Peter, which most early thinkers rejected. Eusebius, an early church historian, early in the fourth century, states that the Gospels, Acts,

---

5. On the Muratorian Canon or Fragment, see Benjamin Laird, "Muratorian Fragment," in LBD, no page, Logos edition. It is the oldest NT canon in existence. It was discovered by Ludovico Antonio Muratori in Milan and is a Latin mss from the seventh to the eighth century. It contains an incomplete eighty-five-line description of the NT writings, including some content and background. While a few scholars date it in the fourth century, most date it between AD 170–200. Luke and John are mentioned, and references to Mark and Matthew are lost. Also important is that the writer sees Luke as a traveling companion of Paul, identifies thirteen Pauline letters, including the Pastorals, but notes that there were two circulating that were spurious—to the Laodiceans and Alexandrians. It also notes that Revelation's authority was disputed.

the fourteen letters of Paul (including Hebrews), 1 John, 1 Peter, and perhaps Revelation were the "acknowledged" works of the church. Those he lists as disputed include James, Jude, 2 Peter, 2–3 John, the Acts of Paul, the Shepherd of Hermas, the Apocalypse of Peter, the Epistle of Barnabas, the Didache, perhaps Revelation, and the now lost Gospel of the Hebrews. By this time, he tells us the early church rejected the gospels of Peter, Thomas, and Matthias, along with the Acts of Andrew and John, among others.[6]

By the mid-third century, the "canon" was becoming concrete. The twenty-seven-book canon was finalized in the fourth and fifth centuries.[7] Evangelicals accept that God governed this process through his Spirit in producing the documents and in the church councils as they chose those works to be included. God ensured that his truth was established in these twenty-seven books held as sacred in the church today.

The Text of the Documents

Initially, all the NT documents were written in Koine Greek ("common dialect"),[8] the dominant language of the Macedonian and Roman Empires. Finding the original text of each biblical document is called Textual Criticism. In this scientific art, scholars closely study the multiple texts, versions, and citations. They seek to discern the original autograph of the work (see Part 3). While some

---

6. H. Y. Gamble, "Canon (New Testament)" in AYBD 1:856.
7. Gamble, "Canon," 1.852–58.
8. Introduced by the armies of Alexander the Great and common even among Jews in Israel at the time of Christ. See G. Hadjiantoniou, *Learning the Basics of New Testament Greek* (Chattanooga, TN: AMG Publishers, 1998), 3.

passages are debated, we can be confident that the text used to translate the Bible into our language is very close to the original.

Then, faithful Christians work together in translation committees to translate as best they can the Hebrew, Aramaic, and Greek writings into the Bibles we read today in our native tongues. There is a range of translations today covering many of the world's languages, with a plethora of English ones. These translations have different purposes. Some more literal translations seek to be close to the original text (e.g., NASB, ESV). Others seek to be faithful to the text but are more interpretative and literary in their approach (e.g., NIV, NRSV, NKJV, NET Bible, LEB). Some are paraphrases that try to make the text easy to read. These productions take more liberties with the original text to ensure the meaning is grasped (e.g., The Message, Living Bible, GNB). These translations and paraphrases are all useful and add to our tools for conveying and understanding God's Word.

The Content and Structure of the New Testament

The Books of the New Covenant Community

The word "testament" derives from *testamentum* (Lat.), and this translates *diathēkē* (Greek), meaning a "covenant" or a "contractual agreement." It thus speaks of God's legally binding agreement with humanity through Jesus. Many covenants feature in the OT, and Jeremiah dreamed of a "new covenant" (Jer 31:31–34), which Christians believe has happened in Christ. The New Testament documents, then, are the writings of the New Covenant community. They are made up of writings that faithfully represent God's actions in this new phase of salvation history. "Through these books, God speaks, we respond, and we enter a covenantal relationship with God."[9]

The New Testament as a Library of Books

The New Testament was not originally a book but a compilation of twenty-seven individual documents grouped by early Christians to form one work.[10] We can break the NT into four groups and genres (forms) of literary material. First, there are the four "gospels" (*euangelion*, "good news"). These each recount the story of the central character in the Christian movement, Jesus. The four accounts are likely fashioned from the Greek Bios genre.[11] They give us four viewpoints of Jesus' life, ministry, death, and resurrection.[12]

---

9. Keown, *Discovering the New Testament*, 1:2.
10. It is also called the "Second" Testament in relation to the "First Testament."
11. On ancient Greek biographies (*Bios*), see R. A. Burridge, "Biography, Ancient," in DNTB 167–70.
12. Many other gospels have been discovered, some of which have become of interest to popular culture (e.g., the Gospel of Thomas, Gospel of Mary Magdalene, Gospel of Judas, Gospel of Peter, Gospel of Matthias, Gospel of Philip, etc.). These are almost certainly second-century AD and later gospels falsely written in the name of a famous early Christian (pseudonymous) reflecting gnostic thought. They are very unreliable witnesses to the historical Jesus and reflect more the theology of those who compiled them. See further, Richard J. Bauckham, "Gospels (Apocryphal)," in DJG 286–91, discussing the Gospel of Thomas (he dates it at the end of the first century), the Gospel of Peter (from before the middle of the second century), Papyrus Fragments of Unknown Gospels (P. Oxy. 840; P. Egerton 2; Oxy P. 1224; Fayyum

The first three in the NT, Matthew, Mark, and Luke, are called the Synoptic Gospels and have similar structures and much common material.[13] The third Gospel, Luke, forms the first half of a longer work of history that includes Acts. Luke tells the story of Jesus to his ascension, and Acts tells of the spread of the movement that grew around him. The fourth Gospel, John, has a different theological tone and tells of many things Jesus did in Jerusalem. Each of the four Gospels similarly outlines Jesus' life and death. He was an itinerant preacher, miracle worker, and people-gatherer who was arrested, tried, and sentenced to death by crucifixion. Each Gospel claims he rose from the dead and appeared to many of his disciples, his brother James, and one fierce opponent, Paul.

After the Four Gospels is the Acts of the Apostles, the sequel to Luke's Gospel. Acts accounts for the expansion of the Christian faith through the work of the Spirit through early believers. The shape of the historiography is Acts 1:8: (1) the Jerusalem Church (Acts 1:1–8:4); (2) the faith's expansion into Judea, Samaria, and the beginnings of the mission to the ends of the earth (Acts 8–12); and (3) the spread of the faith to the Rome from where the mission to the ends of the earth will continue (Acts 13–28).

The rest of the New Testament includes letters to churches and

---

Fragment; Strasbourg Coptic Fragment), Jewish Christian gospels (*Gospel of the Hebrews*; *Gospel of the Nazarenes*; *Gospel of the Ebionites*), the Gospel of the Egyptians, the *Secret Gospel of Mark*, birth and infancy gospels (*Protoevangelium of James*; *Infancy Narrative of Thomas*), *Gospel of Nicodemus*, and post-resurrection revelations. Others include the *Gospel of Truth*, the *Gospel of Philip*, the Coptic *Gospel of the Egyptians*, the *Gospel of Eve*, and the *Gospel of Mary Magdalene*.

13. Called Synoptic because they can be placed alongside one another in a Synopsis—i.e., viewed simultaneously because they contain common material (see Patzia and Petrotta, PDBS 110).

individuals.[14] These include the letters of the apostle Paul to churches (Romans, 1 and 2 Corinthians, Ephesians, Galatians, Philippians, Colossians, 1 and 2 Thessalonians) and coworkers (1 and 2 Timothy, Titus, Philemon).[15] Then comes Hebrews, which was considered by some early thinkers to be Paul's letter but is now generally agreed to be an unknown author other than Paul. It exhorts Jewish Christians who are under pressure to return to Judaism.[16] James is traditionally held to be written by Jesus' brother, encouraging and challenging diaspora Christian Jews.[17] The two letters ascribed to Peter are written to churches in west Asia Minor (Anatolia, modern Turkey). There are three letters from John written to churches and individuals. The letter of Jude, another of Jesus' brothers, challenges false teaching and urges perseverance.1[18] Collectively, aside from Hebrews, the non-Pauline letters are entitled the General or Catholic Letters.

Finally, while Revelation is written in letter form and contains prophecy, it is an example of Christian apocalyptic writing. Such apocalyptic writings were produced between 200 BC and AD 200, written to people under pressure, encouraging them that God would triumph. Such writings, like Revelation, include a range of ideas such as good versus evil, signs and wonders, conflict, woes of

---

14. There is great debate about whether Paul wrote 1–2 Timothy and Titus and about whether Peter wrote 2 Peter. There is also some debate over whether Paul wrote Ephesians, Colossians, and 2 Thessalonians.
15. Note in a number of these books, there are co-authors/co-senders (e.g., 1 Cor 1:1; 2 Cor 1:1) or secretaries (e.g., Tertius [Rom 16:22]).
16. Apollos and Barnabas are the most popular candidates as authors, but this is speculation.
17. The "diaspora" refers to the significant number of Jews who were scattered in the Gentile world beyond Israel.
18. Hebrews, James, Peter's letters, John's letters, and Jude, are also called "Catholic Epistles" or "General Epistles."

wrath, visions, symbolism, and imagery. Such writings are difficult to interpret, but when read in their context become understandable as writings to comfort God's people and give them hope. Revelation is written to the seven churches of Asia Minor suffering under persecution and encourages them that God has got this. Harmful stuff will happen, but Jesus will come, evil will be destroyed, and the earth will be restored as heaven descends.1[19]

The Dating of the New Testament Documents

The dating of the various books is a matter of great controversy and debate. However, we can generally date them in relation to the life of Jesus as follows:

---

19. Apocalyptic literature is full of vivid symbolism, addresses people in need of hope, has a strong sense of good and evil, judgment and reward, and speaks of the present and the future (see later Revelation). The word is drawn from the Greek *apokalypsis* indicating something unveiled (i.e., a vision of the hidden future).

Date	Event
ca. 6–4 BC	The birth of Christ in Bethlehem
ca. 4 BC	Death of Herod the Great (allowing us to date the birth of Christ after)
AD 30/33	The death and resurrection of Jesus (disputed between the two years)
AD 33–35	Conversion of Paul traveling to Damascus
AD 48–67	The early letters of Paul (Gal; 1 & 2 Thess; 1 & 2 Cor; Rom)
AD 55–75	The Gospel of Mark
AD 60–70s	Hebrews
AD 60s–80s	The Gospel of Luke1[20]
AD 60s–80s	The Gospel of Matthew
Late AD 60s–90s	The Gospel of John1[21]
AD 60s–90s	Revelation1[22]

20. Some date these later in the 80s; we will discuss this as we come to these books.
21. Most place John in the 80s but a case can be made for the 60s.
22. Some would argue James was written earlier; similarly, Hebrews.

Part 2: The Place of the New Testament

The Story of Salvation

The New Testament grew out of Judaism. Jesus and all the first disciples were Jews. Aside from one or two exceptions, the Gospels' events occurred in the ancient land of Israel. The New Testament writers saw Jesus as the fulfillment of the promises of God to Israel. They saw Jesus as the transition point of history, whereby God established his long-awaited reign and the new covenant through him. Their writings are full of references to the OT. As such, the NT cannot be abstracted from the whole story of God found in Israel's sacred writings. Indeed, the NT is the continuation of salvation history. With these things in mind, any serious NT reader must also study the OT and God's workings in Israel. The OT is not merely an introduction to the NT; it is part one of the story that culminates in the return of Jesus and the new heavens and earth.

We can trace this story. It begins with God, omnipotent, omniscient, omnipresent, and self-sufficient. He creates our world and sets the natural order ablaze with beauty. He creates people, us, in his image and commissions us to fill the world, subdue it, work it, and care for it. Doing this remains our human vocation when we come to Christ. Hence, everything we do is necessary, and God's world is to be cherished as we build human society.

Having placed the first humans in the garden of Eden and blessed them with the freedom to eat from any tree, Adam and Eve violated the one law given to them, eating from the tree of good and evil. This set loose sin and corruption, and they were banished. Still, humankind expanded but became increasingly corrupt, leading to God flooding the world and starting again with Noah's family. From Noah descended the nations of the world, scattered through it by

God, each with its own language. Just as humans spread with their technological innovations, sin and social injustice spread through the world.

Then God acted, calling an Arab from what we call Iraq near the Arabian Gulf by the name of Abraham. He promised that he would bless him, give him a land, and through him, bless the nations (Gen 12:1–3). The story of his descendants is astonishing as they traveled, faced famine, and were welcomed into Egypt, only to become enslaved. Then, with a series of outrageous miracles, through Moses, God led them out of Egypt (Exodus) to the promised land of Canaan. En route, God met Moses on Mt Sinai and made a covenant with Israel stating his terms in law and warning them of the consequences of failing to heed them. After forty years of wandering, led by Joshua Son of Nun, they entered the land, overcoming the Indigenous people and establishing their nation.

They lived first under Judges but demanded a king. God granted their request, and the kingdom of Israel began under Saul and then David. David established peace, and his son Solomon built the temple, which quickly became the spiritual and political center of the nation. After Solomon, the nation split into the kingdoms of Israel in the north and Judah in the south. The north spiraled into decay and ruin with a series of poor leaders and idolatry. Prophets of God rose, warning them of the consequences of failing to heed the covenant. They were rejected, and the Assyrians destroyed the north and exiled many of its people. The southern kingdom lasted longer, with some leaders more faithful to the covenant and prophets to some extent heeded. Yet, eventually, the south also, due to its idolatry, injustice, and sin, fell to Babylon. The temple was looted and destroyed. Israel's best people were taken into exile.

Still, the exile of the south was not permanent. Some six decades later, fulfilling his promises through Isaiah, the Medo-Persians under Cyrus overcame the Babylonians, and Judah's people were released to return to the land. They rebuilt the temple and the wall around Jerusalem and remained in the land until the coming of

Christ. The glory had filled Solomon's Temple, but the new buildings were an empty shadow.

Yet, at this time, they were oppressed, subjugated first by the Medo-Persians and then by the Macedonians (Greeks). In the mid-second century bc, led by the Maccabees, they rebelled, gaining semi-autonomy and establishing their own kingdom (the Hasmonean Dynasty). This empire ended when Pompey led the Romans into the land. Again, those living in the land and region were subjugated to a foreign power.

As we come to the turning of history from bc to ad, Jesus was born in the city of David, Bethlehem, a seemingly insignificant event. He is born into a nation yearning for God's intervention. As Israel and then Judah had plunged into decadence and had gone into exile, prophets had begun declaring that God was going to act in a new way. A range of confusing and disconnected prophecies pointed to "The Expected One" (Theo), who would usher in an age in which Israel would live faithfully to God in peace and prosperity. Through him, God would reign in Israel, and it would be free of the Gentiles. Jerusalem, with its glory-filled temple, would be the world's capital. All the world would yield to God; his law would be their law and inscribed on the hearts of the faithful. The Spirit would come. The nations would bring tribute, and God would finally rule his world. Eventually, the faithful dead would rise, the wicked destroyed, and the world would be the Garden of Eden God initially established.

Before Jesus, the first prophet since Malachi, nearly 500 years prior, emerged crying out to the people that Theo was coming. The last prophet, John the Baptist, pointed *forward* to Theo, who would call Israel to repent of sin and prepare for the day of the Lord. Recognizing that Jesus, or better, Joshua, is the one, he baptized him. As Jesus was baptized, heaven was torn asunder, the Spirit fell on Jesus, and the new Joshua was commissioned as king. From the waters, he set about his ministry of bringing in the reign of God. He drew followers who expected him first to cleanse the land and then, having established God's kingdom, would subjugate the nations with God's power and people. Yet, Joshua, Son of God, had come in a unique way—he was Theo, but he was clothed in the ideals of Isaiah's Servant who would conquer through love, his death, his defeat of sin, and would rise to be Lord and God of the Cosmos. He would establish a new covenant, not with the blood of animals or Israel's enemies, but by his own precious blood. He would be King, Son of God, Son of Man, Christ (Messiah), the Prophet, the Savior, the Son, High Priest, the Lamb of God, the destroyer of evil, sin, and death, Christus Victor, and the Lord. But the path to this exalted status that played out was not as expected.

The NT and Theology

At the time of Jesus, Israel was a land of competing theologies and ideas. Different interpretations of Israel's scriptures are hardly surprising because the OT is an amazingly diverse book with multiple possible ways of drawing together its threads and ideas. The OT Scriptures were interpreted in diverse ways as theological thinkers pondered how to interpret the times and the coming of God and Theo. All believed in the one God, a confession they made daily (the Shema). All recognized the need to maintain their relationship with God through careful observance of the Sabbath, circumcising boys, attending Synagogue, and, if possible, participating in temple feasts, eating the right food, maintaining distance from anything unclean, and cherishing the temple. Yet, beyond this, there were various ideas concerning God and his intervention in their context.

Some focused on the Torah only and had little confidence in such an intervention. They awaited the coming of a Prophet after Moses (Sadducees), as did the Samaritans, who called this figure the Taheb. Others, who accepted the full story of God in the OT, understood that legal observance would usher in God's reign (Pharisees). Yet others saw Israel and its institutions as entirely corrupt and withdrew into the wilderness by the Dead Sea, creating a community of the faithful to which God would come through his Messiah (Essenes, Qumran). Others looked back on redemptive heroes Moses, Phinehas, Joshua the son of Nun, David, Elijah, and the Maccabees, believing that if they could draw the people together, God would enable them to take over the nation and establish God's reign (Zealots, Revolutionaries). Other ideas swirled—did Moses die on Mt Nebo? Would he return? Would Elijah (who was taken up to God in a whirlwind) return, as Malachi indicates? Would the figure be like the Son of Man in Daniel? Or perhaps he would be more akin to the Anointed One, the Messiah (Christ), a descendent of David? Or perhaps, he might be a prophet like Moses? Most held that God's intervention would see the Romans driven out like the Canaanites, and God would rule his world forever. None saw that the Servant figure in Isa 53 was this person. Not one recognized that Ps 22 foretold the suffering and death of the coming Messiah. Such an idea was not in their worldview.

Then Jesus entered the world, and everything changed. He is the heart of our theology, our starting point, its center, and the focus of the future. Because he came, we can know what God is like, for Jesus is God's Son, his very image, embodying God in the world. He died for our sins, rose from the dead, and welcomed us into this new age. He interpreted Israel's Scriptures, showed and taught us how to live, and told us more clearly how this age will end—when he returns and judges the world, extinguishes evil, and we are his forever in the fully restored cosmos.

Theology then is forever changed by his coming. The Apostles' writings in the NT, understood in continuity with the story of God in the OT, form our canon. From this corpus, we think theologically. Our musings will be forever Trinitarian, as we now know that the one God is revealed to us in the three persons of the Godhead—Father, Son, and Spirit. At the center will always be Jesus, the Christ, for he came to be God among us and to rise and ascend to be the exalted Lord of the world. Christology, then, lies at the heart of our Theology. The focus of Pneumatology is also Christ, for the Spirit's work is to take us to Christ and form us into the image of the invisible God seen most clearly in Christ. Christ informs our anthropology, for he became *anthrōpos*, so we know what it means to be truly human. He reveals God the Father to us by his Spirit.

Theologians since Christ have come and gone. The great ones are those who continually summons us to consider Jesus—who he is, what he has done, what he will do, what he wants from us, how he reveals God and connects us to him, and how he sent his Spirit to shape us into the people of God we were created to be. They seek to explain the cross, Christ's redemptive atoning death, and how we are newly created in him. They recognize and unravel what it means to be God's people, the church, in Christ, his body, the temple of His Spirit, and the family of God. They consider deeply how we are to live in a world that crucifies God's people, how we are to take up crosses and follow him in the Christoform life. They may become so famous that their name becomes a movement, e.g., Calvinism, Arminianism, Barthianism, etc. Yet, as Paul did, they declare to us, "I follow Christ!" There is only Christianism or "Jesusism." Indeed, all theologians who do God's work appropriately stand and point us to Jesus, as did John the Baptist, who declared, "he must become greater, I must become less" (John 3:30). They read the world through the lens of Jesus. There is no other way to do theology.

The NT and The World

The Bible is the most sold and read book in history.[23] Of ancient books, it is by far the most copied and transmitted work of ancient

---

23. "Best-selling Book," *Guinness World Records*, https://www.guinnessworldrecords.com/world-records/best-selling-book-of-non-fiction.

literature.[24] Its influence is unrivaled. The Old Testament is a sacred text to Judaism, Islam, and Christianity. The New Testament is a hallowed work to over thirty percent of the world's population.[25] The Roman Empire adopted Christianity as its religion in AD 380, sixty-seven years after Constantine's adoption of the faith and fifty-five years after the Council of Nicaea. Christianity then became the primary religion of Europe and is still a dominant ideology governing western thinking to this day. It spread in the missionary expansion of the last four hundred or so years to be, arguably, the most influential ideology in the world. Its central figure, Jesus, is adored by billions. In eastern polytheistic religions, he is an honored figure. He remains central to western ethics. His teaching has contributed immensely to our notions of compassion, egalitarianism, inclusion, concern for the marginalized, justice, and education. While individuals like famous Greek philosophers, Julius Caesar, Confucius, Buddha, Mohammed, Karl Marx, Albert Einstein, and many others have been significant, no person has influenced the world like Jesus. There have been many bestsellers by Shakespeare, Marx, Tolkien, Dan Brown, J. K. Rowling, and others but the Bible outstrips them all. It is not only studied by Christians but by others as ancient literature and history. The study of the NT should be compulsory for all people simply because of its influence. It is indispensable for disciples and "students" of the kingdom of God.

24. "New Testament Manuscripts and Why They're Important," *Logos*, https://www.logos.com/how-to/study-nt-mss.
25. "The Global Religious Landscape," Pew Research Center (2012), https://www.pewresearch.org/religion/2012/12/18/global-religious-landscape-exec/#:~:text=The demographic study – based on the world as of 2010.

Part 3: Interpretative Methodologies

This chapter introduces a range of approaches to biblical study used today.[26] These arose through the historical-critical period. While they often led to doubt and uncertainty about the history of the Scriptures, they have added to our ability to plumb the depths of the Bible, which is made up of divine and human writings. As a person begins their academic study of the Bible, some basic concepts must be grasped to make the most of the study.

Exegesis

In Chapter Five, we will explore exegesis in some detail. Here, I introduce it briefly. "Exegesis" is a word derived from *exēgeomai*, a Greek term that means "to set forth in detail, to expound."[27] The term is found in John 1:18, where Jesus, the Word made flesh, "exegetes" or "expounds, makes known" God. We use the term in biblical studies to describe the process of drawing out the meaning of a Bible verse or passage, often with verse-by-verse or phrase-by-phrase exploration of that passage. Sound exegesis seeks to be faithful to the biblical author's intent and considers how the reader hears it. It seeks to explain the passage's meaning in its original context within the writing in which it is found, in relation to other works by the same author, and regarding its historical and social setting. Exegesis draws out the meaning and avoids eisegesis, whereby one interprets the text from a presupposed tradition or perspective.

---

26. For more detail, see Keown, *Discovering*, 1:99–109 (Ch. 4).
27. BDAG, 349.

Hermeneutics

Hermeneutics will be discussed in Chapter Two. It is sufficient to say here that the term comes from *hermēneia* and means to "translate" or "interpret."[28] In 1 Cor 12:10 and 14:26, related terms are used to interpret or translate tongues. In biblical studies, hermeneutics is the art of interpreting Scripture. While exegesis focuses on drawing out the original meaning of a passage, hermeneutics includes exegesis but uses a wide range of interpretative methods relevant to the genre, context, very importantly, considers how we are to apply the teaching of the passage to our various situations today. "Put simply, it speaks of how to interpret Scripture for daily living."[29]

Textual Criticism

Textual Criticism is the study of establishing the original autographs of the biblical text from the many textual witnesses we have at our disposal. As we Christians hold that the Bible is the sacred text through which God speaks, this is an important exercise. Sadly, we do not have the actual original documents of the Bible. The earliest we have is P52, a papyrus fragment from around AD 125 that includes a few verses from John's Gospel.[30] Many variant readings

---

28. BDAG, 393.
29. Keown, *Discovering*, 1:100.
30. Roger L. Omanson and Bruce Manning Metzger, *A Textual Guide to the Greek New Testament: An Adaptation of Bruce M. Metzger's Textual Commentary for the Needs of Translators* (Stuttgart: Deutsche Bibelgesellschaft, 2006), xi. Much of this section is drawn from pp. xi–xvi.

were passed on as the Bible documents were copied and distributed. Most errors were caused by copyists who labored in producing duplicates of the documents. One example is Mark 1:1, where some versions include "and Son of God," while others do not. In such instances, the textual critic must decide whether "and Son of God" was original by weighing the readings—did it drop out, or was it added?

To decide such things, textual critics consider two main text types. First, they consider the 5400 Greek manuscripts ranging from whole books (3000 continuous text mss exist) to passages (2,403 lectionary mss). These are either manuscripts of papyrus or animal parchment.[31] Such mss have a P label like P52, indicating it is Papyrus 52. Second, textual critics consider the many citations of the Bible in early church writers that show us the text they used.

Textual Criticism is a vital foundation for establishing the original text. Those who learn koine Greek can read the Greek text and see the variants in the textual apparatus. They can consult other scholars, consider how they weigh them, and develop their skills in Textual Criticism. For those who do not go this far in their study, better Bible translations include footnotes with the main textual variants, and it is essential to observe them and to read how experts assess them in commentaries. *The Textual Commentary* by Metzger is a great resource where students can get an excellent summary of how the UBS translation teams considered the variants.[32]

---

31. Papyrus mss are made from pressed strips of papyrus plant (116 exist today). Parchments are made from animal skins and found from around fourth-century AD (around 3000 exist). Many are Uncials, written in Greek capital letters.
32. Bruce Manning Metzger, United Bible Societies, *A Textual Commentary on the Greek New Testament, Second Edition a Companion Volume to the United Bible Societies' Greek New Testament* (4th Rev. Ed.) (London; New York: United Bible Societies, 1994. See also Omanson and Metzger, *A Textual Guide*.

Historical Criticism

Historical Criticism[33] arose in the seventeenth century as interest in science developed and Christianity lost dominance. Historical Criticism is an approach that seeks not only to study the text of Scripture but the historical situation in which it arose. The focus is on reconstructing how the text came to be as it is—its origin and development. That is, it focuses on the history *in* the New Testament text and the history *of* the said text.[34] Understanding the historical setting and how it is reflected in the text is sensible as we seek to understand its original meaning. However, another aspect of Historical Criticism is constructing how the text often developed with a view that what we have is a mythological development of an event, often without any supernatural dimension. Many people lost confidence in the Bible as its historical integrity was questioned.

While historical Criticism claimed to be neutral, it tended to be skeptical, seeking to explain away the miraculous with complex reconstructions of how the event recorded came to be in the Bible. Often it was supposed that extraordinary claims, such as feeding 5000 people, rising from the dead, or miraculous healings, were creations of the early church or the Gospel writers. Many of the methods that will be explained in what follows carry this skepticism. While evangelicals rejected such approaches in the earliest stages of the critical period, now evangelical biblical scholars recognize the value of considering the text's historical setting, development, and other background aspects. As we explore these, new insights can be gained about the Bible without the skepticism of earlier

---

33. It is also called "the historical-critical method" or "higher criticism."
34. Bruce Corley, Steve W. Lemke, and Grant I. Lovejoy, *Biblical Hermeneutics: A Comprehensive Introduction to Interpreting Scripture*, 2nd ed. (Nashville, Tenn.: Broadman & Holman, 2002), 150 (italics theirs).

historical critics. Understanding them in their historical setting is a significant first step in applying the Bible today. Historical Criticism helps us understand what the Bible books did in their context and help us determine what they cannot mean.[35] Reading the Bible in its historical setting safeguards us against imposing contemporary ideas on the text that violate its original intent.

Source Criticism

Source Criticism, as the name suggests, looks for the sources of the information found in the Gospels and Acts. Searching for sources is a crucial aspect of Historical Criticism. It asks, where did Matthew, Mark, Luke, and John, get the material they include in the Gospels and Acts? Until the period of Historical Criticism, it was assumed that Matthew and John were apostles, and the Gospels reflect their material. Based on early church traditions, it was believed that Mark drew on Peter's recollections and Luke on Paul and other eyewitnesses to get his material. However, in the historical-critical period, more attention was paid to the similarities and differences between the Gospels. The skepticism of the period led people to question whether Matthew and John were written by apostles, whether Mark drew on Peter's ideas, and whether Luke had any access to Paul. Scholars debated whether Gospel writers drew their material from one or more Gospels and whether they accessed other documents. Some consider that many sources were not original, but traditions developed like Chinese Whispers in the church community. What has been left behind from these debates are some core ideas that shape contemporary biblical studies that will be discussed in Chapter 9 (The Synoptic Problem) and as we briefly introduce each of the Gospels and Acts. While contemporary

---

35. Patzia and Petrotta, PDBS 58 (italics theirs).

evangelical scholars have some divergent ideas concerning how the material in each Gospel relates to the others, they have established sound reasons to trust the historicity of the Gospels and Acts.

Form Criticism

Form Criticism is a foundational historical-critical approach that looks to locate the oral tradition behind the existing Gospel texts and then categorizes them into fixed forms (*Formgeschichte*, "history of forms"). Such classifications include things like parables, miracles, pronouncement stories, and legends. Assuming that the events recorded in the Gospels are not to be trusted, they looked to establish where the events and sayings originated in the life of the early church—the *Sitz im Leben* (life setting). Key figures included Martin Dibelius, Rudolf Bultmann, and Vincent Taylor. These thinkers developed criteria of authenticity that helped them assess whether or not they occurred.[36] For example, if the event is in all

---

36. See C. L. Blomberg, "Form Criticism," in DJG 248–49 for a list of criteria and assessment: 1) Criterion of dissimilarity—where Jesus says or does something different to Judaism and the early church, it is likely authentic; 2) Criterion of multiple attestation—if something is found in multiple sources (Mark, Q, M, L, John) it is likely authentic, e.g., feeding of the 5000; 3) Criterion of Palestinian environment or language—if the action or saying is very Semitic in style or background, rather than Hellenistic, it is more likely genuine; 4) Criterion of coherence—if the text aligns with another authenticated by the first three, it is more likely authentic. These sound okay but, in fact, say nothing of historicity. Jesus was capable of originality. Something found in one Gospel may still be historical. Further, the criteria are not applied in all cases. So, Form Critics did not accept that Jesus fed 5000 miraculously despite it

four Gospels, something happened (e.g., the feeding of the 5000). They also rejected the miraculous aspects of the story and imagined how an actual event came to be understood as it is in Scripture.

For them, the origin of these supposed miracles was the early church, where legends grew out of small events in the life of Jesus. The stories blend the actual event and amplify it through ancient mythological perspectives. They expanded over an extended period of oral tradition into the stories we have in the NT. As they were heavily influenced by seeking natural explanations, they wrote of miracles and other supernatural phenomena as myths. As such, they drew a sharp distinction between the Jesus of history and the Christ of faith; essentially, myths developed in the church. Their influence has not faded with the Jesus Seminar and significant voices who carry on this approach. While evangelical biblical scholars reject much of their approach, they have found value in classifying the biblical texts and considering the life setting in which the NT occurred. This process did not occur in the early church for evangelicals but in first-century Israel, where Jesus and the disciples existed. Surprisingly, the criteria of authenticity have helped argue for the historicity of Jesus' miracles, as many are found in multiple Gospels.

Redaction Criticism

The term "redaction" refers to the process used by a redactor to edit preexisting material. As such, Redaction Criticism, which grew out of Form Criticism, shifted the attention from the development of NT stories in the early church to the work of the evangelists

being in all four Gospels. Further, miracles are found in all five sources and yet are rejected by many. See Blomberg for further critique.

(Matthew, Mark, Luke, and John). The early redaction critics continued the skepticism of Form Critics, arguing that the Gospels were historical fiction created by the Gospel editors. Assuming Mark's Gospel and the so-called Q document were first and fictitious and legendary, they considered how these had come to be as they focused on the evangelist. They considered the theology of Mark as evidenced by the edited form. They then considered Matthew and Luke noting how they used Mark, Q, and other material they accessed and how they shaped their Gospels. Their interest was how the evangelists selected their material (what they left in, left out) and how it was then arranged and edited. Then they sought to understand their theological perspectives.

This approach was taken up without the same skepticism by evangelicals in the mid to later twentieth century (e.g., F. F. Bruce, I. Howard Marshall, Leon Morris). They found that they could use this method positively to consider how the evangelists formed their material and were able to discern their theology. Doing this launched the new movement of evangelical biblical scholarship that continues to this day. Commentaries, articles, essays, and monographs exploring how the evangelists have expressed the story of Jesus and the early church have exploded from this time. Indeed, "the rise of Redaction Criticism has seen the rise of a new era of biblical scholarship which continues today through the many faithful evangelicals producing magnificent biblical scholarship around the world."[37] As you study the NT, much of what these redaction critics established is foundational to contemporary biblical study.

---

37. Keown, *Discovering*, 1:105.

Narrative Criticism

Historical Criticism no longer dominates the study of the Gospels and Acts. In the final decades of the twentieth century and with gathered momentum in the twenty-first century, there has been an increased desire among biblical scholars to move beyond asking questions about the historicity of the text (which often ended inconclusively) to consider the texts themselves as narratives. While most scholars still seek to read the documents in their historical setting, they focus on reading them as literature (Literary Criticism) rather than unanswerable historical questions. The Gospels and Acts are read in their own right as narratives or stories (not fictional), considering the placement, plot, and characterization and how that contributes to the theology of the work. Such a narrative approach frees the biblical scholar to interpret the Gospel rather than prehistory. While there is an acknowledgment of the use of sources, what is in the Gospel becomes the focus, not how it came into existence and whether the events happened. The best narrative critics acknowledge the setting, sources, and the evangelist's work. But their interest is the content of the document itself, what is being said by the writer, and how it applies today.

Social Scientific Approaches

Another aspect of Historical Criticism that has recently gained more popularity is reading the Bible against the social setting using methods from the social sciences. With this approach, scholars explore the social setting of the NT and how the people of the Greco-Roman world, in its various parts, understood life and social relationships. Then, the Bible is explored with careful consideration of the broader milieu. Such approaches have spawned a whole raft of studies from the perspective of politics, gender, family relationships, race, class structures, gender, the rhythms of ancient life, and more. Biblical people lived in a world like ours, and the more we know about its social structures, the more we can make sense of its material and apply it sensibly to our own context.

Rhetorical Criticism

The approaches above have mainly been applied to the study of the Gospels and, to a lesser extent, Acts. Rhetorical Criticism is an approach used in interpreting the twenty-one letters of the NT. Rhetorical Criticism is premised on the idea that the NT letters were constructed as speeches from the author to be delivered by an emissary. Such an approach is appropriate based on the importance of speech-making in the Greco-Roman world. Rhetorical critics have carefully studied Greco-Roman rhetorical principles developed by Aristotle and others and used across the Roman world by elite men who were brought up to be skilled in public speaking. Rhetorical Criticism assesses the NT epistles against their form, structure, and devices. Three primary forms are considered.[38]

1. Forensic Rhetoric: The speaker/writer defends or accuses the hearers/readers regarding their past actions and seeks to move them toward the right action.
2. Deliberative Rhetoric: The speaker/writer exhorts or dissuades them from the desired future action.
3. Epideictic Rhetoric: The speaker/writer affirms shared communal values using praise or blame to move them toward the correct response.[39]

---

38. Another approach is protreptic, which is a hortatory approach that calls the audience to a new and different way of life. Many scholars consider Romans to be an example of protreptic rhetoric.

The letters are assessed and classified. Scholars who do this have diverse understandings. For example, some scholars consider Galatians to be forensic rhetoric (Betz), while others see it as deliberative (Witherington). Philippians is seen as deliberative rhetorical (Watson, Witherington), and 1 Thessalonians is understood as epideictic (Jewett). Rhetorical critics have different views, while many scholars reject approaching the letters this way. Most scholars recognize some influence of rhetorical forms but find the NT letters evade such close classification.

One of the beneficial aspects of rhetorical critics is how they break down letters into distinct parts within the overall rhetorical approach. "There are usually six parts: (1) introduction (*exordium*); (2) narration (*narratio*); (3) proposition (*propositio*); (4) confirmation (*probatio*); (5) refutation (*refutatio*); and (6) conclusion (*peroratio*)."[40] Each part leads to the overall goal that differs depending on the approach used.

Another positive contribution of Rhetorical Criticism is identifying well-known rhetorical devices in the letters. A good example is a chiasm, a device used in the OT (e.g., Gen 6:9–9:29) and often used in the NT. It is based on the Greek letter chi (X) and has an A-B-C-B2-A2 structure whereby A correlates linguistically or thematically with A2 and then B with B2 (and so on). The emphasis usually falls on the center. An example of a macro-chiasm (big one) is 1 Corinthians 12–14.

A   Spiritual Gifts (1 Cor 12)
    B   The Most Excellent Way—Love (1 Cor 13)
A2   Spiritual Gifts (1 Cor 14)

Another shorter example is Phil 3:8–10:

A   that I may gain Christ and be found in him,

---

39. See G. W. Hansen, "Rhetorical Criticism," in DPL 822.
40. Keown, *Discovering*, 106; see also Patzia and Petrotta, PDBS 101.

> B   not having a righteousness of my own that comes from the law,
>> C   but that [righteousness] which comes through faith in Christ,
> B2   the righteousness from God that depends on faith
A2   that I may know him and the power of his resurrection, and may share his sufferings, becoming like him in his death,

The emphasis here is the central plank—righteousness by faith in Christ (or the faithfulness of Christ). Many such rhetorical devices will come up in your study.

Conclusion

Many other approaches to biblical study will become more familiar as students go deeper into biblical studies. What intrigues me is how methods initially used to challenge the truth of the Bible have become essential tools to help us understand and apply God's Word better.

Textual Criticism has been a brilliant tool to help us find out more accurately what was initially written in biblical documents. We can now say that we are confident that the text used for most contemporary translations is remarkably close to the original (NA28; USB5).

Historical Criticism has forced us to read the Bible in its original context and not impose our culture and perspective on the text (although that is never entirely avoidable). It is an invaluable initial principle in any biblical study.

Source Criticism has helped us identify the relationship between the Gospels and their material and forced us to consider carefully how the stories in the Gospels and Acts came to be as they are. Form Criticism has encouraged us to consider the various forms of NT writings and their original life setting. Redaction Criticism has been especially foundational in drawing our attention to the literary skills and theology of the different authors. Narrative Criticism has led us to read the NT documents with our best literary skills, bringing the stories of God's Word alive. Social scientific approaches have enabled us to know more about the social world of the NT and make sense of the biblical documents in this regard. With the best approaches, we can read the Gospels and draw out their meaning with increasing confidence.

Finally, Rhetorical Criticism has helped us recognize that the letters were written to be spoken and heard and has helped us identify ancient rhetorical forms illuminating biblical texts' meanings. God is amazing in his capacity to allow people to come at his Word with skepticism and even malicious intent to deconstruct its power, and yet in his sovereignty, through people with renewed minds, what emerges is new and creative ways to read his Word and even the power of the Word is enhanced and unleashed in new ways. Social scientific approaches are equally crucial to epistle research as we get into the world behind the text and the people and world of the text come alive.

2. Principles of New Testament Study

Introduction

The term "hermeneutics" is derived from a set of Greek words associated with the Greek term ἑρμηνεύω (*hermēneuō*). The terms are found twenty-one times in the New Testament (NT) for translating words from other languages or their interpretation.[1] Our English term, "hermeneutics," has become a technical term for:

The discipline of interpreting texts, with special reference to the principles and procedures involved.[2]

In this short paper, I will outline some of the basic principles of interpretation with an eye on the New Testament aspects of the discipline.

---

1. Including the verb μεθερμηνεύω (*methermēneuō*), "translate." It is used of translating Hebrew words into Greek, including *Emmanuel* translated (in English from the Greek), "God with us" (Matt 1:23); *talitha koum* translated "little girl, I say to you, get up!" (Mark 5:41); *Golgotha* translated "Place of the Skull" (Mark 15:22); *Eloi, Eloi, lema sabachthani* translated "My God, my God, why have you forsaken me?" (Mark 15:34); *Rabbi* translated "teacher" (John 1:38); *Messiah* translated "Christ" (John 1:41); Barnabas translated "son of encouragement" (Acts 4:36); *Bar-Jesus* translated Elymas (Acts 13:8). The verb ἑρμηνεύω (*hermēneuō*) is also used of translating Hebrew words, including *Cephas* translated "Peter" (John 1:42); Siloam translated "sent" (John 9:7); Melchizedek translated "King of righteousness" (Heb 7:2). The verb διερμηνεύω (*diermēneuō*), is used of interpreting—as in Jesus interpreting the Scriptures concerning himself on the Damascus Road (Luke 24:27). It can also mean translate, as in *Tabitha* translated Dorcas (Acts 9:36). It is also used of the interpretation or translation of tongues (1 Cor 12:30; 14:5, 13). The cognate noun *hermēneia* is also used for the interpretation or translation of tongues (12:10; 14:26, 27, 28). The adjective δυσερμήνευτος (*dysermēneutos*) is also used to mean "hard to explain" (Heb. 5:11).
2. DeMoss, PDSNT 66.

Part 1: Hermeneutical Principles

It is God's Word

The most fundamental aspect of NT interpretation for believers is remembering that the NT and the Old Testament (OT) are God's Word to the world.[3] In Protestantism, the books involved are the thirty-nine books that make up the Jewish canon[4] and the twenty-seven books the early church agreed were faithful to the apostolic tradition.

Paul wonderfully articulates how Scripture should be understood in 2 Tim 3:16:

> All scripture is God-breathed and profitable for teaching, for reproof, for correction, for training in righteousness, in order that the person of God may be competent, equipped for every good work" (my translation).

Just as God breathed life into Adam, he breathed his life-generating power into and onto the Scriptures as faithful descendants of Adam wrote them down. The Scriptures are then Spirit-inspired and breathed, the inspired Word of God.

The Scriptures, as God's written Word, lead us to the Living Word, Jesus Christ (John 1:1), and the salvation that God offers us in him. The divine nature of the Scriptures means that when we come to

---

3. This is fresh material, not published in Keown, *Discovering*, or *The New Testament A Taster*.
4. For Roman Catholics, these books include the Apocrypha, which was also included in the Greek translation—the LXX. All Christians agree with the divine inspiration of the sixty-six books included in the Protestant Bible.

interpret the Bible, both OT and NT, it is a sacred thing. The Spirit was on those who wrote it down and those who preserved it. The same Spirit was hovering over the church as our forebears grappled with which writings to include as inspired and which to reject as uninspired. As believers have sat to read the Scriptures over the centuries, God's Spirit has mantled them, illuminating the Word and enabling them to interpret it for their situations. The creeds and canons of the church (where consistent with the Bible) were formed by people filled with the Spirit for their times, enabling the preservation and dissemination of God's Word and keeping his people faithful to him.

As God's inspired Word, the Scriptures are our canon or rule of life. Through them, God speaks and guides us into the life he has for us and the eternal existence to come. We are corrected from false ideas and directed toward others that are trustworthy and reliable. We are encouraged by the Scriptures to persevere in suffering. We learn the gospel we are called to share with others by continually immersing ourselves in Scripture. As such, we should approach Scripture like the Bereans in Acts 17:11,

> But these people were more open-minded than those in Thessalonica. They eagerly welcomed the Word, investigating the Scriptures every day to see if these things were so (my translation).

In my view, as God's Word, the Scriptures are untainted, untarnished, unblemished, inviable, infallible, and inerrant. They are unique among all writings as God's message to us for life as his faithful people. They are as God wanted them exactly written—true, factual, non-fictional, historical, perfect, exact, consistent, coherent, correct, pure, holy, and divine. We can trust them. Forming our theology begins with the Scriptures, and our theology, as it develops, should be bounded by their teachings. As Paul puts it brilliantly in 1 Cor 4:6, we must not go beyond what is written.

It is a Human Word

The Scriptures are God's Word to the world. Yet if we stop with the recognition that the Bible is God's divine Word, we make the mistake of failing to see that they also have a human side. We can liken the Scriptures to Jesus, who is simultaneously fully God and fully human. Similarly, the church forms God's holy people (the family of God,[5] the body of Christ,[6] the temple of the Spirit),[7] yet it is a human institution made up of people like us across the world who gather in small groups. The church is divine yet very human.

Similarly, the written Word of God was penned by everyday people. They wrote across thousands of years as God's faithful people, in each setting and context to a specific group for a particular godly reason. Hence, good interpretation trusts that the Bible *is* God's Word. Still, at the same time, it delights in exploring the people, the places, the historical situation, the social contexts, the events happening at the time, the situations of the writers and their intent, and the situations of the readers. God chose to reveal himself in a book, recording peoples' encounters with him, so we should use the best reading skills we can manage to interpret it well. We never lose sight of its divine nature, but then, like time travelers, we explore the world of the book in question, getting behind and inside what is written within. We discern what the same Spirit, who inspired the writing of the words of the Bible, is saying to us now for our times and situations. We then rise from reading and live out what we have heard, empowered by the Spirit who impels us into God's work.

What tends to happen when we study theology at a tertiary

---

5. Rom 8:29; 1 Tim 2:15; 3:14; Heb 4:9; 11:25; 1 Pet 2:9; 4:17. See also Gal 6:10.
6. 1 Cor 12:27; Eph 1:23; 4:12; 5:23, 30.
7. 1 Cor 3:16; 6:19; Eph 2:19–22.

college or seminary is that we who have previously read the Bible as God's Word to us discover the human dimensions of the text. Then, as we dig into this new dimension, we find hidden depths to the Word, and God speaks to us in fresh ways. Be warned, however, as this can be a disruptive time as we often experience some degree of disruption to formerly held ideas as we explore the Bible by reading it from both a divine and human perspective. Yet, the experience of those who have gone before assures us that if we persevere in learning to read the human side of the Bible, knowing it is God's Word, it comes alive in new ways. We find its power to change and grow us. We are changed and for the better. We then become people who, as Paul desired for Timothy, are "approved" workers who are unashamed and are "rightly handling the Word of truth" (2 Tim 2:15, ESV).

It is an Act of Worship

Because the Bible (OT *and* NT) is God's written Word, studying Scripture is a holy act of worship. As we, filled with God's Spirit (1 Cor 12:13; Eph 5:18), sit to read the Spirit-inspired Scriptures, we worship God. We speak to him and hear his voice as he whispers into our minds and hearts through his Word. We must never lose our sense of wonder and excitement at what God will say next. It is an act of prayer, for prayer is a conversation between God and us, and the primary way God speaks to us in that conversation is through his Spirit-breathed words. He shapes us to be more like him and his Son, conforming us to who he created us to be as his image bearers (Gen 1:26–27; Rom 8:29). He guides us to hear what he needs us to hear, reprimanding us, correcting us, encouraging us, comforting us, and leading us.

Of course, the worshipful act of studying Scripture does not end with reading but with obeying what is learned. We must not be mere listeners of the Word but do what it says, as James tells us (Jas

1:22–24). If we do not do so, we have missed the point and have failed to worship as is appropriate. Worship is not merely responding to God in prayer but it being obedient in our attitudes, actions, and words. As such, we should begin our Bible study in any situation and time by praying and asking God to speak so that we hear and respond. We ask him to shape us into his image. We read it well and take note of what he teaches us. We rise, go, and practice what we have been instructed to do.

It is an Act of Research

The Bible is not merely God's Word dictated directly for us personally and individually to simply read, interpret, and respond to it. It is made of writings that people originally wrote to others, and the more we can know about the situation of the writing, the better we will understand its message. Consequently, good biblical readers delight in "going back" into the world of the original reading and understanding it. We want to know who the writer was, why they wrote what they did, and what they were trying to say. Similarly, we want to know the audience and their situation. We need to understand as much as possible about the context in which it was written and what was going on in the world, group, or church at that time. We want to know the historical setting and social situation. We want to be aware of the background cultural norms and social practices.

As we do, we find that the Scriptures come to life in a fresh way. As we learn of the culture and social setting of the situation, we often discover surprises and even shocks in the story that we would overlook unless we studied the historical setting of the Scriptures. Every encounter with Jesus has some cultural shock or surprise, which can only be known when we do our homework concerning the situational context.

When we read a verse or set of verses, we should explore how it relates to the whole piece of writing. When we come across an OT quotation, allusion, or echo, that should send us off exploring the OT and its Jewish setting. When a historical figure is mentioned, we can explore that person's story in Scripture and non-biblical writings. Many people are from the wider world, like Augustus (Luke 2:1) or the figures mentioned in Luke 3:1. There are social customs to be explored, like the traditions of Mark 7:1–23.

However, we must do all this research without losing sight of the fact that the Bible is God's Word, and at some point, we must stop and ask him to highlight what he is saying to us and what he wants us to do as a result. We then get up from our time of reading and prayer and do it.

The NT is to be Interpretated in Relation to the Whole Bible

Another essential thing to note is that the New Testament is part two of God's great book gifted to humankind to know his truth. God's story includes the thirty-nine books of the Old Testament and must be interpreted in terms of the unfolding revelation of God. The story of God in the world, especially Israel, is assumed because the God in whom Jesus and the NT writers believed is the same God the patriarchs and Israel worshiped. Jesus did not come to abolish God's Word but to affirm and interpret it correctly. As such, our overall task is not to interpret just the NT but the whole story of God as it unfolds.

This concern for the whole Bible has a general dimension to it as we recognize the flow of God's great story, including Creation, Fall, Flood, Babel and the confusion of languages and spread of nations, Abraham and God's covenant with him, the Patriarchs, the Exodus, the Sinai Covenant, the law, the sacrificial system, the Wilderness, the Conquest, the period of the Judges, Monarchy, temple, the Davidic Covenant, the Prophets, Exiles, and the restoration and eschatological hopes of Israel. The NT continues this story and must be read in this light as containing the subsequent phases of God's work in the world: Jesus, the Spirit, the church, mission, and the consummation of new creation.

The more specific dimension of interpretation, where the OT is concerned, is where and how the NT writers use quotations, allusions, and echoes of the OT in their writings.[8] When we come across an OT recollection, we must look closely at how the OT feeds into our understanding of the specific NT passage and the overall message of the writing. So, in sum, the first principle of New Testament interpretation is understanding its place regarding the OT—it continues the same narrative of God and his world, fulfills many of its hopes, and looks forward to the climax of history itself.

It Must Be Read Forwards and Backwards

The previous section focused on the Bible as one unfolding narrative. As such, it needs to be read forward consecutively, and then we can summarize the gospel. However, on its own, this is not enough. In Hebrews 1, we are told God spoke many times in the past but has now spoken through his Son—his Word is the ultimate

---

8. Some scholars like Richard Hays distinguish between explicit quotations of OT texts (whether from the Hebrew Masoretic Text or the Greek LXX); an allusion, which is an "indirect, imprecise or passing reference in which verbal correspondence to the source text is relatively remote" (DeMoss, PDSNT 17); and an echo—which is even more remote. See Richard B. Hays, *Echoes of Scripture in the Letters of Paul* (New Haven; London: Yale University Press, 1989). An example of a quotation is Romans 3:11–18 (a series of quotes, a catena); an allusion might be 1 Pet 3:20 (Noah), and an echo might be John 1:1 (recalling Genesis 1:1).

message of God for humankind (Heb 1:1-2). John describes Jesus as "the Word of God." He is God's message to the world (John 1:1). In fact, John goes on to say that no one has seen God, but now Jesus (who he describes as God) has made the Father known (or in Greek, exegeted God; John 1:18). On the Mount of Transfiguration (Matt 17:1-13), when Jesus stood with the two great prophets, Moses and Elijah, God's booming voice echoed forth, stating, "listen to him." "Him!" Jesus *is* the turning point of history when God came to earth as his Son, embodied as a human, to become the ultimate interpreter of every aspect of God's revelation to the world. As such, central to our hermeneutics is Jesus Christ, God's Son, the Lord, and our Savior.

Hence, good hermeneutics privileges Christ in terms of interpretation. An excellent example of how that works is the Sermon on the Mount (Matt 5-7), where Jesus says something like, "You have heard that it was said," and then Jesus interprets the intent of God's law for his hearers. Jesus, then, is the lens through which we interpret the OT. We must not only read forward but also backward, reading the OT Scriptures through the lens of Christ.

Furthermore, after Christ's death, resurrection, ascension, and exaltation to the right hand of God as Lord, through him, God poured out his Spirit on his people (Pentecost; Acts 2:1-13). The Spirit is that of Christ in God's people, his body, the temple of the Spirit (1 Cor 3:16-18). The Spirit led the early Christians to declare the gospel to the world and to put it into writings that the church now recognizes as consistent with the Jesus who came among us. Moreover, some writers of the NT lived with Jesus for his earthly life, heard from him, and sought to live out his injunctions being led by the Spirit.[9] Paul was well acquainted with Christian claims through

---

9. Assuming the traditional authorship, these include Matthew, John, Peter, James, and Jude. Mark may have encountered Jesus if Mark is the fleeing naked man of Mark 14:51, and he was certainly a member of the first Jerusalem Church community (Acts 12:12; Col

his interrogation of persecutors, and shortly after his conversion, he traveled to Jerusalem to meet with Peter and James (Jesus' brother) and would have learned more of the traditions associated with Jesus (Acts 9:26-30; Gal 1:18-19). The messages of the apostles were written down as the apostles approached death to ensure that the gospel was not distorted. As such, it is not only the teachings of Jesus recorded in the Gospels that have a particular priority, but the whole NT.

Overall, then, we need to read the Scriptures Christocentrically, recognizing the epochal event of the coming of Christ, and therefore our theology must be a new covenantal theology. Such an approach means that every word in the OT is equally inspired. Still, as we interpret, we not only seek to understand the OT in its initial moment, but we look at the reception history of the OT into the teaching of Jesus and the early church. The writings of the apostles in the NT have a specific priority when formulating our complete understanding of the faith. Interestingly, many contemporary heresies depend on OT ideas for their defense, with less regard for the NT.[10] To avoid this, we allow Jesus by his Spirit to be the primary interpreter to ensure we appropriately preserve God's gospel.[11]

4:10). Luke joins Paul in Troas but travels to Jerusalem and Rome with him giving him access to the eyewitnesses he relied upon (Luke 1:2; Acts 16:10; 21:10; 27:1).

10. Possible examples are using Abraham's wealth as a premise for prosperity theology (ignoring his generosity and the NT witness that rejects prosperity theology); the demand for tithing in the contemporary church (noting it is a law from the OT which is rarely mentioned and that NT giving speaks of something more radical than a certain percentage).

11. See John 16:13a–c: "But when he comes—the Spirit of truth—he will guide you into all truth" (my translation).

It Must Be Interpreted in the Community

One of the most significant problems people of the so-called "Western world" face is rampant and almost narcissistic individualism. Most European cultures are "me" and not "we". Individual rights and freedoms are fiercely asserted and defended.[12]

Inadvertently the evangelical church has been corrupted to an extent by this individualism. In our zeal to help Christians grow in their faith, we have told individual people to read the Bible *for themselves* and check everything out in the Bible. Concern for individual interpretation is a good thing. However, if we stop at our *own* research and work everything out for *ourselves*, we fall prey to the idolatry of self, whereby we think we decide truth from God, and we can become prone to not listening to others. Christianity is about us becoming believers and joining an immense multitude of other believers who have received the Spirit and can interpret Scripture. Researching Scripture is not an individual "sport" but a team one. Furthermore, while we become God's children when saved and receive the Spirit, we remain prone to errors (including interpreting the Bible). Hence, the importance of genuinely hearing the views of others, remembering James 1:22–24 mentioned above, and Philippians 2:3: "but in humility, consider others above yourself" (my translation).

Good hermeneutics does not merely involve me reading the Scriptures but hearing the views of others who have also received the Spirit of God. We should want to hear how people of other denominational traditions read the Bible. The writings of Christians throughout the centuries—church history and church traditions—are also essential to help us grow. Hearing the

---

12. Defending individual rights can, however, be a good thing, depending on what is being defended and the actions and attitudes of the people doing the defending.

interpretations of other cultures, age groups, genders, and people with specific interests deepens our understanding. We should be as hungry to hear what other people are discovering in the Scriptures as actually doing it ourselves.

Of course, we will encounter false ideas, but we will also discover our tendency to misread at times and hear ideas that will deepen, broaden, and balance our theology. The Bible is also so diverse and detailed that one person cannot fully understand its every aspect and interpret it. As such, we need others who do the hard work considering diverse aspects of interpreting Scripture for us to grow in understanding.

We need those textual experts who work on the many texts from which the Bible is put together, those who know the original languages, are experts in aspects of the social and historical settings, those who understand our cultural context well, and those who have studied the significant figures of biblical interpretation across the story of God's people. We are sadly mistaken if we simply read the Bible and think we can be self-sufficient and know everything about God and his will through individual study. We fall victim to syncretizing the gospel to two great sins of this age—individualism and pride. We must read and interpret Scripture with other people.

It Must Be Interpreted with Humility

The previous point leads to one of the most important principles of interpretation—humility. Assuming we are the arbiter of all knowledge through self-study is arrogant and wrong. The Scriptures call us to the very opposite, humility. We must acknowledge our limitations, biases, lenses, and capacity to distort God's message. Concurrently, our minds must always be open to listening to what others are discovering about God and human life in Scripture. This principle is especially important for those who study the Bible at an increasingly advanced level. It is not uncommon for such people to become very judgmental of others and their views. Indeed, there is a time to identify an idea as false where Scripture is clear. However, we should always do so with humility (and love) and an openness to hear God saying something fresh through his Word. We get into grave danger when we think we have sorted it all out and atrophy, not hearing God's voice.

Such deafness was the problem in Israel when the Prophets called God's people to repent or face exile. They believed they knew what was right, rejected the Prophets' summons, and went into exile. Without exception, the people at the time of Christ failed to recognize who he was and heed his message. For this reason, Judas betrayed him, Peter denied him, the disciples deserted him, and Israel's leaders conspired with the Romans to crucify him.

We must always be open to fresh takes on God's Word, and where we think we have encountered something flawed, we respond with humility and grace, even if we must take a firm stand against it. The Scriptures declare that there is a time to resist false ideas, as we see in the Prophets, Jesus, the early Apostles, the NT writers, and the likes of the Reformers since. However, hermeneutical humility is always our starting point.

It Needs to be Interpreted Regarding the Original Languages

The Old Testament was originally written mainly in Hebrew, with a few sections written in Aramaic.[13] The New Testament was written in Koine Greek, the dominant language of the Roman Empire at

---

13. Those OT sections in Aramaic include Dan 2:4–7:28, Ezra 4:8–6:18, 7:12–26, and a few other words and phrases across the OT. See Brendan Kennedy, "Biblical Languages," in LBD, n.p.

the time. In addition, a Koine Greek translation of the Hebrew Old Testament exists, called the LXX or Septuagint (written several centuries before Christ). Hence, when we read the Bible in our own language, we read a translation of the original language. Ideally, interpreting biblical books well is best done in the original languages. Working from biblical languages is important because things are always lost in translation. We get closer to the intended meaning of Scripture when we read it in the original languages (the languages God inspired the writers to write it in).

Without a doubt, reading the Bible in the original language is ideal for biblical study. However, it is painstakingly challenging work to learn the biblical languages, as many have found over the years (although with Bible software and other tools, learning the languages is far less challenging). Furthermore, keeping them alive when you have learned a language is also demanding work, as one needs to use it consistently to retain it. However, learning the biblical languages and keeping them alive for the long term can be helped by joining reading groups and utilizing resources such as the Biblical Language Centre—which specializes in teaching Hebrew and Koine Greek with lots of picture lessons, class interaction, and a smaller amount of textbook work.[14]

Still, as one who has learned how much is gained by reading the Scriptures in their original languages and knowing countless others who agree, I want to encourage as many as possible to learn biblical Hebrew and Greek. If it is hard to fit into a one-year diploma or three-year degree, why not learn them over a year after completing the qualification? Furthermore, those who wish to study the Bible at the postgraduate level must demonstrate competence in interpreting the Scriptures from the original languages.

Still, if learning a biblical language is not for you, all is not lost. There are thousands of resources available for those serious about

---

14. "Biblical Language Center."
https://www.biblicallanguagecenter.com/.

God's Word to gain insights from those who have studied in the original languages. These resources include quality Bible dictionaries, original language lexicons, commentaries on distinct parts of the Bible ranging from the critical to the easy to understand, books written on parts of the Bible and themes, and countless articles.

Today, there are also excellent biblical software packages like Logos or Accordance to help study the Scriptures. Another clever idea is not just to read one translation, e.g., the NIV. We should choose one we prefer but also consult and compare other versions of the Bible that show the translation choices of others, such as the ESV, LEB, NRSV, NASB, and so on. There are also excellent Study Bibles with notes accompanying the text to fill out your knowledge. Still, nothing beats learning the biblical languages and being able to read and interpret Scripture from the original text (as we best have it).

Another terrific way to grow in our biblical understanding is to take trips to Israel/Palestine, Italy, the Balkans, Greece, and Turkey. Such travel is a fantastic way to deepen our biblical knowledge and connect more with the world of the text.

It Must Be Interpreted in Historical and Social Context

As discussed, the Bible is God's inspired Word, written by people like us. They lived at a particular time when God's people faced many challenges. When we set about serious Bible study, we try to immerse ourselves in that situation, the context. Who was the writer? Where were they writing? Why were they writing? To whom were they writing, and what was their audience's situation? What was the historical setting, and what were the cultural and social norms of the people in broader world history (like the Roman

Empire)? What do we know about the city (e.g., Corinth for the Corinthian letters and the church itself there)?

The more we can discover, the better. The Bible itself becomes a superb resource as we study and learn. Understanding Jesus' activities and teaching take us into the world of the Old Testament and many resources written in what is called the Intertestamental Period (the Apocrypha and Pseudepigrapha). There are also other Jewish writings like those of the historian Josephus, the Jewish philosopher Philo, and the writings of the Qumran community (the Dead Sea Scrolls), all of which fill out the backdrop. As the NT was written in the Roman Empire, the other writings of Greeks and Romans become essential to fill out the picture even more (e.g., Plato, the history and social customs of the Greco-Roman world). Those who have done a classical education will find extra depth in their biblical study through what they learned in that discipline.

Matthew and Luke used Mark's Gospel to formulate their accounts of Jesus. As such, we can study how they have used Mark and discern how they are shaping the story of Jesus for their respective audiences. An example is the many times Luke adds the detail that Jesus was praying to Mark's Gospel—this highlights that Luke wants his readers (and us) to be always prayerful.[15]

When we encounter letters from Paul, we can learn a lot about the interpretation of a letter by studying his other letters, especially where there are common themes. For example, when resurrection is mentioned, we can spend some time in 1 Corinthians 15, where Paul devotes a whole chapter to the theme. The book of Acts is also vital for understanding Paul's letters, as they tell us the story of the origin of his churches and his encounters with them.

Luke's account of the lives of Peter and Paul (in Acts) illuminates our understanding of Mark's Gospel (traditionally associated with Peter) and Paul and Peter's letters. John's Gospel should be read alongside the letters of John and Revelation (although some dispute

---

15. See, for example, Luke 3:21; 6:12; 9:28–29.

the same John is behind all these writings). The social customs and cultures of the people of the Bible are also invaluable resources when it comes to interpretation.

One of the greatest dangers of biblical interpretation is reading back from our setting into the Bible as if it were written directly to us in the twenty-first century in our cultural setting. The first step is always to read it in its original context. Then as we consider it and study our situation well, we can interpret and apply the Bible faithfully and well to our contexts.

It Must Be Interpretated in Its Own Literary Context

When we study a specific NT book, having gained a good feel for the historical and social setting, we study the book in its own right.

So, for example, when studying Romans, we consider Romans! When we seek to interpret Matthew's Gospel, we isolate the Gospel and explore the text we are interested in, in terms of Matthew's overall structure, purpose, message, and movement. If Matthew is using Mark's material, that leads us to another layer of interest—how does Matthew use Mark? We explore the OT context where an OT text is quoted, alluded to, or echoed in the text. We might explore Paul's use of an idea across his letters. Yet, after doing such things, we still come back to ask, what is Matthew saying here? How do we interpret Matthew? The same principle applies across the whole NT (and OT).

When interpreting Scripture, we look at how a specific text fits into the letter or Gospel narrative. This process is called researching the literary context of a text. An example is Philippians 1:27–2:4, which is the first direct appeal of the letter. Philippians 1:1–26 leads into it with themes like imperialism, the gospel, evangelism, opposition, and suffering. As we explore these things, we build a picture of how Paul seeks to persuade the Philippians. We see that

Paul restates what is in 1:27–2:4 throughout the letter and reinforces it with examples. So, we can conclude that the passage is a propositional statement for the letter. If we look at Romans, we see that Romans 1:16-17 functions analogously in that letter.

When we consider a passage, we carefully look at it regarding the broader purposes of the Gospel, letter, or Revelation; how it fits into the flow of the writer's appeal; what immediately precedes it; what comes after it. When we are interested in a theme in the passage, e.g., the gospel in Philippians 1:27, we go through Philippians looking for other uses of gospel language or parallel ideas like the Word in focus.[16] Doing so fills out our understanding of what Paul is saying in the letter about the gospel. The basic principle is that we interpret a piece of writing in its own right; otherwise, we risk not understanding what the human author (and God) wanted (and wants) to convey.

This section and the previous one on the historical background illustrate the two significant aspects of biblical interpretation—reading the text in its historical and social setting and reading the writing in its own right—in these two ways, we do our initial work of interpretation. Doing this is the essence of exegesis. But wait, there is more, to which I now turn.

The Fuller Picture of Biblical Interpretation

Careful and detailed interpretation of biblical texts is foundational for sound biblical interpretation. To get a complete picture of who God is, what he wants from us, and where we are heading, we need to do this for the entire Bible. By doing this throughout a book, say 1 John, we get a good picture of John's message in the letter. Then,

---

16. This is where Bible software tools and knowing the biblical languages can be especially beneficial.

we would want to do the same for John's other writings: his Gospel, 2 and 3 John, and if we think John wrote it, Revelation. By doing this, we can put together a Johannine theology. Constructing this is complex, as each document has its particularities and is written to its community. Hence, some scholars have produced ideas like the Johannine Community.

We would do the same for Paul's letters, constructing a theology of Paul from his thirteen letters (which, for some, is complicated by arguments against the authorship of some of his letters). As Luke-Acts is a united work, we can create a Lukan theology from the two works studied as a unity. We can do the same for the other writings: Matthew, Mark, Hebrews, James, Jude, and Peter's letters.

Still, even then, we are not done because we must bring this all together into a New Testament theology that will explain the common main threads and note the distinctives of each author's thoughts. As we synthesize the material, we discover a coherent NT center and space for their different ideas or expressions.

Yet, this is still not a complete theology because we need to bring this together with the Old Testament, observing how the whole story may be constructed into a biblical gospel. We can see how themes are tracked through the Bible to produce a biblical theology of a particular idea, like, "the temple."

Still, we are not there yet, because we need to engage with the whole of Israel's and Christian history and the ways that people have interpreted and put together their theology. They have done so for parts of the Bible and the whole thing—there is so much to explore. Such analysis is the work of systematic theology, where we seek to study aspects of the Christian gospel in conversation with the writings of people before and since Christ and, of course, Christ himself.[17] Today, wonderfully, theology is becoming global and no

---

17. One device used for theological interpretation is the Wesleyan Quadrilateral, whereby we bring to our interpretation these four things: Scripture, Tradition, Reason, and Experience. Still, Scripture

longer dominated by elite white males. Hence, we live in a time that gives excellent opportunities to read hermeneutical ideas from all humankind. And that is good because all people are made in God's image (Gen 1:26–27; 5:1).

There is yet one more aspect: how we live today. All the above is nonsense unless it ends with us responding to God in worship, service, planting and nurturing more vital churches, being the people of God that he dreams we will be, doing the works of social justice God has for us, and giving witness to God in the world. Theology that ends with people sitting around and talking and never getting up and doing anything of worth is dead.

And, of course, when we rise and get to work, we encounter others with different ideas and interpretations of Scripture. Such fresh perspectives send us back to Scripture, and we continue to ponder and discuss so that our interpretation always leads to new thoughts and ideas. We get into what has been termed the hermeneutical spiral, where we explore Scripture, encounter something, go back and explore again, and so on. The work is never done. One person cannot imagine they can do more than touch the sides. We need others, and they need us. Moreover, fresh challenges arise, and we must respond faithfully and intelligently.

Still, we continue the same way as we begin: opening Scripture, studying it closely, formulating a synthesis of ideas, closing the book, and getting on with being God's people. And so, this will go on long after we have died, or until Jesus returns—now that is an excellent hermeneutical question!

is the most important aspect of this. A contemporary approach to reading Scripture is "Theological Interpretation," whereby we interpret the NT through a theological idea (e.g., the Spirit, Third Article Theology) or work from Scripture to theological interpretation.

Part 2: Exegetical Principles for New Testament Study

Exegesis comes from the Greek term *exēgēsis*,[18] meaning "exposition, account, explanation, interpretation, translation."[19] The term is not found in the NT but is used in the LXX of Judges 7:15 concerning the "telling of a dream" and in Sirach 21:16 of a fool's talk. In the Apostolic Fathers, it is used for an explanation (1 Clem. 50:1; Herm. Vis. 3.7.4) or for the exposition of something like Jesus' sayings (Frag. Pap. 3:1; 15:1; 16:1; 18:1). The cognate verb, *exēgeomai* means to "explain, interpret" and is used of the explanation of experiences like Jesus' appearance on the Road to Emmaus (Luke 24:35; Acts 10:8; 15:12, 14; 21:19) and Christ making God known (exegeting God, John 1:18). As such, exegesis means to expound, explain, or interpret something. Where it has the sense of interpreting something, the prefix *ex* implies drawing *out* the meaning. So, in Biblical Studies, exegesis is "[t]he act or result of drawing out the meaning of the biblical text and explaining it; interpretation."[20]

The converse is reading something *into* a biblical text rather than something "out of." This approach is commonly called "eisegesis," compounding *eis* ("to, into") with *exēgēsis*.[21] Eisegesis is a common issue among those who have not learned the art of exegesis. They read ideas back into the text from their situation, experience, or

---

18. This is fresh material, not published in Keown, *Discovering* or *The New Testament A Taster*.
19. See BrillDAG n.p.
20. DeMoss, PDSNT 54.
21. This is a creation as the original Greek term εἰσήγησις, *eisēgēsis* means introduction, the act of proposing, proposal, and motion, and has nothing to do with this created idea. Still, it is a useful construct to warn against reading ideas into Scripture.

tradition that are not intended in the biblical passage. Eisegesis can occur through naïve popular interpretation—reading from life today into the text[22]—scholars and others reading a strong view into a passage and making the text conform to it,[23] and people defending a theological or ethical idea from a tradition.[24] Exegesis is a better way to read Scripture as it is based on the notion that God speaks to us through the text. Led by the Spirit, using appropriate methods of exegesis, we draw out of the text what it (and so God) says. Through

---

22. I was guilty of this before studying the Bible—I tended to read back contemporary things into the Bible from my own life, assuming it was written directly to me.
23. In my view, a good example of this is women in ministry. Two texts suggest Paul forbade women from leading and teaching men (1 Cor 14:34–35; 1 Tim 2:11–15). These become the core texts for many to prohibit women from such roles. However, when we read all of Paul's letters within the biblical story, we find that these are two passages written to two specific contexts where Paul says such things. There are, in fact, a whole lot of women working alongside Paul in his letters (Rom 16:1–16; 1 Cor 1:11; Phil 4:2–3; Col 4:15; Phlm 1; Acts 16:11–40). Also, when observed closely, women are allowed to speak publicly in 1 Cor 11:5, and so 1 Cor 14:34–35 is not a general prohibition but a specific command not to participate in the chaotic worship practices in Corinth. A look at the wider Biblical narrative supports reading these two texts as outliers, not a prohibition of women. Galatians 3:28 presents the social vision of the new covenant.
24. I remember doing this with the secret rapture, which I believed was found in Luke 17:22–35 and Matthew 24:36–41. However, I vividly remember being shown that it is not, in fact, the unbelievers who are left behind in these passages but the believers (like Noah). I was shocked at how I had read back a theological idea into the passages without reading them closely and seeing that this was flawed.

this, God's Word shapes and leads us. Our job, then, is to obey rather than resist its message because we have read our perspective into the text.

So, how do we do exegesis appropriately? What follows are some basic principles of exegesis (with some overlap in the previous material concerning hermeneutics). I will illustrate the ideas using Philippians. We should read the chosen passage (text, pericope) considering the following factors.

The Historical, Social, and Cultural Context

The first step in exegesis is considering the background of the letter in which the chosen passage stands. One aspect is the historical setting. Here, we discuss who wrote it, when it was written, to whom it was written, and any background we can discern concerning these things. So, in the case of Philippians, the author is named Paul (Phil 1:1). Now, in some NT letters, some scholars argue that despite Paul's name being there, he did not write some of his letters. This suspicion applies to the six disputed letters of Paul[25] and most of the General Epistles. In Philippians, Paul is named with Timothy (1:1), so we would seek to discern what role Timothy had

---

25. Mostly because, for some scholars, some letters are too different from the undisputed letters for their liking: Ephesians and Colossians (which are similar, so may have a different common author); 1 & 2 Timothy; and Titus. 2 Thessalonians is questioned because it is seen as a poor replica of 1 Thessalonians with some divergent theology. There are good reasons to reject such views, but they perpetuate today among many scholars. See Mark J. Keown, *Discovering the New Testament: An Introduction to Its Background, Theology, and Themes: The Pauline Letters*, Vol. II (Bellingham, WA: Lexham Press, 2021), 87–94.

in the letter (either co-writer, co-sender, or amanuensis for the letter).[26]

Identifying the writer in many NT writings is not as easy as one imagines, sitting in the pews, never having studied the Scriptures closely. None of the Gospels have a clear author's name. Hence, we rely on the prescripts added to them (sometimes in the second century) to know who wrote them.[27] The early church's reliability is a point of contention, so some are skeptical. Many evangelicals consider it likely they were right about something as crucial as authorship. In the case of James and Jude, while tradition holds these are Jesus' brothers, the names were prevalent, and it could be that it is other people with those names from the NT, or otherwise, it is simply unknown who wrote them.[28] Some scholars delight in challenging these things, and when we exegete, we need to consider where we stand, as that helps us understand the background of the writing.

---

26. An amanuensis is a secretary who composed the writing on behalf of someone.
27. Scholars debate when they were added. Martin Hengel argues for the early second century when the four Gospels began to be grouped. Others argue for later in the second century. Either way, none of the original Gospel autographs had the names on them, and we rely on tradition for who we think wrote the Gospels.
28. In the case of James, it is unlikely to be James the son of Zebedee, as he died ca. AD 43 (Matt 10:2; Acts 12:1-2). James, the son of Alphaeus, is a possibility (Matt 10:3), as is James the brother of Joseph [James the Younger] (Matt 27:56; Mark 15:40). Jude cannot be Judas Iscariot for obvious reasons, but could be Jesus' brother (Matt 13:55), Judas the son of James (Acts 1:13), Judas of Straight Street (Acts 9:11), and Judas called Barsabbas (Acts 15:22). He is like the same person who is the prophet in 15:22). This highlights why scholars do not immediately assume the name mentioned is that which tradition holds.

In the case of Paul's letters, we try to locate the letter in Paul's mission—its date and point of origin (provenance). Acts is an immense help for this as Luke gives an account of Paul's mission. Philippians is interesting because Paul is in prison (Phil 1:7). We can search Acts and the letters to see where this might be. Scholars have produced three main ideas, two of which are taken most seriously. The first is that he is in Caesarea, mentioned in Acts 23–26. If so, Philippians is to be dated AD 60–61. Few scholars think this fits the data. The second idea is that the great suffering mentioned in 2 Corinthians 1:8–9 refers to imprisonment in Ephesus (also 1 Cor 15:32). If so, it is dated AD 53–55, as we can work out when he was there from Acts 19. Ephesus is quite popular, especially among non-evangelicals. The third and most held view across history is that this is in Rome—the imprisonment mentioned in Acts 28:16–31. If so, it was written in AD 60–63. Many still hold this today, including myself and most evangelicals.[29]

The letter recipients must also be considered and are usually clear from the details in the prescript and sometimes other points in the letter. In the case of Philippians, it was obviously written to the church in Philippi in ancient Macedonia (see Phil 1:1; 4:15). We then explore all we can find about Macedonia and Philippi to get a sense of who the recipients were. Other Greek and Roman writers can be explored here to learn more about the city and its people. We can also look at references to Macedonia and Philippi in Acts and the other epistles.[30] If we look at one city with multiple letters (Thessalonica, Corinth), the other letter to the same city becomes valuable to aid interpretation. We can also explore Timothy in the other Paulines, Acts, and Hebrews to learn more about him.[31]

---

29. See Keown, *Discovering*, 2:250–52.
30. See mentions of Philippi or Macedonia in Acts 16–17; 19:21–22; 20:1–6; Phil 1–4. Also see Rom 15:26; 1 Cor 16:5; 2 Cor 1:16; 2:13; 7:5–9; 8:1–7; 9:2–4; 11:9; 1 Thess 1:7–8; 2:2; 4:10; 1 Tim 1:3.
31. See mentions of Timothy in Rom 16:21; 1 Cor 4:17; 16:10; 2 Cor 1:1, 19;

Principles of New Testament Study | 63

To aid interpretation, we want to know about Philippi's culture and social situation. Doing this will include knowing about the Roman world and Macedonia's history but also matters specific to Philippi. Bible Dictionary articles introduce this material, while commentaries and focused monographs often have more detailed discussions of these things. Advanced scholars will read Greek and Roman resources to learn more about the region. At this point, our study overlaps with historical and sociological research from specialists in the Greek and Roman worlds.

When doing this work, we find things illuminating the text's meaning. For example, Philippi's involvement in Rome's civil war and status as a favored Roman colony backdrop the use of military and citizenship language in the letter (esp. 1:12–30). Compared to other parts of the Empire, there was a greater degree of freedom for women in Macedonia. Knowing this helps explain the prominence of women like Lydia, Euodia, and Syntyche (Acts 16:11–40; Phil 4:2–3). We can background the planting of the church in Acts 16 and one or two of Paul's other visits there in Acts 19–20, which cross-reference nicely to 2 Corinthians (esp. 8:1–4).

We also engage in what is called "mirror reading" as we interpret NT letters. We seek to discern Paul's concern from a close analysis of what is explicit and implicit in the letter's details. In the case of Philippians, unity in the gospel is a prominent issue, and there is a range of other challenges to delve into, like persecution and false teachers. We note the names of the Philippians mentioned in Acts and the letters. From them, we gain a better sense of the town's and region's demography.[32] Greek and Latin inscriptions in the city

---

Phil 1:1; 2:19–25; Col 1:1; 1 Thess 1:1; 3:2–6; 2 Thess 1:1; 1 Timothy–2 Timothy; Phlm 1; Heb 13:23.

32. These include Lydia and her family (Acts 16:14, 40), Epaphroditus (Phil 2:25; 4:18), Euodia, Syntyche, and Clement (Phil 4:2–3). There are others not named like the Philippian jailer and his family (Acts 16:23–36), and if she was converted, the exorcised slave girl (Acts

can be considered at an advanced level. The better commentaries all have a wealth of information for us to read to get a sense of the background of Paul's situation and that of the Philippians. Monographs and focused academic articles on specific themes and passages are also invaluable for research.

The Integrity

The term "integrity" here is used by scholars to speak of the "unity" of NT writing. Some older scholars questioned whether some of the letters of the NT were originally multiple letters from the same author to the same recipients but fused into one letter. Integrity is discussed where 2 Corinthians and Philippians, and to a lesser extent, 1 Corinthians, are concerned. They note that these letters involve dramatic shifts of theme and tone at specific points. Rather than accept that the writer shifted themes and tone intentionally, they argue that these shifts indicate the letter is a composite of multiple Pauline letters.

So, in the case of 2 Corinthians, some consider it is three Pauline letters fused into one. The first is 2 Corinthians 1:1–6:13; 8—9, the second is a short letter in 2 Corinthians 6:14–7:1, and the third is in 2 Corinthians 10–13. If so, the prescripts (beginnings) and postscripts (endings) are constructs. Similarly, some scholars argue much the same for 1 Corinthians, and a few believe Philippians is made up of three letters from Paul to Philippi., stitched together: Letter A (Phil 1:1–2:30), Letter B (Phil 3:1–4:9), and Letter C (Phil 4:10–20).

When you exegete such disputed letters, this needs to be considered. Are these scholars correct? Why? Why not? In the case of Philippians, multiple scholars have argued against this

16:16). Philippians 4:3 implies a reasonably sized group of coworkers in Philippi as well.

partitioning of the letter, showing that the themes found in each part are consistent. Few scholars hold this partitional view of 1 Corinthians. 2 Corinthians remains the most contested. In my view, there are excellent reasons to conclude that there is, in fact, no evidence that these letters once existed as multiple separate letters, so we should interpret them as a whole.[33] Still, serious exegetes will consider this as they prepare to exegete a piece of Scripture.

The Writer's Other Writings and Movements

When we are exegeting an NT text, as will be discussed, the most important thing is the book in which it stands. Still, the writings and mentions of the writer across the whole NT are helpful.

So, in the case of Philippians, Paul is clearly the primary author. We can explore Paul's missionary movements through Acts and the letters. We can also consider the theological ideas in Philippians in terms of his other letters and their teaching. For example, in Philippians 2:1-11, Paul speaks of the example of Christ. He invites people to cruciformity (living in accord with Christ's attitude in serving in humility, to the point of death on a cross [*crucis*]). Exploration of Paul's discussions of a theme in other letters can inform his intent in our letter of interest. In the case of Philippians, he mentions resurrection and the transformation of the body in Phil 3:20-21. It is natural, then, to consider this passage with regard to his more extensive discussion of the resurrection in 1 Corinthians 15. Still, this is only useful in informing how we read Philippians itself.

---

33. If you are interested in this, you can read the sections in the chapters on 1 Corinthians, 2 Corinthians, and Philippians on integrity in Keown, *Discovering the New Testament*, Vol. 2, and see a little more. For more detail, consult technical commentaries on these parts of Scripture.

However, as we do this, we must be judicious to ensure we are not distorting Paul's theology by assuming he is saying the same thing.

At a secondary level, we consider Paul and his teaching in Acts. In older scholarship, some scholars were happy to accept that what was said by Paul in Acts is authentically Paul. Now, scholars recognize that Luke gives summaries of Paul's teaching shaped to Luke's purposes (in his own voice). Hence, when seeking to understand Paul's perspective, while considering Paul in Acts is helpful, it does not carry the same importance as what Paul *himself* says.

We must not import ideas from a different NT writer, assuming Paul thinks the same. Hence, when exegeting Philippians, we might find something in one of the Gospels or Acts, the General Epistles, and Revelation that illuminates something in Philippians. However, we cannot assume Paul is considering it identically. An example is "the Book of Life" in Philippians 4:3. The idea is found in different ways in Luke (10:20) and Revelation (e.g., 20:12). We can compare and evaluate the way the idea is used but without assuming the same meaning.

We also examine the original text and context where OT quotes, allusions, and echoes are concerned. We need to see whether it is based on the Hebrew text or the Greek (LXX). Then we can read the original closely, compare it with the NT, and see how Paul uses the passage. We consider how much of the OT passage is being picked up by Paul and how he applies it. A fascinating example of this in Philippians 2:10–11 is his use of Isaiah 45:23. Paul takes Isaiah's hope of all people bending the knee and confessing Yahweh's lordship and applying it to Jesus. We see that Paul considers Jesus to be God's Son who is fulfilling the hopes concerning God in the OT.

When studying Luke, we focus on Luke and Acts, written by the same author. Where John's writings are concerned, our interest is primarily in John's Gospel, the letters of John, and Revelation (if you are of the view that he wrote them all), i.e., the Johannine literature. Hopefully, you get the picture.

The Recipients

Biblical books were all written by someone to others. Another key focus is the recipients of the letter. Some of the things we will explore will fit into the letter's background mentioned earlier. We explore the non-biblical writings of the ancient world, the New Testament, and the letter itself using mirror reading to learn as much as possible about them. We learn about the origins of the church from Acts. Yet, there is also material about the beginnings of NT churches in the letters. For example, 1 Corinthians 2:1–5 tells us about Paul's preaching in Corinth, while 1 Thessalonians 2:1–12 tells us how he behaved among the Thessalonians. We learn that teaching on sexual holiness was an aspect of his initial teaching to them in 1 Thess 4:1–8. Where Philippi is concerned, aside from Acts 16 and 20, we read in 1 Thessalonians 2:1–2 that Paul was severely persecuted and shamed in Thessalonica (which fits neatly with his illegal flogging and imprisonment in Acts 16). We learn that the Macedonian churches were suffering poverty during his collection for the poor in 2 Corinthians 8:1–4 (which is consistent with their generosity mentioned in Philippians 4:10–19). Still, the focus letter is the primary source of information concerning the church.

I mentioned "mirror reading" earlier. We can read the letter as one email in a series of unique communiqués from Paul to Philippi and from them to him. We seek to imagine what is going on in the church. So, in Philippians 1:28–30, there are opponents of the Philippians who treat them in the same way Paul was previously treated in Philippi (Acts 16) and presently in Roman prison (described in Phil 1:12–26). He warns of false teachers in Phil 3:2 (dogs, Judaizers) and 3:18 (enemies of the cross). We must consider who they are from a range of possibilities and whether they are the same group in each instance; or whether they are different groups. If the latter, we discern what we can about the groups from the letter and broader context. Philippians 4:2–3 indicates some women in the church were falling out, and Paul calls them back to unity in the Lord. The sending of money from Philippi to Paul dominates 4:10-19.

We are trying to discern as much as we can about the recipients to inform our understanding of the situation and how the readers would experience the letter. How did their culture and social situation affect their interpretation? Overall, the more we can learn about the background of the recipients, the better—it helps us make sense of its message and apply it to ourselves.

The Genre of the Writing

A crucial aspect of biblical exegesis is considering the genre of the material under consideration. It is common in popular Christianity to argue that every part of the Bible must be read with the same approach. So, often Genesis 1 is read literally, as is Revelation 13 concerning the Beasts. Yet, biblical scholars consider this naïve. The Bible comprises diverse types of writing (genre), and we should consider this when interpreting it well (just as we would when considering C. S. Lewis's fantasy writing in the Narnia chronicles in comparison to his Christian books like *Surprised by Joy*).

The New Testament comprises a range of genres, including "Gospels," believed to be based loosely on the Greek *bios* (biography) genre. Luke writes self-consciously in the historical genre. Within the Gospels, there are parables—which should be read carefully concerning their symbolism and analogical aspects. Indeed, they have been the subject of great controversy as people have allegorized them in the past, often with a very eisegetical approach.

Another NT genre is apocalyptic writings—books full of symbolism and good versus evil found between 200 BC and AD 200. Revelation is a fantastic example, and other sections of the NT are also in that form (e.g., Mark 13 and parallels; 1 Thess 4:13–5:10; 2 Pet 3:1–12). We cannot simply read these writings literally (because of their genre). Instead, they must be read considering their genre, intent, and symbolism, and what they would have meant to first-century Christians in Asia Minor.

Letters are a particular genre that must be discerned (Epistolary Criticism), and to complicate matters, writers often employ rhetorical techniques found in Jewish and Greco-Roman writings. Hence, some consider they should be read as speeches (Rhetorical Criticism). There were also diverse letter forms in the Greek and Roman world. Some scholars approach NT letters in this regard. For example, Fee thinks Philippians is a friendship letter, Alexander a family letter, Holloway a letter of consolation, and Witherington considers it a deliberative rhetorical speech to persuade the Philippians. Doing our best to consider these things helps us be more confident in our interpretations and faithful to the original intent.

The Immediate Context

There are various aspects of the context of an NT passage. First is its context in the Bible and God's mission. How does Philippians fit into the unfolding narrative of God in the world? Interestingly, 333 years or so before Christ, a Macedonian, Alexander the Great, conquered Israel. From then until the Romans conquered in 63 BC, Israel was Macedonian or Greek. Consequently, Macedonian and Greek culture influenced Israel immensely as it was Hellenized.

When Philippians is written, Christ has lived, died, risen, reigns as Lord, and has poured out the Spirit. Early apostles were spreading the good news throughout the world. The gospel had reached places like Philippi, an entirely Gentile town without a male Jewish presence. While this is not something we will discuss much in an exegetical piece, it is also good to think in such broad terms.

Second, there is the broader context of Paul's letters (or, in the case of Luke, Luke-Acts; in the case of John, the Johannine literature, etc.). We can set Philippians in the context of Paul's mission, life, and letters. It is probably his ninth letter, the last before he goes on one further trip (disputed). On this trip and in Rome before his death, he wrote 1 and 2 Timothy and Titus. It is one of Paul's letters to churches (along with seven other letters), a prison epistle (so too Ephesians, Colossians, Philemon, 1-2 Timothy, Titus), one of his three Macedonian letters (1-2 Thessalonians being the others), and an undisputed letter. All these things can contribute to considering the meaning of the letter.

Third, there is a wider context within the letter to the Philippians. Exegesis involves us considering the letter's structure and form. Then, we can discern how the sections relate to each other. The immediate context includes the passages immediately before and after. The wider context is the whole letter. Often in long letters like 1 Corinthians, the sections are clearly delineated.[34] We work out where the passage in question lies. So, in the case of Philippians, we can isolate these units (1:1-26; 1:27-2:18 [made up of three sections]; 2:19-30 [made up of two sections]; 3:1-21; 4:1-9, 10-20, 21-23). So, if we are studying Philippians 2:5-11, we will notice how it continues the thrust of 1:27-2:4 and is then picked up with a "therefore" to lead into the next section, 2:12-18. Observing this helps us place the particularities of the passage in the immediate context of Paul's wider purposes in the letter.

The Literary Features

Another thing that is good to do when looking at a biblical passage is to consider whether it has any distinctive literary features. Modern

---

34. 1 Cor 1-4; 5-6; 7; 8-10; 11; 12-14; 15; 16. Some see the end of Ch. 4 as the beginning of what follows. Others put Ch. 7 with Chs. 5-6 as it involves matters of sexuality and marriage. Often Ch. 11 is linked to Chs. 12-14 that all address issues related to worship.

English writers love to use figures of speech and creativity, and the ancient Hebrews and Greeks were no different. When we have a passage, we look closely to see if there are any creative literary features in it. Often, they are found in the original languages and lost in translation. Hence, it is good to look at some commentaries that look closely at such things to see what scholars have found.

One example in Philippians is found in 1:7. In the first part of the verse, Paul says, "It is right for me to feel this way about all of you" (NIV). He then explains why: "since I have *you in my* heart" (NIV). However, when you read the Greek of the second clause, you discover that it can equally mean "since *you have me* in your heart." Because of this uncertainty, we must consider whether Paul meant the NIV reading or the alternative. Scholars discuss this. It is also feasible that Paul intentionally wrote it as a literary device. If so, the Philippians would note that it can be read either way. They would potentially recognize he is speaking of their mutual affection. This shared love would then be a feature of the partnership in the gospel Paul experiences with the Philippians (1:5). We are encouraged by Paul to emulate how they hold each other in their hearts. Good exegetes will consider these things.

Another example is the use of *chiasm*. A chiasm (or chiastic structure) is based on the Greek letter *chi*, the same as the English letter X. It is a framing device with a center and has distinct parts that correlate. Here is an example of a large one (macro-chiasm) in 1 Corinthians 12–13.

    A   1 Corinthians 12 (Spiritual gifts)
         B   1 Corinthians 13 (Love)
    A2   1 Corinthians 14 (Spiritual gifts).

The framing device (A and A2) correlate, and the emphasis falls on the center—Love, the most excellent way all things must be done! Paul uses many of these across his letters (people imagine some; some are real). An example in Philippians is Phil 3:9–11, which has two overlapping chiasms:

    A   and found in him

    B   not having a righteousness of my own which is from the law

        C   but one through faith in Christ,[35]

    B2   the righteousness from God based on faith,

A2   to know him

Parts A and A2 focus on relationship with Christ. Parts B and B2 speak of two contrasting types of righteousness. Part C is the center—faith in Christ is the basis of righteousness (not the law, as the opponents claim).

Then, there is another chiasm in 3:10

A   to know him and the power of his resurrection

    B   and the fellowship of his sufferings being conformed to his death

A2   if somehow to attain the resurrection, which is from the dead.

Parts A and A2 focus on the resurrection. The center and emphasis are sharing in Christ's sufferings and death.

There are oodles of such rhetorical features in the NT, and one of the fun things to explore is what they are. These include repeating words, plays on words, puns, allegory, metaphor, repetition of sounds (alliteration, assonance), hyperbole, onomatopoeia, parallelisms, and many more. When we exegete, especially from the original language, we notice these things, and we consider how they help us draw out the meaning of the text.

The Content and Message

What matters most is drawing out the content of the writing and interpreting its message accurately and well. We hear God through the voice of the author as a reader. Everything discussed thus far

---

35. Or "the faithfulness of Christ," as some scholars read it.

helps in this process, but nothing beats reading the letter repeatedly and allowing it to sink into us. Exegesis is drawing out what is there. It is like going to the beach, taking a bucket, and filling it with water. We then pour it out. The Bible is like the ocean; no matter how many buckets you take out, we will never exhaust its message. Incidentally, knowing this should encourage us to be humble as we interpret and listen to the ideas of others. No one knows it all except God himself.

Where Philippians is concerned, it becomes apparent that specific themes are critical. These are highlighted by the crucial terms that are often repeated. Noticing this yields a rich array of threads we can take up and discuss. These include, at least, joy, the gospel, citizenship language, thinking ideas, evangelism, unity, Christ, military metaphor, athletic metaphor, work language, opposition and suffering, service, prayer, love language, death, eschatological ideas, witness, sacrifice, generosity, righteousness by faith, imitation, salvation, and destruction. These ideas can each become the focus of an article, thesis, chapter, or book.

We also notice the letter's structure—how Paul uses his usual greeting (Paul ... to ... Grace and peace). As usual, Paul goes to thanksgiving and prayer (as in most letters). We see that he then does not launch the body of the letter but gives a report of his situation (more on this below). The letter appeal starts in 1:27, and through the letter, Paul oscillates between exhortation to the Philippians and giving examples. He weaves his travel plans into the letter. We notice that Philippians 3 shifts away from a joyful appeal to a somber warning—there are real threats to the church. He returns to his appeal in 3:15, which carries on to 4:9, and then he thanks them for their gifts (4:10–20). He ends as usual with greetings and blessings (4:21–23). From the structure, we learn heaps of his intent.

We find all sorts of other things that pique our interest in Philippians. It is the only Pauline letter that addresses leaders directly: "along with the overseers and deacons" (Phil 1:1). Hence, Philippians is the only New Testament letter or document that is written with a specific focus on leaders. This means that Christian leaders should pay special attention to the letter. Indeed, it is written by God's apostle, seeking to demonstrate quality leadership in his appeal. The central focus is Jesus Christ, especially in the Christ hymn in Philippians 2, where readers are to emulate his mindset (2:5). So, the letter has a special appeal to the leaders in the city, especially Euodia and Syntyche who have fallen out. Still, the Greek of 1:1 specifies that the letter is addressed to all the saints in the city as well. Hence, lay Christians are not off the hook when they read the letter.

Right from the start, Paul speaks of Christians unified in mission. This stress on unity begins with "Paul *and* Timothy" who are both "slaves *of* Jesus Christ" (Phil 1:1), "God our Father *and* the Lord Jesus Christ" (1:2), and their "partnership in the gospel" (1:5). The letter, from its beginning, is summoning the Philippians to such unity. So, he reminds them of their partnering with him in the thanksgiving and then prays for more love (1:3-11).

When he reports on his situation in prison, he mentions the advance of the gospel and two groups of people preaching from different motives (truth or pretense, Phil 1:15-18). Already he has an eye on the Philippians where two missional leaders are falling out—he is subtly summoning them to follow the example of the well-motivated ones (1:12-18). Through the letter, there are other examples given of believers who are unified in mission with the right attitudes, including himself (esp. 3:1-17), Timothy (1:1; 2:19-25), Epaphroditus (2:25-30; 4:18), and the Philippians themselves in their history (1:5; 4:3, 10-14).

We notice Paul's attitude to his trial where he faces death—he wants to be released to have more evangelistic fruit and to build up the Philippians (Phil 1:19-26) —the Philippians who are being persecuted are to do the same. The first appeal comes in 1:27-2:4, where Paul uses the idea of them as citizens of heaven, warriors, and athletes of God and calls them to emulate his attitude but with the ethics of God (not false motives like the evangelizers mentioned above).

Philippians 2:12-18 restates the appeal of 1:27-2:4 (forming a chiasm around the Christ-example in 2:5-11), but with different emphases. The Philippians hear about working out their salvation with fear and trembling—but not through their own strength—through God's! That is, the Spirit!—by whom, God in Christ is in them. They are to stop arguing and complaining like Israel in the wilderness and be untarnished lights of the world in Macedonia, offering the Word of life to all people. This work requires effort like that of an athlete or laborer—they, with Paul, are poured out in sacrifice, yet together, they must rejoice.

At the same time, sharing his travel plans and giving Timothy and Epaphroditus as missional partnership examples (Phil 2:19-30), Paul repeats earlier warnings of enemies in Philippians 3:2, 18. Some people preach a false gospel of law-observance, and that yields nothing. What matters is gaining Christ, knowing him, being found in him by faith, and walking in the cruciform pattern of Jesus (3:1-11). Paul does this, believing he is not there yet, but will ultimately gain the prize. The Philippians are to emulate him (3:12-17). They are not to be like the enemies of the cross. He outlines the future hope of all heavenly citizens—the savior's return, resurrection, and bodies of humiliation transformed into bodies of glory like Jesus' amazing spiritual body (3:18-21).

In Philippians 4, the contending women leaders are called to unity. Paul outlines the attitudes and devotional practices that will reinforce this—hope, gentleness, joy, prayer, right thinking, and emulation of Paul's practices (4:1-9).

Then, Paul finishes the letter body by thanking the Philippians for their financial gifts, commending them, and ensuring they do not feel obligated to send more. As he does this, he instructs readers concerning the right attitude to money—trust and contentment because, through all financial suffering, God strengthens his people and provides for their needs(4:10-20).

He finishes the letter with his usual greetings, but one has the assurance that the gospel has penetrated Caesar's inner circle—wow! The evangelization of Rome that will culminate in

Constantine and what followed is underway (4:22). The letter ends with grace—grace frames the letter (4:21–23, cf. 1:2).

Sound exegesis discovers such things and more as we move verse by verse through the letter, considering each part. We try to get to the heart of what Paul was saying to the Philippians and allow God to speak through his words to us 2000 years later. Everything he says to them applies to us, and we are challenged to obey, as were the Philippians. And their lives and ours are changed forever.

Synthesis

Exegesis should include a synthesis of the passage and its core ideas. Such a summary does not have to be complicated but concise and to the point. It is good to produce a one-line proposition or slogan that encapsulates the passage in synthesizing ideas. If you are preparing a sermon or Bible study, this summary can be the launch pad for this. It is good to break it down into the three or four main things gleaned from the passage. These could end up as subheadings in a sermon or presentation. Such things require our reflection and consideration.

Biblical Theology and Systematic Theology

It is also good after exegeting a passage to consider how it informs our understanding of the whole story of God and its inner connections and critical threads. We can go beyond this and consider how it speaks to our theology. Doing these things is vital, as when we study a passage of Scripture closely, there are always ramifications for our broader theology. Questions we can ask are, what does the passage teach us about:

The Triune God and Members of the Trinity?

The Story of God in the World?
Sin?
Salvation?
The Church?
Worship?
Ethics?
Eschatology (end times)?
Discipleship?
Marriage, gender, sexuality, and family?
Mission?
Interaction with culture(s)?
Government and secular authority?
Covenant?

To be fair, there is no end to the possibilities! One important question is, how has this passage changed the way I view these things?

Our Setting Today

One might ask, "so what?" We end exegesis by asking this question: What does it mean for today, for me, and for the church? Indeed, as important as reading the text closely in context and judiciously drawing out its meaning is what it says for today. We call this *application* to a contemporary setting. How do we apply what we have learned appropriately today? Doing this overlaps the previous section as we synthesize what we find in the passage and then think of how it might impact the way we live. How should we live now in light of the study? We must carefully consider our culture and church contexts and then, led by the Spirit, imagine how we should take what we have learned and apply it. Modeling this is especially important for preaching and leading Bible Studies as we want people to hear God's Word and apply it in their lives.

So, in the case of Philippians, what does it say about worship and prayer? What does it say about the way we Christians should relate to others? What does it say to the church about money, mission, and so on? Doing this also gets personal—what does it say to me? What does it mean to live by the cruciform pattern of Christ? What does that mean in pastoral, youth, or missional leadership? What might it mean for how I relate to my wife, husband, and children (if I have them)? How should I worship and serve God? Prayer becomes crucial as we pray and ponder on the passage and ask and allow God to speak. It is good to get up from exegesis and go to those places where we find God. Dwell on it and ask him to bring home what he has for us. The end of exegesis is worship and service.

Part 3: The Jewish Setting for the NT

The New Testament begins in Israel, or as it was at the time, Judea, Galilee, and Samaria.[36] This land is what we call today "Palestine" or "Israel and Palestine" (for simplicity and historical accuracy, I will call it "Israel" in these notes).[37] Its central character, Jesus, was a Jew. The prominent early figures Peter, Paul, and the other leading apostles and disciples were Jews. The thought world was Jewish. As seen by the many OT references and the dominant theme of promise (OT) and fulfillment (NT), the NT is written as a continuation of the Old or First Testament. The NT writers continue Israel's story, which is also the story of the world. So, all the Jewish ideas of Creation, the Fall, Abraham, Exodus, Covenants, Moses,

---

36. See for more detailed analysis, Keown, *Discovering*, 1:14–56 (Ch. 2).
37. Technically, the name Palestine was used for the area after the Bar Kochba revolt in AD 135. Hence, it is inaccurate to term the region Palestine until that date. It should probably be called "Galilee, Samaria, and Judea," but that is too clunky.

Law, Wilderness, Conquest, Exiles, Restoration, and Hope come to their fulfillment in the NT. Hence, we are looking at Part 2 of the remarkable story of God and his world. To understand the NT, one must be immersed in Israel's story.

Geography

Israel is a Middle Eastern country. It is hot in summer and could be cold in winter. At the time of Christ, it was separated into three parts: Galilee to the north, Samaria in the center, and Judea to the south. Galilee was a diverse region, also called Galilee of the Gentiles. Samaria was the area of the Samaritans, despised by the Jewish population, with their own version of belief in Yahweh. To the north were Cilicia and Phoenicia (Lebanon) and to the east over the Jordan were the Decapolis (ten cities) and Perea. South was Egypt. To the east lay the Great Sea (Mediterranean). The whole area is not large, about the size of Northland in NZ (north of Auckland).

Distinctive geographical features included the Judean desert where Jesus was tempted, mountains on which events occurred (e.g., the Transfiguration), the River Jordan, which marked the country's eastern boundary, and the Sea of Salt (Dead Sea). The main center was Jerusalem, the capital, where the temple was, and so the center of Israel's political, economic, and religious life. Other important centers include Caesarea Maritima on the western coast, a prominent center for Roman occupation, Sepphoris near Nazareth, Tiberias on the eastern shore of the Sea of Galilee, Caesarea Philippi in the north where Peter confesses Jesus' messiahship, and Jericho, near Jerusalem. The population of Israel at the time was around 2 million, with 200,000 to 300,000 in Galilee, 80,000 in Jerusalem (which swelled considerably in festivals), and 5,000,000 Jews living outside Israel (the so-called Diaspora, Dispersion).

Ethnocentricism

While the Jewish majority had diverse ideas and interests, some important generalizations for NT study can be made. They saw themselves as Jews and the rest of the world as Gentiles and tended to discriminate against non-Jews. Gentiles were required to Judaize to become a member of God's people. They did this through circumcision and other rituals. The need for such boundary markers becomes vital in the story of the gospel spread to Gentiles (below).

Monotheism

Unlike many modern Westerners and most people in history, Jews (like all ancient peoples) believed in God. Unlike the Greco-Roman world, though, for them, there was one God, Yahweh, whose name they tended to avoid uttering as it was so sacred. The idea of God having a divine Son was ridiculous. They confessed this every day in the sacred Shema based on Deut 6:4–5.

Covenant

Israel's history includes a string of covenants between God and Israel. Some scholars consider the first of these to be an Adamic covenant. In support, some translations of Hosea 6:7 speak of an Adamic covenant,[38] Paul understands Jesus as the new Adam who undoes the failure of Adam (Rom 5:12–21), the pattern of the Noahic

---

38. The Hebrew can refer to a place "Adam" (NIV) or the transgression of the covenant "like Adam" (LEB, ESV).

covenant recalls creation (Gen 9:1-17), and the whole structure of the redemptive story climaxes with the new heavens and earth that recall creation (Rev 21-22).

The covenant with Noah is made after the flood, where God, in his grace, promises never to flood the world again (Gen 9:8-17).

The OT covenant that shapes the biblical story is the Abrahamic covenant, where God begins to resolve the problem of the fall through his gracious election of a wandering Aramaean (Deut 26:5). God promises to bless Abraham and make his name great, grant the land to his descendants, through him bless the nations, that his seed would bring God's promises, and that he would be the father of many nations with a multitude of descendants (Gen 12:1-3; 15:18-21; ch. 17). The first part of the promise plays out in the OT, as God establishes Israel in the land, and they walk in relationship with him. In the NT, Jesus is Abraham's seed (Gal 3:16), and God's promises to bless the nations are fulfilled through him.

The Sinai covenant is also critical as God lays out the terms of the covenant in the Mosaic law (Exod 20; Deut 5). This law defines the nation from that point on. Premised on the curses and blessings of the covenant (Deut 27-28), Israel's fortunes rise and fall as they, at times, are faithful to a degree, but at other times, fail dismally and go into exile. By Jesus' birth, the law dominated Israel's life, especially those that marked them off from the Gentiles. Jesus fulfills the law and completes it. Sinless, he died for the world's sins and rose to new life. He becomes the end of the law, and the period of Sinai is complete (Rom 10:4; Gal 3:15-22; Heb 101-18). Now that Christ has come, the law merely enslaves and exposes people to their need for God as they see what God wants from them but fail to live it.

The other great OT commandment is the Davidic covenant, in which God promises David that through him, he would establish an eternal Davidic kingdom (e.g., 2 Sam 7; Isa 9:1-7). This figure would be the anointed one, the Messiah, the Christ. He was expected to establish God's reign with brutal force. Jesus comes as this Messiah but does what no one expected. He was crucified bearing the curse of the law and sin (Gal 3:13). He rose to cosmic lordship, and God's promise to David was fulfilled in him.

Finally, the new covenant is predicted by Jeremiah (31:31–34). This covenant is established in the new Adam, the seed of Abraham, the one who fulfills the Mosaic law, and the Davidic King. All covenants are ratified by blood, which is established in the blood of the high priest who sacrifices himself for the world's sins. In this covenant, people come to God through Christ by faith. They receive the Spirit. They remember this covenant each time they meet with the Lord's Supper (Luke 22:20; 1 Cor 11:25). God enacts this covenant in Christ by the Spirit (2 Cor 3:6). This covenant ends with people living forever with God in the world as he always planned.

Law (Torah)

All of Israel's life, including many of the legal expectations placed on the people, was governed by the laws of Moses. These were extremely important for preserving the status quo, pleasing God, and hopefully bringing redemption. The ten commandments were the heart of the law, but as we read in Exodus, Leviticus, and Deuteronomy, there was a vast range of laws to be kept. Sacrifices needed to be made at the right time. Tithes were expected. Sabbath-keeping and circumcision were obligatory. The festivals were important. Some laws delineated Israel from the nations and are sometimes called boundary markers. Although Israel recognized God chose the people through grace, they were bound up in keeping the law. Christianity is set against this legalism and especially the boundary markers. These are reframed in the teaching of Christ, Paul, and the apostles.

Temple

Jews loved their religious rituals, primarily centered on their cycle of feasts and the significant role of the Jerusalem Temple. Solomon originally built the temple. After its destruction by Babylon and a period of exile, it was rebuilt. God's glory did not descend, and Israel yearned for this to occur. In a sense, Israel was still in exile until this came to pass. The temple was being rebuilt at the time of Jesus by Herod the Great and was finished in the early 60s AD, a few years before the Romans again destroyed it. The place heaved during festivals and daily prayer times. Many areas would be messy and bloody with their sacrifices, crowds, and heat. The feasts, especially Passover, the Feast of Booths, and Pentecost, play essential roles in the NT story. These retold the story of Israel and kept them strong in their faith. The temple becomes vital in the story of Jesus as he challenged its system in his final week and stated that it would be destroyed and rebuilt (Mark 11:15-19; John 2:19-22). This prediction was taken literally and misused to have Jesus killed (Mark 15:58). Jesus meant that he was establishing a new temple in his being, a people of God formed into a temple that would surpass the physical space in Jerusalem. In all the Gospels, the temple is a place of debate between Jesus and his opponents. Paul picks up the idea of the people of God as the temple of God (1 Cor 3:16; Eph 2:19-22).

Feasts

A series of feasts mark Israel's calendar. These include Passover (Lev 23:4-8), where Israel remembered the Exodus when God passed over the firstborn of Israel because of blood and delivered them from Egypt. Christ died on the Passover as the Passover lamb, so Christians remember our exodus from sin into the life God has for us (cf. John 1:29; 1 Cor 5:7).

After this is the seven-day feast of the unleavened bread (Lev 23:6). This recalls their making unleavened bread as they fled Egypt. Each Passover, yeast is removed from the homes of Israelites as they remember. In the NT, this becomes a metaphor signifying the removal of sin (1 Cor 5:6–8).

The Feast of the Firstfruits is a harvest feast in which they thank and honor God for his provision (Lev 23:10). The idea of firstfruits becomes symbolic of Christ's resurrection as the firstfruits of the great harvest of resurrected people to come at the eschaton (1 Cor 15:20).

Pentecost, or the Feast of Weeks, is held seven weeks (fifty days) after the Feast of Firstfruits (Lev 23:16). This is the second of the three harvest feasts, where people brought the first grain to the Lord. In the NT, it is the day when God poured out his Spirit on humankind (Acts 2). This Spirit is the firstfruits of the fullness of resurrection life to come.

The Feast of Trumpets is a time of rest when people offer food offerings to God (Lev 23:24). They commemorate it with blasts from their trumpets. In the NT, the trumpet blast signals the return of Christ (1 Cor 15:52).

The Day of Atonement is a day when Israel confessed their sins and received God's forgiveness. The High Priest made the necessary offerings and entered the most holy place with blood to atone for Israel's sins (Lev 16; 23:26–32). In the NT, the curtain marking off the most holy place was ripped when Jesus died (Mark 15:38). Jesus is the High Priest whose blood opened the way to the most holy place forever. He has now entered it and opened it for those who believe in him so that people can worship in the throne room of God (Heb 9).

The Feast of Tabernacles or Booths recalls Israel's wilderness wandering in which they lived in tents. During the seven days of the Feast, Israel lives in tents to recall that journey (Lev 23:34). In the NT, Jesus is the tabernacle of God's presence (John 1:14). The church and individual Christians in him are also tabernacles of God's presence because of their purification in Christ and the giving of the Spirit (1 Cor 3:16; 6:19; Eph 2:19–22).

The other feast of note in the OT is the anticipated eschatological feast in which the nations will dine at the table of God, and he will destroy death (Isa 25:6–8). This hope is fulfilled in the people of God invited to God's great banquet and wedding feast, and they dine with him forever with death defeated eternally (Matt 22; Luke 14:14–24). Jesus was also the friend of sinners (Matt 11:19) who hosted banquets for all who wanted to come (Mark 6:44; 8:9). The Lord's Supper anticipates this momentous day.

Synagogues

There were synagogues scattered throughout the country and in the cities of the Diaspora. These were more like the community centers of the Māori marae than simply places of worship. There, young boys learned the Torah and memorized vast portions of it until their coming of age at twelve. The synagogues were not an all-Jewish affair. Especially in the Roman world, but also in Israel, some Gentiles were drawn to Judaism. Some converted and became Jewish proselytes. Others would attend worship with limited rights. These were called "worshipers of God" (God-fearers, devout people) in the NT. Examples include Lydia and Titius Justus.[39] The patterns of early Christian worship came from the synagogue, where worship centered on praise, prayer, and preaching.

---

39. Acts 13:43, 50; 16:14; 17:4, 17; 18:17.

Prayer

Israel had a formal prayer ritual. Prayers were held in the morning and evening sacrifices. Sometimes people prayed at midday. Each day they recited the Shema, stating that God is one and he is to be loved with all they have (Deut 6:4–5). This confession is the Great Commandment of Jesus' teaching (Mark 12:29–30). They also prayed the eighteen benedictions each Sabbath. When absent from Jerusalem, they prayed toward the temple. Modern patterns of Islamic prayer give us an idea of this kind of thing. Prayers were said at Festivals and on each Sabbath. The prayers were spoken at the temple, in Synagogues, in the homes over meals, and at other significant times. Prayer was essential to Jewish life.

Sabbath

Every Saturday, the Sabbath is a sacred time of worship and rest. It runs from darkness on Friday night to sunset on Saturday. Even today, for Jews, work is strictly forbidden. The Sabbath laws were a key point of contention as Jesus was healed on the Sabbath.[40] His claim to be "Lord of the Sabbath" was exceptionally provocative as God created the Sabbath and demanded it is a day of rest for Israel (Gen 2:1–3; Exod 20:8–11).

Circumcision

Aside from the temple, synagogues, festivals, and Sabbaths,

---

40. E.g., Mark 2:23—3:6.

circumcision was essential to Israel. The rite was also practiced in other ancient cultures. It became obligatory for Israel in Gen 17 when Abraham was commanded to circumcise the men in his clan. From then on, circumcision was expected for all Jewish boys (Lev 12:3). All boys were circumcised when they were eight days old. Any male proselyte must be circumcised (e.g., Acts 6:5). This requirement became a huge issue when the gospel expanded to Gentiles (esp. in Galatia). It was resolved (at least in principle) at the Jerusalem Council with new converts no longer circumcised (Acts 15). The removal of the obstacle allowed the gospel to spread more rapidly. However, early Christians used the idea of heart circumcision and baptism (e.g., Rom 2:25-29; Phil 3:3; Col 2:11).

Religious Purity

Also important were matters of religious purity. Israel's law was premised on keeping oneself ritually clean, which meant avoiding that which contaminates—the dead, the wrong food, Gentiles, the disabled, sinners, the cursed, and so on. Holiness was critical and needed to be maintained. Hence, one ate the right things, washed one's hands in the right way, avoided dead bodies, kept away from sinners, avoided the marginalized, including the ill and disabled (as God had supposedly cursed them), did not enter the homes of Gentiles, the women were not to enter holy places while menstruating and after childbirth, and more. Jesus challenged Jews concerned about purity concerning these things. He was prepared to touch dead bodies, eat with unclean hands, dine with Gentiles, hang out with the disabled and sinners, go into the home of a Roman, and so on. He challenged this idea directly, calling for inner holiness rather than external cleanliness—which is neither here nor there. Jesus' position on these things made him very popular among those at the margins and equally unpopular among those who wanted to protect the status quo of Judaism.

Language

There were four languages used in first-century Israel. Latin had been introduced by the Romans and was used among the Roman elite and their circles. Hebrew was the historical language of Israel, dominates the OT, and was used in synagogue and temple worship. The primary language was Koine Greek, introduced by Alexander the Great when he conquered the region, and the lingua franca of the Greek and then Roman Empires. It was the most critical language for life, trade, and commerce. Among Jews, Aramaic was the primary language of conversation. It is similar to Hebrew. Young Jews were multilingual and grew up familiar with Aramaic, Greek, and Hebrew through the Scriptures and worship. We see this in Paul, who speaks to crowds in Aramaic and Hebrew and writes in Greek. Fishers like Peter, Andrew, and the sons of Zebedee would use Greek in trading. Tax collectors would also use Greek in their trade. They may also be familiar with Latin. Although some scholars argue Jesus taught in Greek, his teaching was likely in Aramaic. As Greek was not his first language, our records of Jesus are translations and shaped by those who crafted the Gospels. So, our absolute certainty concerning the exact words of Jesus is a little blurred. However, these writers sought to record his words with great care, and the sense of his teaching is clear.

Wealth and Poverty

At the time of Christ, Israel's people were mainly poor, living hand to mouth. The wealthy elites were the Romans and those who supported them, including the leading priests. Many wealthy property owners had large chunks of land farmed by Israel's struggling poor (tenant farmers). The majority struggled; the vagaries of the climate and other natural disasters were a continual threat. They paid Roman taxes, tithes, and temple taxes. In a world with rudimentary health care, they were vulnerable to sickness. Life expectancy was thirty-five to forty years of age, with high infant mortality and many women dying during childbirth. Such vulnerability makes sense of the enormous crowds coming to Jesus. Here was someone who fed them and healed them.

A Subjugated People Hoping for Deliverance

A few things need to be clearly understood to understand Israel's social situation at the time of Jesus. First, Israel was divided into north and south in the tenth century after Solomon's reign. The north was Israel, and the south was Judah. This division remained intact even during the time of Christ.

Second, both kingdoms, Israel and Judah, had declined then and became increasingly syncretistic, blending Judaism with foreign religious ideas (e.g., the Baals). They worshiped false gods and neglected the social justice called for in the Mosaic Law. This covenant violation compromised them deeply, and prophets appeared to critique the king and other leaders who did not do enough to solve the problems. Eventually, due to their sin, the northern kingdom was destroyed by Assyria and went into exile in the eighth century. Although the south withstood Assyria, the same happened when Babylon destroyed Jerusalem and exiled many from Judah in the sixth-century BC.

After these exiles, Israel remained a nation under foreign rule, aside from one period in which they had more autonomy. After Judah's exile, the Medo-Persians allowed the people to return from Babylon, and the temple was rebuilt (read Ezra, Nehemiah, Haggai). It was never as glorious as the First Temple, and God's glory did not fill it. Those who returned rebuilt the nation, but the Medo-Persians ruled the nation. In the fourth-century BC, Alexander the Great claimed the nation for the Macedonian (Greek) Empire, and they ruled it. Then, in the mid-second century BC, led by a Judean family, the Maccabees, there was a revolt (160–67 BC). This rebellion was, to an extent, successful, leading to a period of self-rule and determination: the Hasmonean Empire (140–37 BC). This period is important when we come to the NT, as it seems many saw John the Baptist and Jesus as deliverers who would complete what the Maccabees sought to do.

In 63 BC, the Romans conquered the area. They had bases in Caesarea Maritima and Jerusalem in particular. Soldiers like Cornelius were stationed in Caesarea and all over the country. In Jerusalem, adjoining the temple was the Fortress Antonia, from which Roman soldiers could move quickly into the temple to suppress uprisings. So, Israel was under Roman rule.

Israel also had the writings of the prophets, which predicted a time when God would move and deliver his nation from foreign rule. Indeed, he would not only liberate the nation, but he would ultimately conquer the world. They hoped for a time when all nations would believe in the Jewish God, its males circumcised, with Jerusalem the world's capital, and the Jewish law as the legal basis for all human life. They had a range of expectations concerning what would happen.

In some scenarios, God himself simply intervenes in history to seize control. In others, a human or semi-divine agent would bring redemption. The main ideas included the Messiah (the Anointed One, or Christ, a Davidic King), a Son of Man, a Prophet like Moses, or Elijah. All would be warrior figures like Moses, Joshua, David, or Elijah and would be supernaturally empowered. They would raise Israel's armies empowered by God and his angels and then liberate Israel from the Gentiles. It is likely that Jesus' disciples were full of such hopes and expectations and saw in Jesus the person of a new Joshua, Moses, or David, who would bring this dream to pass. The story of the NT is that he did, but not in an expected way. The idea of a crucified Messiah, Son of Man, or Prophet, who would bring redemption through his death was, to them, an oxymoron. For Israel, any such figure crucified on a tree was cursed by God and not God's savior (Deut 21:23; Gal 3:13). This problem of a crucified Messiah is a big obstacle that Paul defends.

Religious Parties and Groups

There was a range of religious ideas in Israel at the time of Christ, expressed in different "parties" among the religious elite.

Pharisees

The first group was the Pharisees. While some were priests, most were not. They were religious scholars. They accepted the OT canon and Halakhah, a written law to ensure Israel kept God's Torah. They saw themselves as the gatekeepers of Judaism, and they were offended by Jesus, who challenged them on issues of eating protocols, Sabbath, and forgiveness (which he claimed authority over). They believed in a Messiah, resurrection, predestination, free will, angels, and demons. Their theology aligns with Jesus and Paul (a Pharisee) in many ways. But, at the same time, their theology is reframed through Jesus and Paul. They dreamed that Israel would become more holy, and this would bring deliverance. They thus accepted Roman rule as God's judgment. They hoped for better things. The ideas of the Pharisees became the basis of the Rabbinic writings of Israel after the Fall of Jerusalem in AD 70, the Mishnah, and other writings. The Scribes were linked to the Pharisees—kind of like junior lawyers.

Sadducees

The second group is the Sadducees. They were mostly priests, and many were in the Sanhedrin, the ruling council of seventy-one Jews, under the high priest. They only accepted the Torah, the first five books of the Bible, as authoritative. They did not believe in angels, demons, resurrection, and the Messiah. Hence, they show little interest in Jesus, only confronting him once over resurrection and marriage. However, they were important politically , accepting Roman rule and dominating Israel's political scene.

Essenes

A third group is the Essenes. The Essenes are known from the Qumran Community, a group of Jews who lived monastically beside the Dead Sea. Their writings were found between 1946 and 1951—the Dead Sea Scrolls (DSS). They were dissatisfied with the Jewish religious system of priests and the temple. They opted out, preferring to establish a community hoping God would come. They shared their financial resources. They lived in community. Some think John the Baptist was one of them; some even claim the same for Jesus and others. Yet, such links are tenuous. Their existence does show that Jesus was not the only one who critiqued Israel's religious system. There was much dissatisfaction at the time.

Herodians

It is also important to be aware of the Herodians. Herod the Great was a friend of the Caesars and a puppet or client king with limited control. The Herodians formed a vital part of the political elite. He is the one who tried to kill Jesus (Matt 2). He also is responsible for many magnificent buildings, including the temple and Caesarea Maritima. Any visitor to Israel and Palestine finds evidence of this everywhere. After his death around 4 BC, his sons were given control of various parts of the area. Most important is Herod Antipas, who governed Galilee, as most references to Herod in the Gospels, including at Jesus' death, refer to him. Other descendants feature in Acts, especially Herod's grandson Agrippa I, who put James to death and then died after declaring himself a god (Acts 12). Then, later in Acts 24–25, Agrippa II interrogates Paul and is interested in Christian things. These Herodians were corrupt Roman-like rulers who were not widely loved but were given significant political power. The Roman Caesars and Herodians starkly contrast the real King, Jesus, and help us understand how radical he is.

Sanhedrin

As noted above, the Romans allowed the Sanhedrin (sometimes known as the Seventy or the Ruling Council) to govern the religious world and some aspects of civil life. The Sanhedrin was made up of a ruling group of seventy men, mainly Sadducees, priests, and some Pharisees, plus the High Priest (e.g., Caiaphas), who the Romans appointed at the time. They were not permitted to put people to death; hence, when they condemned Jesus, they handed him over to Pilate. At times they violated the law in this area, e.g., the killing of Stephen (Acts 7). Joseph of Arimathea and Nicodemus (John 3), who buried Jesus, were members of the Sanhedrin. Paul was associated with it, holding their coats as Stephen was stoned (Acts 7:58) and having the High Priest's approval to destroy the Christian movement (Acts 9:2).

An Agrarian World

Other features of Israel's culture and social setting are important, especially compared to ours. First, it was a rudimentary, pre-industrial, and agrarian world, with all the challenges that such a context brings. Jesus spent most of his time outside the cities, in the towns and their environs. There he mingled with the likes of farmers and fishers, and his stories about seeds, harvests, and fishing are contextually appropriate to everyday life. Many people were poor. Life was slower, with no modern gadgets. Walking was the primary mode of transport. People ate off the land. Comparatively speaking, life was extremely basic.

Patriarchy

The ancient world was very patriarchal. Men dominated everything. The central sphere of influence for women was the home. Jewish women were not permitted to learn the Torah. All official positions were held by men, whether Pharisees, Sadducees, leading Essenes, priests, Levites, politicians, or educationalists. Women were chaperoned everywhere. They covered their bodies carefully and guarded their virginity zealously. Menstruation and childbirth made them unclean and marginalized them at times. They were concerned with women's matters (menstruation, childbirth, and lamenting death). Society was sharply divided, with a limited association between men and women in broader society. Many criticize early Christianity, especially Paul, for being patriarchal. Still, when we realize what the context was like, they were revolutionaries building societies in which women could learn and contribute in unprecedented ways.

Collectivism

The cultures of the ancient world were more collective than individual in orientation. Families were not nuclear (mum, dad, two kids) but were more like the Māori idea of a family. The family leader was the oldest living male, elders were highly respected, and the seniors held power. While this societal structure brought stability, it made bringing change exceedingly difficult. Young upstarts, like Jesus, were problematic. The family links were many. Genealogy was important. Children were seen and not heard and expected to uphold the family name. Life was about the collective—family, tribe, and nation.

Honor-Shame

The ancient cultures were honor-shame based rather than guilt-freedom based, as ours often are. What mattered was upholding the status quo and maintaining one's honor and that of the collective (family, tribe, nation). Honor came through upholding religious and social expectations. Shame was to be avoided and came through failure to uphold the group's expectations, as this disgraced both the individual and the group.

Reciprocity

Reciprocity was vital in these cultures. If one gave, the recipient reciprocated. Reciprocation could be positive, whereby one gave a gift and then expected something in return. The notion becomes extremely important in NT understandings of reward and retribution. Christianity is counter-cultural in that it is not based on personal reciprocity. Instead, God reciprocates on our behalf.

Hence, if one is on the receiving end of violence, one does not take an eye for an eye. Instead, one responds with blessing and prayer and leaves justice to God. Similarly, if one gives to the needy, one does not expect reciprocation from that person, as God will reward the giver.

Hospitality and Food

In the first century, hospitality was paramount, and life revolved around meals. In this sense, the culture was like Māori, Pasifika, and some other non-European cultures in NZ today. When one's people needed help, it was given. Hence, the shock when Joseph and Mary were rejected in Bethlehem before Jesus' birth. Large portions of three chapters in Luke's Gospel occurred at meals (Luke 7; 11; 14). Eating together means becoming one family and people; community is forged at meals. Jesus is the host of two open meals and commands his disciples to feed the crowds (Mark 6:30–44; 8:1–10). The Lord's Supper lies at the heart of Christian worship. Christian mission is portrayed as God's servant inviting the world, including those at the margins, to the Great Banquet (Luke 14:15–24). In this passage and others, eternity is envisaged as a great eschatological feast (Isa 25:6–8). As we come to Acts, the Christian home is the venue for the early churches.[41] Jesus is envisaged as food, and Christians offer the bread of life to the world (John 6:33–51). Hospitality and eating together spiritually and materially are at the heart of being God's people.

---

41. Rom 16:5; 1 Cor 16:19; Col 4:15; Phlm 2.

Marriage and Sexual Immorality

Marriage is etched into the creation narrative, with men and women becoming one flesh and filling the world (Gen 1:27; 2:24). Jesus and Paul endorsed these texts as fundamental to being human and Christian (Mark 10:7-9; 1 Cor 6:16; Eph 5:31). Consequently, Israel had strict laws concerning marriage. Marriage was understood as something between heterosexuals. While there is polygamy in the OT, monogamy was the ideal. The critical text was Deut 24:1, which forbids divorce except where there is unfaithfulness. This passage was interpreted by some strictly, others more liberally, allowing a man to divorce his wife for minor misdemeanors. Jesus was caught up in this debate endorsing marriage and faithfulness (Mark 10; Matt 19, cf. 1 Cor 7:1-16). A woman could not divorce her husband. Sexual immorality was anything outside of a faithful heterosexual marriage with severe consequences (Lev 18; 20). The sexual immorality of the pagan world was ridiculed and rejected.

Angels, Demons, Magic, and the Occult

Angels feature in the OT. By the time of Christ, angels and demons were a prominent aspect of their cosmology. The apocalyptic writings of Israel are full of encounters between angels and demons. Exorcisms were performed. While people believed in God, they also believed in spirits. Magic and sorcery were theoretically forbidden, but there is evidence that some dabbled in such things.

Abortion and Exposure

One of the features of the Roman world was the practice of abortion and exposure, whereby a father decided whether a child was kept or left to die (exposed). Abortion was condemned in Jewish writings, and although it is not specifically forbidden or mentioned in the NT, other early Christian writings utterly reject it.

An Oral or Aural Culture

In the modern world, at least until the digital revolution, we mostly learn through oral teaching and reading (books and other written literature). We increasingly use a combination of oral teaching, reading, AV, and other digital resources. In the ancient world, life was learned primarily through hearing and observing. Life was imparted through oral teaching and example. We see this with Jesus. He called his disciples to follow him, taught them verbally, ministered before them, sent them out to do the same, and lived with them, passing on the patterns of the kingdom of God by example and instruction. Sons learned from their fathers, as Jesus learned to be a carpenter from Joseph, and daughters from their mothers. Rabbis passed on traditions to disciples. There were sacred scrolls, which the educated could read and pass on. Often, these were memorized, processed, and the traditions passed on by those chosen to do this. The Gospels, and undoubtedly the OT traditions, began as oral stories. These were joined together to form the Gospels as the apostles neared death. Their teaching, which spread orally in the first period, became sacred scrolls, were copied, and passed on in mainly oral form in churches and across the empire. Eventually, Christians developed the book (the Codex), and Bibles were created (initially in Greek). Then, these were passed on across the Empire. However, aside from the educated literary elite, life was passed on orally until the printing press age. The printing press revolutionized the ability to pass on information as much through reading as speech. Now we are all living in the dawn of a new digital revolution. God knows where that will take us.

3. Setting, Then and Now, and the Synoptic Problem

Part 1: The Greco-Roman Setting of the New Testament

As ancient cultures were similar in many ways, many of the things mentioned concerning Israel are relevant to the Greco-Roman world. Some of these include the premodern nature of the preindustrial world, patriarchy, collective cultures, honor and shame, reciprocity, and hospitality. However, there were many other distinctive features.[1]

Cities

The city was significant across the Roman world. Cities such as Rome, Corinth, Athens, Thessalonica, Ephesus, and Syrian Antioch, were crucial centers for life. Jesus did most of his ministry outside the main centers of Israel, other than Jerusalem, which he visited for festivals. Paul, on the other hand, focused on cities in his mission. They were cosmopolitan and more open to change. There were synagogues in most of them, enabling him to start his mission among Jews and Gentiles who gathered there. The gospel could spread fast and penetrate the cities quickly.

While the wealthy had villas, most people lived in insulae, which

---

1. See for more detailed analysis, Keown, *Discovering*, 1:57–99 (Ch. 3).

were large apartment blocks. These were densely populated, even more than modern Asian cities like Kolkata. Often, there were shops on the lower level. These apartment blocks circled the agora (the marketplace) and were the centers of life. There were other places people gathered—fountains, baths, gymnasia, and for the Jews, synagogues. Many cities had regular games like the Olympics (e.g., Corinth). The insula was a place for sleeping and storing possessions, as life was mainly lived outdoors. Hence, everyone's business was there for all to see.

The cities were sizeable in some instances. Rome is said to have been a city of one million people. Alexandria, Antioch, Ephesus, and Corinth had about 500,000 people, and Thessalonica was around 200,000. Corinth was a young city, having been demolished by the Romans in the mid-second century bc in the Roman-Achaian wars, and rebuilt in the mid-first century bc by Caesar. As a young city, it was a haven for people trying to gain wealth and rise up the social ladder.

Polytheism and Religious Rituals

Unlike Israel's monotheism, the Greeks and Romans believed in multiple gods and goddesses. They both had a pantheon of twelve parallel divinities (e.g., Zeus and Jupiter), but they also believed in many other gods and goddesses. As polytheists, they were always open to new religions like the mystery religions of the east (e.g., Mithras). They had gods for most parts of life (e.g., Bacchus or Dionysus were the parallel gods of wine for Romans and Greeks), and they also worshiped the Emperor, the so-called Imperial Cult. Multiple temples were dedicated to gods, goddesses, and Emperors and their wives. They worshiped with sacrifices and libations led by various priests and priestesses. Prophetic oracles were especially important, such as the famous oracle of Delphi. They were highly superstitious, into magic and occult, and life was devoted to keeping the gods and the spiritual forces happy. The peace of the gods was maintained through careful religious rituals. Maintaining the status quo was critical; thus, keeping the *Pax Deorum* (peace of the gods) and *Pax Romana* (peace of Rome) was vital. When things went wrong, the gods were consulted. While other religions were welcomed, they could be blamed for adverse events, upsetting the spirits. Exclusive religions believing in one God, as in Judaism, clashed with Greco-Roman polytheism. Yet, there was also an attraction for many to Judaism with its solid ethics and family life.

Philosophy

Philosophy was critical to the Greeks and Romans. They had a great heritage of great thinkers like Socrates, Plato, and Aristotle, who were preceded and followed by many others. Many of the ideas that undergird western civilization come from them. The Greeks, followed by the Romans, who were enamored with them, privileged the mind over the body. It was believed the soul was immortal, from God, and placed in the mind. Philosophy was the path to fully being what one was created to be. Hence, they were extreme rationalists. Emotions were viewed negatively as unreliable, and women were criticized for being too emotional. The body was also seen negatively.

There were distinct groups among the philosophers: Stoics, Neo-Platonists, Epicureans, and Cynics. Stoics tended to focus on seeking virtue as the means of happiness. Hence, they tended to be more rigorous in their views. Epicureans went the other way, seeing pleasure as the highest good found through living modestly, gaining knowledge, and limiting desire. Cynics were traveling preachers who tended to be critical of the state. They begged for a living, often lived in squalor, and could be disgusting in their behavior. Some have argued that Jesus and his apostles were Cynics; however, most biblical scholars consider this implausible.

One of the great traditions of philosophy is logic and rhetorical argument, taught to all young elite Roman men as they grew up. Many modern biblical scholars consider how NT writers used rhetoric in their writings (Rhetorical Criticism). Undoubtedly, the NT writers used methods and ideas gained from philosophy, although there is ongoing debate concerning to what extent.

Roads and Travel

The Romans were great road builders. For example, they built roads that ran from Rome to the bottom tip of east Italy (Via Appia) and from western Greece (Illyricum) to what we call Istanbul (Byzantium). The roading system was great for trade, communication, and the movement of the military. Paul used these roads as he traveled around the Roman world. They also had a sophisticated shipping system, avoiding travel from mid-autumn and winter. At times, they made errors, as in the shipwreck journey of Paul in Acts 27 (which was preceded by three shipwrecks earlier in Paul's missions [2 Cor 11:25]). The combination of ship and road meant movement of goods was possible. Vast amounts of food were required for the great city of Rome, and this was possible with such a system.

Social Status

The ancient Roman world was very "classist." One was born into one's position. A child of a slave was born into slavery. A member of the elite senatorial or equestrian classes was born into privilege. To be a member of these groups was not easy and depended on being part of an old family with great prestige and wealth. From these classes came Roman leaders, born into privilege and leadership. Old money and the aristocracy were where the power was held. These people controlled politics, were elected to the Senate, and held positions in city leadership. Slaves could gain their freedom by buying it or being gifted it. They then became citizens, which was cherished. While some slaves gained good positions, slavery was not freedom and was reviled by the freedom-loving Romans.

The status system was linked in with honor and shame. One sought to gain honor through military service and benefaction (below). Such things helped one move up the Roman social ladder. Finding ways to do this was critical. Hence, boasting was a vital art whereby, without blowing one's own trumpet too loudly, preferably through others, one sought to climb the social ladder. One also sought to bring down enemies to elevate self. It was a brutal political and social world.

Elite Romans had lots of slaves, and so did little menial work. The idea of elite Roman tentmaking was appalling. Although a citizen, Paul's work with leather would marginalize him from those in the upper echelons of society. His tentmaking may have contributed to negative views of him in Corinth (2 Cor 10:10).

Patronage

The Roman world revolved around the wealthy giving to the needy and for civic enhancement. Giving in this way sounds noble, but it was part of a carefully orchestrated system to gain prestige and enhance one's status. So, people made contributions not just to improve the city but to enhance their status. A good example is Erastus, mentioned in Rom 16:23, who was the Corinthian city treasurer. The first-century Erastus inscription in Corinth states that a particular politician called Erastus gifted a piece of road. Some scholars consider this to be the same person. In NZ, we have this sort of thing where prominent people contribute financially to build libraries, sports facilities, medical facilities, and other things that enhance life. Doing this is terrific. However, Christians are not meant to give publicly to improve their status. Rather, they give quietly to improve the situation of others.

There was also personal patronage which functioned under the rules of reciprocity. Wealthy patrons gave as they willed to people in need. These people would then repay in kind. Sometimes writers received patronage. Some consider Theophilus may have been Luke's patron, paying him as he wrote (Luke 1:3; Acts 1:1). The poor would also gather at the homes of the wealthy in the morning, hoping for a handout. Such people would then be expected to support their benefactors in any way they could as they sought prominence. The Emperor was considered the *paterfamilias* and patron of the empire. Without the complex state-sponsored social welfare systems today, patronage was critical for maintaining the state. However, it ran a bit like the mafia. If a rich man looked after you, you looked after him or paid the price.

Marriage and Sexuality

Marriage was seen as the basic unit of life. Unlike in Israel, women could divorce their husbands and vice versa. Families tended to be much smaller (usually two children), as they exposed and aborted unwanted infants. Sexual immorality was much more prevalent and even encouraged at times of celebration. However, men had far more freedom in this regard than women. Women were expected to be chaste for marriage, and men were encouraged to "sow their wild oats." Same-gender relationships were legitimate, although it was preferable to be the dominant male (sodomite), not the one who played the passive role (catamite).

The elite, including the royals, were famous for their sexual liaisons. An example is Nero, who, after his third marriage to different women and one to a man, castrated a boy (Sporus) and married him. Prostitution was a part of the religious system whereby people could worship with sacral prostitutes. Prostitution appears to have been an ongoing problem in the Corinthian church (1 Cor 6:12–20). Paul's warnings against sexual immorality across his letters speak to its prevalence. Alcohol abuse was also a significant problem throughout the Roman world, linked to sexual immorality and debauchery. As the Western culture moves away from its Judeo-Christian mores, we see our society becoming increasingly like this. While there were always people who violated biblical ethics, largely speaking, the early church refused to compromise the ethics of Christ, Paul, Peter, and the other NT writers as they encountered such things. Neither should we.

Resurrection

The Greek distaste for the body meant that they viewed death as a blessed release from the cage of the body. They believed in an afterlife, but this was spiritual and non-corporeal. They believed in Hades, a grey world ruled by Hades, the Lord of the dead. Those who lived well got to live in Elysium, but the wicked went into the deeper pit of Tartarus. Those who lived well would experience pleasure and bliss. Remembering the dead was necessary, so they lived on in the memory of the living. The Jewish idea of resurrection was foreign to them. The body was dispelled at death. 1 Corinthians 15 is probably written to Christians who accepted the bodily resurrection of Jesus but who did not accept their own bodily resurrection. The NT is clear; the body is raised and freed from sin, decay, and death. The resurrection of the body is reflected in Jesus' bodily appearances and in 1 Corinthians 15. As with sexual immorality, even though the surrounding culture rejected resurrection (as in Athens when they laughed at Paul), the Christians never compromised their belief. Over time, many Romans were drawn to this belief.

Diaspora

Reference was made earlier in this chapter to the diaspora (dispersion) of Jews worldwide. Many Pacific nations today have more of their people living in other nations, such as NZ and Australia. Similarly, most Jews (about five million) did not live in Israel but in the diaspora (dispersion, two million). Under the Romans, Judaism was a legal religion. One of the strategic aspects of the Romans was to allow locals and migrants from other cities to maintain their cultures and religions as long as they were not a threat to the stability of the city and state. So, wherever Jews went, and if there were more than ten males, they set up synagogues. We see them in almost all the cities Paul visited, aside from Philippi, where a group of women met outside the city, indicating there was no synagogue in the town (Acts 16). The synagogues were the center of Jewish life in the cities. They tended to live near each other in ethnic enclaves to maintain their culture and belief. Older scholars believed that Palestinian Judaism was pure and diaspora (Hellenistic) Judaism was corrupted. Such a contrast is now widely rejected. Hellenism certainly influenced Judaism, but across the Empire, Judaism was much the same.

The synagogues of the diaspora were critical for the gospel's spread. Paul always began his mission in the local synagogue, knowing there would be a congregation including Jews, proselytes, and God-worshiping Gentiles. As was inevitable, he always managed to gain a few converts and start a church after they were driven out. These people, familiar with the Jewish Scriptures and ethics, became the leaders of the new churches. He would leave them to it and move on. Many of the first converts were Jewish and Gentile people who gathered at the synagogue. It meant the gospel could get a foothold in each context, the church could engage in the mission after he left, and Christianity spread.

Households

As noted earlier, the family was the core unit of the Roman world. Like Israel's families, this meant a more expansive family than the European nuclear family. The oldest male was paterfamilias, the head, with significant power. The family included the wife, children, slaves, other family members, and sometimes others. The home was also a place of worship, with shrines established. As the church developed and was driven out of the synagogue, the homes of the wealthy became the centers of the church's worship and life. So, we see churches in women's homes (Lydia and Nympha) and those of married couples like Priscilla and Aquila. These homes were likely larger villas, with a pool used for washing which became a baptismal, and an atrium that housed up to thirty for worship.

Mealtimes were also important as often, at the main evening meal, a speaker (e.g., a philosopher) would be welcomed to speak. Early Christian missionaries like Paul likely spoke on these occasions. The gospel would have moved primarily through family groupings in households and moved from household to household as people were converted. The church was more like the underground church of China than the basilica-like church buildings across western cities. This approach allowed Christianity to spread subtly, subversively, and spontaneously. Such a movement was hard to stop even when authorities saw it as a threat.

Part 2: The Contemporary Setting of New Testament Study

The purpose of this part of the chapter is to consider our current setting today with the Jewish and Greco-Roman first-century contexts in view.² Doing this is vital as we consider how we apply the Bible to life today. I will focus on NZ as this is where I have lived my life; however, NZ is part of the wider western anglophone world, and much of what is said applies to other western countries. If you read this from a different setting, I encourage you to think deeply about the similarities and differences with your situation.

The most obvious first point is that we live in far more technologically advanced societies than in the first century. Travel by foot, animals, or sea was slow and limited. As such, ancients tend to stay in their cultural contexts, especially those in the rural world. Without much exposure to others, rural people tended to be inward-looking and suspicious (as they are to a limited extent today). The major urban centers were more cosmopolitan and diverse and more like our western world today, with people from all over the Empire coming into them for work. Still, compared to our western context, ethnic and racial suspicion was extreme and commonplace (e.g., the divisions between Jew and Gentile, Greek and barbarian).

Further, communication is far quicker and more diverse today. The invention of the printing press, the internet, computers and cellphones, mainstream and social media, and globalization means we have massive resources to learn about the world and other people quickly. There is no need to send letters carried and read out by a courier; we can send an email or message in an instant.

In NZ, there are diverse understandings of God or the gods. Before colonization, Māori, Pacifica, and Asian peoples were like the Greeks and Romans in that they explained reality with a pantheon of gods and spiritual forces who controlled the natural world. Christianity came to NZ with the Europeans, and other religions have come with other people. With the rise of atheism, agnosticism, "no religion," and diverse spiritualities, unlike the ancients who

---

2. This is fresh material, not published in Keown, *Discovering* or *The New Testament A Taster*.

assumed the existence of spiritual forces and gods, we cannot assume that Kiwis believe in divine beings or see them as influential in any way.

Christianity was only emerging and beginning to spread as a new faith in the first century; now, it is nearly 2000 years old. Most Kiwis are, to some extent, familiar with its aspects. The faith as expressed in NZ today sets the backdrop for other ideas that have become popular. It is seen by many as a corrupt religion, ancient myth, or foolishness (cf. 1 Cor 1:22) and to blame for many of the problems in the world today. Those of us who want others to believe in our God face resistance and ideas about the faith in part caused by our checkered history of failure and distorted perspectives on the faith that cause people only to see the failings and not the extraordinary advancements that Christianity has catalyzed in our world.

Sharing the Christian faith in the first century required believers seeking to persuade other believers of the gods or God to adopt their perspective. Converting a Jew required convincing them that Jesus is the long-awaited Messiah and God's Son. Doing this was no easy feat for the Jewish world revolved around Torah and tradition, but it was a more precise and focused task than evangelization today. Converting a Greek or Roman means convincing them of the superiority and exclusivity of the Christian God; again, something that was not easy for their societies was ordered around their gods, but it was focused apologetically. Still, while sharing the faith was more focused, doing so was dangerous. In Jewish and Roman contexts, restrictions, imprisonment, and death awaited those who destabilized the political, religious, economic, and social order.

Although we do not face the same danger of persecution and death in our western countries, extending the faith is complex and personal, as one cannot assume what any western person believes. They might be vehemently anti-Christian, adherents of another faith, atheists, agnostics, new-age spiritualists, knowledgeable or ignorant about matters of faith—we cannot assume anything. One-size-fits-all evangelism is now out of the question. Whereas the church was a subversive faith of small groups in homes, church buildings devoted to worship now dot the nation. They are diverse in their theology and liturgy, and this further confuses witnessing.

Different public expressions of the faith confuse the public understanding of the faith. Some conservative fundamentalists expect members to tithe and are strongly outspoken against abortion, non-traditional sexualities, and government. Others are fully open, inclusive, and liberal, with a range of groups between the two extremes. One can hardly blame unbelievers for having no absolute certainty about Christians and the faith. Aside from a general appreciation for Christian social concern and some rare positive moments, Christianity features in the public space through public opposition to this or that legislation, Christmas and Easter (although these are secularized), and misdemeanors. Over the 2000 years, diverse philosophies such as capitalism, Marxism, social humanism, and neo-liberalism have also arisen, and the rapid spread of information further complicates things. Sharing the faith today is an incredibly challenging thing indeed.

Christianity started in Judaism and the Roman world in which people engaged with Jewish political and religious structures within Israel and the Diaspora synagogues and with the blends of local politics and Roman rule throughout the rest of the Empire. The Roman political system was imperial, with an Emperor to be worshiped, Roman provincial governors to be respected, local political rulers like client kings (e.g., Herod), and varying local structures. The system had aspects of democracy, but only among elite wealthy males who held office. The vast majority were disenfranchised. Autocratic leadership and imperialism were dominant.

Today's NZ is different. It is part of an empire, but the leadership is benign and of no consequence other than to give us a shared identity with other Commonwealth countries. Ours is a parliamentary democracy in which people are invited to vote, participate in the democratic process in numerous ways, and run for office. Whereas the ancients had no say, unless they were from the tiny elite and powerful senatorial and equestrian classes, they had no way of participating. The government was a monstrous beast, prepared to subjugate and use force, bestowing favor on the complaint and punishing those who resisted. After Constantine, Christianity had a considerable influence on the State and the shape of life. Now, it is thrust to the margins, and Christians struggle to function in what is now not a welcoming place.

The challenge is further complicated because, in many Western cultures, Christian values are now modified by de-Christianized secular humanism that has taken what it wants from Christian ethics, leaving the power that drove it behind (2 Tim 3:5). The Judeo-Christian ethic in terms of sexuality, the sanctity of life, marriage, and the family, no longer dominate political discourse. While most Kiwis desire that the marginalized are cared for, since the Great Depression, this has increasingly been taken over by the State. Where the church is active in this space, it often works with the government and its funding. There is often no apparent Christian ethos and caring for those in need loses its missional power. Many local churches fill the gaps in the State social welfare system, but this is rarely acknowledged and varies depending on the church's capacity. The church struggles to find its place in such a space and loses its distinctiveness.

We also grapple with the problem of colonization subjugating our Indigenous people and the Treaty of Waitangi, which envisions a partnership between the Crown and Māori, and the critical work of ensuring that Tangata Whenua[3] flourishes. However, distinct groups of Kiwis within the church and beyond imagine how this might happen differently, which can easily cause misunderstanding and tension. With such things and others in view, Christian engagement with the State is complex and requires our best thinking.

Another feature of our culture is its hyper-individualism. Individual human rights are a pillar of our social imagination, and

---

3. The indigenous Māori people of New Zealand.

we struggle to find ways to express healthy collectivism. More akin to non-western cultures, ancient societies, to varying degrees, were all collective, based on expansive family, tribal, and national interests—collectivism held sway over individualism. Corporate responsibility rather than individual rights was dominant. There is tension in the church between faith self-determinism and church traditions. Christianity brought a revolution in religion whereby a person's individual faith determined their destiny, not their participation in the prevailing religion (e.g., Judaism). Essential to the story of God we are embedded in is our personal conversion, baptism, receipt of the Spirit, and maturing as a disciple. Yet, without doubt, we have dislocated individual salvation from the summons of the gospel to participate in a people. We saved into a community in which we must value the views of others in history (tradition) and our communities. The church is a family, and unity and togetherness are supreme virtues.

The ancient societies were patriarchal, ethnically and racially divided, layered with a few elites holding most of the wealth and power, with the vast majority of people living close to the breadline. Christianity exploded into this world, shattering its social conventions. Suddenly, slaves and freedpeople could be citizens fully participating together in the faith community. Indeed, Jesus was a non-citizen (as evidenced by his crucifixion), and most of the first Christians were humble nobodies (1 Cor 1:26).

The mission to win all people to faith meant women were encouraged to become educated and to pass on their faith to others. The great ethnic and racial divisions were shattered as Jews, Barbarians, Gentiles, Scythians, Arabs, Syrians, Greeks, and Romans came together to form God's people bound together in Christ. Caring for the marginalized meant the socioeconomic situation of the poor was transformed. They were no longer seen as those cursed by the divine but as God's precious image bearers to be fed, loved, and nurtured. They, too, could be full participants in God's people. Now, most in the west live in wealthy societies where, although the gap between rich and poor remains (and is growing), our societies are committed to these things. Hence, unless it is radically and openly focused on eradicating social injustice, the church does not look that different to the world. Whereas the church filled social gaps, now it is etched into our political structure that the government is to do this.

The church, then, struggles to find its place in such a social situation. Still, we also live at a time where the secular utopia western civilization yearns to bring to pass through its political structures is coming apart. Their doing so gives new opportunities for the church to continue to worship our God passionately and in culturally appropriate ways, build strong communities of faith that embody the social vision of the gospel, preach the Word with words that are wise, full of grace, and seasoned with salt, and reach out into our communities with the attitude of Christ and acts of compassion.

In conclusion, I encourage you to think deeply about how the tiny Christian community of 120 that met in Jerusalem after Christ's resurrection changed the world, beginning with the Roman Empire. As we reflect on the challenges of today and their extraordinary Spirit-impelled commitment, and as we get on our knees and pray and rise to do our absolute best thinking, we too can change the world. Or better, through us, God will continue to do so. Kia Kaha, stay strong, and be the people of God!

Part 3: The Synoptic Problem

A Gospel is an account of the good news, the *euangelion*.[4] The Bible includes four Gospels: Matthew, Mark, Luke, and John. These are

---

4. See for more detailed analysis, Keown, *Discovering*, 1:110–128 (Ch. 5).

all from the ancient genre of biography (*bios*), in which a prominent person's life is narrated. In this case, the person is Jesus! They are all narratives. They continue the OT story. Sometimes people today do not get why there are four Gospels. Why not harmonize them into one? Some in the second-century ad had the same problem. Tatian wrote a harmony called the Diatessaron based on John, including material from the other four Gospels.[5] When the church debated making this their sacred text, it was roundly rejected.

The four Gospels give four views of Jesus. In Jewish thought, two to three witnesses must agree to prove a legal point. The four Gospels are then essential to give credence to the Christian claims. Further, early Christians did not see a problem with the four Gospels. They not only gave credibility to the Christian claims, but they give four eyewitness perspectives. Imagine one goes to a sports ground to watch a major sports event. Later, you ask a person from each of the four main grandstands to narrate their story of the game. There will be many of the same things in the accounts, especially the key moments. However, there will also be differences in detail, perspective, and different points. The four Gospels are like four views of Jesus. They are also written for audiences at different times facing different issues. Hence, they have differing emphases, depending on the points the Gospel writer is trying to make. Many skeptics note that a range of other gospels should be given equal privilege (e.g., the Gospel of Thomas). There are other gospels, but the early church was careful to preserve those that were written early, are based on eyewitness tradition, and preserve the authentic apostolic gospel. These other gospels are much later and not to be trusted.

A casual observer will notice that the first three Gospels, Matthew, Mark, and Luke, have a lot of similar material. They are thus labeled the Synoptic Gospels. The term "synoptic" is formed by

---

5. See "Diatessaron," *Early Christian Writings*, http://www.earlychristianwritings.com/text/diatessaron.html.

syn (with) and *optic* (sight), meaning they can be laid side by side and read simultaneously. Hence, they can be read in a synopsis.

This commonality has led to vast swathes of scholarship as people try to determine how they are related. Here is a summary of the main views, with the final one dominant in scholarship.

1) An Oral-Tradition Relationship: as noted earlier, the Gospels were formed from circulating oral traditions. A few have tried to argue that there is no literary relationship between the Gospels and that their commonalities are due to shared oral traditions. This idea is unlikely as the correspondence between the three Gospels is too close to be purely oral.

2) Matthew's Gospel First: Advocates of the Griesbach Hypothesis, like Augustine, consider that Matthew was the first Gospel. Mark and Luke are then based on Matthew. Mark abbreviates Matthew. Luke uses Matthew and perhaps Mark and creates his own story with a few extras. This position is held by few today.

3) Mark's Gospel First, Matthew Second, Luke Used Both: Some scholars today see Mark as first, followed by Matthew and then Luke. In this view, the Farrar-Goulder Hypothesis, Mark's Gospel was written at the end of Peter's life by Mark. Matthew used Mark and other material to write his Gospel. Luke used both Mark and Matthew to write his. This minority position is gaining traction today.

4) Mark's Gospel First, Luke Second, Matthew Third: Some reverse the previous, arguing Mark was first, Luke wrote with Mark's Gospel and other sources he found himself in his research, and Matthew wrote using Mark and Luke. This view is the Wilke Hypothesis and is not widely held today.

5) Mark's Gospel First, A Common Source Q (Quelle), Matthew and Luke Wrote Independently using Mark, Q, and Their Sources: This perspective is dominant today. It is argued Mark was written toward the end of Peter's life, sometime in the 60s to early 70s. The material common to Luke and Matthew is said to be from an early lost document called Q (from the German *Quelle*, "Source").

Matthew and Luke wrote their Gospels using a combination of Mark, Q, and the material they gathered (M and L). Some see Q as a combination of oral and written sources.

The final view above is the main view of scholarship. Is it important? At one level, not at all. On another level, it is crucial to interpret Matthew and Luke. If we believe Luke and Matthew used Mark for their version, we can study how the two evangelists adapted and used Mark to discern their perspectives. We can see what they left in, left out, and how they reword it to make a point. For example, Luke will often add a detail that Jesus was praying when something happened (e.g., his baptism). We realize that prayer is essential in Luke's story of Jesus. The implication is that he wants readers to pray! For those who wish to advance in biblical study beyond an introductory level, the Synoptic Problem is essential for understanding a passage and the author's intention in telling the story the way they do.

4. The Synoptic Gospels—Mark and Matthew

Each Gospel will be briefly introduced in this section, and their distinctives will be noted. This material is elementary, and fuller detail can be gained from Chs. 6-7 in Vol. 1 of *Discovering the New Testament*.[1]

Part 1: The Distinctives of Mark's Gospel—Background Matters

As noted in the previous section, the three Synoptic Gospels are related in some way. Likely, Matthew and Luke used Mark's account as the basis for their Gospels. Matthew and Luke's use of Mark shows its preeminence in the early church. Early church tradition also states that Mark's Gospel was put together at the time of Peter's death in the mid-60s and represents Peter's kerygma, his proclamation. While the three Synoptics have commonalities, there are distinctives, and some of these will be discussed in what follows.

Mark's Gospel was likely written in the 60s or 70s AD. Some scholars do not consider John Mark to be the writer of Mark's Gospel, producing various alternatives to the traditional view. However, the traditional understanding of Mark's Gospel has significant early church support.

Papias, a second-century bishop of Hierapolis, in what we would call western Turkey, notes that Mark was Peter's interpreter.

---

1. Keown, *Discovering*, 1:128-215 (Chs. 6-7).

Mark wrote down with some accuracy what he recalled of Peter's proclamation concerning the things done by God. His account is not ordered chronologically but is an account arranged for his purposes (Eusebius, *Hist. eccl.* 3.39.15–16). Mark is traditionally understood to be the John Mark of Acts, a member of the early Jerusalem Christian community (Acts 12:12), and a relative of Barnabas (Col 4:10). He traveled with Paul for a period but returned to Jerusalem (Acts 12:25–13:13), and in the aftermath of this, he and Barnabas fell out with Paul, and he engaged in mission with Barnabas (esp. Acts 15:36–41). He is connected with both Peter and Paul in Rome in later life (Col 4:10; 2 Tim 4:11; Phlm 24; 1 Pet 5:13). The writer may be found in the narrative of Mark as the young man who fled naked in the Garden of Gethsemane (Mark 14:52). Traditionally, Mark's Gospel is connected to Roman Christianity where it is likely Mark wrote the material near Peter's death. During this time, Nero was Emperor, and Christians were severely persecuted when Nero blamed them for the fire of Rome (Tacitus, *Nero*, 15.44). While many dispute that the writer is this Mark and the link to Peter on the basis that the evidence is flimsy, the early church was in no doubt, and there seems no good reason to dispute it from this distance.

Mark's Gospel is a fast-moving account of Jesus indicated by the continual use of "immediately" (*euthys*, forty-two times). He entitles it a Gospel (*euangelion*), a declaration of the good news of God's salvation. Without a doubt, the central theme is Jesus the Messiah, the Son of God (Mark 1:1). There is no infancy narrative. Still, it begins with John in the wilderness crying out from Isaiah and Malachi that he is the long-awaited herald of the Messiah. Jesus appears abruptly, is baptized as Servant King, tempted by Satan, and launches his ministry as the Messiah.

The central theme of Jesus' ministry is the kingdom of God. In the backdrop are two sets of presuppositions. First, there are the Jewish expectations of a military Messiah who will cleanse the land of evil, i.e., the Gentiles. If Jesus were this Messiah, he would be expected to raise an army and do just that with God's power. He is named Jesus,

Greek for the Hebrew name "Joshua" (God saves), which provokes memories of the OT Joshua.

The second point of background is the things happening in the Roman world during Nero's despotic rule in the mid-60s. It was written before or after the Neronian persecution. This period was a time of persecution for Christians who were "taking up their crosses," The story of Jesus is in vivid contrast to Roman imperialism based on the dynastic rule, luxury, military force, and political machinations.

This Jesus gathers twelve disciples, recalling the tribes of Israel—a renewed Israel is being launched. Rather than military conquest, he sets about his ministry of healing, deliverance, feeding, preaching the good news of the kingdom, summoning disciples, and inviting people into it through repentance and faith. These show what the concerns of the kingdom are. This kingdom will grow like a mustard seed and become huge so that the nations enter it. The first half of the Gospel is the revelation of this Jesus.

Through the Gospel, secrecy is demanded when anyone recognizes Jesus as the Messiah, whether a demon or a person. This recurring limitation is called the "Messianic Secret" and is likely because Jesus did not want to excite ideas of revolution, which were associated with Messianic hopes. Hence, he urged quietness from all who recognized him.

The crucial point of Mark is the confession in Mark 8:29, where Peter states: "you are the Messiah." In the rest of the Gospel, Mark's Jesus unpacks what this Messiah and his kingdom are about—not military power but the power of service, love, prayer, holiness, sexual fidelity, and mercy that will change the world. As a result, we see Jesus hanging out with all the wrong people, like children and blind beggars, repudiating the world's political systems, challenging the rich and powerful alike, calling for the disciples to be servants and like children, and predicting the destruction of the temple and Jerusalem. This event marks the end of Judaism as it is known and its continuation in Jesus and his people.

The climax of his demonstration of what it means to be the

Messiah is his death for the world as a ransom for many people. He is Isaiah's Servant, Messiah, Son of Man, and Son of God, all tied up in one, and his modus operandi is servanthood. Jesus died on a cross deserted by almost everyone, with the only confessor of his Messiahship in Mark being a Roman soldier. Rather than destroy the Roman world, he dies for their sins and invites them into his kingdom to be his disciples, prepared to count the cost of following Jesus.

The earliest texts of the Gospel end abruptly in Mark 16:8 after the angel announces Jesus' resurrection. The longer endings are important historically but are not part of the original Gospel. The readers are left with questions at the surprising end of the Gospel: "who is this man?" And "What are we to do?" The Gospel's answer speaks powerfully to Romans at the time who are indeed doing this; the call of the gospel is to "come and die," as German theologian (and martyr) Dietrich Bonhoeffer has said.[2]

Part 2: Key Themes of Mark's Gospel

Mention has been made of the kingdom of God as a central theme in Mark's account. As significant space is given to the central Synoptic themes in Chapter Five, I will summarize the themes here as most apply to Mark and Matthew and Luke.

The most apparent theme is Jesus, as the Gospel gives an account of his life. Jesus is Theo, the expected one. He is the Messiah and Son of God. His coming fulfills the prophets' hopes, and he is the King around whom the kingdom revolves. God has sent him, and he has

---

2. Dietrich Bonhoeffer, *The Cost of Discipleship*, trans. R. H. Fuller and Irmgard Booth (London: SCM Press, 2001), 44: the full quote is: "When Christ calls a man, he bids him come and die."

come to declare that the kingdom of God is breaking in through him. The Gospel gives a succinct summary of his ministry of preaching and teaching in parables, miracles, and calling disciples. It moves inexorably to the events leading to his death, his crucifixion, and the mystery of the empty tomb when a young man declares that he is risen and summons the women to meet him in Galilee.

As mentioned in the previous section, the kingdom of God is a core theme. Jesus comes as Messiah and Servant proclaiming the inbreaking of God's reign. The kingdom is seen in his power, as people are restored, forgiven, and joined to God's people as disciples. The king's death is utterly surprising but is crucial as Jesus gave his life as a ransom inaugurating the new covenant for the forgiveness of sins. His resurrection signals that sin and death are overcome and that salvation has come. People are invited to enter the kingdom through repentance and faith. The parables envisage the kingdom extending through the preaching of the Word and eventually expanding to be the most influential movement in the world—this has happened in the twenty-first century.

Mark has a constant stream of miracles of deliverance, healing, feeding, and astonishing power over creation itself. Mark's Jesus is a powerful man through whom the power of God is manifest on earth, undoing sin and its consequences. The miracles fulfill the hopes of the OT (e.g., Isa 29:6; 35:5; 42:2), signal the presence of the power of God to restore, and point forward to the nature of the age to come—a world free of evil, illness, demonic forces, chaotic and destructive natural events, hunger, and death.

Discipleship is a central theme in Mark's Gospel. A disciple repents and believes, and follows Jesus. Such a person is prepared to give up all their possessions and past lives to follow Jesus. They take up their crosses, deny themselves, and give themselves entirely over to serve the King as he extends the kingdom. Disciples include women, and within the group are leaders chosen by God. The Greek for "disciple" (*mathētēs*) indicates a Jesus-follower is a student or a learner. Consequently, they must be devoted to studying and growing in knowledge and the wisdom of God. They understand that the path of discipleship is pathed with suffering but also know that eternal life awaits.

Mission is a subliminal yet prominent theme. The Gospel begins by recalling the mission of the prophets to prepare the way for the Lord, and now he has come. John the Baptist ends that missional period, and then Jesus takes center stage as the Missio Dei becomes the Missio Christi. He enters Israel with the expectation of a mission that will see the nations pummel into submission and Israel at the center of the world. Instead, he declares the gospel to all people summoning them to yield to him and his Father willingly. His mission involves restoring people to relationship with God, with one another, and with the created order. His death ends the mission, but his resurrection declares that it has only just begun. The Gospel imagines the message of God preached to all nations before the end coming—this is the work of the disciples after his resurrection (13:10).

There is a range of other themes which could be mentioned. Please read the next chapter and see more about the themes that dominate the Synoptic Gospels.

Part 3: The Distinctives of Matthew

Matthew's Gospel includes ninety percent of Mark and continues the same narrative with some distinct emphases. While it is disputed, Matthew is a former tax collector and disciple of Jesus, also called Levi (Matt 9:9; 10:3). Papias is again helpful, telling us that Matthew wrote down his *logia* (words) in the Hebrew language. This reference could mean that he wrote an original Hebrew Gospel, drew on Hebrew sources, or that his Gospel is Hebrew in flavor. It is also possible that the document in question is the Q document used as a source for Matthew and Luke. As with the authorship of Mark, there seems no reason to dispute the general agreement of the early church that Matthew is the author. It is believed he wrote in Syrian

Antioch after Mark, sometime in the 70s and 80s. In this area, the church flourished among both Jews and Gentiles (Acts 11-13). Like Luke, Matthew draws on Q and his own material, drawn from his own experience of Jesus and that of his disciple colleagues.

Whereas Mark and Luke's Gospels feel more Greco-Roman, his Gospel's emphasis is decidedly Jewish. He writes an apology for Jesus genuinely being the Messiah of Israel; something Mark implies but does not make explicit to the same extent. He writes at a time when Jewish and Christian relationships were strained as Christianity emerged from the chrysalis of Judaism after Jerusalem's destruction in AD 70. His Gospel is ideal for training disciples, especially to read Jesus against the OT Scriptures and defend Jesus against Jewish opposition.

Matthew's Gospel is a passionate defense of Jesus' messiahship, full of OT quotations demonstrating that Jesus is the fulfillment of the hopes of Israel. Indeed, Matthew is a repository of OT texts pointing to Jesus. Often, he mentions the text using a fulfillment formula, e.g., "in order to fulfill."[3] His Gospel strengthens Jewish Christians being persecuted for their belief in Jesus. It has the evangelistic power to draw Jews to Jesus as they read the story. It equips those who engage in mission among Jews.

Matthew fills out Mark's story, adding an infancy narrative written from the perspective of Joseph, Jesus' earthly father (unlike Luke, which seems drawn from Mary) (Matt 1-2). He adds the details of the temptation (Matt 4:1-11). He also includes many other parables and fresh incidents from Jesus' life, many of which are unique, while some are found in Luke's Gospel.[4]

Matthew emphasizes eschatology, pointing forward to the culmination when Jesus returns. Mark includes one chapter on the events surrounding the destruction of the temple and the return of Christ (Mark 13). Matthew also includes this, making it clear that it

---

3. Matt 1:22; 2:15; 3:15; 8:17; 12:17; 13:35; 21:5, cf. 5:17.
4. Matt 13:1-50; 18:10-14, 21-35; 20:1-16; 21:28-44; 22:1-14; 24:32-25:46.

applies to both the fall of Jerusalem and the return of Christ (Matt 24). Then he adds the parable of the ten virgins, the parable of the talents, and the sheep and goat's judgment scene to summon disciples to be faithful until Jesus' return (Matt 25:1-46).

Mark summons people to take up crosses, but Matthew emphasizes discipleship and its cost. He adds challenging material, e.g., Matt 8:18-22 (as does Luke, as we will see). He highlights God's judgment against false Christians and those who reject the faith; indeed, many of his parables end with darkness and the gnashing of teeth.[5]

He also emphasizes mission, giving a whole discourse on mission (Matt 10:5-42) and climaxing his Gospel with the Great Commission, whereby the gospel goes global (Matt 28:18-20). Gentiles feature throughout, e.g., the wise men who worship Jesus (Matt 2:1-12) and the Roman soldier (Matt 8:5-13). He fills out the Markan narrative of the resurrection (Matt 28:11-20), telling readers what came next—the women delivered the news to the apostles, and Jesus appeared to some of them. Matthew's Jesus is also harshly critical of the Jewish leadership (esp. Matt 23:1-36).

Although the kingdom is central to his Gospel, Matthew prefers to use the kingdom of Heaven rather than the kingdom of God. This descriptor does not speak of something different but is driven by the Jewish desire to avoid using the personal name of God, Yahweh.

His Gospel is traditionally seen as being arranged in five discourses and is not so much a Gospel as a catechism for teaching and training Christians.

1. The Sermon on the Mount (Matt 5-7): a gathering of many of Jesus' sayings, teachings, and pithy parables. Along with the Sermon on the Plain in Luke (Luke 6:17-49), this gives us the best material to understand the ethics of the kingdom.
2. The Mission Discourse (Matt 10:5-42): a gathering of Jesus'

---

5. Matt 8:12; 13:42, 50; 22:13; 24:51; 25:30.

teaching on mission into one chapter built on the sending of the Twelve, which focuses on mission.
3. Kingdom Parables (Matt 13:1–52): this includes the parables of Mark 4 with some additional extras ramping up the teaching on the kingdom.
4. The Church (Matt 18): this focuses on matters of church life, focusing on humility, resisting sin, caring for the lost sheep, discipline, and forgiveness toward others.
5. The Return of Christ (Matt 23–25): The fifth and final discourse includes a sharp critique of the Jewish leadership and being prepared for the future return of Jesus.

The final discourse is followed by the account of Jesus' death, resurrection, and the Great Commission. The Great Commission in 28:18–20 concludes Matthew's Gospel. This passage shows that Matthew did not write his Gospel merely to prepare people for discipleship but for mission. He knows that after Jesus' death, God will use readers to spread the Gospel throughout the world, and his account of Jesus, nicely built around the five discourses, prepares them for the task. They then are to preach the gospel through which people will be won to Christ by repentance and faith. They are then to baptize them in the name of the Triune God and teach them the teachings of Jesus. The teaching manual for this is Matthew's Gospel. Essential to their discipleship is preparing new converts for ongoing mission whereby they are disciples who make disciples. This way, the Gospel will spread through the world, and Christ will return (24:14).

Matthew's Gospel stands in contrast to that of Luke. Matthew's interest is in Jewish Christians. Luke's interest is in Greeks and Romans, especially Theophilus, who is from the well-educated citizenry of the Roman world. As such, they give us ideas for contextualizing the Jesus story depending on our audience.

5. Luke and Synoptic Gospel Themes

Part 1: The Distinctives of Luke's Gospel

There is only one Luke named in the NT; Luke the physician (Col 4:14).[1] It is almost certain that he wrote the third Gospel. It is hard to date, with theories ranging from a time just after the point of the end of Acts (ends in AD 61) to the 80s and even the 90s. I sense that it is earlier, as there is much not included from the 60s, including the deaths of James in AD 62 (recorded in Josephus, *Ant*. 20.197–201) and Paul and Peter under Nero (AD 66–68), the Roman-Jewish war and fall of Jerusalem (AD 66–70). It seems strange that these are not included in Acts if Luke's writings were written later.

Luke addresses his Gospel to a certain "most excellent Theophilus," which may be a cipher for "friend/lover of God" or, as is most probable, an elite Roman. He may have been involved in Paul's situation in prison in Rome. He may also be a patron of Luke. He appears to be a Christian but at the least has a good understanding of Christianity, and Luke writes to strengthen this.

Luke's preface is most helpful as it tells us he consulted other accounts in writing his. He spoke to eyewitnesses and ministers of the Word. He is not a first-generation Christian but a Gentile (see Col 4:11–14). That is amazing—a Gentile was one of the four Evangelists. Luke's account is also distinctive because it is a two-part work; he writes an account of both Jesus (Luke) and the early church until Paul is imprisoned in Rome (Acts). Many believe that

---

1. See for more detailed analysis, Keown, *Discovering*, 1:215–59 (Ch. 8).

the two-part narrative is one story only separated due to scroll length. As such, his presentation of the gospel includes the story of Christ from his birth to Luke's present situation.

If Matthew has a Jewish feel, Luke is decidedly Greco-Roman in orientation. He writes to an elite Roman, and the way he presents the story of Jesus, he is seeking to challenge Roman ideas of status (humility)—the poor, the marginalized, and patronage—and to challenge Roman Christians to live out of the pattern of Christ rather than being conformed to the patterns of the world.

He uses Mark and Q, or perhaps Matthew, and he writes as a historian. Luke was well-positioned to gather material. The four "we passages" of Acts (where the writer shifts from the third person "they" to the first person "we") indicate that he was with Paul for extended periods of his mission. He joined Paul in Troas in Acts 16:10, traveled to Philippi with him, remained behind (Acts 17:1), and re-joined Paul on his third Antiochian mission in Macedonia (Acts 20:6). He traveled with Paul to Jerusalem. He would have had a terrific opportunity to gather material from eyewitnesses for his work. He also traveled with Paul to Rome (Acts 27:1; 28:10). In Rome, he would have had contact with a wide range of people who had traveled with Paul and even with Peter himself and others. He writes a historical biography of Jesus and an account of the early church, focusing on the gospel's spread through the Roman world.

Luke includes a distinctive infancy narrative because it is written in Greek using a style similar to the LXX—the Greek OT Scriptures. Luke seemed to set out to continue the Septuagint (LXX) intentionally. He then takes sizable portions of Mark, blends it with common material from Matthew (Q), and adds significant other material. He includes his version of the Sermon on the Mount, the Sermon on the Plain, which is presented as the basis of an ethic for the new covenant.

Luke's material has many of the same things found in Mark and Matthew: calling disciples, healing, casting out demons, teaching, and preaching. Jesus is the Davidic Messiah King who came to gather God's lost sheep and feed them materially and spiritually.

Many see Luke 4:18-20 as critical to understanding Luke's Jesus. Here, Jesus stands in the Nazareth synagogue and preaches. He draws on Isa 61:1-2 with a clip from Isa 58:6. He is the anointed one Isaiah predicted. This figure will proclaim good news to the poor—not just preaching but feeding them with physical and spiritual food. He has come to set people free and open their eyes. His coming inaugurates the year of Jubilee (cf. Lev 25). This passage sets the program for Luke's Gospel. Later, he will more succinctly state his mission: "For, the Son of Man came to seek and to save the lost" (Luke 19:10). This is what Jesus is all about for Luke. Empowered by the Spirit at Pentecost and subsequent experiences, believers are to join in this ministry until the completion of the mission.

The turning point of Luke is Luke 9:51 when Jesus turns to Jerusalem to die as God's Servant. Through his entry to the city recorded in 19:28-44, Luke mainly uses original L and Q material. Also dominant is the theme of money and the poor; the reader is challenged to care for the lost. Central to this section are the three lost parables in Luke 15—the lost sheep, coin, and son stories. There are many other parables and encounters where Jesus calls believers to be radical disciples.

Discipleship is a core theme. Like Matthew, Luke includes the summons to take up crosses and follow Jesus twice (Luke 9:23-26; 14:27). Other passages call believers to do more than merely believe; they must live out this gospel. The cost is great, but the reward is more significant (e.g., Luke 9:57-62; 14:25-35).

Luke's story is full of unlikely heroes. There is the commendable Roman centurion (Luke 7:1-10) and the sinful woman who anoints Jesus' feet (Luke 7:36-50). Startlingly, given the cultural situation, women traveled with Jesus, ministering to him, and may have engaged in God's mission to other women. These include Mary Magdalene, who had been delivered from seven demons, and Herod Antipas' household manager's wife, Joanna, a woman of significant social status (Luke 8:1-3). Although despised, Samaritans and not Jews are heroes in the parable of the Good Samaritan and the healing of the ten lepers (Luke 10:25-37; 17:11-19). Mary is another unlikely hero as she does not participate in the expected hospitality protocols but sits at Jesus' feet as a disciple (Luke 10:38-42). She paves the way for women to be disciples, something forbidden in Judaism.

Another feature of Luke is meals. In Ch. 7, 11, and 14, Jesus is eating in the homes of Pharisees. He powerfully challenges them in each case—only a brave person invites Jesus for dinner. In chapter 14, he tells the story of the Great Banquet, which speaks of God sending out invitations to the Great Eschatological Banquet (cf. Isa 25:6-12). People are all invited and welcomed if they accept the invitation by faith. The invitees are then sent to invite others which is our mission.

Luke's interest in mission is strongly signaled by his inclusion of the missions of Jesus, the Twelve (Luke 9), and the Seventy-two (Luke 10). Only Luke includes these two sending narratives. Later, in Acts, the mission began with the Twelve, especially Peter and John (Acts 3-5), then the seven, especially Stephen and Philip (Acts 6-8), and then the whole church was thrust out of Jerusalem, sharing Christ (Acts 8:4, cf. 11:19-21). Dynamos, like Apollos, emerge from nowhere (Acts 18:18-19:1). We see that the Spirit is the primary evangelist, thrusting people out to continue the work of Jesus, extending the kingdom into the world.

Luke includes Jesus' death and resurrection, as do Mark and Matthew. He tends to play down the Roman role in his death, perhaps being sensitive to the concerns of Theophilus and Roman readers. He includes different accounts of Jesus' appearances, including two travelers on the Emmaus Road and Peter. The Emmaus Road account is filled with accounts of Jesus' teaching from the OT that the Son of Man must suffer, die, and rise according to the Scriptures. In particular, Jesus is the Suffering Servant of Isaiah (Luke 24:25-26, 46).

Luke also includes his version of the Great Commission, which focused not on making disciples as in Matthew but on preaching repentance and forgiveness of sins throughout the world. They are to wait in Jerusalem for God to imbue them with power for this (Luke 24:46–49). Then they are to go. It ends with the ascension and worship at the temple (Luke 24:49-52). These themes are all reframed again in Acts 1:1-11, after which part two of the story is launched.

Luke-Acts is excellent because we have the story of Jesus *and* an account of how the first Christians lived out his commands. We are also part of the story, as the same Spirit is in us, and we continue the great drama of God.

Part 2: Synoptic Themes 1—The Kingdom of God: Expectations, Reign, and King

The Kingdom in the Hopes of Israel

For Israel, God is King.[2] He is enthroned above the world. His kingdom is Israel. However, Israel has failed him, and he has allowed other nations to rule over her. They were (and remain) convinced that God will, at some time in the future, deliver them from foreign rule, restore the nation, rebuild the temple, subjugate the world, and the world will experience the pax-Theos, the Shalom of God. There were diverse expectations, including God coming sovereignly to establish his reign through a human or semi-divine agent. As mentioned earlier, the most popular expectations were the Davidic Messiah, the Prophet, and the Son of Man. Whoever it was, it would involve God liberating the nation from Roman and Gentile rule.

Another aspect of Israel's worldview was a common idea that the voice of the prophets had gone quiet since Malachi. They longed for and expected God to speak again, perhaps through an Elijah-like

---

2. See for more detailed analysis, Keown, *Discovering*, 1:417–59 (Ch. 11).

figure (Mal 4:6). This explains why there was so much excitement when John the Baptist turned up, summoning Israel to repent and baptizing people for the forgiveness of sins. He did not go unnoticed, and in John's Gospel, Jerusalem's religious leaders asked him if he was the expected one. He denies this powerfully, pointing to one coming after him. This man will be the one who will baptize with the Spirit and fire, of whom John is not worthy.

Hence, when Jesus turned up, there was again great excitement. Indeed, the hope was far greater because Jesus was full of the power of God to heal. One of the signs of the messianic age was God again doing miracles, as he did with Moses to liberate them from Egypt, through Joshua as he led Israel into the land, and through Elijah to liberate Israel from the Baal prophets. Jesus was full of such power. It was likely that the leaders were waiting for Jesus to do some authenticating miracles as Moses did when he came from Midian to Egypt for the great Exodus.

However, Jesus did nothing of the sort. He began gathering a motley group of disciples, including, first of all, four fishers. Next, he called a tax collector, one of the despised Israelites who had sold out to the Romans and fleeced his people for the Gentile oppressors. He welcomed Simon the Zealot and others. He chose twelve, a very provocative number considering his name was Joshua.

Jesus, however, at no point sought to convince the general populace of Israel's leaders that he was the Messiah. He quietened down any hopes. He used his power only for the good of others in genuine need—healing, casting out demons, feeding them, calming a threatening storm, and walking on water. All these miracles point back to OT moments and hopes, all speak of God's power in the present, and all are windows into the world God is creating in Jesus—a world without hunger, pain, illness, evil spirits, death, and natural disasters. Jesus refused to use his power for his ends. He refused to arrogate himself before the world openly as King.

Yet, he did announce the coming of the kingdom of God. Mark 1:14-15 sums up his message:

> Now after John was arrested, Jesus came into Galilee, proclaiming the gospel of God and saying, "The time is fulfilled, and the kingdom of God is at hand. Repent and believe in the gospel."

The kingdom is the central theme of the Synoptic Gospels. Jesus is the Messiah, the Son of God, the Son of Man, and God's ruler to establish his reign.

As he went about his business, in many ways, Jesus disappointed those who were waiting for Israel's redemption. His disciples were a bunch of nobodies. He never used his power as they wanted. He refused to perform signs on demand. He spent time with sinners and people clearly under the curse of God, as evidenced by their sicknesses and demon possession. They were so frustrated that they accused him of being an emissary of Satan himself. He also said things that offended their religious views. He dared to forgive sin. He healed on the Sabbath, claiming to be the Lord of the Sabbath. He refused to wash his hands at mealtimes ritually and ate with sinners. He even broke bread in a Gentile territory as he fed the 4000. His miracles were great, but never enough for those religious leaders who knew that if he were God's deliverer, he would come knocking at some point. Yet, he openly ridiculed Israel's leadership in debate. They saw him as a threat to God's self-revelation through Moses. He then dared to challenge the temple system, speaking of its destruction and clearing it in a breathtakingly daring challenge to the center of Israel's worship. Believing themselves to be defenders of Judaism akin to Phineas of the OT, they had to kill him.

The final ignominy was his death on a cross—Messiahs kill and are not crucified, hung on a tree, and accursed. Even on the cross, they cried out to him to prove himself. Other than assuming the words of David in Ps 22:1, pointing them one final time to his identity, he refused. He died refusing to respond to the challenges to use his power to save himself. Shockingly for a Jew, he died at the hands of Gentiles. This is no Messiah to them; he is a false prophet and Christ.

Jesus was a failed Messiah according to their expectations. He held promise but fell well short of their hopes and dreams.

The Kingdom as Reign

Israel's worldview was locked up in their belief that they were God's elect, chosen by God through their father, Abraham. As such, the problem with the world was not them; it was the nations full of idolatry and gross violation of the law of God. They were not perfect, but God would move and establish them as he had at the Conquest, and this time for good, to rule the world on his behalf. Their view of God's reign included the world, but it had to be subjugated, and this was to come. Hence, their view of the kingdom was a classic ancient imperial concept of a geographical kingdom.

The stories of the ancient kingdoms speak of expansion. It begins with the uprising of a warrior-deliverer (e.g., David, Alexander the Great, Julius Caesar). They become king of their locality, be it Israel, Macedonia, Greece, or Rome. Such empires then extend their reign, claiming the territories adjoining them. This expansion involves war as armies move north, south, east, and west, claiming territory. There are two paths to victory—the easy way of surrender or the hard way through being devastated by invading armies. The territory expands, and the kingdom gains more wealth and subjects. The kingdom must establish itself in these lands, winning the subjects over with benefaction (e.g., citizenship and positions of honor) or punishment (e.g., crucifixion)—again, the easy and hard ways.

Israel's expectations of the kingdom of God were locked in such ideas. God or his agent would come. With God on his side, he would gather the best of the men of Israel and first drive out the Gentiles. He would then extend the territory by taking nearby nations—Egypt, the Nabateans, and others in Africa, the Parthians to the east. Armies would march through Syria, Anatolia (Turkey),

Greece, to Rome. Conquest would continue until the world was subjugated. Such events were possible because God was on their side. Insurmountable odds mean nothing. This process of subjugation would continue until the world was God's. Israel would be restored, and the world as God wanted.

If we consider the kingdom from the outcome's perspective, it will look like what is described. Evil will be vanquished. The enemies of God, spiritual and otherwise, will be gone. No one who refuses to yield to this King will live in this world.

In one sense, the kingdom's geography is the world, including all nations, the ends of the earth. Yet, the process of getting there does not involve taking geographical territory. It is extended as people enter it by yielding their hearts and lives to God. It grows as a reign within the nations without becoming a geographical kingdom. Even where most people in a nation claim to be Christian, it is not fully established. When Jesus returns, the whole world will be wholly God's kingdom.

The good news of the inbreaking of God's kingdom through the King, Jesus, is spread to the world. Many people hear this gospel and reject it with indifference or direct opposition. They continue to live in the world but not *in* the kingdom. They are citizens of the world and its kingdoms (allowed to live on by the grace of God in enmity to him, in the hope that they will turn and be saved). The correct response is to yield and submit to this King, give him our allegiance, repent, believe, and follow him. Those that do are then members of God's kingdom people, his subjects, part of his purposes, working for the King.

As such, it is better to talk about the kingdom of God in this period between its beginning and its consummation as the reign of God. The kingdom is found where God's rule is not only exercised but also where it is accepted. It is a kingdom of hearts and minds involving people who love this King and God with their inner beings and bodies. It becomes a community of people, wherever two or three come together in the king's name to worship him and do his will and work. It exercises its influence as these people work in the world for the King and the kingdom. Like salt and light, the kingdom's power permeates the world through the actions and words of God's people. It spreads, not geographically, but in human hearts.

Yet, there is a geographical dimension as the gospel moves from land to land. It began in Jerusalem with 120 people (Acts 1:15). By the Spirit-power of the King, through his subjects, it spread into the Roman world. It has now penetrated vast swathes of the world. Yet not everyone in these places has yielded to the king. Such rejection is found in NZ, where there are many Christians and many who are not. The kingdom is here in NZ, in the sense of God's reign and his subjects who set up colonies of the kingdom of heaven on earth. Yet, it is not complete. It is now, but not yet.

Recognizing that the kingdom is not a geographical concept is vital in ecclesiology (the study of the church). The church is not a building but a people who acknowledge the reign of God and his Son and gather to worship and serve him, love one another, and engage in mission in the world. We do not go to church on Sunday in the sense of a building; we go to gather and be the people. We are bound together as one when we are separated geographically. Buildings are helpful, but they are not the church. Those in Christ are the church.

The Kingdom of God: The Now and Not Yet

The kingdom of God is the reign of God exercised across the world. Another significant area of debate in the history of biblical scholarship is to what extent the kingdom has arrived. Some emphasize its presence. The kingdom has come in Jesus and is here. It will expand and come to completion. They play down any future dimension. Others do the opposite. They see what is happening now as a mere prelude to the main event. They focus on the return of Christ instead of recognizing God's work in the present. I will now consider the present and future dimensions of the kingdom.

God as Reigning King, God as Coming King

Before addressing the now and not yet of the kingdom, it is good to take a step back and think of the kingdom in the biblical story. The day God created the world, he was King. He is King. So, in a sense, the entire world has been, is, and always will be his kingdom. He is the reigning King and always has been.

Yet, while this is true and confirmed in Israel's Scriptures, he is also the coming King. That is, at the fall of humankind, humanity chose another ruler—themselves. Unwittingly, in usurping God, they also gave themselves over to the dominion of the evil one and his minions. They became subject to sin. They preferred their own dominion over God. The work of Jesus is to take back what is, and always has been, God's. I will now consider to what extent the kingdom is "now" and "not yet."

The Kingdom Inaugurated in Christ—the Now

Over time, scholars settled on the concept of an inaugurated eschatology to resolve the dilemma. In this schema, Jesus' birth was the beginning of the kingdom of God. Or one can say it was the point at which he became King waiting for his inauguration (below). So, Gabriel tells Mary concerning Jesus: "and he will reign over the house of Jacob forever, and of his kingdom, there will be no end" (Luke 1:33). He is the one Isaiah sang of: the son born and given, on whom the government will rest, the "Wonderful Counselor, Mighty God, Everlasting Father, Prince of Peace" (Isa 9:6, ESV). We also see this in Matthew's birth narrative, where the king of the Jews is born, magi come from the east, Herod the Great is disturbed and challenged, and he seeks to kill Jesus (the stuff of ancient kingdoms). He fails, and Jesus, the King, begins his life. He is raised in the home of the Davidic descendant Joseph (Matt 1:1-18), to be inaugurated officially as the King eventually.

Jesus' inauguration (coronation, crowning, anointing) as King came at his baptism. In Israel's story, the king must be anointed by a prophet. So, Samuel anointed Saul and then his replacement David (1 Sam 10; 16). Nathan anointed Solomon (1 Kgs 1). Even Joshua was anointed by the prophet Moses (Num 27:18-20; Deut 34:9-12). Through the prophets, God gave his choice and approval to the king.

John the Baptist is the last of such prophets. He came from nowhere, God making his move to establish his reign by sending him to prepare the way and to inaugurate his king. Therefore, the Gospels all begin with John. The Gospel writers recognized that the true Davidic King would be preceded by a prophet who would authenticate him.

The prophetic authentication occurred at Jesus' baptism. Unlike the earlier prophets who poured oil over the king's head, John baptized Jesus. He dunked him in the Jordan. Jesus came up, the heavens opened, and God anointed him as Israel's King, the new Joshua. He must conquer his world by freeing it from corruption. God calls out: "You are my beloved Son; with whom I am well pleased" (Mark 1:11). The language of Sonship speaks of his royal role. So, in Ps 2:7, God says of the king: "You are my Son; today I have begotten you" (ESV). Here, God authenticates Jesus. This instant also calls to mind Isa 42:1, where God speaks to the Servant of Yahweh, whom we now know to be looking toward Jesus. He says: "Behold my servant, whom I uphold, my chosen, in whom my spirit delights; I have put my Spirit upon him; he will bring forth justice to the nations" (ESV).

Notably, the heavens were opened at that moment, and the Spirit was released. This moment marks the beginning of the inbreaking of God's rule into the world—the Spirit-filled Jesus. He led Jesus in his mission from start to finish. His first job was to find a way for humankind to receive this Spirit and be similarly anointed. That would require dealing with sin and corruption.

So, Jesus' baptism was the moment when the King was

inaugurated. The kingdom began when God commissioned this King for his mission. His first move was not to go out to win subjects for the kingdom. That came later. His first move was to be thrust out by the Spirit to fight his ultimate foe, Satan (Matt 4:1–11; Mark 1:12–13; Luke 4:1–13). This encounter recalls Adam and Eve in the garden (Gen 2–3). Jesus succeeds where Adam and Eve failed. He defeats Satan, resisting Satan's attempts to appoint him "king" without conflict (the easy way) (esp. Matt 4:8). This happens in the wilderness. After the Exodus, Israel was tested in the wilderness by God. They were unsuccessful, constantly succumbing to complaints and contention. Jesus does not. He is the new Israel. He is its rightful King. He will spend his life taking back those under bondage to Satan throughout Israel (Acts 10:38). In him, and by his Spirit, we also do so throughout the world.

After his first victory, Jesus returned in the power of the Spirit and began to preach, teach, heal, deliver, feed, and raise the dead (Luke 4:14, s.a. 7:22). He was the new Joshua, coming to deliver the world from the dominion of darkness (Col 1:13), not by might, not by power, but by the Spirit (Zech 4:6).

As noted earlier, he preached that the kingdom is nearby. That is, it is here in his person. Its full inbreaking is near as he goes to the cross, dies, rises, ascends, and the Spirit is poured out. Israel must repent and believe the good news (Matt 4:2, 17).

Jesus was a man with a plan. His strategy was not to win the world in one fell swoop but to win people, one by one, beginning in his own nation. He summoned Israel to yield to God's reign through repentance and belief. Some responded. Many were attracted. But most did not yield to him.

The presence of the kingdom is seen in his ministry. His miracles spoke of the inbreaking of God's reign. His pithy parables taught people the nature of the kingdom. His love drew the lost and broken, and his kingdom expanded as people yielded to his reign.

Jesus had followers, but they were sinners, and sin must be dealt with for God to dwell permanently with people. Israel's sacrifice system sets the agenda—the blood of an unblemished animal temporarily deals with sin. The blood of the unblemished Son of God, the Lamb of God, must be shed. Jesus fulfilled the requirements by living a sinless life, despite being tempted in every way as we are and yet being without sin. He died. His broken body and shed blood inaugurated the new covenant dreamed of by Jeremiah (Jer 31:31).

Jesus looked like an abject failure on the cross. Yet, his death was the victory over sin God required. Hence, death could not restrain him, as sin brings death, and he had no sin. He rose, launching a new creation and new humanity. The empty tomb is a metaphor for the coming day when the graves of the dead will open, and God's people will be raised.

In giving his life as a ransom for many, those who repent and believe in him are cleansed of sin and, despite having to die physically, are freed from sin's power and consequences. They are ready receptacles in which the God, who cannot dwell with evil (Ps 5:4), can now reside, temples of the living God (2 Cor 6:16). They are also bound together as one temple in Christ filled with the Spirit (1 Cor 3:16).

As such, the Spirit was poured out at Pentecost. By this time, Jesus had ascended and was (and is) seated at the right hand of the Father, King of the Cosmos, Lord, and Christ, God the Son. His Father, through Jesus, poured out his Spirit repeatedly on God's people through the book of Acts. The Spirit is poured out upon anyone who yields to God as King. In this way, the kingdom is extended.

As Luke emphasizes in his Gospel, the Spirit is the key. He fills us and empowers us for this mission, the extension of the kingdom. After Jesus' death, the gospel exploded out of Jerusalem into Judea, Samaria, and the Roman world. By the time of the apostles' deaths, the gospel was established in the regions around the Mediterranean. Over time it moved through Europe and now has reached most of the world.

The Kingdom Consummated

There is an essential future dimension to the kingdom; the consummation of the kingdom, when all our hopes and dreams of a world rid of evil and God's reign unopposed will be complete.[3] Jesus must reign until all enemies are subjugated under his feet—the consummation of the kingdom will be that day (1 Cor 15:24–28). On that day, with a loud angelic cry, the trumpet of God, and blazing fire, Jesus will return with his angels (1 Thess 4:16). The dead in Christ will rise. With those believers alive at the time, the risen in Christ will be taken up to meet him in the air, and they will welcome him as King and Lord (1 Thess 4:17). Heaven will come to earth; the new Jerusalem (Rev 21–22:5). God will judge humanity and all those who have not yielded to his lordship, will be swept away in eternal destruction (Matt 25:41–46; Rev 20:11–15). We will be transformed in an instant from perishable mortal beings to immortal and imperishable people with bodies like that of Jesus, and we will live on with God (1 Cor 15:50–54; Phil 3:20).

The not-yet of the kingdom will come to pass when God decides the time is right. It will be when his mission is completed to his satisfaction when the gospel has been made known in every nation.

The Tension

We live in the tension between the two great moments: 1) the inauguration of the kingdom in the first coming of Jesus and 2) the

---

3. For a fuller discussion, see Mark J. Keown, "The Consummation of the Kingdom," https://www.academia.edu/92023729/The_Consummation_of_the_Kingdom.

consummation of the kingdom in the second coming of Jesus. In the interim, we live by the pattern of Christ's life in his first coming—his ethics and mission. We live ever prepared for the consummation, even if we do not know the day or hour (Mark 13:32-37). We do so by being faithful servants, finding our place in his mission, and persevering to the end, knowing that our labor in the Lord is not in vain.

We must avoid what is called over-realized eschatology. This inadequate view is found where people falsely assume that the blessings that believers are destined to experience in the consummated kingdom can be fully experienced now. An example is prosperity theology, which claims that if we are obedient, we will be rich in the present. Such a perspective is incorrect as it does not conform to the Christ pattern. The sacrifice made at Jesus' circumcision is evidence he began life poor (Luke 2:24). He died naked, deserted, and bereft. Neither did Paul live like a king. Indeed, he mocked the Corinthians, who seemed to think they should live like royalty (1 Cor 4:8-14). Paul lived in weakness and suffering. If we are blessed financially, it is not to gain possessions but to use what we have been given to serve God and his reign.

We must not make false claims concerning the present experience of the kingdom. We should try and live the life of the resurrection now—out of love and holiness. Yet, we work hard, knowing that God is storing our future inheritance. Our call, in the meantime, is to get on with the King's business. That is what good subjects do. They are faithful to their sovereign. Our job is to be available to God so that he can extend his reign through us.

Part 3: Synoptic Themes 2—The Kingdom of God: The King, Power, & Parables

The Kingdom of God: The King

Every kingdom needs a king.[4] In our case, God is King. Completely sovereign, he sent his Son into this world to be its King on his behalf. He now rules through his Son, and his Son willingly rules on his behalf. Our primary human vocation is to yield to Jesus and, by doing so, to his Father. We do his bidding, whatever we are called to do.

There is a range of important titles used for Jesus in the NT. The focus of this section will be on the main ones used for Jesus. Then, consideration will be given to Jesus being both human and divine.

The Christ

The Davidic monarchy ended in Babylonian exile, led by Nebuchadnezzar. As the prophets predicted, Israel and then Judah were destroyed because of their sin. The penultimate Davidic King was Zedekiah, before whom Nebuchadnezzar slaughtered his sons, blinded him, and took him to Babylon in chains. When Israel returned from exile, the Davidic monarchy was not re-established. The prophets dreamed of this coming to pass as they dreamed of a

---

4. See for a fuller discussion, Mark J. Keown, "Who is Jesus?" https://www.academia.edu/91877704/Who_Is_Jesus_Introduction.

new Davidic King, a fresh branch.[5] Contrasting other terms (Lord, Son of God, Savior), and like "Son of Man," *Christos* is very much a Jewish idea. Outside of Jewish literature, it was never used for the Emperor or gods in the Greek world. Unlike "Son of Man," it became one of the most important titles for Jesus in the church.

In the NT, Jesus is recognized as the Christ (Heb. Messiah) or Anointed One, the Son of David. In the Synoptic Gospels, the great moment is when Peter confesses that Jesus is the Christ (Mark 8:29, s.a. Matt 16:16; Luke 9:18–20). Peter is saying that Jesus is the anointed one, God's Messiah, the longed-for Davidic King who has come to save his people.

In Matthew and Luke, Jesus is born in Bethlehem, the city of David's family, fulfilling the expectations of the Messiah born there (Matt 2:1; Luke 2:1–7). In all the Synoptics, Jesus is not open about this, shutting down anyone who says this aloud, including demons (e.g., Mark 1:25, 34) and Peter himself (Mark 8:30). This is likely because he did not want to excite a revolution. We see this in John 6:14–15, where after feeding the 5000, the crowds perceive Jesus as the Prophet (see below) and seek to make him King by force. Jesus slips away, not interested.

The story of the Synoptics is that after the confession, Jesus teaches the disciples what sort of Messiah he is. He is not a King who has come to be served but to serve others and give his life as a ransom for many (Mark 10:45). He values children, the poor, and the marginalized and acts on their behalf. He came to take up a cross and die and rise again. Jesus tells them three times of his death and resurrection (Mark 8:31; 9:31; 10:33–34). He has come to be a crucified Messiah, his body broken for his people, his blood the blood of the new covenant (Luke 22:20; 1 Cor 11:25). He is the

---

5. Pss 89:4–4; 132:11–12, 17–18; Isa 4:2; 9:7; 11:1, 10; 16:5; 55:3; 23:5; 33:15–17; Ezek 34:23–24; 37:24–25; Hos 3:5; Amos 9:11; Zech 3:8; 6:12; 12:7–13:1, s.a. Pss. Sol. 17:4, 32.

ultimate Passover Lamb, given for the sins of the world (1 Cor 5:7; John 1:29).

The claim to be the Christ contributed to his condemnation. The High Priest asked Jesus whether he was the Christ, the Son of the Blessed One. Jesus answered, "I am, and you will see the Son of Man seated at the right hand of the Power and coming with the clouds of heaven" (Mark 14:61–63). His blasphemous response caused the High Priest to tear his clothing and condemn him to Pilate (14:63).

At the center of the sermons in Acts is the claim that Jesus is the Christ.[6] What had radically shifted in the disciples' thinking is that Jesus would not come to inflict suffering as he claimed back his world, but that he would suffer and die to save the world in a unique way (Luke 24:26, 46; Acts 3:18; 17:3; 26:23).

After his conversion, Paul the Pharisee, who had rejected Jesus' messiahship, broke from others and accepted that Jesus is the long-awaited Messiah. In fact, he used the name Christ more than any other term (383 times, cf. Jesus 212 times, Lord 273 times, Savior thirteen times, Son of God fourteen times, Son of Man zero times). Jesus is the climax of Israel's story and hope, her King and Lord of the world.

Paul recognized that the problem of a crucified Messiah was a stumbling block to Jews (Gal 3:13; Deut 21:23). Yet, he reframes the idea by acknowledging that Jesus was accursed on the cross for our sake as he took the curse of the law and sin on himself. He recognizes the importance of his suffering and death as the path to redemption.

The Lord

Jesus is *kyrios*, the Lord. Unlike Christos, *kyrios* is at home in both

---

6. Acts 2:31, 36, 38; 3:18, 20; 4:10; 5:42; 26:23, s.a. 17:3.

the Roman and Jewish worlds. *Kyrios* and the feminine *kyria* were used for deities and the Emperor. In the Jewish world, *kyrios* translated the Hebrew *Adonai* in the LXX some 6,000 times for God. Using *kyrios* of Jesus, from both Greco-Roman and Jewish perspectives, suggests his divinity.

The use of the term was daring, considering Jewish monotheism. Christians took verses from the OT in which *kyrios* referred to God and applied it to Jesus. An example is Phil 2:10–11, where the world bowed to Jesus as Lord, whereas in Isa 45:23, God is in view (s.a. Rom 10:13; 15:11). Hence, to call Jesus Lord crossed the line of monotheism. Similarly, in the Roman world, to say Jesus is Lord was to challenge the supremacy of the Emperor. Christians then would get it from both sides.

Kyrios is used of Jesus through the Gospels, sometimes with the sense that he is an important person with the power to heal (e.g., Luke 5:12), and at other times, especially in Luke, speaking of him as cosmic Lord (e.g., Luke 6:5; 17:6; 24:3, 34). "Lord" is Luke's favorite designation for Jesus in his Gospel and Acts. In Acts, Jesus is the cosmic Lord, seated at the right hand of God, sharing his rule (Acts 2:25, 34). This idea is found in Paul and through the remainder of the NT. "Lord" implies Jesus' complete sovereignty over the world. The NT usage builds on Ps 110:1, the verse quoted the most in the NT. In discussing this verse, Jesus identifies himself as the Lord (*Adonai*) (Mark 12:36–37). He reigns from heaven as Lord until the completion of the subjugation of God's enemies, which will come to pass finally upon his return. Other writers in the NT continue to use *kyrios* for Jesus (over 250 times Paul).

The Son of Man

Jesus' favorite self-designation was "Son of Man."[7] Yet, in the rest of the NT, it is used only four times.[8] The term is ambiguous, often used for a prophet (93x Ezekiel, s.a. Dan 8:17). It is used for humanity in general (Ps 8:4; 144:3; 146:3). It is also used for a figure at the side of Yahweh, who is strengthened to act to save Israel (Ps 80:17).

The latter idea is also found in Daniel, where one "like a son of man" comes to God and is given authority to rule the world (Dan 7:13–14). This idea is developed in 1 Enoch in a section written between c. 105–64 bc. In this Book of Similitudes (1 En 37–71), this Son of Man is also the Messiah and the one who rules, judges, deals with sinners, rewards God's people, and much more. He is a mighty, transcendent, and semi-divine figure.[9]

Jesus used this term of himself. He may have done so for its ambiguity, as it would not excite the same kind of messianic expectations created by *Christos* (Messiah). He used it impersonally, "the Son of Man …," making it unclear whether he was even talking about himself in some instances. The figure could be a human or all humankind. It could point to a prophet. We know, looking back, that he meant it in the sense of Dan 7:13–14 and with some of the ideas of 1 Enoch. Yet, listeners would have been puzzled.

Overall, it points to Jesus being a human, but more, the Human, the Son of Man, the one of whom Daniel prophesied, the one who would be given all authority over the nations.

---

7. 14x Mark, 30x Matt, 25x Luke, 13x John.
8. Acts 7:56; Heb 2:6; Rev 1:13; 14:14.
9. See 1 En. 46:2–4; 48:2; 60:10; 62:5–14; 63:11; 69:27–29; 70:1; 71:17.

The Servant

There are four passages in Isaiah that many scholars call "the Servant Songs of Isaiah." They predict a servant figure whom God would delight in; God will raise him and anoint him. He will bring justice to the nations and preach God's Word. He will be despised, maltreated, and killed. He will be buried with criminals and restored. He will be a covenant for the people, a light to the nations, and through him, salvation will go to the ends of the earth. Before him, kings will fall.[10]

In Judaism, these passages were not associated with the Messiah; instead, the Servant was seen as the prophet or Israel herself. In the Gospels and Acts, Jesus is identified as this figure.[11] Paul also describes Jesus as being in the form of a slave, invoking the same ideas (Phil 2:7).

As we read the Gospels, all other titles given to Jesus are mediated through the figure of this image. He is the Christ but in the form of a Servant. He is the Son of Man but in the form of a Servant. And so on. The writers have an interlaced Christology in which they bring these ideas together.

We need to grasp this very clearly. Jesus came as God and King of the world, yet he came washing feet (John 13) and serving humankind in need. We are called to follow this path and are told that greatness comes from service.[12] His self-humbling is our call. The path to greatness is service.

---

10. Isa 42:1–9; 49:1–7; 50:4–11; 52:13–53:12.
11. Esp. Matt 12:18–21, s.a. Matt 20:28; Mark 10:45; Luke 1:69; 14:17–23; Acts 3:13.
12. Matt 20:26–27; 23:11–12; Mark 9:35; 10:43–44; Luke 22:26.

The Son of God

In the OT, angels, people, and the king were all sons of God. For the Greeks and Romans, kings were the sons of God. There were not many Jewish prophecies expecting a Son of God, but for most, it was another way of thinking of the Messiah. However, in the NT, Jesus is more than just a king; he is God the Son. The devil calls him the Son of God (Matt 4:3, 6). He claims God as his Father and that he is the only one who knows him (Matt 11:27, s.a. Matt 24:36). People confess that he is the Son of God, including the Roman centurion (Mark 15:39, s.a. Matt 14:33; 16:16; 27:54). Jesus' claims to be the Son of God were part of the reason he was killed (Mark 14:61–62). In the Parable of the Tenants, he distinguishes himself from the prophets as the Son who is killed and thrown out of the vineyard—a prophecy of his death (Mark 12:6–8). The identification of Jesus as the Son is most frequent in the writing of John, where right from the start, Jesus is God and the one and only unique Son of God (John 1:1, 18, 34, 49). Jews seek to kill Jesus for calling himself God's Son.[13] God has given him all things (John 3:35), and he is the personal revelation of God. One is saved by believing he is God the Son (John 3:36; 11:27).

The Greeks believed in the gods copulating and having children. Jesus is not to be understood in this way. He is not the product of God's procreation but God's Son, who existed before the world's creation. He is God in person, and his Word made flesh without such things as divine procreation. He is eternal. Jesus' divine sonship is found throughout the rest of the NT.[14] John writes in 1 John 5:20 that Jesus is the Son of God, who is the true God and eternal life.

Christ's sonship leads to believers also being God's children in a derivative sense. We never take his place and become divine, but we

---

13. John 5:18; 10:36–39; 19:7; 20:31.
14. E.g., Acts 9:20; Rom 1:4; 2 Cor 1:19; Gal 2:20; Heb 1:8; 4:14; Rev 2:18.

are considered children of God by faith in him.[15] We know what it means to be a Son of God, for God's Son has shown us in his example and by the Spirit. It means to live with total obedience to our Father, emulating his humility, service, and love, and seeking the kingdom of God and his righteousness above all things.

The Prophet

Another very Jewish idea was the hope of a prophet. The prophetic expectation is derived from Deut 18:15-19. God will raise a prophet like Moses, and he will be God's spokesperson. Israel must listen to him or die.

This idea is swirling in the NT. Jerusalem religious leaders asked John the Baptist whether he was the Prophet, something he immediately denied (John 1:21). The Samaritans were anticipating a Taheb, a figure based on Deuteronomy. In the conversation Jesus has with the Samaritan woman in John 4, she likely means this when she considers Jesus the Messiah (John 4:25-26). The crowds consider Jesus the Prophet in John 6:14 and wish to enthrone him and start a revolt. In Acts 3:22-23, Deut 18 is cited, with Jesus fulfilling the Mosaic prophet figure (s.a. Acts 7:37). Jesus is King and Prophet. In Hebrews, he is also the High Priest (e.g., Heb 5:10). He fulfills the three-fold leadership of Israel.

The Kingdom of God—Power and Miracles

A miracle is something that occurs that violates the natural order

---

15. E.g., Matt 5:9; John 1:12; Rom 8:14-21; Gal 3:26; Phil 2:15; 1 John 3:10; 5:2.

of things.[16] Jesus is famous as a miracle worker. In Israel's story, he is not unique in this. Moses performed miracles authenticating his mission, including the plagues that enabled Israel to leave Egypt, the destruction of the Egyptians in the Red Sea, and a few others. Joshua also performed miracles like stopping the flooded Jordan River to cross it, the destruction of Jericho, stopping the sun, and so on. Elijah and Elisha performed miracles of provision, military victories, and the reanimation of the dead. It was hoped that the age of the Messiah would bring miracles (Isa 29:6; 35:5) and the Servant would open the eyes of the blind (Isa 42:7) and bring healing—"and by his wounds we are healed" (Isa 53:5, LEB).

Jesus was unique in the vast number of miracles he performed. His miracles included miracles of provision, including turning water to wine and feeding enormous crowds (John 2:1–11; Mark 6:30–44; 8:1–10); exorcisms where he casts out demons (e.g., Matt 4:24); a wide range of healings (e.g., Matt 8:16); raising the dead (Mark 5:21–43; Luke 7:1–10; John 11:1–44); miracles over nature including walking on water and calming a storm (Mark 4:35–41; 6:45–52); and prophetic predictions such as the destruction of the Jerusalem Temple (e.g., Mark 13:2). John's Gospel revolves around the seven signs (see on John earlier). All the Gospels indicate that Jesus was a miracle worker. Even the Jewish writer Josephus mentions it (Josephus, Ant. 18:63–64). Other Jewish sources also credit Jesus with miracles. The miracles have a three-fold impact.

The Past: Fulfillment

First, they point back. I have noted above some of the OT texts that looked forward to miracles in the eschatological age. The miracles

---

16. See for more detailed analysis, Keown, *Discovering*, 1:460–510 (Ch. 13).

themselves also point backward in different ways. Jesus' miracles of calming the weather and sea recall God's creative power, his chaos dominance, and Joshua stopping the sun. Through them, Jesus brings Shalom where there is chaos. The provision miracles recall God through Moses providing manna (see esp. John 6) and Elisha and Elijah providing for the needy (1 Kgs 17:8-16; 2 Kgs 4:4-7, 42-44). The healings fulfill the hopes of Isaiah.[17] The revivification of the dead points to the OT's hopes of resurrection and Elijah and Elisha raising the dead (1 Kgs 17:17-24; 2 Kgs 4:18-37). The prophetic predictions speak of the hope of God raising a prophet like Moses (see the previous section).

The Present: The Breaking in of the Kingdom

The miracles also say something about the inauguration of the kingdom and who Jesus is for his people in the present. In Jesus, we see the inbreaking of the power of God making right the world wracked with evil, poverty, sickness, death, and despair. God's power is present in Jesus. He can heal, provide, deliver, raise, and bring hope. In that Christ has given his people the Spirit, and the gifts of miracles and healing are distributed, we should pray and expect God to act in the present. However, we must not overstate this, as we are still all subject to decay and death, and miracles are temporary fixes. So, we pray passionately for them, hoping God will act. He will, but this will not fix our larger problem. We need to die and rise for this to happen.

---

17. Isa 29:6; 35:5; 42:7; 53:6.

The Future: The Consummation of the Kingdom

The miracles are also enacted parables telling us what the kingdom is about and what it will be when fully consummated. They are signs of the kingdom. John rightly recognizes this, calling them signs. They point to who Jesus is. They point to God's ideals for us. They give us glimpses of the nature of the consummated kingdom. They summon us to join God in bringing this closer.

The provision miracles are a window into a world free of famine and poverty, the haves and the have-nots. They also summon us to work for this in the interim between Jesus' comings. As Jesus says to the disciples in feeding the 5000, "you give them something to eat" (Mark 6:37).

The exorcisms point to the day when Satan is finally destroyed. His power is reduced as demons are driven out (see Luke 10:18). We are to withstand evil in the meantime, not giving Satan a foothold (Eph 4:27, cf. 1 Pet 5:8).

Jesus' healings look to the end of sickness. While personal sickness is not necessarily a result of personal sin (see John 9:1–3), sickness is a symptom of the decay that blights God's world through sin (Rom 5:12; 8:19–23). Jesus' healings show his power to end illness. The world to come will be free of all such things; we will be immortal and imperishable.

The resurrections from the dead performed by Jesus and his resurrection show the power of God to raise the dead. The final enemy to be defeated is death (1 Cor 15:26). People who have given allegiance to God and his Son will live forever, amazingly transformed from bodies of humiliation to bodies of glory like Jesus (1 Cor 15:50–54; Phil 3:21).

Prophecy gives us glimpses of God's future for us, often with warnings for the present. In the age to come, prophecies will end, for we will know and be fully known (1 Cor 13:8–9).

Faith and Miracles

Often faith is associated with miracles. For example, "your faith has delivered you" (Matt 9:22; Mark 5:34; 10:52; Luke 7:50, s.a. Matt 15:28). This has led to some Christians thinking that faith is required for miracles to occur and leads to people believing they are not healed for deficient faith. However, while they show that faith can be a factor in healing on occasion, there are also situations where faith is not mentioned (e.g., Matt 4:24; 8:16). In John's Gospel, faith is never mentioned as a reason for healing. Instead, miracles produce faith. However, this belief is not a salvific faith but needs to flower for salvation (e.g., John 2:23–25). We must also remember that no amount of faith can stop decay and death. These can be hindered if God chooses to intervene. But death cannot be stopped. Jesus' healings and raising of the dead were fleeting moments of restoration. Also, both Jesus and Paul experienced God saying no to their deliverance prayers (Mark 14:32–42; 2 Cor 12:7–9). God did so as he willed. Our call is to believe in God's ability to answer prayer, pray for those in need, trust God to do what is best, accept his decision, and continue believing in him whatever he does.

The Kingdom of God: Parables

Parables and Their Interpretation

In the Synoptic Gospels, Jesus taught in parables.[18] The word "parable" comes from *parabolē*, which has at its root "comparison." It is used in Jesus' teaching of a range of sayings and short stories

---

18. For a fuller discussion, see Keown, *Discovering*, 1:511–48 (Ch. 13).

he used to convey the message of the kingdom. Parables are found in the OT. One of the best examples is that told by Nathan to David after he had Uriah killed and married Bathsheba. The parable exposed David's sin and duplicity (2 Sam 12:1–15). Solomon had 3,000 parables (1 Kgs 4:28 [LXX]).[19] Jesus used a range of them. His parables were concerned with explaining the kingdom of God to his listeners. They have two levels of meaning: 1) the obvious surface daily life level; and 2) the kingdom of God level. They function to summon people to respond to the kingdom and the point(s) being made.

Parables have been the bone of a lot of contention in biblical studies. Throughout the history of interpretation, they were taken allegorically. The most famous example is Augustine's allegorization of the Good Samaritan, in which he reframed the parable into the gospel story.[20] Doing this meant the challenge of the parable to love one's enemy was lost. Rampant and contextually unsound allegorization led scholars away from this to reading them like Aesop's Fables, in which one point is made. As such, the discussion was based on what one interpretation is to be found.

However, since then, others have found a middle ground

---

19. This is found at 1 Kgs 4:32 in the English Bible, and the Greek translates the Hebrew *maschal* (translated proverb) as "parable."
20. See K. R. Snodgrass, "Parable," DJG 591: the injured man = Adam; Jerusalem = the heavenly city; Jericho = the moon and our mortality; the robbers = devil, and demons who take away the man's immortality and beat him by persuading him to sin; the priest and Levite = the corrupt priesthood and OT ministry; the good Samaritan = Christ; the binding of the wounds = the restraint of sin; the oil and wine = the comfort of hope and the encouragement to work; the animal = the Incarnation; the inn = the church; the next day = after Christ's resurrection; the innkeeper = the apostle Paul; the two denarii = the two commandments, or, the promise of this life and that which is to come (Augustine, *Quaest. Evan.* 2.19).

recognizing that many parables are allegorical, as seen by Jesus explaining them (e.g., Parable of the Sower and Weeds, Matt 13:1–30, 36–43). Others, like the Parable of the Banquet (Luke 14:12–24), the Prodigal Son (Luke 15:11–32), and the Parable of the Talents (Matt 21:33–44), are also allegorical. In these parables, the main characters correlate with God, the prophets, Jesus, Israel, and so on. The key is not trying to impose onto the parable later ideas, such as a particular form of the gospel. Instead, we need to consider the kingdom and discipleship aspects each character represents.

Parables also cannot be seen as having one meaning. There may be an overall point, such as "love your enemies," in the Parable of the Good Samaritan. Yet, one must think more carefully about the more complex parables. Even in the Good Samaritan, differing points are being made. We are not to be like the priest and Levite who ignored the injured man on the side of the road, whatever our reason. We are to be like the Samaritan, despite his being a despised figure in his world.

Each parable must be carefully considered, and the possibilities of interpretation must be carefully assessed. Here are some core principles of interpretation.

1. How would they have been understood in Israel at the time? First, we must interpret it in its original context and then apply it thoughtfully to our situation.
2. What cultural, historical, and social ideas help us understand the parable? For example, an older man would not run to his son as the Father does in the Parable of the Prodigal. Hence, this enhances his love for his son.
3. What is Jesus trying to teach about the kingdom of God? Doing this is more straightforward in those parables that begin, "the kingdom is like …" Yet, we should ask this about all the parables. What do they teach us about the King? The kingdom? What does it mean to be a subject of the King?
4. How does its material align with his other teaching? We should look through the content of the Gospel in which it stands and

see how it connects. So, for example, the Good Samaritan parable enacts Jesus' command to "love your enemies" (Luke 10:25–47, cf. 6:27, 35).
5. How do they connect with the broader biblical story, particularly the OT? Sometimes there are links to the OT. So, the Mustard Seed parable can be read with the tree of Ezekiel 17 in mind.
6. Who do the characters potentially align with from a first-century Jewish perspective? In the Prodigal: the father aligns with God. The older son with Israel. The younger son with the sinful marginalized Jews and Gentiles. In the Banquet: the banquet host aligns with God. The servant is Jesus and later missionaries. Those invited include the poor and disabled. Those further distant point to the Gentiles.
7. How does the parable end? The ending often points to Jesus' intended meaning. So, in the Parable of the Tenants in Mark 12, Ps 118 is quoted, and the Jewish authorities seek to arrest Jesus. They recognize that they are the tenants whom Jesus is challenging, the prophets are the servants, and Jesus is the loved son.
8. How do the preceding and following material help in interpretation? We must always read Bible passages in context. How does the parable fit into the whole Gospel? What section is it in, e.g., the Travel Narrative of Luke? What comes before and after the parable?

Theology

Drawing theology from Parables requires a bit of thought. Parables are stories, and we cannot assume that the image given is to be taken as pure theology. So, for example, in the Parable of the Rich Man and Lazarus, Abraham and Lazarus are in Paradise while the rich man is in Hades. Are the people Hades and Paradise existing in the final state? Such things need careful thought. As the remainder of Luke's Gospel and the wider NT do not indicate that people in eternal destruction and eternal life will be able to see each other, we should not instantly suggest so simply from the parable. We must form theology from a broader range of texts as parables are stories first, and the theology we draw from them should parallel Jesus' other teaching.

Why Did Jesus Teach in Parables?

Mark 4:11–12 suggests Jesus may have taught in parables to intentionally blind people to who he is. Yet, this is a misunderstanding of this passage. There is a little "so that" which starts v. 12. This is a *hina* in Greek. *Hina* usually indicates purpose or result. If the *hina* here is purposive, then Jesus did intend to blind people with his esoteric teaching. However, this is most probably a result *hina*—Jesus did not intend to blind them; his parabolic ministry resulted in them not understanding. They were genuinely invited to believe in him through the parables. He knew they would not and would kill him.

It is likely Jesus taught in parables because of their genius. Parables draw on real life and are easily understandable even for a child and people without higher education (as were the majority at the time). Parables draw us to basic ideas from life (coins, seeds, fishing, banquets, priests, fathers, sons, and so on). They have a deeper layer than we can perceive if our hearts are open. Jesus was using stories to give people a vision of a different world. We are invited into them and challenged to accept or reject the vision.

Stories are critical to cultures, especially oral cultures like that of Jesus. Stories bring laughter (e.g., logs hanging out of eyes). They bring shock (e.g., a Samaritan hero). They bring surprise (e.g., a super-large harvest as in the Parable of the Sower). They make us think about meaning (e.g., what does it mean for Christians to be the salt of the earth and lights in the world?). They grip us in a way that propositional teaching does not. We should think deeply about the meaning of the parables and how we might use stories when we preach.

6. More Synoptic Gospel Themes

The Death of Jesus in the Gospels

The most crucial moment in the account of Jesus is undoubtedly his death.[1] All four Gospels lead to this moment. In the Synoptics, Jesus told the disciples three times that he would die. He would be rejected by the Jewish leadership and be killed by the Gentiles (Mark 8:31; 9:31; 10:33–34). He had come as God's Servant "to give his life as a ransom for many" (Mark 10:45). He knew his ultimate purpose. He is the beloved son the tenants would kill and throw from the vineyard (Mark 12:6). He is the shepherd who was struck, and the sheep scattered (Mark 14:27). At the Last Supper, Jesus explained the reason for his death. His body was broken, and his blood poured out for the forgiveness of sin and to inaugurate a new covenant (Mark 14:22–25; Matt 26:28; Luke 22:14–23).

In John's Gospel, Jesus knows he will die. For John, he is the lamb of God who takes away the sin of the world (John 1:29). In John 3:14, Jesus tells hearers that just as Moses lifted the snake on a pole in the wilderness so that Israel would be delivered from the serpents attacking them (Num 21:9), Jesus, the Son of Man, would be lifted up. In so doing, Jesus is how they can be delivered from the eternal consequences of sin through faith (s.a. John 8:28; 12:32, 34). He referred to his going away to prepare a place for his people. Some cannot come (resistant Jews), but his people will join him, for

---

1. For a fuller discussion, see Mark J. Keown, "The Death of Christ," https://www.academia.edu/91884498/The_Death_of_Christ.

he is the way. And, when he goes, he will send the Spirit.[2] When Philip and Andrew brought some Greeks to Jesus at the Passover, Jesus predicted his death as his glorification. He likened himself to a grain of wheat that falls into the dirt, dies, and becomes a plant bearing much grain. Troubled of heart, he refers to his hour to come when he is to be uplifted. Through his death, he will draw all people to himself (John 12:20–34).

The story of Jesus' betrayal, arrest, trial, denial, and death is like a brilliant, horrific Netflix *Game of Thrones*-like drama in which the forces of evil and fallen humanity conspire to kill him. Satan is involved, inducing Judas to betray Jesus (Luke 22:3; John 13:2). Jesus is betrayed by Judas for money (Matt 26:15) and with a kiss (Luke 22:47–48). Jesus knew this was coming, yet he still broke bread with him (Matt 26:21). He still washed his feet (John 13:5). We see the unconditional love of Jesus.

We see Jesus deeply anguished in the Garden of Gethsemane, pleading with his Father to release him from the horrors of what is to come. God refuses. Instead, he strengthens Jesus for the death that would change the world (Mark 14:32–42).

The Jewish leaders, who were usually divided over matters of theology and law, came together to conspire to destroy him by stealth (Mark 14:2). They harnessed false witnesses to create a pretext to kill him. The best they had was the charge that Jesus would destroy the temple. Such destruction is unthinkable for one man with a small group of disciples. At the meeting of the whole council were two members who would later turn and bury Jesus: Joseph of Arimathea and Nicodemus, shafts of light in the darkness of this meeting (Mark 14:53–65).

Despite his bravado, Jesus' leading disciple, Peter, also denies him. He is the bravest of the men, following Jesus at a distance. Yet, he fails the challenge of denying himself, taking up his cross, and following Jesus (Mark 14:29–31, 54, 66–72). James and John are

---

2. John 8:21; 14:3–7, 28; 16:7.

nowhere to be seen. They have failed to drink from Jesus' cup and to be baptized with him at this right and left hand (Mark 10:37-39). The only ones who do not wholly desert Jesus in the Synoptics are the women who watch from a distance (Mark 14:40-41). In John's account, the women are much closer to the beloved disciple (John 19:25-27). Whichever is closest to the truth, the women put the men to shame.

The Romans are involved. The Sanhedrin had no power to kill Jesus lawfully (John 18:31). Hence, they handed him over to Pilate—Jews and Gentiles colluding! In Jewish law, the alliance of the clean and the unclean is questionable. Pilate interrogates Jesus asking if he is the king of the Jews. Jesus is, as usual, ambiguous, responding, "you say so" (Mark 15:2). Pilate is intrigued and ambivalent about Jesus, who he realizes is no threat. He looks for a way out.

Consistent with the practice of the governor releasing a prisoner, he offers them a choice between Jesus and a revolutionary, Barabbas. Barabbas means "son of the Father." In some ancient witnesses, in Matt 27:15-17, his full name is Jesus Barabbas. So, the crowd's choice is Jesus Christ, the Son of God, or Jesus, the father's son. Incited by the Jewish leaders, they opted for the revolutionary. Jesus will go to his death between two of his revolutionary partners. The real Son of God is crucified while the real revolutionary goes free. Pilate then had Jesus crucified for political expediency to appease the Jews and end any question of a revolt.

Jesus' death is horrific. He is flogged, beaten, and mocked as a king with a crown of thorns and a purple robe. He was then forced to carry his cross (or crossbar) to his death. Some unknown in the crowd (who we know from Mark to be Simon of Cyrene) is conscripted to carry it for him when Jesus is too tired. We see the humanity of Christ. We also see the first person who carries a cross for him. He is a Gentile. His sons are named, suggesting they became a part of the church (Mark 15:21; Rom 16:13). It is a Gentile who helps Jesus carry his cross; the disciples are again nowhere to be seen.

Jesus is crucified, meaning he is nailed by his hands (or wrists) and feet to the cross. He is lifted up, as he predicted in John. Soldiers gamble over his robe. The crowds mock Jesus, challenging him to come down from the cross and save himself. Jesus speaks only seven statements from the cross. He cries out the words of abandonment from Ps 22:1. This is Israel's last chance to recognize that he is the one predicted by David in this Psalm. They misunderstand him (Matt 27:46; Mark 15:34). In Luke 23:34, in a disputed text that is likely authentic, Jesus prays for his killers, asking God to forgive them for their ignorance. Again, in Luke, one of Barabbas' revolutionaries recognizes Jesus as a crucified King, pleading that he remember him when he comes into his reign (the first to recognize a crucified Messiah). Jesus promises the thief salvation on that day (Luke 23:43). In John's account, Jesus gives his mother over to the beloved disciple for his care (John 19:26–27). He cries out his thirst (John 19:28). His final words in Luke are to commit his spirit to his Father (Luke 23:46). In John, it is *tetelesthai*, "it is completed"—Jesus has finished the work he has come to do (John 19:30).

There is then a three-hour period of darkness (Mark 15:33); evil seems to have won! Yet, the curtain hiding the Holy of Holies in the temple is ripped asunder (Matt 27:51; Mark 15:38; Luke 23:45). Access to God is now open for all humanity through Jesus. In Hebrews, Jesus himself is the curtain (Heb 10:20). Some tombs are cracked open, and dead saints are seen in the city (Matt 27:52-53).

And after his death, the Roman centurion confesses: "surely this man was the Son of God" (Matt 27:54). He is the first Christian of the new era, recognizing in Jesus' death that the true savior of the world is not Caesar, but Jesus Christ, despite his crucifixion. He is a foretaste of a Roman world that would, in 300 or so years, adopt faith in this crucified Messiah as its state religion.

What does the death of Christ mean? The meaning is not fully explored in the Synoptic Gospels, where the writers focus on telling the story. It is John, in his Gospel, Paul, especially in Romans and Galatians, and other NT writers (e.g., Hebrews; 1 Peter) who draw out the theological and ethical implications of the death of Christ. Four things stand out.

Our Forgiveness and Salvation

The death of Christ is the willing sacrifice of an unblemished human to deal with sin once and for all. He is the completion of Israel's sacrificial system (and any other such system in the world). No more animals need to be killed. Jesus' death is the solution to sin. Jesus was sinless. He died for us. If we believe, his death brings complete forgiveness for sin for all humankind.

It brings our justification before God. We are declared righteous by God if we believe because Jesus is our substitute, our representative, and the one who conquered sin and death.

It opens the way for the Spirit to be poured into us. When we believe we are cleansed of sin and declared holy so that the Spirit can be given to us, as the Spirit can only dwell in the holy. This holiness comes through Jesus' holiness, imparted to us. We receive his anointing, we are sealed for redemption, and the Spirit is deposited as a guarantee.

We are then redeemed, ransomed, and our life purchased. We are no longer slaves of sin, law, death, and eternal destruction. God's wrath is propitiated and dealt with where there is faith. He will act to cleanse the world of evil, removing its every vestige when the time is right. But this will not include those who believe in him, for the cross dealt with our evil.

The cross also reconciles us to God. It deals with the problem of sin, which separates us from an intimate relationship with God. Now God has dealt with sin. We have peace with God through our Lord Jesus Christ.

Our Death

As such, the death of Christ becomes our death. Paul develops the idea of being "in Christ," in which we participate in Jesus' death, burial, and resurrection. As we are "in Christ," we can say with Paul: "I have been crucified with Christ" (Gal 2:19 [Greek text]). We have crucified our old natures (Gal 5:24). When we die physically, this will merely be a transition to eternal life. Hence, in a sense, while we live on, we are dead in Christ and alive to God in Christ Jesus (Rom 6:11).

A New Covenant Inaugurated

At the Last Supper, Jesus speaks of his blood as the blood of the new covenant (Luke 22:20). The writer of Hebrews states the premise that every covenant is established with blood, including the Mosaic covenant (Heb 9:18–22). Christ's death is the blood inaugurating the new covenant. He has been offered once for all to bear the sins of many (Heb 9:28). His blood is "the blood of the eternal covenant" (Heb 13:20). This covenant is the fulfillment of Jeremiah's vision of a new covenant in which God would inscribe his law on the hearts of his people and forgive their sins permanently enabling people to walk in close relationship with him (Jer 31:31–34). It speaks of an agreement between God and all humankind whereby he will be King, and people who yield to his reign have their sins forgiven. Then they will receive eternal life in his everlasting kingdom.

Our Life-Pattern

Most of us know that "Christ died for our sins" (1 Cor 15:3), and we are saved through his death. Yet, the NT says something more about the death of Christ that we must grasp deep in our beings so that we can be the people God calls us to be. It is this: Christ's death is the pattern by which we should live. The term used for this is cruciformity—to be conformed to the pattern of the *crucis* (cross) of Jesus. We are to live *via crucis*, by the way of the cross.

The cross is the summit of Jesus' life and sacrifice. Despite being King of the cosmos, his life was one of humble service in which he used his immense divine power only in the service of others—healing, feeding, comforting, raising the dead, liberating, giving sight and hearing (spiritual and physical)—and seeking and saving the lost. He never used his power for his own ends. He was totally devoted to the good of others. As Paul puts it, "he emptied himself ... taking the form of a slave ... he humbled himself and became obedient to death, even death on the cross" (Phil 2:7). He poured himself out for the world.

Our call as God's people is to take up our crosses and follow him—a summons to walk in the way of the cross. Wherever we are, among the people we are placed, we are there to live out of Christ's humility, serving them in whatever station God has placed us. This imperative applies to dads at home, kids at school, women at work, church, and everyone at play—anywhere we are. We ask God to show us how to see the world and people as he does and live cruciformly.

We are to do what Jesus did and spend ourselves for his kingdom, his people, and the world. It will be hard. Suffering is essential to the journey, for the path to glory is participating in Christ's sufferings (Rom 8:17). Yet, the reward is great. We already have it: eternal life. We are to press on to win this prize, working out the salvation we already have (Phil 2:12-13; 3:12-14). Put another way; we are to take up our towels and follow Jesus, washing the feet of the world (John 13:1-15).

We each walk in a parent-child relationship with God. We are to spend time with him, allowing him to guide us and shape our lives. We live out of his direction, not our desires, which are always flawed. As we live in this way, whatever the challenges are, we do so cruciformly. We live by the pattern of the cross: humility, service, sacrifice, suffering, love, seeking justice, and a million other virtuous attitudes. We renounce the patterns of this age but are transformed with renewed minds. The key is the Spirit in us, transforming us to be increasingly like Jesus. We are to yield to the gentle nudging of the Spirit, which is the impulse toward cruciformity.

The world will respond again to Christ when it sees people living in the pattern Jesus laid down for us. Such a life is what Jesus was driving at in John 13:35: "By this, all people will know that you are my disciples: if you love one another."

The importance of the death of Christ makes communion a highly significant ritual. When we celebrate communion, we proclaim Christ's death until he comes (1 Cor 11:26). We remind ourselves of the main event that shapes us, the cross, which is our salvation and life pattern. Alongside the proclamation of the Word, communion is the center of worship.

The Resurrection

If the death of Jesus is the most critical moment in the Jesus story, then its unexpected aftermath, the resurrection, is arguably the most momentous moment in history. All the Gospels tell the same story with some detailed variations.[3]

The Burial

First, Jesus is buried late the day before the Sabbath begins at sunset (Friday of Passover) in the tomb of Joseph of Arimathea. A group of women sees the burial (Matt 27:61; Mark 15:47; Luke 24:55). Matthew

---

3. For a fuller discussion, see Mark J. Keown, "The Resurrection of Christ." https://www.academia.edu/92023663/The_Resurrection_of_Jesus.

records that a guard is set to ensure the body is not stolen and that the tomb's entry is covered with a stone (Matt 27:62–66).

The Women at the Tomb

Second, the women go to the tomb early on the following Sunday, the third day from Friday (inclusive), and find the stone rolled away from the tomb. In Matthew, Mark, and Luke, the women are met by an angel (or two) in white who tells them Jesus has risen.

Sent To Tell the Others

Third, in all the Gospels, the women are the first evangelists of the resurrection who took the message to others. They are the apostles to the apostles. There are different details in each Gospel at this point. In Matthew and Mark, they are instructed by the angel to tell the other disciples to meet Jesus in Galilee. Mark ends at this point. Yet, we know that the women told the others because Mark's Gospel exists, and Christianity had spread into Rome at this point. Matthew's Gospel tells us that they went and met him and were commissioned to take the gospel to the world. In Luke, they remember Jesus referring to his resurrection and go to tell the men, who then see for themselves. In John's Gospel, Mary Magdalene tells Peter and John, and they run to the tomb to see for themselves.

Appearances

Fourth, aside from Mark, each Gospel features Jesus appearing to his disciples.

Mark

The original early ending of Mark has no appearances. However, the longer ending from the second century supports that the early church accepted that Jesus appeared to two on the Emmaus Road (Mark 16:12, cf. Luke 24:13–32). It also includes Jesus appearing at a meal (s.a. Luke 24:36–49) and commissioning his disciples to preach to the world and its fulfillment. It retells Luke's commission and recollects tongues speaking and miracles in Acts (Mark 16:14–20; Acts 2:1–11; 28:3).

Matthew

Matthew adds an appearance to the two women named Mary (Matt 28:9-10) and the Great Commission appearance in Galilee (Matt 28:11-20).

Luke

Luke has the Emmaus appearance and names one of them as Cleopas, an appearance to Peter (Luke 24:35), and a meal appearance with the disciples where he commissions them to preach to the world (Luke 24:36–49).

John

John includes an appearance to Mary Magdalene (John 20:11-18), the disciples minus Thomas where they receive the Spirit (John 20:19-23), the disciples with Thomas (John 20:26-28), and seven disciples (Peter, Thomas Didymus, Nathanael, James and John, and two others) meeting Jesus at the Sea of Galilee.

Acts

Acts includes Jesus appearing over forty days, proving his resurrection, and he commissions them to be his witnesses, a retelling of Luke 24:36-49). Luke tells the story of Paul's experience of the resurrected Christ three times (Acts 9:1-18; 22:1-21; 26:12-23).

Paul

Paul has a neat summary of some of the appearances in 1 Cor 15:5-8: 1) Peter; 2) the 12 apostles (actually, the 11, as Judas was gone); 3) an appearance to a great crowd of 500; 4) James; 5) to all the apostles; 6) Paul (s.a. Gal 1:16).

Synthesis

Overall, with moderate harmonization, we get something like this list of appearances:

1. An appearance to Mary (and another Mary) (Matt 28:9-10; John 20:11-18).
2. The Great Commission appearance in Galilee (Matt 28:11-20).
3. The Emmaus appearance, including Cleopas (Luke 24:13-32, s.a. Mark 16:12).
4. Peter (Luke 24:35; 1 Cor 15:5).
5. A meal appearance to the disciples in which he commissions them to preach to the world (Luke 24:36-49, s.a. Acts 1:4-8; Mark 16:14-20; Matt 28:11-20).
6. The apostles minus Thomas (John 20:19-23; poss. 1 Cor 15:5).
7. The disciples with Thomas (John 20:26-28; poss. 1 Cor 15:7).
8. Paul (Acts 9:1-18; 22:1-21; 26:12-23; 1 Cor 15:5-8; Gal 1:16).
9. Jesus appears to a great crowd of 500 people (1 Cor 15:6).

10. James (1 Cor 15:7).

World Mission

Fifth, the disciples are commissioned to engage in mission throughout the world on Christ's behalf.[4] In Luke's second account of the resurrection period, he again emphasizes the mission to the world (Acts 1:8). He includes Paul's commission to the nations (Acts 9:15; 22:21; 26:16-18). (See further on mission later in this chapter).

Importance

The resurrection is vital theologically. Jesus' resurrection begins God's fulfillment of the hopes of resurrection in the OT.[5] It fulfills the hope of the resurrection of the Servant (Isa 53:9-10) and in Judaism.[6] At the time of Jesus, although the Sadducees rejected an afterlife (Acts 23:8; 26:8; Josephus, *Ant.* 18.14; b. Sanh. 90b), the Pharisees expected resurrection and eternal reward for the righteous (Acts 23:6-8; b. *Sanh.* 90b; b. *Ketub.* 111b).

Jesus' resurrection is a victory over sin and its consequences (1 Cor 15:55). Being in Christ, we have died in him, and we are raised (Eph 2:5). Presently, this resurrection is spiritual, Christ's Spirit regenerating our inner beings while our bodies decline. It will be our complete restoration at his coming. His resurrection is

---

4. See Matt 28:18-20; Luke 24:46-49; John 20:21, s.a. Matt 24:14; 26:13; Mark 13:10; 14:9; 16:14-20.
5. E.g., Job 19:25-27; Ps 16:10; 49:15; 73:24; Isa 25:8; 26:19; Ezek 37:1-14; Hos 13:14; Dan 12:1-3.
6. E.g., 2 Macc 7:10-11; 14:46; 1 En. 22:13; 46:6; 51:1-2; Pss. Sol. 3:11-16; 13:9-11; 14:4-10; 15:12-15; Sib. Or. 4:176-82.

the firstfruits of a harvest of people to be raised (1 Cor 15:20). His resurrection guarantees our resurrection (1 Cor 14:22). He is the first of a new humanity and renewed creation (cf. 2 Cor 5:17; Gal 6:15). His resurrection body is a prototype of ours (Phil 3:21). He ate after being raised (Luke 24:42). He remains human. However, as flesh and blood cannot inherit the kingdom of God (1 Cor 15:50), he is no longer flesh and blood but flesh and bones (1 Cor 15:50; Luke 24:39). He bears the scars of his suffering (John 20:25-27). His body is a spiritual body (1 Cor 15:44); still a body but empowered by the Spirit. We will receive the same body of glory he has. Our bodies of humiliation will be set free from bondage to sin and death (Phil 3:20). We will be transformed instantly when the perishable becomes imperishable and the mortal immortal (1 Cor 15:50-54). Unlike those raised from the dead in Israel's story, Jesus' ministry, and the wider NT, ours will be final and eternal as is Christ's.

Did it happen?

Did the resurrection happen? Something happened, for the world has never been the same. While there are differences in detail, the early church saw no reason to remove these as they formed the canon. They let the variations stand, demonstrating that the early Christians did not conspire to produce a neat, tidy story. Instead, they let the witnesses give their recollections. Other things add to an argument for historicity. Women's testimony is included, even though in the ancient world, it carried no weight. There is also a diversity of witnesses, which is astonishing. These disciples were determined to tell the world, even though they would be persecuted and martyred. People might die for a lie to protect their reputations and families, gain wealth, or something similar. However, there was no reason for the early Christians to die for the conviction Jesus was resurrected. All it gained them was suffering. Monotheistic Jews converting to believe in the divine sonship of Jesus must also be explained. Also requiring explanation is the acceptance of the bodily resurrection by the Greeks and Romans, who denied its possibility. The simplest explanation for these transformations is that Jesus has risen.

Then there is the problem of a decent alternative. Having been speared through the side, Jesus was undoubtedly dead when placed in the tomb. A Roman custodia and a huge rock also guarded his tomb. He could hardly have got himself out of the tomb. Nor could others get in. The idea that the women had the wrong tomb is dumb, as they were witnesses to his burial.

Further, the body would be produced to dispel the myth that it lay in a tomb in Jerusalem. No one produced it. The idea that their experiences of Jesus were hallucinations is hardly likely when one considers the number of people involved and the geographical spread of the appearances. Without a doubt, the best explanation is that Jesus did indeed rise.

Response

The resurrection does not prove Jesus' divinity but strongly suggests it. The correct response is that of the women who worshiped him (Matt 28:8, 17). Also appropriate is going to tell others that he has risen (Luke 24:32, 46–49; John 20:21; Acts 1:8). We are called to cry out with the angel, "he has been raised" (Matt 28:6, 7; Mark 16:6; Luke 24:6). With Thomas we should declare: "My Lord and my God" (John 20:28). Just as the eucharist is important to recall the death of Jesus, so baptism is vital as a marker of new life in Christ (Rom 6:3–4). We must celebrate each new conversion to Christ with it.

The Mission of the Kingdom

The kingdom of God is God's great mission project. Jesus comes as God's King and heralds the kingdom.[7] The proper response is to repent and believe the good news (Mark 1:15). Moved by compassion (e.g., Matt 9:36; 14:14), Jesus moved through the nation of Israel, preaching, calling people to join him, feeding the poor, healing, driving out demons, and raising the dead. He is God's anointed King, his sent one (e.g., John 3:34), preaching good news to the poor and releasing people from bondage (Luke 4:18–20). His mission is to seek and save the lost (Luke 19:10). He sought out the lost sheep and brought them home (Matt 9:36; Luke 15:3–7). He invited people to the banquet of God (Luke 14:16–24).

He was not satisfied with doing this himself. Twelve apostles were selected. An apostle is a "sent one, a person sent into mission. The Synoptics all record this initial sending. The disciples are to take nothing much with them, relying on God's provision and people's hospitality—a short-term training exercise. Mark's account is brief, focused on their casting out of demons (Mark 6:7–13). Luke's account involves the deliverance of demons, healing, and preaching the kingdom (Luke 9:1–6). Matthew's account also includes exorcism, healing, preaching the kingdom's nearness, and even raising the dead (Matt 10:1, 8). Matthew adds an entire discourse on mission, equipping readers for their participation in the mission of God (including us).

The mission does not stop with Jesus and the apostles. In Luke 10, there is a second short-term mission assignment with the Seventy-Two (or, in some texts, the Seventy) sent out. This exercise may have involved the Twelve gathering teams of five others and leading them into mission as Jesus had led them. These people are told that "the harvest is great, but the laborers are few" (Luke 10:2). They are urged to pray for Christ (the Lord of the harvest) to send out laborers,

---

7. For a fuller discussion of the mission as per the Gospels, see Mark J. Keown, "The Mission of God's People (The Gospels)." https://www.academia.edu/41159857/THE_MISSION_OF_GODS_PEOPLE_THE_GOSPELS.

for the mission begins in prayer.[8] They are sent again to rely on hospitality, heal, and proclaim the kingdom (Luke 10:9). When they return, Jesus sees Satan fall from heaven; the mission is the progressive defeat of Satan (Luke 10:18).

Each of the Synoptics ends with mission commissions. The original ending of Mark has the women sent to tell the men that Jesus has risen (Mark 16:6). Earlier in the Gospel, the good news will be preached to the entire world before the end (Mark 13:10, s.a. 14:9). Matthew's Gospel ends with Jesus sending the disciples to make disciples of all nations, teaching and baptizing them (Matt 28:18-20). Luke also includes a Great Commission narrative; the disciples sent, empowered by the Spirit, to preach repentance and forgiveness of sins to the entire world (Luke 24:46-49). John's Great Commission involves Jesus sending the disciples as he was sent. He breathes the Spirit on them. He sends them to grant forgiveness of sins on God's behalf (John 20:21-23). In Acts 1:8, Luke's retelling of Luke 24 includes the disciples receiving power from the Spirit to be Christ's witnesses to the ends of the earth. The story of Acts is the story of this mission. It concludes with Paul in Rome, which is not the end of the earth but its center. Rome will be the locus from which the mission will be completed.

Like the restoration of Europe after WW2, the mission of the kingdom is a wholesale restoration of the world. It began with the seed of Jesus' incarnation, God the Son becoming flesh and beginning the work. It will end with the world transformed into what it was always created to be—a world free of evil, sin, decay, death, and pain (Rev 21:1-4).

Jesus preached. At its heart is the salvation of people. The core work of mission is that they come into God's salvation. They hear the good news of the kingdom. They repent and believe. They follow Jesus. They are his. So, its core mission must include the proclamation of the gospel understandably and clearly, people

---

8. Luke 10:3, s.a. Matt 9:38; Acts 4:29-31; Eph 6:18-20; Col 4:3.

submitting to its God, and receiving eternal life. This activity is commonly called evangelism.

Yet mission is also more than verbalizing the message, important though this is. Jesus trained his disciples. The mission involves training new disciples, caring for them, and ensuring they grow in the faith. The mission includes discipleship.

Jesus fed the poor. In the feeding of the 5000, Jesus said to his disciples, "you give them something to eat" (e.g., Mark 6:37). Many other texts support that we are to do the same (e.g., Matt 19:21; Luke 14:13, 21; 16:19–31; 19:8). The early church in Acts took this seriously as they ministered to the poor among them (Acts 4:32–37) and so must we. Preaching good news to the poor (Luke 4:18) is not purely verbal; it includes acting as Jesus did.

Jesus healed the sick and cast out demons. By the same Spirit, we are to lay hands on the ill and demonized and pray that God will heal them. He will act as he wills. Where someone is healed and set free, we praise God. Where God, in his wisdom, chooses to leave a person in a state of unwellness (as in the case of Paul, 2 Cor 12:7), we are to continue ministering to them. We are to care for those in need. The nations will be judged based on how they care for Jesus' people (Matt 25:37–40). It is obvious we are to do this. The marginalized are invited to the banquet, and whether healed and set free or not, they are invited to dine, and we are to care for one another (Luke 14:12–24). The mission involves social justice.

Jesus built a community. He called people to him, and aside from the demoniac sent home to tell his testimony to his people in the Decapolis (Mark 5:1–20), all who wanted to join Jesus were welcome. A good example is Bartimaeus, who followed Jesus along the way (Mark 10:52). The ethics of the kingdom are to be lived out in the Christian community. We gather to love God (worship). We gather to love one another (*koinōnia*). We disperse into the world weekly to be the salt of the earth and the light of the world (Matt 5:13–16). The mission is to build authentic Christian communities in every context filled with love. By this love, they will know that we are Christ's disciples (John 13:34–35).

Jesus went. When a group of people genuinely imbibe the principles of the kingdom, the church can become great. Such churches can be amazingly missional as people are attracted to the faith. This attraction is what missiologists call "centripetal mission" (mission to the center, mission by attraction). While this is what God wants (John 13:34-35), "centripetal mission" is not enough. There must also be "centrifugal mission" (like a centrifuge, mission from the center, mobilized mission, going out). The Great Commissions do not tell people to sit and wait for the world to come. We are sent people. We are to go. Like Jesus, we are to have sinners as our friends. We are to participate in families, workplaces, sports and social contexts, and broader society, flavoring, leavening, and lighting the world. We are to share Jesus as we go with the attitudes of Christ, good works of justice and kindness, and with winsome, wise, and salty conversation (Col 4:5-6). Western Christianity has lost its sense of going. We must regain it, going into our nation with the good news and reclaiming our place as the world's leading sender of missionaries.

We must also remember our call to mission regarding the big picture of what God is doing on planet earth. We are created in God's image to rule over and care for the world. Looking after God's world involves building human society worldwide, using God's resources wisely, and preserving the world's ecology. I call this the Great Cosmission of God—his mission to build a cosmos, a world.

Sadly, sin has seen this dream marred deeply. The world is built but flawed, rife with corruption and sin, broken and hurting, subject to decay and death, and full of brokenness.

Even in the garden of Eden, God the Missionary began the restoration work, clothing Adam and Eve and allowing them to produce children. He called Abraham, from whom he would save the world. Abraham became a nation, and God blessed them and foretold his future intervention to transform the world into what it should and could be. Jesus is his intervention. He has come, and the new creation and humanity are launched.

We are his people, filled with his Spirit. Each of us is to take up our role in the Great Cosmission—to build God's world. Hence, work is essential. Not all of us are sent to be full-time missionaries or ministers. We are to go out and do work that builds God's world. This engagement involves all sorts of work, from digital production to the very pragmatic trades, from IT to accounting to education to science, art to politics, and so on. We must be creative, designing, creating, and renewing with all that God has given us. We are to do so in a way that nurtures God's world and humankind.

We also carry with us the Great Commissions referred to above. We are about evangelism, discipleship, feeding the poor, social justice, social transformation, love, exorcism, healing, and more. We build churches, schools, hospitals, and more. We do whatever God summons us to do.

Our prayer lives are most important so that we hear his call to do our part in the mission. In prayer, we discover our gifts, and the Spirit guides us in mission. And we always do mission cruciformly. We are here to serve the world and are always humble, taking up our crosses. We are to be God's people emulating the Master Jesus and taking our part in his mission.

The mission will end when God, Father, Son, and Spirit, are satisfied that the good news has penetrated the nations to God's satisfaction (Matt 24:14; Mark 13:10). Then, Jesus will return, and the final work of restoration will be completed. We will be as we are created to be, and the world will be liberated from its bondage to decay (Rom 8:21). Heaven and earth will merge, evil vanquished, and we will live forever in the new heavens and earth (Rev 21–22).

Perhaps then our mission will be complete. Or will it? What does the God of universes have in store for us? Only time will tell. In the meantime, "go and make disciples from all nations" (Matt 28:19).

Ethics, culture, and leadership

Ethics

Ethics is about moral principles for life.[9] Ethics are fundamental in the OT, found in Israel's complex legal code. The emphasis in OT ethics is holiness and being ritually clean. The concern was contamination, which could come through a range of things such as a dead body, a menstruating woman, the wrong food, a person with a skin disease, unclean hands, and so on. Personal holiness was indispensable, and although Deuteronomy called for the circumcision of the heart (Deut 10:16; 30:6), Israel tended to be overly concerned with external holiness. However, Israel's law was also concerned for people and was full of injunctions to care for the poor and socially marginalized.[10] The second great commandment, to love your neighbor as yourself, is also found in Lev 19:18. In context, it applies to love for one's fellow Jew. However, in Lev 19:34, this includes love for the immigrant.

The prophets of Israel were heavily critical of Israel's leadership and people for their failure to care for the poor and needy.[11] These seers called Israel to show the mercy and love of God to the marginalized (e.g., Isa 1:17; 58:6-7; Jer 22:3; Zech 7:10). Their God "executes justice for the fatherless and the widow, and loves the sojourner, giving him [or her] food and clothing" (Deut 10:18, ESV).

---

9. For a fuller discussion on ethics in the Synoptics, see Mark J. Keown, "The Ethics of the Kingdom," https://www.academia.edu/41159580/THE_ETHICS_OF_THE_KINGDOM.
10. E.g., Exod 22:22; 23:3, 6, 11; Lev 14:21; 19:10, 15; 23:22; 24:17, 19, 20; Deut 15:4-11; 24:14; 27:29.
11. E.g., Isa 1:23; 3:14-15; 10:2; Jer 2:34; 5:28; Ezek 16:49; 18:12; Amos 2:7; 4:1.

Jeremiah urged people to have circumcised hearts (Jer 4:4). The Messiah would preach good news to the poor (Isa 61:1).

The summons to yield allegiance to Jesus the King includes a call to a particular lifestyle. It stands in continuity with the fulfillment of the OT law, not its abolition. Yet, its focus is a holiness of heart and mind expressed especially in love (Matt 5:17-20). It is not merely coming to faith and then doing what we want (see Rom 6). We are called to live by the value system of our King and kingdom. The supreme virtue is love which is drawn from Lev 19:18 and 34 (cited above). For Jesus, one's neighbor is anyone we meet on life's journey, including our enemies (Matt 5:43-48; Luke 6:27-36; 10:25-37). Paul and John emphasize love for one's neighbor.[12] Such compassion cannot be mere sentiment but is expressed with action on behalf of the other (1 John 3:16-18). For James, living by the royal law means caring for orphans, widows, and the poor (Jas 1:27-2:26). For Matthew, love is expressed in the golden rule: doing for others what we want them to do for us (Matt 7:11).

Other great ethical principles are humility and service, as seen in Jesus' summons to take up one's cross and follow him. Living this way means being devoted not only to our good but also to the good of others.[13]

Matthew and Luke's Sermons on the Mount and Plain have the most extensive collections of Jesus' ethical teaching (Matt 5-7; Luke 6:20-49). These passages summon people to be pure-hearted, show mercy, seek reconciliation, and care for the poor, the grieving, and others in need. Believers are to renounce fits of anger, retaliation, and sexual immorality, be faithful in marriage, and always keep their word (Matt 5:21-42). They are to give lavishly to the needs of others, not for public recognition, but quietly, and God will reward us (Matt 6:1-4; Luke 6:38). They are to be utterly devoted to God, his kingdom, and his righteousness, and not money and possessions,

---

12. E.g., Rom 13:8-10; 1 Cor 12:31-13:13; Gal 5:14; John 13:34-35.
13. Mark 8:34, s.a. Matt 10:38, 39; 16:24; Luke 9:23; 14:27.

trusting God to provide for our needs (Matt 6:19-34). They are also to hold themselves accountable, not focusing on the failings of others (Matt 7:1-5; Luke 6:37, 39-42).

Doing this is not merely an ethic to be lived when we are together as kingdom people. It is to be lived 24/7 in the world. As the salt of the earth, we are to bring flavor, preservation, and healing to broader society. We are, similarly, the light of the world who are to shine brilliantly before the world through good works (Matt 5:13-16). Such lives are to be bathed in prayer, fasting, and forgiveness of the other (Matt 6:5-18; 7:7-11; Luke 6:37). Doing is premised on cultivating a solid relationship with God (Matt 7:21-23). It is living by the teaching of Jesus (Matt 7:24-27; Luke 6:46-49).

There is a vast range of other ethical things across the NT. Paul, especially, recognizes the Spirit is the key to living in line with God's ideals. We receive the Spirit at conversion, and by the Spirit, God transforms us if we are willing. We are to be people of personal holiness in every aspect of our lives. Socially, we are to be governed by love for everyone we meet. We are to be non-discriminatory, full of grace, merciful, compassionate, kind, gentle, humble, servant-hearted, constructive of speech, sexually pure, and give witness to the world of the patterns of God's kingdom. Great societies form where these are lived well, and the world is transformed.

Culture

The coming of Jesus inaugurates a cultural revolution. The world that Jesus came into was highly ethnocentric. The Jewish worldview divided the world between Jews and Gentiles. Jews were God's people. While there was the hope of the Gentiles eventually submitting to God's rule, until that happened, the Gentiles were idolatrous sinners. They needed to become Jews to be God's people. Becoming a Jew is called Judaizing, whereby a person not born into Judaism converts to the Jewish faith. Converting involved circumcision (for men), ritual cleansing (a kind of baptism), and submission to the laws of Moses, especially the boundary markers: Sabbath, ritual purity, eating protocols, the Jewish calendar, and so on. Being a member of God's people involved conforming to Jewish culture.

The rest of the world was also highly ethnocentric. Romans loved Greek culture and absorbed it. They saw themselves as Greeks and the rest of the world as uncivilized barbarians. The term "Barbarian" is derogatory, formed by onomatopoeia to imitate the babbling of other languages. While some Gentiles respected Judaism and Jewish culture, there was widespread anti-Semitism. Jewish concern for circumcision and their aversion to pork were especially ridiculed.[14]

In the ancient world, religions were predominantly tied to culture. Judaism is associated with Israel and Jews; Hinduism with Indian culture; Buddhism with SE Asian cultures; and so on. Christianity marks something new. No longer is religion ethnic. People of every nationality and culture can convert while retaining the ceremonial aspects of their culture that do not violate the gospel.

Jesus could be critiqued for focusing only on Israel. So, in Matt 15:24, he says to the Canaanite woman: "I was not sent except to the lost sheep of the house of Israel" (NET). He also told the Twelve to limit their apostolic mission to "the lost sheep of Israel" (Matt 10:6).

Yet, while Jesus did have a focus, we cannot ignore Jesus' radical relationship with Gentiles. The first worshipers of Jesus in Matthew are Gentile magi from the east (Matt 2:1–12). When a Roman

---

14. Richard Berchman, "Pagan Philosophers on Judaism in Ancient Times," in *The Encyclopedia of Judaism*, ed. Jacob Neusner, Alan J. Avery-Peck, and William Scott Green (Leiden; Boston; Köln: Brill, 2000), 3:1041: notes that for some: "Jewish religious rites such as circumcision seemed barbaric, the dietary laws appeared ridiculous, and the refusal to acknowledge other gods was impious atheism."

centurion approached Jesus to heal his servant, Jesus was prepared to break cultural rules and go into his home. His entry into the Roman home is only prevented by the centurion, who did not want Jesus to do so, trusting him to heal his servant from a distance. Jesus commends his faith as superior to that of the people of Israel (Matt 8:3–13; Luke 7:1–10).

Although Jesus' statement concerning the dogs is puzzling, he commends the faith of the Syro-Phoenician woman and heals her daughter (Matt 15:21–28). He willingly healed people from the Gentile region of the Decapolis (Matt 4:25; Mark 3:8; 5:1–20). He entered Gentile territory, including Tyre, Sidon, and the Decapolis (Matt 15:21; Mark 7:24–31). While in Gentile territory, he fed the 4000, breaking bread with Gentiles without concern for uncleanness (Mark 8:1–10). In Luke, he challenged the ethnocentricism of his people in Nazareth with stories of the widow of Zarephath and Naaman from the OT—both Gentiles (Luke 4:26–27, cf. 1 Kgs 17:9; 2 Kgs 5:1–14).

John also mentions Greeks approaching Philip wanting to see Jesus at Passover. Philip and Andrew came to see Jesus. Jesus then predicts his death through which he will draw *all* people to himself (meaning every nation, not every individual). He encourages them to believe and receive eternal life (John 12:20–36).

As has been noted, Samaritans were hated by Jews. Yet, Jesus is prepared to stay in a Samaritan town, only to be rejected. Their refusal led James and John to seek to destroy the town with fire from heaven. Jesus utterly repudiated this with a strong rebuke (Luke 9:51–56). Twice, Samaritans are the heroes in Jesus' ministry. First, the Good Samaritan is commended, while the Jewish priest and Levite are tacitly rebuked (Luke 10:25–37). Second, the only grateful leper who returned to thank Jesus after he healed the ten was a Samaritan, commended by Jesus (Luke 17:11–19).

Then there is the stunning story of the Samaritan woman in John 4. She is also an adulterer and perhaps a prostitute. Yet, Jesus willingly asks her for a drink, prepared to partake of what her supposedly unclean hands offered him. Later, he accepts an invitation to stay in Sychar, and many come to faith in him. In the first-century Jewish context, this is stunning.

Throughout his ministry, Jesus was unafraid to hang out with tax collectors, despite their rejection as traitors to Rome (e.g., Matt 9:10–11). Indeed, one of his disciples was Levi, a tax collector who is almost certainly the Matthew who wrote one of the Gospels (compare Mark 2:14 and Matt 9:9; 10:3). Then there is the remarkable story of Zacchaeus, who accepts Jesus into his home and finds salvation demonstrated in his radical generosity to the poor and defrauded (Luke 19:1–10).

Jesus also spoke of people from every nation becoming disciples who are taught and baptized (Matt 28:19). The gospel will be preached throughout the world (Matt 24:14; Mark 13:10). The disciples were to preach repentance and faith throughout the world (Luke 24:46) and be Christ's witnesses to the ends of the earth (Acts 1:8). Jesus is the savior *of the world* (John 4:42).

In Acts, the gospel began among Jews in Jerusalem. The Spirit fell, and they spoke in the tongues of the nations (Acts 2:1–11). God was beginning the reversal of the scattering of the world and confusion of languages at Babel (Gen 11:1–9). Eventually, the gospel spread after Paul's persecution, and they began preaching to non-Jews in Syrian Antioch (Acts 8:4; 11:19–21). Peter led Cornelius and his family to Christ, and the uncircumcised received the Spirit showing God's acceptance of them as his children (Acts 10–11; 15:8). The church had to work through whether a new Gentile convert had to Judaize as well as believe in Jesus. The Jerusalem Council roundly rejected the idea. All Gentile converts require is sincere faith, just like all Jewish Christians (Acts 15).

Paul neatly sums up the Christian attitude to culture in Gal 3:28: "for in Christ Jesus there is neither Jew nor Greek." We are one in Christ, bound together by faith and the Spirit. Our fundamental culture is the fruit of the Spirit with which we love one another and the world (Gal 5).

The kingdom story ends with people from all the nations gathered around the throne of God, worshiping God and his Son, the lamb who was slain (Rev 5:1–14; 7:9–17). The city of God descends to earth, and in the new heavens and earth is the tree of life, and its leaves are the healing of the nations (Rev 22:2).

The gospel brings a cultural revolution. There is no longer Jew and Gentile, Roman and Barbarian, and Pakeha and Māori. Our cultures are still, in many ways, unique and wonderful. Culture is to be celebrated. Yet, we are not to be divided culturally. All are welcome to come to Christ as they are. We are bound together as one by faith. No culture can be allowed to dominate another.

The cultural imperative of the gospel needs to be carefully considered in each context. Any church has a dominant culture, whether a particular ethnicity (e.g., Korean) or a particular way of doing church (e.g., Presbyterian). Our challenge is to break open our churches so that no culture dominates. We need to be open to the different, the other, and embrace them as they come. All they need is to come and belong. To be a full member of God's people requires genuine faith. Cliquey groups, dominant cultures, "the way things are done around here," and rules that divide churches must be challenged. The vision of God is not many people of the same ilk hanging out feeling cool. It is the wide variety of people coming together as one and, despite our differences, being one people united in the gospel. Such a vision is more challenging than hanging out with our mates and people like us. But this is the gospel's challenge, and we must take it up.

Leadership

The undisputed leader of the kingdom of God is God the Father. It is his kingdom. He has appointed his Son King, anointing him through his prophet John, by the Spirit. Jesus leads his kingdom as Christ, Lord, Son of God, and King of kings.

Jesus appoints leaders. In his life, he appointed the Twelve. These were designated apostles, a Greek political term, speaking of an emissary who travels on behalf of a ruler. The task of the apostle was to establish faith communities of God throughout the world. Others were commissioned with leadership roles in Luke's Gospel; the seventy-two were similarly sent into mission (Luke 10).

The appointment of the Twelve in Luke's Gospel (Luke 6:12-16) is followed by the Sermon on the Plain (Luke 16:17-49). The implication here is that the ethics espoused in the Sermon are integral to the life of an apostle and Christian leader. They must be devoted to embodying the kingdom ethic and being an example to others.

The fundamental call of the Christian leader is to lead, as did Jesus. After Jesus is recognized as Messiah, the following verses teach what it means to be a Christian leader. Fundamentally, leaders are to deny themselves, take up their cross, follow Jesus, be prepared to lose their lives for his sake, and never be ashamed of Jesus and his words (Mark 8:34-38). They are to listen to Jesus (Mark 9:7). They are to lead by example in their worship lives, in how they treat others, and in their missional desire.

They are to renounce selfish ambition and concerns for greatness in the eyes of others. They are to be as humble as children, servants, leading through servanthood (Mark 9:33-35). Unlike John, who was threatened by the presence of others in ministry, they are to be permission-giving leaders, releasing people into their ministries (Mark 9:38-41). They are to be holy, but not holier-than-thou people; determined to please God but not self-righteous and judgmental (Mark 9:42-50; Matt 7:1-5). They are to seek sexual purity, faithfully celibate or married (Mark 10:1-12). They are not to get in the way of people coming to Jesus, whether old or young but open the pathway to the Lord (Mark 10:13-16). They are not to be covetous of wealth; they are to serve God and not money (Mark 10:17-31, cf. 1 Tim 6:3-10, 17-19).

One of the NT's most significant passages on leadership is Mark 10:35-45. James and John came to Jesus, demanding he does their bidding. Herein we see their fundamental problem—although they know Jesus is Messiah, they have not grasped what that means. They want *their* way when all that matters is the way of Jesus! They think that they can tell Jesus what to do. It is the other way around for a Christian leader.

Jesus goes along with them. He asks them what they want. They arrogantly ask for the premier positions of power on his right and left when he enters his glory. Jesus challenges whether they can go through the suffering he is about to. They probably thought Jesus was referring to war with the Gentiles, and as the "sons of thunder," they were overly confident of their ability. Of course, Jesus is not talking about killing others but about his crucifixion. Jesus, however, does not grant their wish, telling them that this is up to God. Hearing this is important for us too. We may aspire to leadership or a particular role. God decides who does what. Our job is to do what he tells us, not what we want from him.

Understandably, the other ten disciples are annoyed at the arrogance of James and John. They likely felt miffed—why them? Why not me? Jesus then takes the opportunity to teach them about leadership. He points them to what they know—that the Gentiles rulers, the Caesars, and the Herods rule autocratically.[15] They are despots, ruling arrogantly, with masses of attendants and servants who they rule by intimidation, might, and power. We have the likes in the world today, ruling North Korea and other totalitarian contexts. Some western leaders also behave more like them than Jesus.

However, the Christian leader is not to be like this. Greatness is found in the service of all others. Even Jesus came as a servant to serve others and give his life for them, not to be served by others.

The challenge of Christian leadership is to have the courage to lead, yet to lead through service. Doing this means not simply demanding people do what we demand when we expect it done and how we want it completed. It is about building teams, cultivating

---

15. Herod the Great became a Jew by conversion but was originally a Gentile, the son of an Idumean and an Arab woman. He was never fully accepted by the people as a Jew.

imaginative approaches, and working together to build community. Doing this is a slower process than dominating autocracy. Yet, it is God's way.

God could have sent Jesus as a Gentile leader, with armies, demanding the world submit. However, he would not have had our willing allegiance. He would rule by fear with coerced responses. God's way is to lead by service and love.

Through Acts and the rest of the NT, we see first the apostles leading with courageous example, prepared to be obedient even when punished for their stand. When the work of feeding the poor widows in the community became too much for the apostles, a new leadership group was formed. Commonly called "the Seven," they focused on caring for widows, two of which became great evangelists: Philip and Stephen. Stephen is the first martyr of the church.

God chose Paul. He plucked him from persecuting Christians to be the leader of his mission to the world. Paul chose a range of men and women co-workers to work with him. He summoned them to "imitate me" (e.g., 1 Cor 4:16, Phil 3:17), recognizing that authentic Christian leadership is more caught than taught. He called men and women to live cruciformly, led by the Spirit, leading out of love, leading by example, holy, faithful, and filled with the Spirit.

7. John's Gospel

Part 1: Background Matters

Authorship

John was written by the "beloved disciple" or "the disciple Jesus loved" (John 13:23; 19:26; 20:2; 21:7; 21:20).[1] He is also likely the other disciple in John 1:40; 18:16; 20:2-4, 8. The identity of this disciple is vigorously debated. It is agreed that a certain John wrote it, but which "John" is debated. There are two main ideas—John the Apostle and John the Elder, referenced in Papias. With the greater focus on Judea rather than Galilee and the author's relationship with the High Priest (John 18:16), a good case can be made for the author being an otherwise unknown disciple from Jerusalem (e.g., Bauckham).[2] The traditional view that John the Apostle is the author is also defendable. His identity can be seen by cross-referencing with the Synoptics. Most scholars believe the author is the "other disciple" who was with Andrew in John 1:35-42. From the Synoptics, this is probably John the Apostle (see Mark 1:16-20; Luke 5:1-11). The author is also referenced at the Lord's Supper, reclining beside Jesus (John 13:23). The best alternative candidates for this person are John's brother James or Peter. However, James was dead when John was written (Acts 12:1-2). Peter is ruled out as he motions to the beloved

---

1. For a fuller discussion, see Keown, *Discovering*, 1:260-318 (Ch. 9).
2. Richard Bauckham, *The Testimony of the Beloved Disciple: Narrative, History, and Theology in the Gospel of John* (Grand Rapids, MI: Baker Academic, 2007).

disciple at Jesus' side. Hence, knowing James and John sought the places of prominence beside Jesus in the Synoptics, including at the Lord's Supper (Luke 22:24–30, s.a. Matt 20:20–28; Mark 10:35–45), by far the best candidate for this is John the Apostle. Early church tradition also supports John the Apostle. Whichever of the Johns wrote it, it is a skilled eyewitness account of the life of Jesus.

Date

The dating of John's Gospel can be as early as the 60s if it is written before the temple's destruction, either by the Apostle or another John (the Elder?). Some scholars date the Johannine writings to the reign of Nero. However, tradition places it in the reign of Domitian (AD 81–96). There are indications that 1 John was written after John's Gospel,[3] and so John was written in the 80s. As such, it is the latest of the Gospels. One or more of the Synoptics were likely written and well circulated by the time of the Gospel.

Provenance and Recipients

For those who reject that John was written by the Apostle John, a range of ideas have formed from John being written in Israel, Egypt, and a range of other places. The unanimous early church tradition suggests John settled in Ephesus and died as an older man there. As such, the Gospel most likely originated from John in Ephesus and

---

3. See, e.g., the new commandment of John 13:34–35 has become an "old commandment" (1 John 2:7). Also, there is clear evidence of a heretical movement that is not explicit in John's Gospel.

was circulated first through the churches mentioned in Rev 2-3 and then distributed throughout the Christian churches.

Relationship to Synoptics

When one reads John after the three Synoptics, it is clear John is not singing from quite the same hymn sheet. It is still about Jesus, and many of the same characters are there. He is in the same parts of the world, although in Jerusalem a lot more than Galilee. John the Baptist precedes his ministry. Jesus preaches, heals, teaches, raises the dead, and encounters harsh opposition from his people (the Jews). He is arrested and tried before the Sanhedrin, condemned to die, and sent to his death by Pilate. He rises from the dead and appears. He sends his disciples into mission. So, it is clearly about the same guy.

Yet, there is much that is different. Scholars explain the differences in varying ways. Some think John had no idea of the other Gospels and wrote from independent sources. Others consider that John knew Mark and probably Luke and that he wrote to tell the story differently. His writings use ideas found in Paul, e.g., faith and love. He recasts the Jesus story, blending his experiences of Jesus with theological ideas in the church, some of which he takes to a new level. He tells us stories of Jesus in Jerusalem, especially at festivals. This material supplements the Synoptic stories and fills out our picture of Jesus.

The call of the disciples in John 1 involves radically different material. In addition, Jesus is in Jerusalem a lot, encountering opponents (the Jews) with whom he is in constant debate. He does not teach in parables but in long discourses often built around deep "I am" sayings. Yet, while not teaching in parables, he uses a range of parabolic ideas and images: living water, the bread of life, the way, the truth, the life, light of the world, the resurrection and the life, the good Shepherd, the vine, and more. The central theme is not the kingdom of God, although this is mentioned (John 3:3, 5), but eternal life. The right response is not to repent and believe, but faith and belief are required (e.g., John 3:16).

Part 2: Structure & Overview

The Prologue (1:1–18)

The story begins with a bold declaration that Jesus is God in the prologue (1:1–18). Jesus is the Word who is God, the creator, and light of the world. The Word becomes incarnate—he is made flesh (v. 18).

The Call of the Disciples (1:19–51)

From there, as with the Synoptics, John focuses on the ministry of John the Baptist, and we learn new things about the prophet and Jesus. The first disciples, Andrew and the other disciple (undoubtedly the author, John), initially followed the Baptist. Yet, they are sent by John to Jesus. Andrew finds Peter, who joins the group. Jesus calls Philip, who calls Nathanael. Chapter One ends with a group of five disciples following Jesus.

The Book of Signs (2–12)

Then begins what scholars call the Book of Signs, which runs from Ch. 2 to the end of Ch. 12. It is called the Book of Signs because of the stunning seven miracles Jesus performs.

The Cana Cycle (2:1–4:54)

The first miracle is in Cana, where at a wedding, somewhat reluctantly, Jesus turns water into wine (2:1-12). The second is also in Cana, when Jesus heals the royal official's son (4:46-54). Some scholars, therefore, label the section the Cana cycle. In between, Jesus visits Jerusalem and clears the temple. As this event is placed at the beginning of the Passion account in the Synoptics, Jesus either cleared the temple twice, John recorded the actual occasion at the beginning of Jesus' ministry, or John moved the story from the Passion to this place for theological reasons. While some scholars hold all three views, the latter seems probable, pointing to the importance of the temple theme in John. Jesus is the tabernacle of God (1:18), clears the temple, and later becomes the temple in which people abide (2:18; 15:1-17). Also significant is Jesus' encounter with Nicodemus, who lacks spiritual insight, launching a long Johannine discourse declaring Jesus the means of salvation (3:1-21), the ministry of John and Jesus (3:22-36), and the encounter with the Samaritan woman who has spiritual insight and becomes a mass evangelist, despite being from the despised Samaritan community—in stark contrast to Nicodemus (4:1-45).

Galilee and Jerusalem Festivals (5–12)

After the Cana cycle with its two miracles, from John 5-12, Jesus moves from Galilee to Jerusalem several times, and most events take place in Jerusalem at festivals (whereas in the Synoptics, they take place in Galilee). Throughout the book of signs, there are the other five miracles: the healing of the man by the pool (5:1-16), the feeding of the 5000 (6:1-15), Jesus' walking on water (6:16-21), the healing of the blind man (9:1-7), and the raising of Lazarus (11:1-44). The Book of Signs is also punctuated with long discourses in which

Jesus declares the truth to the Jews and two of the "I am" sayings of John—"I am the bread of life" (6:35) and "I am the light of the world" (8:12). These link neatly to the feeding of the 5000 with bread and fish (*bread* of life, John 6) and the healing of the blind man in John 9 (*light* of the world).

The Book of Glory (13–20)

After the Book of Signs, attention turns to the death of Jesus in what scholars call "the Book of Glory." This part of John runs from Ch. 13 to the statement of the purpose of the book at the end of Ch. 20. This half of John is so named because, for John, the cross of Christ is his exaltation and glorification.

The Last Supper Discourse (13–18)

The first three chapters are focused on the Last Supper, where John's Jesus demonstrates the nature of his kingship as servant leadership by washing the feet of the disciples. His disciples are to do the same (13:1–15). Then attention turns to the Supper, focusing on his betrayal (13:21–30). After this begins a long discourse in which Jesus prepares the disciples for his death and their suffering, summons them to love one another, and tells them of the coming of the Spirit. The Spirit is described as "the Paraclete" (comforter, counselor, advocate) of God (13:31–16:33). Jesus also declares the other five "I am" sayings, in which he identifies himself as God (*the I am*, Exod 3:14), and summons people to live in him: "I am the gate" (10:7), "I am the good shepherd" (10:11, 14), "I am the resurrection and the life" (11:25), "I am the way, and the truth, and the life" (14:6), and "I am the vine" (15:1). John 17 has the great prayer of Jesus for his people in the world. The focus of the prayer is perseverance and unity.

The Passion and Resurrection (18:1–20:29)

John 18 and 19 include the Passion account, which is clearly the same story found in the Synoptics, even if there is much additional information that adds to our knowledge of the death of Jesus. These include Jesus declaring himself the "I am" when confronted by his arresters. They fall at his power (18:5-6). We learn that Peter struck off the ear of Malchus. He is likely named as he became a member of the early church and perhaps an eyewitness source (18:10). John records that Jesus appeared before two high priests, Annas and Caiaphas (18:12-14, 19-24, 28-32). John includes the memorable conversation between Pilate and Jesus, culminating in Pilate asking, "What is truth?" (18:33-38). The Gospel's answer is Jesus! (14:6). John records that the sign above Jesus on the cross was written in three languages, Aramaic, Latin, and Greek (19:20-22). Unlike the Synoptics, the author and three women named Mary are near the cross, demonstrating their courage. Jesus' concern for the care of his mother is seen as he urged John to care for her, which tradition suggests he did (19:25-27). Jesus' final words are "it is finished," speaking of the completion of his life and mission (19:30). We read that Jesus was dead and so his legs were not broken; however, his side was pierced, and the separation of his blood confirmed his death (19:31-35). The separation of his blood rules out Jesus merely being asleep and escaping the tomb. Finally, we learn that Nicodemus was with Joseph at his burial and that he provided spices for his burial (19:38-42). This mention is the third reference to Nicodemus, and we can trace through the Gospel his journey from inquiry to disciple by the end of Jesus' life (3:1-9; 7:50; 19:39).

The Resurrection (20:1–29)

This passage narrates the resurrection leading into the purpose statement of the Gospel (below). We learn new things from the passage. First, John testifies that Mary Magdalene came to the tomb, reported the resurrection to himself and Peter, and the duo ran to see its emptiness (20:1-9). Second, John records Jesus' appearance to Mary Magdalene (20:10-18). Third, Jesus appears to the disciples aside from Thomas. He sends them to continue his mission of pronouncing God's forgiveness empowered by the Spirit (20:19-23). Fourth, Jesus again appears to the disciples, including Thomas, who believes and declares Jesus Lord and God (20:24-29).

The Purpose of the Gospel (20:30–31)

The resurrection appearances of Jesus are then interrupted by John telling readers why he wrote his Gospel (20:30-31).

> So then, on the one hand, Jesus did many other signs before the disciples, which are not written in this book. But these have been so that you may believe that Jesus is the Christ, the Son of God, and that by believing, you may have life in his name.

John writes that readers may either come to believe in Jesus or continue believing, depending on who is reading. He tells us that believing in Jesus brings eternal life, whereby we will be raised on the last day to live with God forever (John 5:25-29). His message is summed up gloriously in John 3:16 (s.a. John 3:36). As we read it, John wants us to believe in Jesus and never give up.

Epilogue (21)

The epilogue first continues with a fifth dimension of the

resurrection account—the appearance of Jesus to the seven fishing by the Sea of Galilee. These include Peter, Nathanael, John, James, and two unnamed disciples (21:1-2). One of these is the author; as discussed, the best indicators lead to John the Son of Zebedee. In Jesus' third appearance in John, Luke 5 is recalled as they are told to gather fish from the right side, and they gather a massive haul of 153 fish. After dining with Jesus, undoing Peter's denial, he is three times commissioned to provide food for Christ's disciples (21:4-19). The Gospel culminates with the focus shifting from Peter to the death of John and the veracity of his testimony contained in it (21:19-25).

There is no messianic secret in John. John boldly declares who Jesus is and then tells the story to demonstrate his claim. It is written as an eyewitness account, a quasi-legal defense of Jesus presented to Jews and Gentiles with different presuppositions that Jesus is the Son of God.

Part 3: Important Themes

We can note here the importance of signs to John's story. John's Gospel is arranged around seven signs: 1) turning water to wine (John 2:1-11); 2) the healing of the official's son (John 4:46-54); 3) the healing of the man by the pool (John 5:1-17); 4) the feeding of the 5000 (John 6:1-15); 5) walking on water (John 6:16-21); 6) the healing of the man born blind (John 9:1-42); 7) the raising of Lazarus (John 11:1-44). Signs are crucial in authenticating Jesus to his challengers. Knowing that Jews were most interested in signs (Matt 12:39; 1 Cor 1:22), this may be to convince them that Jesus is indeed the longed-for one.

There are also seven predicated "I am" sayings, i.e., they have predicates or descriptors (e.g., I am *the life*): 1) I am the bread of life (John 6:35, 48); 2) I am the light of the world (John 8:12; 9:5); 3) I am the gate (or door) (John 10:1, 9); 4) I am the Good Shepherd (John 10:11, 14); 5) I am the way, the truth, and the life (John 14:6); 6) I am the resurrection and the life (John 11:25-26); 7) I am the true vine (John 15:1). Each of these points back to the OT and Jesus as the fulfillment of the hopes of Israel. Each point forward to the hopes of eternal life.

There are also a series of discourses which include debate and Jesus responding with complex teaching which confuses the Jewish hearers: 1) Nicodemus (John 3:1-21); 2) The Samaritan Woman (John 4:1-38); 3) Witnesses (John 5:19-47); 4) The Bread of Life (John 6:26-59); 5) Jesus at the Feast of Booths (John 7:14-39); 6) I am the Light of the World (John 8:12-59); 7) I am the Good Shepherd (John 10:1-39); 8) Greeks and Jesus (John 12:20-36).

John's Gospel does not have the Sermon on the Mount or Plain but has a substantial section of teaching attached to the Last Supper. It includes Jesus washing the disciples' feet and teaching about the coming of the Holy Spirit, the Paraclete, or Comforter, Jesus as the vine, and warnings of suffering and Jesus' death (John 13-16). John does not include Jesus in the Garden of Gethsemane but includes the great prayer of Jesus for the perseverance and unity of his people (John 17).

John's account of Jesus' death is similar in outline but has many different details. He does not include the clearing of the temple in Jesus' final week but places it at the start of Jesus' ministry (John 2:14-22). The placement of the account causes a great deal of debate. Some argue there were two clearings of the temple. Others suggest John has the correct chronology. The third idea is that John placed it early in the Gospel for theological reasons. The latter seems best. John recasts the story of Jesus after the Synoptic perspective was well known. He moves the temple clearing to highlight that Jesus marks the end of the period of the Jerusalem Temple and becomes the new temple of God, the locus of God's presence on earth. He is the living tabernacle in which God lives and reveals himself (John 1:1, 14-18). We are drawn into this temple by faith.

John's Gospel has an exceedingly high Christology stressing Jesus' divinity more explicitly than the other Gospels. He is God in John

1:1, who becomes flesh in John 1:14, and the one and only God who exegetes the Father to the world in John 1:18. The author declares Jesus equal with God in John 5:18. Jesus pronounces himself divine with the multiple "I am" sayings. He is the "I am" who existed before Abraham in John 8:58. He claims oneness with the Father in John 10:30. Thomas pronounces him his Lord and God in John 20:28).

John's Jesus, however, is also human. He is human and engages with others. He shows weakness, getting tired and thirsty (4:6). He wept (11:35) and washed their feet (13:1–14). He died on a cross, and his blood separated, showing his full humanity (19:34). In stressing his humanity and divinity, John is combatting false ideas of Jesus being only human (Arianism) or only divine (Docetism, Gnosticism). He also uses many other terms to describe Jesus, such as the lamb of God (John 1:29), the light of the world (John 8:12), and many others.

8. The Acts of the Apostles

Part 1: The Background to Acts

Authorship and Recipient

The prologue of Acts mentions a former book and the same recipient as Luke, Theophilus, indicating that the same person authored Luke and Acts (Luke 1:3; Acts 1:1).[1] The early church was in no doubt that the author was an early disciple, Luke. Hence, all that was said concerning the authorship of Luke earlier stands. The recipient is the same, most excellent Theophilus, a Roman noble person to whom Luke tells the story of Jesus and the expansion of the early church to Rome. He is likely an official connected to Paul's situation in Rome. As with Luke, Acts is written to the Gentile world. Whereas Luke summons them to believe in Jesus and live a life of radical discipleship, especially social justice, Acts calls them to join the mission of God by his Spirit to the ends of the earth.

Date

The date of Luke-Acts is heavily contested. One school of thought holds that Luke and Acts were written as late as the 80s and 90s to unite disparate Christian factions. However, the best evidence of the date comes with the end of Acts, with Paul in Roman prison around

---

1. For a fuller discussion, see Keown, *Discovering*, 1:319–416 (Ch. 10).

AD 60–61. Luke chooses to end his account here rather than tell the story of the stoning of James the brother of Jesus in Jerusalem in AD 62 (Josephus, *Ant.* 2:200), the Neronian persecution (AD 64–65), the deaths of Paul and Peter (AD 65–67), and the fall of Jerusalem (AD 70). The non-inclusion of these events suggests that we should date the Gospel and Acts sometime in the 60s after the writing of Mark's Gospel. Some reject this idea because they consider there must be a significant period between Mark and Luke for Luke to gain access to Mark. Such an interim is unnecessary as Colossians and Philemon place Mark and Luke together in Rome in the early 60s (Col 4:10, 14; Phlm 24). I consider it likely that Luke-Acts was written soon after Mark's account, and his Gospel is one of the key sources for Luke (Luke 1:2).

Luke-Acts as One Work

While it is possible Luke was written first and then Acts with a good gap between, more likely, Luke-Acts is one work that came in two volumes due to the limitations of scroll length. Knowing this means fully considering Luke's perspective and theology requires careful examination of both books. Seeing them as one work also indicates that the gospel can be proclaimed from the time of John to Jesus and then to the point in history in which the gospel is preached (first-century Rome).

Genre

It is commonly held that the four Gospels are biographies based on the Greek *bios* genre that tells the story of a prominent person's life. However, while Luke bears the hallmarks of a *bios*, the prologue of the Gospel is similar to other ancient historiographies (e.g.,

Josephus, *Ag. Ap.* 1.1–5). So, then, Luke-Acts is not merely a *bios* but the first history of the early church. Volume 1, Luke, focuses on the life of Jesus. Volume 2, Acts, accounts for the spread of the faith attached to his name. In reading both volumes, Theophilus fully understands who Jesus is, what he requires of his followers, and the gospel's spread into the Roman world.

An Open-Ended Story

Luke tells us from the first the agenda for part two of his work. It begins with Jesus charging the disciples to be his witnesses to the ends of the earth (Acts 1:8). It ends with the gospel yet to be preached to the ends of the earth. By its end, the gospel had reached the center of their world, Rome, and had spread through Israel, Syria, Anatolia, Macedonia, Greece, and North Africa. The gospel had to reach the ends of the earth—West to Spain; North to Europe, Britain, Scandinavia, and Russia; south through Africa; and east to China and Southeast Asia. The ancients knew the world was huge (although they did not know about the Americas and the Pacific nations). Acts ends with Paul in Rome, with the gospel poised to go to the ends of the earth from the empire's capital. It looks forward to the completion of the mission and the return of Christ (1:11). Hence, readers are to see that it is an ongoing story and that they are sentences, paragraphs, or chapters in the ongoing book of the spread of the gospel. The story continues today, and we will work out our place in it.

Historicity

Some scholars have read Acts with great historical skepticism. They see it as a construct that has little historical value. Yet, this is a strange perspective. Luke places himself in the story in the four "we passages" mentioned earlier in the discussion on Luke.[2] He was thus a traveling companion of Paul and had access to Paul and his coworkers as he compiled his work. Acts 21 places Luke in Jerusalem with Paul; hence, he had access to the earliest Christians in the city and region. Luke placed himself on the boat with Paul to Rome in Acts 27 and encountered Christians in Rome. As we cross-reference the people mentioned in Acts, like Gallio in Corinth (Acts 18:12-17) and others, we find that these people are referenced in Roman sources, and his account stands up. We can easily harmonize the chronology and movements in the letters with Acts. As such, while Luke wrote a limited account of the early church, carefully selecting what he included, telescoping events, and summarizing speeches, there is no reason to reject it as a fictional and false account of early Christianity. On the contrary, Luke was an excellent and precise ancient historian.

Part 2: Acts—Structure and Content

The book of Acts is carefully structured. The prologue retells the story of Christ's resurrection and the commissioning of the first Christians. The key verse is Acts 1:8, where Jesus tells his disciples that the Spirit will come on them and they will be his witnesses in Jerusalem, to all Judea and Samaria, and the ends of the earth. To a considerable extent, this sets up the structure of the book. After the replacement of Judas with Matthias in Acts 1:12-26, the Spirit falls at Pentecost (2:1-4). The coming of the Spirit launches a period of mission in Jerusalem that ends with Saul's persecution scattering most of the church out of the city (Acts 2:5-8:4).

---

2. Acts 16:10-17; 20:5-15; 21:1-18; 27:1-28:16.

Then, Acts 9–12 tells the story not only of Paul's conversion (setting up what will come in the second half of Acts) but the spread of the gospel through Samaria and Judea by Philip (Acts 8:5–40) and further work in Judea by Peter (Acts 10–11). Peter is the dominant figure in the first half of Acts. After the execution of James and Peter's miraculous release from prison that undoubtedly saved him from the same fate, Peter leaves Jerusalem (Acts 12:1–19). Aside from being at the Jerusalem Council in Acts 15, Peter drops from Luke's account. The Jerusalem church's leadership then fell into the hands of James, the brother of Jesus. The missions of Paul dominate the second half of the book.

Acts 13–28 tell the story of the beginning of the fulfillment of Jesus' commission to the disciples to witness his name to the ends of the earth. Paul dominates the narrative, first with Barnabas and Mark, then with Silas and other coworkers, as the gospel of grace through faith is taken through Anatolia, Macedonia, and Rome. As noted, it ends with Paul in Rome, from where the gospel can go to the farthest ends of the earth.

There is an ongoing movement of the gospel from Jerusalem. The Jewish eschatological expectations envisaged the nations coming to Jerusalem with wealth and for worship. However, Acts sees disciples radiate from Jerusalem into the world, taking the good news to them. Rather than becoming Jews through circumcision and yielding to Mosaic law, people must repent and believe in Jesus to be saved. They are then baptized and join the church and the mission of the Spirit to see humankind saved from sin and its consequences.

Part 3: Key Themes in Acts

As noted, Acts is the second part of Luke's narrative. Having the second work means we not only have Luke's brilliant account of Jesus' life, but we can see how Jesus' followers lived out his injunctions.

It begins with Jesus telling the disciples that "you will receive power when the Holy Spirit has come upon you, and you will be my witnesses in Jerusalem, and in all Judea and Samaria, and to the end of the earth" (Acts 1:8). This sets the agenda for Acts. Generally speaking, part one of Acts occurs in Jerusalem (Acts 1:1–8:4). Part two is based in Judea and Samaria (Acts 8–11). Part three is to the ends of the earth (Acts 12–28). It ends in AD 60–61, not with part three complete, but with Paul in the center of the Roman world, Rome, preaching and teaching the kingdom (Acts 28:31). The implication is that part three will go on as the gospel continues to work its way beyond the Mediterranean rim where it is planted. When the mission is complete, Jesus will return as he left (Acts 1:11). In the meantime, we continue the work.

This chapter will focus on the Jerusalem Church as described in Acts 1–8 in three parts: worship, inner life, and mission. The account of the Jerusalem Church seems intentionally given not only to tell the story of the spread of the gospel but to inspire us to see what church can be if we live as obediently as they did.

Worship

The first Christians were utterly dedicated to living obediently. They had no idea of an unchurched faith. To believe in Jesus meant to belong to the local Christian community. Hence, they gathered daily and in unity (e.g., Acts 1:12–13; 2:1, 42; 3:1; 4:23–31). They met daily at the temple, participating in Israel's prayer life and worship without engaging in sacrifices (Jesus had come!) (Acts 2:46).

As they met, they were filled with awe toward God (Acts 2:43). They praised God together (Acts 2:46). They prayed together a lot (esp. Acts 1:14; 2:42)! These prayers saw terrific results, including the right people being moved into leadership such as Judas' replacement Matthias, and the appointment of the Seven (Acts 1:15–26; 6:1–6). There were many signs and wonders, including people seeking healing by Peter's shadow (esp. Acts 2:43; 5:12-16). Vast numbers of people were converted. The wealthy sharing their possessions with those in need strengthened the church's inner life. For Luke, there is a definite link between prayer and God's resultant action—renewal begins in prayer (esp. Acts 4:23–5:16).

The first Jerusalem believers did not just meet at the temple but broke bread together. Their meals probably included eating together in each other's homes, during which they celebrated the Lord's Supper and remembered Christ's death (Acts 2:42, 46).

They focused on God's Word and learning from the apostles (Acts 2:42). They were determined to be obedient to Christ's teaching and example, even if they were persecuted (e.g., Acts 4:19-20; 5:29).

Throughout the narrative, Luke emphasizes the leading of the Spirit, promised by Jesus before his ascension, and given bountifully across the narrative of Acts (Acts 2:1-4). They also baptized new converts (e.g., Acts 2:38, 41).

The first Christians sought to take seriously the greatest of commandments: love the Lord your God with everything you have (Luke 10:27). This worship life began in a very Jewish way, patterned on the Synagogue as they met at the temple. Such worship included singing the Psalms and new Christian creations and praying prayers drawn from Judaism, like the Shema and the Lord's Prayer. They would have created new liturgical elements to go with their worship. We see potential hymns embedded in the NT, which may have been written at this time.[3] They desired to convert their people

---

3. Some of these might be nativity songs in Luke, like Mary's Magnificat (Luke 1:46-55), Zechariah's Benedictus (Luke 1:68-79), the angels' Gloria (Luke 2:14), and Simeon's Nunc Dimittis (Luke 2:29-32). Paul includes what might be hymn fragments (e.g., Phil 2:6-11; Col 1:15-20; Eph 5:14; 1 Tim 3:16). Revelation is full of songs to the Lord (1:7; 4:7, 11; 5:9-10, 12, 13; 7:12, 13-17; 11:15, 16-18; 12:10-12; 15:3-4; 16:5-7; 19:1-8; 21:3-4). See also Eph 5:19; Col 3:16.

to Christ in these contexts. Over time they were driven out of the Jewish settings and worshiped in homes.

As the gospel radiated out of Jerusalem, Judea, and Samaria to the ends of the earth, a chorus of worship went up to God from diaspora Jews and Gentile believers. This worshipfulness is seen in diverse ways. As the multicultural Syrian Antiochian church gathered for prayer while fasting, God sent believers on further missions to the west (Acts 13:1-3). New leaders were appointed in each church with prayer and fasting (Acts 14:23). Paul and Silas prayed and sang in a Philippian jail, praise that triggered an earthquake, their release, and the conversion of a Roman family (Acts 16:25). The Ephesian elders and Paul knelt in prayer as he bid them farewell for the last time (Acts 20:36). Similarly, Paul and his group prayed as they neared Jerusalem on his third Antiochian mission (Acts 21:5). The power of prayer was seen as God delivered those on the ship to Rome from drowning (Acts 27:29). Healing flowed as people prayed for the sick (Acts 28:8).

The Inner Life of the Church

Not only was the early Jerusalem church a worshiping community, but they were very dedicated to one another in a way few churches today can match. We are profoundly challenged to seek to be more like them in this.

Their commitment to gather daily at the temple and meet in one another's homes is mentioned above. They shared meals, worshiped, prayed, celebrated communion, baptized new converts, and grew as a community. They were very committed to one another. They made decisions through meetings bathed in prayer (e.g., Acts 1:12-26).

Acts 2:42-47 is a rich summary of this shared life devoted to fellowship/*koinōnia* (Acts 2:42). The term is used widely in Greek writings of a range of partnerships, whether marriage, business, or other shared life contexts. It is a crucial term across the NT to refer to partnership and fellowship.

Aside from the shared worship activities already referenced, it is essential to consider their fellowship over meals (Acts 2:42, 46). In ancient cultures and many today, eating together was a highly symbolic and political act of unity. It connotes trust, acceptance, and welcome into the family and people. Indeed, it is at meals that genuine fellowship is experienced.

Another prominent feature of this first church was how they shared their possessions and wealth. They had "*everything* in common" (Acts 2:44). They sold possessions and belongings and distributed what was made to those as they were in need (Acts 2:45–46). This sharing is sometimes called "economic *koinōnia*" by biblical scholars. These Christians took Jesus' teaching seriously in passages like Luke 12:33: "Sell your possessions and give gifts of mercy." They were dissatisfied with the rich getting richer and the poor poorer. They sought to resolve the discrepancy between the haves and have-nots.

More detail is given on this in Acts 4:32–5:11. The church was "one in hearted and soul, and no one said that any of their possessions belonged to him [or her] alone, but they had everything in common" (Acts 4:32). There was no needy person in the church (Acts 4:34). People sold land or homes to finance the care of those in material need (Acts 4:35). The prime example is Joseph a Levite from Cyprus who was renamed Barnabas (Son of Encouragement) for his acts of generosity. The church took this all with deadly seriousness, as seen in the story of Ananias and Sapphira, who made false claims of giving all proceeds while keeping some of the money for themselves (Acts 5:1–11). We can note, too, that this outpouring of radical generosity of the rich for the poor flowed from the prayer of Acts 4:29–31, asking for God to move in signs and wonders. It is a profound wonder when the rich are prepared to make financial sacrifices for the poor. Their generosity challenges us in our consumptive societies.

Their commitment to continue their economic *koinōnia* is seen in Acts 6:1-7. By this time, food was distributed daily to the widows attached to the church. Some were Hebrew-speaking Jewish Christians (Hebrews); others were Greek-speaking Jewish Christians (Hellenists). Inadvertently, the Hellenists were being neglected. The inequitable distribution was brought to the notice of the leaders. In a church committed to egalitarian care, the Twelve were understandably unhappy with this. They gathered all the disciples to resolve the issues—a brilliant example of church decision-making (s.a. Acts 15). They took personal responsibility for the failure, identifying the problem as their inability to organize the distribution of food as well as maintain their core business: preaching and prayer (an essential lesson to those summoned to preach and lead).

The leadership and community agreed to select seven well-regarded, Spirit-filled, and wise leaders to ensure fair food distribution. The criteria show the kinds of people that are appropriate for leadership. The selection of the seven enabled the Apostles to focus on their core missional tasks—prayer and gospel ministry. They chose seven men with Greek names suggesting that they were Hellenists. One was a convert to Judaism, Nicolaus the proselyte (Acts 8:5). Another would become the only person called an evangelist in the NT, Philip, who evangelized Samaria and had a large home with four prophet daughters in Caesarea Maritima (Acts 8:5-40; 21:8-10). Another would also become a brilliant evangelist and Christianity's first martyr, Stephen (Acts 6:8-7:60).

Some skeptical biblical scholars have criticized the concern for the poor seen in the church. They see it as communism. However, this is not communism. Communism is a state-sponsored non-voluntaristic system whereby the state forces people to pay taxes and imposes artificial wage schemes on them. The system of giving at Qumran was much more like communism than Acts. To join the Qumran community, one had to relinquish all private property and put it in a shared purse. Acts does not demand such a sacrifice. Instead, it speaks of voluntaristic giving, where people gave as they desired. It was heart-giving, not forced giving.

Some scholars also criticize the Jerusalem church because later, Paul had to twice collect money for them from other churches to relieve their poverty.[4] Yet, it is undoubtedly unfair to criticize Christians for giving to each other when times are good yet later facing struggles because of their generosity. These things come and go. When this happens, other Christians should move in and support them as Paul does here. Paul's collections prove the point already made—the early Christians were highly committed to giving to each other in need. So, churches in Turkey and Greece gave to the needy in Jerusalem. Such collections are glorious examples of international economic *koinōnia*. Such things are possible today as more affluent Christian communities help those that are poorer across the world.

In the selection of the seven, we see the early church's passion for caring for the poor and interculturalism while maintaining the core tasks of prayer and proclamation. The appointment of the Seven is one of the most critical steps in the movement from a monocultural church to an intercultural one. To be a leader, one did not have to be an apostle or a native Jewish male. Leaders could come from Gentile converts or Greek-speaking Jews. Over time, this would broaden further as women are involved in leadership in Acts, keeping with Luke's citation of Joel's prophecy that daughters and female servants shall prophesy (Acts 2:17–18; Joel 2:28–29). These women include Tabitha (Acts 9:36) and Lydia, the likely initial leader of the Philippian church (see Acts 16:14–15, 40). Then, there is Priscilla, who is usually named before her husband Aquila in Acts (Acts 18:18, 26), and who, with her husband, taught Apollos a better understanding of the faith—a woman instructing a man (Acts 18). We can also note the importance of women in Luke's story of Jesus (esp. Luke 8:1–3; 10:38–42). Paul's letters also mention some women involved in mission. The writer of Luke-Acts was not a Jew but a Gentile. His non-Jewishness is clear in Col 4:7–17, where Paul carefully lists

---

4. Acts 11:26–30; 1 Cor 16:2–4; Rom 15:26–31; 2 Cor 8–9.

his Jewish co-workers, excluding Luke. Amazingly, the Gentile Luke penned 27% of the NT!

The Jerusalem church shows the way in terms of community care. They cared for each other spiritually and materially. We live in a wealthy part of the world. Yet, a growing gap between the rich and poor has been exacerbated by Covid-19. With the costs of living as they are and the wages of Kiwis in many cases not matching inflation, those at the bottom are suffering more and more. If we name Jesus as Lord, we cannot merely pray and care for one another in word. We must do more. The wealthy among us need to consider how best we can use our wealth to better the situation of the poor. The answer is, in part, state-sponsored care, but that is not voluntaristic and is accompanied by the love and compassion of Christ. We must work alongside national and local governments and the many Christian organizations already doing splendid work and build stronger church communities in which the rich care for the poor. Helping those in need is a profound challenge and is only likely to become greater.

Another church worthy of note is the Antiochian church. It was in Syrian Antioch that they first really grasped that the gospel was not only for Jews but for Gentiles (Acts 11:20). The names mentioned in Acts 13:1 suggest a church comprising Jews (Barnabas, Saul, Manaen) and Africans (Niger, Lucius). We see here a multicultural expression of the faith. Then, at the Jerusalem Council, it was agreed that Gentiles were not to be burdened with Jewish cultural laws and protocols. With this decision, the scene was set for the church to explode into the world without the barriers of Jew and Gentile, slave and free, male and female (Acts 15, cf. Gal 3:28).

Mission

Luke gives us glimpses into the quality of the worship and inner life of the Jerusalem Church. In keeping with him telling the story of the gospel's spread, he gives us even greater insight into their extraordinary commitment to the mission.

The two aspects already mentioned, their worship and *koinōnia*, are no doubt contributing factors to the astonishing growth of the church from 120 (Acts 1:15) to 3000 (Acts 2:41) to 5000 (Acts 4:4) and more. People were attracted by what they saw in the passionate worship of the church and the genuine care they had for their needy (centripetal mission). Yet, as with Jesus, Luke does not present a static view of mission as merely attracting people to the church; he tells a story of a church zealous to continue Jesus' centrifugal mission to the world.

As mentioned earlier, Acts 1:8 sets the agenda for Acts. It speaks of the disciples receiving the Spirit and power to be Jesus' witnesses from Jerusalem to the world. We see this in the account of Jerusalem, the first part of Acts.

The Spirit fell at Pentecost (Acts 2:1-4). All people present received the Spirit, including men and women and the young and old. The impact is that they spoke in tongues. The gift is not tongues as a private prayer language to edify oneself (1 Cor 14:2, 4). Instead, the gift is missional tongues allowing the gospel's spread.

Furthermore, it indicates the undoing of the confusion of human language at Babel (Gen 11:1-9). God brought this confusion in the OT to limit the spread of evil. Now that Christ and the Spirit have come, he will begin its reversal by the spread of good. The impact of Pentecost is missional—while some write it off as alcoholic rantings, residents and pilgrims from across the whole Roman world are intrigued as they hear their language being spoken spontaneously (Acts 2:4-13).

Pentecost was the launching pad for Peter to evangelize in response to their inquiry, "What does this mean?" (Acts 2:13). Peter then peaches, the first of many sermons included in Acts by Peter,[5]

---

5. Acts 2:14-41; 3:11-26; 4:8-12; 5:29-32; 10:32-43.

Stephen (Acts 7:1-60), and Paul.[6] These are all generated by moments of opportunity. They all focus on God and Jesus yet are diverse in content depending on the context. Some are very Jewish (esp. Peter [Acts 2-4. 10], Stephen [Acts 7], and Paul's sermon in Acts 13). Others spoken in Gentile situations are different, focusing on God's work in the wider world (Acts 14; 17). Some include snippets of testimony, and Paul's messages in Acts 22-26 are all compelling testimonies. These messages give us an extraordinary insight into the early church's proclamation.

The disciples were utterly devoted to evangelism and were powerful witnesses by the Spirit. This passion for telling the world began in the temple at Solomon's Colonnade as they met daily and spoke the Word in public so that people could hear the gospel (Acts 2:46; 3:1-26; 5:12-14).

A notable example of their courageous commitment is Peter and John, who refuse to be silenced by the Sanhedrin despite being flogged and imprisoned. Their response is that they must obey God and speak of what they have seen and heard (Acts 4:20; 5:29). When the Christians, aside from the apostles, were driven out of Jerusalem by Paul's persecution, *all of them* preached the gospel wherever they went (Acts 8:4).

The key to their mission was the Spirit who led the mission. Pentecost directly leads to the first significant missionary encounter (Acts 2). The healing of the disabled man at the temple leads to the second (Acts 3). Imprisonment catalyzes the messages of Acts 4 and 5, and trials lead to the messages of Acts 7 and chs. 22-26. There is a fantastic period of evangelistic success after their prayer to God in Acts 4:29, indicating God gave them boldness for evangelism and performed miracles through them. This prayer is followed by them evangelizing boldly (Acts 4:31), signs and wonders performed (Acts 5:12), and multitudes coming for healing, even because of Peter's shadow falling on them (Acts 5:15).

---

6. Acts 13:13-52; 14:15-17; 17:22-31; 22:1-21; 23:1-6; 24:10-21; 26:1-29.

Persecution plays a key role, consistent with the view across the NT that bad situations and opposition are allowed by God and used for his purposes (e.g., Rom 8:28). In the first phase of the church, the focus was on the conversion of Jews. One may even be critical of the church for failing to look beyond itself to the Gentile world in this period. Whether this is fair or not, the persecution of Saul is the catalyst for evangelizing the world beyond Judea. Infuriated with Stephen and the Christians, the young Pharisee launched an assault on the church. He drove all Christians out of Jerusalem except the apostles (Acts 8:1-3). However, this only caused the mission to gain momentum as all those who went shared Christ (Acts 8:4). This included Philip, who took the gospel to the "loathed" Samaritans (Acts 8:5-40) and others who took the gospel to Greeks in Syrian Antioch (Acts 11:19-20). Eventually, God would call the same Saul, renamed Paul, to lead his mission to the world (Acts 13:1-3).

Our mission is not just evangelism, although that is very much included. Signs and wonders were a significant aspect of successful evangelism. No doubt, after the radical healing of the disabled beggar, more came for healing (Acts 3:1-9). The importance of signs and wonders is also seen when the crowds came to be healed by the apostles and even Peter's shadow (Acts 5:12-16).

While there is no evidence that they took their economic *koinōnia* directly to the world to try and solve its poverty issues, there is no doubt that where contact was made, they were extremely generous. As noted, this would also have been a great attraction point. Indeed, in the first phase, the church enjoyed the favor of all the people (Acts 2:47). Some no doubt came to experience healing and provision (Acts 2:43-45).

Those of us in ministry should spend a great deal of time considering the life of the Jerusalem community. We see how those on the ground with Jesus sought to live out his teaching. We are inspired afresh to worship God with all we have, to form communities that truly reflect the ideals of God's reign, and engage in mission in our communities to the ends of the earth. The story goes on. Led by the Spirit, we find our place in it.

The church's mission went on after the early phase. Stephen became the first martyr, followed by James. Both men were missionally minded and prepared to die for the faith (Acts 7; 12:1-2). Philip led the mission to Samaria and Judea (Acts 8), and Peter took the gospel to Judea, including the evangelization of the Roman centurion Cornelius and his family (Acts 10-11). Paul's epic missions and other influential early church missionaries dominate Acts 13 to 28. Acts gives testimony to the unstoppable spread of the gospel, and anyone keen to be a part of God's mission (as all Christians should be) should immerse themselves in its pages.

9. Paul's Life, Mission, and Letters

Part 1: Paul's Life

Chronology

Here, I will summarize Paul's life based on harmonizing the data in Acts and Paul's letters.[1]

Date	Event
1–10?	Birth
31–33	Conversion[2] (Acts 9; 22; 26; Gal 1)
31/33–35	Mission in Damascus and Arabia (Gal 1)
35	First mission to Jerusalem (Acts 9; Gal 1)
35–45	Mission in Cilicia and Syria (Acts 9; Gal 1)
42	Paul's heavenly vision (2 Cor 12)
45–48	Famines in Judea
46	Monetary gifts taken to Jerusalem, the second mission (Acts 11; Gal 2)
47	Mission to Southern Galatia (Acts 13–14)
48	*Galatians*
49	Jerusalem—The Jerusalem Council Mission
49	The Claudian Edict (Jews expelled from Rome)

---

1. For a fuller discussion, see Keown, *Discovering*, 2:1–71 (Ch. 1).
2. Scholars debate whether Jesus died in AD 30 or AD 33—this outline assumes the former but recognizes it is disputed.

49–51	Mission to Galatia, Macedonia, and Greece (Acts 16–18)
50	1 *Thessalonians*
50	2 *Thessalonians*
51	Jerusalem, then to Antioch, visit three
52–58	Mission to Galatia, Macedonia, Greece; Jerusalem Collection (Acts 19)
52–55	Ephesus
55	1 *Corinthians*
55	Troas (2 Cor 2)
55	Macedonia
56	2 *Corinthians*
56–57	Achaia
57	*Romans*
57	Jerusalem Collection delivered to Jerusalem (Acts 20)
58–59	Imprisonment in Caesarea
59–60	To Rome (shipwreck trip)
60–61	Roman imprisonment
60–61	*Ephesians, Colossians, and Philemon*
62–63	*Philippians*
64	Final mission to Spain (?), Crete, Asia, Greece
64–67	Final Roman Imprisonment
64–67	1 *Timothy, Titus, and* 2 *Timothy*
66–67	Paul killed in Rome

Paul is a massive figure in the NT. His writings make up 23% of the NT, and his life dominates a quarter of Luke's writings. Overall, around a third of the NT story is concerned with Paul in one way or another. With this in mind, it is evident that biblically minded people need a good basic understanding of Paul.

Pre-Christian Years (ca. AD 1–33)

Birth and Upbringing

Paul was probably born in the first decade of the first century, not long after Jesus. Tradition has it that his family was from Gischala in Galilee and had been taken as prisoners of war to Tarsus. He was raised in Tarsus, an important city in Cilicia (SE Turkey), famous for Stoic philosophy. He was then raised in the Diaspora and knew the Greco-Roman culture well. He learned Greek. However, it is clear that he was also raised as a passionate Hebrew (Phil 3:4-5), a brilliant young man who advanced in Judaism from an early age (Gal 1:14). This means he knew Israel's story through and through. He also had direct access to Synagogues and the freedom to teach. Such an upbringing prepared him well for God's mission.

Citizenship

He was also a Roman citizen. A Jew became a Roman citizen as a gift from the Roman authorities, purchasing it, or being born from a family which already had Roman citizenship. Unlike the Roman Tribune, who had paid for his citizenship, Paul was in the latter category—he was born a citizen (Acts 22:28). This means his parents or others before them in the family had purchased or received citizenship after being set free from slavery. Citizenship gave Paul some crucial rights, especially the ability to move freely, avoid floggings (most of the time, e.g., Acts 16:22-23), freedom from crucifixion, and the capacity to appeal to Caesar (Acts 25:11).

Tentmaker

Paul was a tentmaker (e.g., Acts 18:3). We are not sure where his trade started. As the name suggests, Cilicia was famous for cilicium (Cilician goat hair), with which people made various items, including tents. He may have learned the trade from his father. As a Pharisee, he may have developed his skill as it was not uncommon for Pharisees to have a trade. In other imperial contexts, he probably worked with leather. His tentmaking was a point of controversy in Paul's life. First, his stained hands meant he was quickly identified as someone beneath the upper classes, as no elite Roman would do such a thing. Secondly, and more importantly, Paul used his tentmaking to support himself in his ministry to avoid being manipulated by donors (esp. in Corinth), being a burden (e.g., 1 Thess 2:9), and being seen as a peddler of the gospel (2 Cor 2:17).

Marital Status

Paul may have been married in his pre-Christian life, but if so, he was no longer so in his ministry. There are two reasons for thinking he may have been married. First, as a young Pharisee, he would have been expected to marry. Second, the word he uses in 1 Cor 7:8 concerning his state is *agamos*, meaning "widower" or "single person." It is balanced in this text with the term "widow," and some scholars read it this way. Whether he was married prior, all evidence suggests that he was single in his life of Christian ministry. If he was previously married, his wife either left him after his conversion (cf. 1 Cor 7:15–16) or died.

Pharisee

As a young man, he was taken to Jerusalem, where he studied to become a Pharisee under the Great Gamaliel. Gamaliel was a great Pharisee, some of whose sayings are still around today, and who was a moderate where Christians were concerned, arguing against using violence against them (Acts 5:33–40). Paul then became a Pharisee. Being a Pharisee meant Saul was one of Israel's religious leaders, brilliantly skilled in OT interpretation, and passionate for Judaism and its traditions. Unlike Gamaliel, he was no moderate. He was enraged by the Christians and sought to destroy the movement. He was prepared to drag them into prison and vote for their deaths if necessary (Acts 7:58–8:4; 26:10). With the support of the High Priest, Paul traveled to Damascus to destroy the church (Acts 9, 22, 26). He was a passionate worshiper of God but rejected Jesus.

Christian Career (ca. AD 31/33–66/67)

Conversion on The Damascus Road (ca. AD 31–33)

En route to Damascus, Jesus appeared to Paul. He was blinded and came to believe in Jesus and his love for Yahweh. His world was turned upside down. Jesus was the Messiah, the Son of God, and Lord, even though he had been crucified! Paul realized he had been wrong about the Christians and became one of them. The same zeal he had had for God was now applied to God and his Son.

God also commissioned him to lead his mission to the non-Jewish world, the apostle to the Gentiles (Rom 11:13). Acts 13–28 is focused on his missions to the Gentiles. These are also referenced in his letters. Some people put together the life of Paul purely from the letters, arguing that Acts is unreliable. However, some scholars have powerfully argued that Luke was a careful ancient historian, and his chronology can be trusted. As such, we can harmonize Paul's letters and Acts and piece together the main threads.

Mission to Damascus and Arabia (Acts 9:20–25; Gal 1:17, ca. ad 31/33–35)

It is traditional to talk about Paul's three great missionary journeys and his final trip to Rome. Some also mentioned a fourth missionary journey after Rome. Yet, this neglects the earlier phases of Paul's life in which he engaged in a mission before what is called his first missionary journey from Antioch.

In Galatians 1:17, we are told Paul's first mission was to Arabia. The term refers to either the Nabatean kingdom extending south into the Arabian Peninsula from Damascus or the whole Peninsula. There were likely two emphases on this journey. First, Paul would have spent a lot of time in prayer and study, working out the theology that flowed from his experience of Christ's self-revelation to him. He may have visited ancient Mt Sinai during this period as it lies in the area. Second, Paul would have preached in the cities and synagogues of Damascus (see Acts 9:19–22) and Arabia. Damascus and Arabia represent his first missionary journey. Aside from the mention of ministry in Damascus, this phase is not mentioned in Acts. This omission is not a big issue. Luke does not include everything Paul did in his account of his life. Moreover, a trip to Arabia fits between Acts 9:25 and 26.

Jerusalem Visit 1: Meeting Barnabas, Peter, and James (Acts 9:26–29; Gal 1:18–19, ca. AD 35)

In Gal 1:18-19, Paul went to Jerusalem for fifteen days, during which he met with Peter and Jesus' brother James. According to Acts, he also met Barnabas and engaged in evangelism but was then driven from the city (Acts 9:26-31). This trip was a critical time for Paul to gather first-hand a complete understanding of the details of Jesus' life and ministry. As he preached the gospel on this trip (according to Acts), this should be considered the second mission of Paul.

Syria and Cilicia (Acts 9:30; 11:25–26; Gal 1:21, ca. AD 35–45)

In Galatians 1:21, Paul mentions his mission work in Syria and Cilicia, his third and fourth missionary engagements. This period included mission work in his home city of Tarsus in Cilicia (Acts 9:30). This period was the most extended period of mission in Paul's career. According to Acts, Barnabas brought Paul to Antioch in Syria to assist with the spread of the gospel among Greeks (Acts 11:20-26). Antioch was crucial as the base for Paul's future mission operations as he went from there on his three Antiochian mission journeys.

Jerusalem Visit 2: The Famine Visit (Acts 11:26–30; Gal 2:1–10, ca. AD 46)

While there is no mention of Paul evangelizing in his trip to Jerusalem at this time, this trip should be seen as Paul's fifth missionary journey. The purpose of the mission was to take money to the Judean Christians about to face a famine (Acts 11:28-30).

Some scholars consider Galatians 2:1-10 an account of Paul's visit to Jerusalem to discuss circumcision in Acts 15. Others argue that the Galatians' account aligns better with Acts 11:30 when Paul traveled to Jerusalem to take money because of famines. It is difficult to decide between the two.

In favor of aligning Gal 2 with Acts 15 is the letter's similar feel to Romans and the Corinthian letters, written in the mid-50s. Additionally, there is an apparent concern for the gospel (Gal 2:2–5) and the request that Paul continue to care for the poor (2:10).

Acts 11 is favored by the mention of a revelation (Gal 2:2), which may have been Agabus' prophecy. Moreover, there is no request that the Galatians give to the Jerusalem Collection (cf. 1 Cor 16:1-4; 2 Cor 8-9), and the meeting only involved Peter and James, not the gathering of Christian leaders in Acts 15. Additionally, if Acts 15 matches Gal 2, then Paul would have sent the Jerusalem Council letter to the churches rather than Galatians. Finally, if we accept Luke's chronology, this is Paul's second visit to Jerusalem and aligns with Acts 11.

Hence, while it is not certain, Acts 11 fits better. If so, there were two motivations for his Jerusalem trip around AD 46—to bring money to the struggling Jerusalem Christians and to ensure that Paul's gospel was consistent with the apostolic gospel of Peter and the Twelve. Ensuring the gospel was kosher was important before Paul and Barnabas set off on their three missions through Anatolia, Macedonia, and Greece.

Paul's First Antiochian Mission (Acts 13:1–14:28; Gal 4:13–14, ca. AD 47)

Acts 13-14 include an account of Paul's first great Antiochian mission, often called Paul's first missionary journey. In reality, it was his sixth mission. Moved by the Spirit, Paul and Barnabas traveled from Antioch by sea to Cyprus, through the island, landed in Asia (mod. Turkey) in Pamphylia, and traveled north to Pisidia and east to Lycaonia, evangelizing in the main centers.[3] Mark abandoned Paul and Barnabas for Jerusalem during the trip, leading to a schism between Paul and Barnabas before the second Antiochian mission (Acts 13:13; 15:36–41). Paul was also sick at some point, which became an aspect of his mission (Gal 4:13).

Jerusalem Visit 3: The Jerusalem Council (Acts 15:1–35, ca. AD 49)

After Paul's return from his first mission west of his home region, other Judaizing gospel preachers attacked his new churches and the church in Syrian Antioch, demanding that new converts Judaize by being circumcised and yielding to Mosaic law to be saved and included in God's people (Acts 15:1; Gal 1:6–9). Paul wrote Galatians to the churches, warning them they would be cut off from justification before God if they went down that path. He traveled with Barnabas to Jerusalem to discuss with the Jerusalem leaders who had it right—a law-free gospel (Paul) or the Judaising gospel. After much debate, Paul, Barnabas, Peter, and James, supported by those there, agreed that Paul had it right—new converts were justified by faith alone and did not need to yield to the requirements of the Jewish Torah, including its boundary markers. A letter was drafted asking Gentiles to consider Jewish cultural customs to ensure unity and ongoing Jewish mission (Acts 15). Silas and Judas Barsabbas were chosen to take the letter to Antioch. While there is no account of Paul preaching in Jerusalem on this trip, he went to defend the gospel, a core aspect of the gospel mission. As such, this is his seventh mission.

---

3. For a map, see Keown, *Discovering*, 2:25.

Paul's Second Antiochian Mission: Macedonia and Achaia (Acts 15:36–18:23, ca. AD 49–51)

After returning to Antioch, Paul went on his eighth journey, visiting the churches he had planted and pushing the gospel further west. As noted above, Barnabas and Paul's conflict led to Barnabas and Mark going to Cyprus and Paul taking Silas with him. Paul no doubt wanted to carry the letter from the Jerusalem Council to the Galatian churches to support his earlier letter to ensure they did not succumb to the Judaizers (Acts 16:4).[4]

While in Lystra, Timothy was added to Paul's team (Acts 16:1-3). Paul had him circumcised, not forcing him to Judaize but because he was a Jew already. His circumcision would enable Timothy to enter synagogues and the temple to share Christ with Paul.

Paul also planned to push further west, planting churches. He wanted to go into Asia Minor, where Ephesus was the capital or Bithynia in northern Asia Minor near the Black Sea. However, the Spirit had other ideas and, through a vision, guided him and his team to Macedonia (Acts 16:6-10). Luke joined Paul for this portion of the trip (the "we passage" begins in Acts 16:10).

Paul then moved through Macedonia, planting churches in Philippi, Thessalonica, and Berea (Acts 16:11-17:15), and was persecuted in each city. He then went alone to Athens, where he gave his famous Areopagus message and established a small church (Acts 17:16-34). Paul moved to Corinth, where he worked with Priscilla and Aquila, who were recently expelled from Rome in the Claudius Expulsion. They were joined by Silas and Timothy and ministered there for eighteen months, establishing the church there (Acts 18:1-17). He traveled back by ship, briefly pausing at Ephesus, where he left Priscilla and Aquila behind.

---

4. For a map, see Keown, *Discovering*, 2:42.

Jerusalem Visit 4: Passing Through (Acts 18:22)

Luke records that Paul landed in Caesarea (Acts 18:22). He may have gone to Jerusalem again, although we cannot be sure.

Paul's Third Antiochian Mission: The Jerusalem Collection (Acts 19:1–21:17, ca. AD 52–58)

Paul then returned to Antioch (Acts 18:22). He set out on his ninth trip, traveling again through the regions of the first churches he had planted on his first Antiochian mission (Acts 18:23).[5]

We know from the letters that his purpose was not merely to strengthen his churches but to gather money for the second Jerusalem Collection. Luke does not mention this until Acts 24:17, and only in passing. This omission puzzles some scholars who think it may be because the collection was not well received in Jerusalem. However, Acts 21:17-20 indicates the converse. The collection is mentioned in Romans, and Paul asks them to pray for its positive reception and that he can next come to Rome and onto Spain (Rom 15:26-31). The Corinthian letters confirm that collecting gifts for Jerusalem was the core reason for the journey to Galatia, Macedonia, and Corinth (1 Cor 16:1-4; 2 Cor 7-9). Timothy and Titus traveled with Paul and were sent on errands at various points.[6] Luke also joined Paul in Corinth and traveled with him to Jerusalem (Acts 20:5-21). Paul also gathered representatives from the contributing churches to join his team and support the collection (Acts 20:4).

Aside from strengthening believers and churches and gathering

---

5. For a map, see Keown, *Discovering*, 3:54.
6. Timothy: Acts 19:22; 20:4; 1 Cor 4:17; 16:10; 2 Cor 1:1, 19; Titus: 2 Cor 2:13; 7:6, 13-14; 8:6, 16, 23; 12:18.

the collection, Paul stopped for three years in Ephesus. Building on the pioneering work of Priscilla, Aquila, and Apollos, he established the church in an extraordinary time of mission success (Acts 18:24-19:20). He led a period of intense training of disciples in the lecture hall of Tyrannus from which Ephesus experienced a spiritual revival and the whole region of Asia Minor was evangelized (Acts 19:9-20). No doubt, the churches Peter addresses in 1 Pet 1:1 and the seven churches of Revelation (Rev 2-3) were planted during this time. The churches of Colossae and Laodicea were also established through the work of Epaphras, who was one of Paul's co-workers in Ephesus (Col 1:7; 2:1; 4:12).

Paul also experienced terrible persecution when the gospel's penetration began to affect the sales of idols. A riot occurred, and Paul was brought before the authorities (Acts 19:21-40).

After leaving Ephesus, Paul wrote 1 Corinthians in Ephesus (1 Cor 16:8). He wrote 2 Corinthians in Macedonia or somewhere between Macedonia and Corinth (2 Cor 7:5). There is an earlier lost letter to Corinth which the Corinthians, to some extent misunderstood. Part of the reason for 1 Corinthians is to clarify its meaning (1 Cor 5:9-13). 1 Corinthians confirms he faced severe suffering in Ephesus (1 Cor 15:32).

2 Corinthians also confirms that Paul experienced terrible persecution in Ephesus (2 Cor 1:8-11). It also tells us he traveled from Ephesus to Corinth, a harrowing visit (2 Cor 2:1; 13:1). Some consider the letters of Colossians, Philemon, Ephesians (if a general letter), and Philippians were written in this period from Ephesus. However, there is no concrete evidence Paul was in prison in Ephesus, and tradition consistently places these in his Roman incarceration.

He returned to Ephesus and then traveled through Macedonia, collecting money for the collection. Again, he suffered greatly (2 Cor 7:5-6). He then went to Corinth for three months (Acts 20:3). During this time, he wrote Romans. He planned then to travel to Syria, but due to a death threat, he went to Macedonia again and struck out for Jerusalem with the collection and retinue. The most memorable events of this trip were the resurrection of Eutychus in

Troas (Acts 20:7-10) and the meeting with the elders of the Ephesus' church in Miletus, where Paul delivered his great pastoral sermon (Acts 20:17-38).

Jerusalem Visit 5: Prison (Acts 21:17–23:22, ca. AD 57)

As noted above, Paul was welcomed first in Caesarea at the home of Philip, the evangelist, and then by the Jerusalem church, which was expanding greatly. He was encouraged to fulfill a vow of purity at the temple, which Paul duly did. However, he was recognized and accused of bringing an unclean Gentile into the temple (Acts 21:1-36). He was seized by the crowd who tried to kill him, only to be rescued at the last minute by a Roman tribune and soldiers, who arrested and bound him. Paul was then permitted to speak to the crowds, which he did. His message ended in chaos as the crowd reacted to him speaking of his mission to the Gentiles (Acts 21:37-22:31). He was saved from the crowd and the next day appeared before the Sanhedrin (Acts 22:22-23:11). His relatives uncovered a plot against his life, and he was sent to Caesarea (Acts 23:12-35).

Prison in Caesarea (AD 58–59) (Acts 23:23–26:32, ca. AD 58–59)

Paul spent two years in a Caesarean prison (Acts 24-26). Some think he wrote the letter to the Philippians in this period. However, few agree. Paul faced a series of trials before the governors Felix and Festus. With Jews still seeking his life, Paul exercised his citizen's right to appeal to Caesar (*provocatio*). Festus accepted his appeal, and Paul was sent to Rome.

Prison in Rome (AD 60–61, ca. AD 60–61)

Acts 27 is a fantastic account of the journey of Paul from Caesarea Maritima to Rome, including a shipwreck in Malta, evangelism on the island, and then transport to Rome.[7] Acts ends with Paul in Rome preaching the gospel from his rented accommodation (Acts 28:30-31). This level of liberty shows that his incarceration was initially relatively friendly and that Paul was seen as little threat. In this period of lighter incarceration, Paul wrote Colossians, Ephesians, and Philemon, which Tychicus and Onesimus delivered.

Harsher Imprisonment in Rome (Phil 1:18–26, ca. AD 62–63)

Philippians 1, where Paul's life is very much under threat, indicates that Paul's situation worsened sometime after the end of Acts. This deterioration fits with Christianity becoming more of a threat to the empire as it spread. In this period, Nero married a God-worshiping Gentile woman Poppaea Sabina (Josephus. *Ant.* 20.195). She may also have made Nero more aware of the danger Paul represented. While some scholars consider that Paul died in this period, indications are that he gained release as he expected (Phil 1:25-26).

A Final Mission Journey? (ca. ad 64–66)

If Paul did gain release, he went on a tenth mission journey. We can

---

7. The path of this journey can be viewed here, "Paul's Journey to Rome," *Net Bible*, http://classic.net.bible.org/map.php?map=jp4.

glean from hints in the letters and especially the Pastoral Epistles his possible movements. First, he might have traveled west to Spain, a desire he had expressed to the Romans (Rom 15:24, 28). However, the evidence he got there is fragile. More likely, he went east again, visiting Colossae (Phlm 22), Miletus (2 Tim 4:21), Ephesus (1 Tim 1:3), and Troas (2 Tim 4:14) in Asia. He also went through Crete (Tit 1:5) and mentioned visits to Macedonia, including Philippi (Phil 2:24; 1 Tim 1:3) and Nicopolis (Epirus, western Balkans) (Tit 3:12).[8] Early church tradition holds that he made such a journey.

Death in Rome (c. AD 66–67)

Tradition supports that Paul and Peter died under Nero sometime after the Neronian persecution and before the Emperor's suicide on 9 June AD 68. It is held that Peter was crucified upside down, whereas as a citizen, Paul could not be crucified and so was beheaded.[9]

Part 2: Paul's Mission

Just as Acts 1-8 lays down core principles of what it means to do church, we gain tremendous insight into the basics of mission from Paul's missionary strategy.[10] It is fair to say that Paul shaped contemporary mission more than any other figure, aside from Jesus

---

8. For a map of the possible journey see Keown, *Discovering*, 3:68.
9. 2 Tim 4:6-8, 1-18; 1 Clem 5:4-7; Ign. *Eph.* 12.2; Eusebius, *Hist. eccl.* 2.22.
10. For a fuller discussion, see Keown, *Discovering*, 2:454-506 (Ch. 15).

himself. Here, I will assume that Paul did have a strategy, which it seems obvious he did, and outline its main points.

Led by the Spirit

Paul's mission was Spirit-guided. His first Antiochian mission was sparked in worship as the Spirit spoke: "Now, set apart for me Barnabas and Saul for the work I have called them to do" (Acts 13:2); they were "sent out by the Holy Spirit" (Acts 13:4). He was guided through the mission as well. The decision of the Jerusalem Council was "great to the Holy Spirit" (Acts 15:28). A clear example is Acts 16:6-10, when he wanted first to go to Asia Minor and then to Bithynia, but the Spirit forbade him. He was guided to Macedonia by a vision. Paul had other spiritual experiences that guided his mission. God spoke to him in Corinth, telling him to keep speaking out, for he was with him and would not be harmed (Acts 18:9-10). In Ephesus, Paul "resolved in the Spirit" to travel to Jerusalem via Macedonia and Achaia and then Rome (Acts 19:21). He went to Jerusalem "constrained by the Spirit" (Acts 20:22). The Spirit testifies to him that he would face imprisonment and persecution in every city ahead (Acts 20:23). Agabus by the Spirit warned him that the Jews of Jerusalem would bind him and hand him over to the Gentiles (Acts 21:11). In Acts 23:10, the Lord spoke to him telling him to have courage because, just as he had given witness in Jerusalem, he would give testimony in Rome. On the ship heading for Rome, an angel told him not to fear, for he would stand before Caesar and that God had granted him all those sailing on the ship (Acts 27:23–25). In the letters, Paul speaks of "gospel doors" opened by God, which caused him to remain in situations for ministry (1 Cor 16:9; 2 Cor 2:12; Col 4:3). While Paul had a strategy, it was subject to change on the leading of God by the Spirit, as well as by angels, direct revelation, visions, opportunity, or prophecy.

Moving West toward Rome and Beyond

Overall, Paul moved west in his missionary journeys. His vision was first to plant churches from Jerusalem to Illyricum, a city on the very west of Greece, just across the Adriatic from Rome. When he wrote Romans, he had completed that work (Rom 15:19). He planned to travel to Rome, use it as a base, and then take the gospel to Spain, where it was not yet established (Rom 15:24, 28). Acts ends with him in Rome, the gospel thoroughly established through Pentecost pilgrims (Acts 2:10) and reinforced by his ministry (Acts 28:30–31).

Main Urban Centers

One of the intriguing differences between the missions of Jesus and Paul is that aside from Jerusalem for festivals, Jesus rarely ministered in the major cities (Sepphoris, Tiberias), focusing on the smaller towns and rural areas. Conversely, Paul focused on the cities. His strategy was to plant churches in the leading centers in each region. From there, the gospel could radiate out into the city and region. A fitting example is the Thessalonians who heard the gospel, and then the Word of the Lord sounded forth from them into their region Macedonia, south into Achaia, and elsewhere (1 Thess 1:5–8). Paul was confident the Spirit would continue the work begun in each church and expand its influence.

Gentiles

Paul's specific call was to the Gentiles. He is an example of someone God directs to a specific people group. His particular call began at his conversion, where Ananias tells him he is Christ's instrument to carry God's name before the Gentiles (Acts 9:14). He labels himself the apostle to the Gentiles (Rom 11:13). The Jerusalem leadership affirms this call, alongside Peter's call to lead the mission to Jews (Gal 2:7–9). It is not uncommon for people with a missionary calling to have a specific call to a people group.

Team Ministry

Neither Jesus nor Paul were lone ranger evangelists. They worked with others. Jesus called the 12 and 72 and sent them out. Paul had a whole raft of co-workers throughout his career. The key ones were Barnabas, Timothy, Titus, Silas (also Silvanus), Priscilla (also Prisca), and Aquila.[11] A range of other co-workers are mentioned (e.g., Rom 16; Phil 4:2–3; Col 4; Phlm 1, 24). Paul worked with others; his passion was training them and releasing them into ministry. He believed in partnership in mission (Phil 1:5). He considered the church a body made up of different people with various gifts working in harmony like a great sports team. Faithful Christian ministry is a team ministry. It is collaborative and relational. One person is not enough. On our own, we will be eaten alive by the devil who roams like a roaring lion seeking prey (1 Pet 5:8).

Evangelizing the Lost

You do not have to be a rocket scientist to recognize that Paul was

---

11. Barnabas (Acts 9:27; 11:22–30; 12:25–15:41; Gal 2), Timothy (Acts 16 onwards, and in many letters including 1, 2 Timothy), Titus (esp. Gal 2:1–3; 2 Cor 7–8 and Titus), Silas (also Silvanus, esp. Acts 15–18; s.a. 1 Thess 1:1; 2 Thess 1:1), and Priscilla (also Prisca) and Aquila (Acts 18; Rom 16:3–5; 1 Cor 16:19; 2 Tim 4:19).

an evangelist. It was core to his ministry. He had a keen sense of compulsion and obligation to preach the gospel to the lost (Rom 1:14–15; 1 Cor 9:16). He believed that the preaching of the gospel brought the opportunity for salvation as people heard, believed, and received the seal and deposit of the Spirit (Rom 10:14–17; Eph 1:13–14). Hence, he sought to win people to Christ at every opportunity. A soteriological motivation governed his life, namely, that everything he did in the presence of others would bring them to faith or reinforce their faith. He did this in imitation of Jesus, and others were to assume the same posture (1 Cor 10:31–11:1).

Synagogues

To achieve his strategy of converting the world, in every city Paul went to, he sought first to convert the people of the synagogues. Synagogues for Diaspora Jews were all over the Roman world. In some cities, such as Philippi, there were insufficient Jewish men to form a synagogue (ten men were needed). Yet, he still began there when he could. Starting in the synagogue made sense for a Jewish Pharisee who commanded profound respect among Jews. In each synagogue, he also found some God-worshipers with whom he would share Christ (Acts 16:13). He sought to convince his hearers that Jesus is the Christ they long for (e.g., Acts 17:2–3). He did this because he believed that the gospel should be offered first to the Jews and then to the Gentiles (Rom 1:16). If a Jew were converted, he would have a ready leader, someone who was grounded in the story of God in the Scriptures. As noted previously, some Gentiles had become Jews or proselytes (Acts 13:43). Others, interested in

Judaism, worshiped at the synagogues.[12] These, too, would know God's story and quickly come to grips with Jesus Christ.

Open Air Preaching

It is commonly thought that Paul preached in the centers of each town as would a pagan philosopher. However, this is rightly questioned by many scholars. As a Jew, it is unlikely. Further, he had dirty hands from tentmaking, meaning he was of lower status. However, there is some evidence he may have spoken and healed in public in Lystra (Acts 14:9). He shared Christ in the open air outside Philippi, but this was a specifically Jewish gathering, not an open public event (Acts 16:13). He also mingled among philosophers, debating Epicureans and Stoics at the famous Stoa in Athens (Acts 17:17). Yet, this passage does not say he preached openly. His message at the Areopagus was an invitation to a philosophical guild. Still, in most contexts he preached, he was quickly challenged by locals.

If early Christians did preach openly in the cities of the Roman world, they only did so for a short period. They were shut down as Jews and pagans reacted against their subversive message. We see the same pattern earlier in Jerusalem. They began openly teaching in the temple courts (Solomon's Colonnade). They were persecuted and eventually entirely shut out. Rather than open-air preaching, the gospel spread through social networks, and preaching occurred in specifically Christian gatherings in homes (see below).

---

12. People like the devout women of Pisidian Antioch (Acts 13:50), some in Thessalonica and Berea (Acts 17:4, 11), Titius Justus of Corinth (Acts 18:7), or the Asian Lydia in Philippi (Acts 16:14).

Part 3: Paul's Letters

Most of the NT is in the form of letters from Christian leaders to converts. These include letters from Paul (13), the writer of Hebrews (whose identity is uncertain), James, Peter (2), John (3), and Jude. Revelation is also an exceptionally long letter (Rev 1:4–5). Hence, understanding how to interpret letters is critical to biblical interpretation. In what follows, the focus is Paul.[13] Some comments on the other letters will come in the next chapter. However, much of what is written in the first section below applies to the other letters.

Paul's Letters: Overview and debates

Thirteen letters are attributed to Paul in the NT. Four are written to individuals—1 & 2 Timothy, Titus, and Philemon. The other nine are written to churches or a set of churches—Christians in a given location. Most of these are written to a city: Romans, 1 & 2 Corinthians, Ephesians, Philippians, Colossians, 1 & 2 Thessalonians. Galatians is written to a set of churches in the Galatian region. Of those written to churches, Romans and Colossians are written to churches Paul himself did not plant—the Roman church emerged early in the Christian period through Pentecost pilgrims (Acts 2:10). Colossians was written to two cities, Colossae and Laodicea, in the Lycus Valley in Asia Minor. These churches were planted by Epaphras, one of Paul's co-workers (Col 1:7; 2:1; 4:11).

Letters were used across the Greco-Roman and Jewish worlds to exchange communication. We sense this as we read the NT letters; they are parts of ongoing conversations. For example, in 1 Cor 7:1, Paul writes: "now concerning (*peri de*) the matters about which you

---

13. For a fuller discussion, see Keown, *Discovering*, 2:72– (Ch. 2).

wrote ..." We also know from 1 Cor 5:9 that Paul wrote an earlier letter. Hence, each letter is a moment in an ongoing conversation. Letter carriers were constantly moving back and forth from Paul to his congregations. They read them out to the churches on Paul's behalf (remembering that many early church members were illiterate when they were converted). Hence, a letter in the NT is part of an ongoing conversation. It is a snippet of time. It is like one email in a string of emails, one end of a telephone conversation.

The art of interpreting the letters is to work out what is going on in the backdrop, the story behind the letter. This is a lot of fun, working akin to a detective, reading what is there and what is between the lines. We call this approach "mirror reading," trying to discern the story behind the story from the letter's content.

Doing such analysis leads to a range of ideas we must sift through to settle on the best possible understanding. For this, we consider the letter writer's situation, whether it be Paul, James, Peter, John, Jude, or the author of Hebrews. Where were they? When did they write? What was going on for them? We consider the broader culture and how what is written should be interpreted. We also give thought to the situation of the readers. We try to construct a narrative of the situation being addressed.

The ones we have, are shaped in the usual patterns of the Greek letter form. They usually have the sender's name(s), the recipients, a greeting, a thanksgiving/blessing and prayer, and then the body of the letter. They end with greetings, blessings, and a final farewell.

The contents of the letters vary depending on the points being made. They were carefully written, for ancient letter writing was a slow and expensive process, and they were often dictated to a secretary (amanuensis). For example, Tertius wrote Romans down for Paul (Rom 16:22). Silvanus (Silas) wrote down 1 Peter (1 Pet 5:12). These secretaries had differing degrees of freedom, depending on the situation. For example, when the writer is in prison, they might ask the writer to craft the whole letter on their behalf. Or they would dictate it. Using different amanuenses could explain differing styles across the letters by the same author.

Authorship

Modern scholars challenge the authorship of many of the NT letters. The authorship of seven of Paul's letters is not seriously questioned: Romans, 1 & 2 Corinthians, Galatians, Philippians, 1 Thessalonians, and Philemon. They are not disputed because of vocabulary, style, and theological similarities. Six letters are questioned: Ephesians, Colossians, 2 Thessalonians, 1 & 2 Timothy, and Titus (these final three are called the Pastoral Epistles). Ephesians and Colossians are similar and have a distinctive style and theology. Some think one of Paul's co-workers wrote it, perhaps after he died. The Pastorals have a similar style and perspective, which is again different from the undisputed letters. 2 Thessalonians is considered too similar to 1 Thessalonians, a poor replica written by someone other than Paul. Many scholars will interpret these six letters by assuming that Paul did not write them. They still see them as Scripture and recognize that they may come from a Pauline perspective. However, this affects their interpretation.

Other scholars accept that the early church knew which letters were from Paul and which were not. They argue that the church would not have allowed a non-Pauline letter to bear his name and be honored. Further, Peter writing in AD 65-66 indicates a collection of Paul's letters was in circulation and honors them as Scripture (2 Pet 1:5-16). So, we argue that if Paul's name is there, he wrote it. Also, as no one questioned the authorship of Paul's letters until the eighteenth century, the questions of authorship are a product of modern rational arrogance rather than any concrete evidence.

The differences across the letters are, to some extent, acknowledged. However, these can be explained by Paul using different amanuenses with more freedom as they were written (e.g., the same one for Colossians and Ephesians, and the same person for the Pastorals). The differences may also be due to the context and diverse issues addressed.

Supporters of Paul's authorship of the whole corpus also note that great authors can use differing styles (e.g., C. S. Lewis). We also do not have enough of Paul's (and other NT writers') material to be sure which letters are original and which are not (i.e., insufficient material to make a fair comparison). As such, the letters of Paul (and the other NT writers) likely originate from those named, even if they vary in style and theology. Some of the letters remain contentious as no name is attached: Hebrews and the Johannine letters. 1 and 2 John are similar in style, theology, and tone to John's Gospel, so they likely come from the same author.

The issue of authorship does complicate the interpretation of letters where authorship is questioned. Commentaries include long sections debating the matter. The interpretation that follows this will be affected by that decision. Students of the NT need to be aware of this and know that when they write about a disputed letter, they must deal with the authorship question.

Different Approaches

There is a range of approaches used by scholars to interpret letters. One is to try and find similar letters across the ancient world and compare them. For example, some think Romans is written as an ambassadorial letter (a letter written on behalf of a government from an ambassador, i.e., Paul, see 2 Cor 5:20; Eph 6:20). Quite a few scholars regard Philippians as a letter of friendship.

Another approach is Rhetorical Criticism. The art of persuasion through speech was necessary for the Greeks, as elite young men were trained in rhetoric. Rhetorical handbooks exist, and NT letters are considered from this perspective. The approach makes sense to some degree because, although they are letters, they were also to be read out by the messengers, and so were also speeches.

There are three rhetorical forms identified with NT letters:

1. Epideictic: the writer reaffirms common core values using

praise and blame. Some think 1 John, Ephesians, and 1 Thessalonians use this form.
2. Deliberative: the writer seeks to persuade and convince the audience of what is appropriate and best. Some place Philippians in this category.
3. Judicial: the writer uses legal arguments to establish right and wrong. Some consider Galatians to be judicial.

Those that adopt this approach apportion the letters according to rhetorical categories. The *exordium* is the introduction to the letter (e.g., Phil 1:3–11). The *narratio* is a narrative, an account of what happened over time (e.g., Gal 1:11–2:15). The *partitio* or *propositio* is the proposition, the central proposition of the letter (e.g., Rom 1:16–17; Phil 1:27). The *probatio* includes the main arguments expounding the main proposition. The *refutatio* is a refutation of opposing views. The *peroratio* is the conclusion with final arguments.

All this sounds complex, but budding biblical scholars will run into these ideas and terminology. Usually, an NT letter does not fit the form these scholars argue for, as each uses a blend of forms. Each has a range of rhetorical devices used by the NT writer. A good example is a chiasm (using the Greek letter *chi*, X), whereby the elements mirror one another: A1B1CB2A2. The emphasis comes in the center. These are found in the NT across whole chapters. For example (1 Cor 5–6):

A1   Sexual immorality (Ch. 5)
  B   Litigation before the courts (6:1–8)
A2   Sexual immorality (6:9–20)[14]

1 Corinthians has a number of these macro-chiasms (e.g., 1 Cor 8–10; 12–14 [see earlier]).

14. Scholars do not agree on what binds the chiasm together. One possibility is the church's relationship to the world.

They may also come in smaller units. For example, Phil 3:8–10:

A1 that I may gain Christ and be found in him,
    B1 not having a righteousness of my own that comes from the law,
        C but that which comes through faith in Christ,
    B2 the righteousness from God that depends on faith
A2 that I may know him

There is a range of other devices used in the letters. These help us grasp more closely the point the author is making. As these devices are not always recognized in translations, it is good to learn biblical languages to identify them. Reading good material on each letter written by scholars when preparing a Bible study or sermon is also essential, as this will help deepen understanding. However, it must still be understandable to the hearers, so do not try to baffle them with too much complexity.

10. Paul's Early Letters

Introduction

Paul's early letters were written before he went to Jerusalem and was arrested (Acts 21). Five were written during the period (AD 47–58)—Galatians, 1 and 2 Thessalonians, 1 & 2 Corinthians, and Romans. Although Galatians is arguably Paul's first letter, I will not discuss Galatians at this point but will do so in part three of this chapter, in which we look at Galatians and Romans together as they deal with similar material—the place of the law in Christian salvation, community, and life. As such, the first part of this chapter will focus on the second and third of Paul's letters—the two letters to the Thessalonians. Then, we will consider the Corinthian letters, his third and fourth letters to the same church. Then, attention will turn to Galatians and Romans.

Part 1: The Thessalonian Letters

The Thessalonian letters were written when Paul was in Corinth on what is commonly called his Second Missionary Journey.[1] In his first Antiochian mission, Paul and Barnabas planted churches in Southern Galatia and returned to Antioch in Syria (Acts 13–14). His second great Antiochian journey took him through these regions (where Timothy joined him) and then west.

---

1. For a fuller discussion, see Keown, *Discovering*, 2:289–329 (Chs. 10–11).

Initially, Paul had wanted to plant churches in Asia Minor (esp. Ephesus) and Bithynia near the Black Sea. Instead, God's Spirit sent him to Troas and then to Macedonia (Acts 15:41-16:10). After landing in Philippi's port, Neapolis, he established the church in Philippi and then moved on to Thessalonica, the capital. There, he reasoned with Jews in the synagogue, eventually setting up a church in the city. However, this sparked a violent response from local Jews and Gentiles who attacked the Christians. Paul and his group got away, leaving Jason to withstand the worst of their attack (Acts 16:11-17:9).

He next went to Berea, where there was great interest among Jews concerning his message. However, this was brought to a swift end when Jews traveled from Thessalonica and forced Paul to leave Macedonia for Athens (Acts 17:10-17). Leaving behind Timothy and Silas to continue the work in Macedonia, he entered Athens, explored the city, considered its religiousness, and then reasoned in the agora with philosophers. He then preached his famous Athens sermon based on the unknown God at the philosophical guild, the Areopagus. A few converts were made, and then Paul moved on to Corinth (Acts 17:18-18:1). It is in Corinth that he wrote the Thessalonian letters.

1 Thessalonians

Background Matters

After Silas re-joined Paul in Corinth, concerned for the persecuted Thessalonians, Paul sent Timothy to travel the 450 km or so to Thessalonica to see how they were faring. The letter indicates Timothy had returned with news of their ongoing suffering at the hands of persecutors. Yet, their commendable perseverance and faith (1 Thess 2:17-3:6). He may also have reported to Paul their lack of understanding of what happens to deceased Christians and uncertainties about the second coming of Christ. Timothy may have alerted him that some locals were challenging Paul and his team's integrity. He may also have reported that members of the church were becoming sexually immoral and that some in the Thessalonian church were disorderly, refusing to work for a living, effectively bludging off the wealthy in the church.

With all this in mind, Paul wrote 1 Thessalonians. The letter indicates that Paul held the Thessalonians with great affection (esp. 2:17–3:5). Indeed, when one considers the warmth of the two Thessalonian letters, it is apparent that Paul's relationship with Macedonian Christians was excellent. They were genuinely seeking to be disciples that made Jesus proud. The two letters are interesting because they are written very soon after the planting of the church, as little as three to six months later.

Biblical scholars agree that Paul is the author of 1 Thessalonians. Interestingly, the letter is sent from Paul, Silas (Silvanus), and Timothy, and Paul often uses "we/us" in the letter—the three missionaries may jointly author it. Still, it is undoubtedly one of the undisputed letters. In that Silas is the amanuensis for 1 Peter (1 Pet 5:12), he may have also penned the Thessalonian letters for Paul. A few scholars consider Paul wrote 2 Thessalonians before 1 Thessalonians. However, the vast majority hold the traditional view, even if we cannot be entirely sure.

The letter has the same structure Paul uses in his letters, with some unique features. First, unlike Galatians, which has no thanksgiving or blessing, 1 Thessalonians has a double thanksgiving (1:2–10; 2:13–16). Paul has a lot to be thankful for in this young church community.

Paul wrote this letter to encourage new believers in their faith, to urge them to godly living, to give them assurance about the eternal state of believers who had died, and to defend the integrity of his ministry as an apostle. Thessalonica (present-day Thessaloniki, Greece) was the capital of Roman Macedonia. It was on vital trade routes. Paul, twice identified as the author (1:1; 2:18), visited

Thessalonica on his second missionary journey but was forced to flee because of Jewish opposition. He sent Timothy to work with the predominantly Gentile church there, and Timothy brought him the good news of their faith (3:6). This is one of Paul's first letters, probably written about AD 50–51.

Letter Overview

Prescript (1:1)

By Paul's standards, 1 Thessalonians has a brief prescript other than the description of the recipients. Paul, Silvanus, and Timothy are named with Paul and might be joint authors. The three are known to the Thessalonians as they were all there recently planting the church. Timothy has just revisited them (3:2, 6). Paul does not add any terms to describe himself, like an apostle or a slave. He does not need to assert his authority or appeal to them to give more of themselves in service to Christ.

The recipients are "the church of the Thessalonians in God the Father and the Lord Jesus Christ." He confirms their identity and status in relation to God, their Father, and Christ. His grace and peace greeting is punchy compared to his more elaborate greetings in other letters. It is implied that God, through Christ, is the source of grace and peace.

Thanksgiving 1 (1:2–10)

This section forms the first part A1 of a chiasm, with this passage paralleling 2:13–16, forming a frame of Paul's defense of his ministry in the face of his critics in 2:1–12. In the first thanksgiving, the three writers (we) give perpetual thanks to God for the Thessalonians because they are a commendable church. They also pray for them consistently, remembering before God the Father their work produced by their faith, their labor flowing from their love, and their perseverance in the hope planted in them through the Lord Jesus Christ (vv. 2-3). They are a remarkable church devoted to serving God.

Paul now assures the Thessalonians. They are siblings of the apostolic team, loved and chosen by God (v. 4). Paul's team knows this is true because of how they received the gospel preached to them when they visited the city (Acts 17:1-10). Through them, the gospel came in word, power, the Spirit, and full conviction (v. 5a). Anticipating his longer defense to his detractors in 1 Thess 2, Paul recalls how he and his group emulated Christ and his integrity when among them (vv. 5b-6a). Jason and the other Thessalonians received the empowered word with the joy provided by the Holy Spirit despite being persecuted by unbelieving Jewish and Gentile locals (v. 6, cf. Acts 17:5-10). They became an example to all the believers in Greece and Macedonia in receiving the Spirit with joy and then proclaiming the faith through the region (vv. 7-8). The Christians of the region have heard the stories of their conversion from idolatry to serve the living and true God and to wait for the return of God's Son, who delivered them from God's wrath and whom God raised from the dead (1:9-10).

Paul's Defense of his Ministry Among the Thessalonians (2:1–12)

This passage indicates that opponents in or beyond the city are denigrating the ministry of the Pauline group. The Pauline team reminds his Thessalonian siblings that his coming bore fruit among them (2:1). He confirms Acts 16:11-40 and Phil 1:28-30, which speak of persecution in Philippi in v. 2—they suffered and were shamefully treated as Roman citizens. Still, despite this, they boldly preached the gospel of God in Thessalonica despite the great conflict. Paul calls God to give witness that they did not use duplicitous methods such as a distorted gospel, impure motives, deception, people-pleasing, flattery, greed, or glory-seeking. Instead, they were faithful to God and sought to please the one who had entrusted them with the gospel (vv. 3–6a).

Although they could have made demands on the Thessalonian converts as Christ's apostles worthy of their hire (cf. 1 Cor 9:1–16), they were as gentle to them as a nursing mother to her children (vv. 6b–7). Full of affection for the beloved Thessalonians, they shared the gospel and their lives with them (v. 8). They labored and toiled night and day as they not only preached the gospel to them but worked to provide for themselves in their tentmaking and other occupations (v. 9). Now he calls the Thessalonians to give witness along with God concerning their holy, righteous, and blameless conduct among them (v. 10). Not only did they care for them as a nursing mother, as a father with his children, they exhorted, encouraged, and admonished them to live in a way that is worthy of the God who calls them into his kingdom and glory (v. 12).

Thanksgiving 2 (2:13–16)

Paul and his team again assure the Thessalonians that they give thanks for them constantly. Again, he recalls their receipt of the gospel (cf. 1:6). They received the message as God's Word at work among believers and not some human creation (2:13). He also specifies their acceptance of the gospel despite suffering and their imitation (cf. 1:6–7). They not only imitated Christ and the Pauline team, but they emulated the Judean churches that were severely persecuted when they heard the gospel in the early days of the church (cf. Acts 3–8, 12). Whereas the Judeans suffered at the hands of Jews who displeased God and opposed humankind by killing Jesus, the prophets, and driving out the church, the Thessalonians were persecuted by their people (vv. 14–15). There is an irony here, for Paul was the architect of the expulsion of the church from

Jerusalem (Acts 8:1-3). Such people hinder Christians from spreading the gospel to the Gentiles so that they can be saved. As such, they are filling up the measure of their sins, and God's wrath is coming on them to the last.

This passage is debated. Some consider it a non-Pauline interpolation because they are uncomfortable with its antisemitism. Others accept it as Paul's but disagree concerning whether it points to the fall of Jerusalem, eschatological punishment, or both.

Pleasing News of Their Perseverance (2:17–3:5)

This section describes events between the planting of the church and the present time of writing the letter. Paul narrates how his team, having been ripped away from Thessalonica (and Berea) due to persecution (Acts 17:5-17), sought eagerly to find a way to see them face to face (v. 17). However, despite trying repeatedly, Paul and the others were hindered by Satan (v. 18). We do not know the specifics here. Still, we see the power of the evil one to disrupt mission plans. Verses 19-20 show the profound pride Paul, Timothy, and Silas feel for the Thessalonians—they are his hope, joy, a crown of boasting, and glory—now and before Jesus returns.

Thwarted repeatedly and unable to bear it any longer, Paul chose to remain in Athens alone (Acts 17:15-18:5). He sent his brother and God's coworker in the gospel, Timothy, to confirm and encourage them in their faith to ensure none are moved by their afflictions (3:1-3a). Verse 3b confirms that Christians are destined for such suffering—something he told them on his first visit among them (v. 4). It was his concern because of their suffering that caused him to send Timothy to learn how they were going in their faith, afraid that somehow the tempter/tester (Satan) had tempted/tested them so that the hard work of Paul and his team was wasted (implying a fear that they had fallen away).

Verse 6 narrates Timothy's return to Paul with the good news of their faith and love that they remember Paul and his team fondly and their mutual longing for one another. As such, the Pauline team is comforted because of their faith through suffering (v. 7). As the Thessalonians stand fast in the Lord, they experience God's life (v. 8). This leads Paul to express his thanksgiving to God for them because of the joy they feel for the Thessalonians before God (v. 9). His team expresses this gratitude as they pray night and day fervently to see them and supply to them anything lacking in their faith (v. 10). Paul moves in v. 11 from talking about prayer to praying that God and Christ will open the way for them to come to Thessalonica. He prays in v. 12 that Christ the Lord will increase the already loving Thessalonians (1:3; 4:9–10) so that they overflow with love for one another and everyone else (including the lost)—just as Paul and the others love them. He prays this so that God may establish their inner beings blameless in the holiness of their God and Father when Jesus comes with his saints (v. 13).

Being Sexually Holy (4:1–8)

In most letters, at some point, Paul urges his readers to be sexually pure. His appeal is because of the sexual immorality that was a feature of the Greco-Roman culture. It seems the Thessalonians were no different.

In 4:1-3a, Paul is general in his injunctions, urging the Thessalonian siblings in Christ to live out the teaching they had previously received from the Pauline team to walk in a way that pleases God more and more and be sanctified. In v. 3, he specifies that they must abstain from sexual immorality. This appeal exhorts each church member to control their own "vessels" in holiness and favor. The term "vessel" here can mean their wives, bodies, or sexual organs. They are not to live out of passionate lust, as do the Gentiles who do not know the Christian God (vv. 4–5). Verse 6 hints at some of the Thessalonians engaging in sexual immorality within the church, so Paul warns them not to transgress and wrong each other. He warns them that the Lord (Christ) is an avenger in all these things, as Paul, Timothy, and Silas previously warned them. This warning suggests Christ acting in judgment against those who violate others sexually. Verse 7 reminds them of God's call to holiness, not purity. Verse 8 warns them again—anyone in the church who disregards Paul's teaching disregards God, who gives his Holy Spirit to his people to sanctify them. This passage shows that sexual immorality is not a secondary offense for Paul—the Triune God calls believers to sexual holiness.

Instructions for Love and Life (4:9–12)

Before coming to the eschatological matters that will dominate the end of the letter, Paul gives them a series of instructions for living in the church and the world. As they love their Christian siblings in Macedonia, they are to love one another more and more as God has taught them to do (vv. 9-10). They are to live quietly, mind their affairs, and work with their hands, as they were instructed when Paul was with them. This injunction is so that they may walk appropriately before outsiders and depend on no one (vv. 11-12). This appeal anticipates the problem of disorderliness and laziness that is mentioned in 5:14 and that features in 2 Thess 3.

The Dead in Christ with the Lord Forever (4:13–18)

While this passage is critical to our eschatology and understanding of Christ's return, the presenting issue is the fate of those who have died in Christ. The Thessalonians and other believers need not grieve like those with no hope. The information about Christ's return and the resurrection of the dead supports the premise that believers need not grieve, as do unbelievers (v. 13). Christians share the belief that Jesus died and rose again. So, through Jesus, God will bring with him those who have died (v. 14). This can sound as if God brings with Christ the dead in him; however, verses 15–17 detail what Paul means. He declares it to them as a word from the Lord Jesus. Those who are alive when Christ comes will not go before the dead (v. 15). Paul explains—Christ (the Lord) will descend from heaven with a commanding cry from the voice of an archangel and the sound of God's trumpet. At that sound, the dead in Christ rise first (v. 16). Then those alive will be caught up with the raised dead into the clouds to meet the Lord in the air (v. 17). What Paul means is debated. Some consider believers are raptured and meet Christ, who takes them into the heavens for the intermediate or final state. Others hold that the Greek "meet" (*apantēsis*) has the meaning "meet and welcome in," as in the case of a dignitary being welcomed into a city (e.g., Acts 28:15). They hold that Jesus is welcomed into the earth, and they live forever with him in the restored world. Either way, they will be with the Lord. Further, they are to encourage each other with these words (v. 18).

Be Ready for the Day of the Lord (5:1–11)

What follows should again be read as Paul's answer to the question of the fate of the Christian dead but focuses on how Christians are to live in the present as they await that day. Paul does not need to go into detail about the eschaton as they know that the day of the Lord will come suddenly and unexpectedly—like a thief in the night (vv. 1–2).[2] This event will happen when unbelievers (as v. 3 indicates) are confident of "peace and security." However, sudden destruction will come upon them as labor pains come upon a woman about to give birth, and they will not escape (v. 3).

Verse 4 contrasts things for Christians. They are not in the dark about the Lord's day and will not be surprised. They are not surprised because they are all children of light and of the day, who

---

2. See Matt 24:43; Luke 12:39; 2 Pet 3:10; Rev 3:3; 16:15.

are not in the dark (v. 5). They must be awake and soberly ready, not asleep and drunk (vv. 6–7). They must be armed with Paul's great triad: faith, love, and the hope of salvation (cf. 1:3; 1 Cor 13:13). Unlike unbelievers in the dark, God has not destined believers for his wrath but to obtain salvation through their Jesus Christ (v. 9). He died for them, so that they might live with him while sleeping or awake. As in 4:18, they must continue encouraging and building each other up.

Injunctions, Prayers, and Assurances for Christian Life (5:12–28)

Most of the passage is a series of ethical injunctions, many in the form of easily remembered maxims for the Christian life. Verses 12–13 urge the Thessalonians to know their leaders in the Lord and consider them above all else in love because of their labor. They are to admonish the disorderly and idle, encourage the small-souled, help the weak, and be patient with all believers (v. 14). They are not to retaliate against evil but always respond with goodness to fellow Christians and unbelievers (v. 15). They are always to rejoice, pray without ceasing, and give thanks in all situations, as God wills for them in Christ Jesus (vv. 16–17). They must also always be thankful, as God wills (v. 18). They do not extinguish the Spirit's fire or despise prophecies but test everything (vv. 19–21a). They must hold fast to what is good and abstain from all evil (vv. 21b–22).

Paul ends the letter proper with a prayer that the God of peace fully sanctifies them so that they will be utterly blameless at Christ's coming (v. 23). Verse 24 assures them that God is faithful and will do this. Finally, they are to pray for Paul and his team, greet one another with a holy kiss, and read the letter to all the church (vv. 25–27). Paul ends with a grace blessing from Christ for the church (v. 28).

2 Thessalonians

Background Matters

While 1 Thessalonians is agreed to be Paul's, the authorship of 2 Thessalonians is disputed. Some consider the letter to be pseudonymous because they see it as a poor replica of 1 Thessalonians, as there are differences in the Greek, and some consider the man of lawlessness passage clashes with what Paul says about the day of the Lord in 1 Thess 5. However, most evangelicals and many others find these arguments unconvincing and accept Paul as the author. The man of lawlessness passage is seen to fill out what Paul says in the first letter, not contradict it. Furthermore, there is continuity in themes from the letter, such as disorderliness, persecution, perseverance, and eschatology. As noted earlier, a few scholars see 2 Thessalonians as the first letter; however, the overwhelming majority accept the usual order.

The letter is attributed to Paul, Silvanus, and Timothy, as is 1 Thessalonians. The recipients are identical—the church of Thessalonica in God and Christ (1:1). As with 1 Thessalonians, two thanksgiving prayers punctuate the letter (1:3–12; 2:13–17). Three matters dominate the letter and explain why it was sent. First, the Thessalonians continue to experience persecution (1:4). Second, false teachers are saying that Christ has arrived, or his coming is imminent, and claiming revelation and Paul's support in this regard (2:1–2). Third, some in the church are being disorderly and refusing to work for a living, as Paul had instructed them to, emulating his example of being a self-supporting missionary (3:6). Paul responds to these things in the letter.

Letter Overview

Prescript (1:1–2)

The letter begins with the same threads as 1 Thessalonians. It has the same writers and senders, Paul, Silvanus (Silas), and Timothy. The addressees are also the same: the church of the Thessalonians in God our Father and the Lord Jesus Christ (v. 1). The only difference is the longer full greeting Paul uses in eight other letters (v. 2).

Thanksgiving 1 (1:3–4)

As with 1 Thessalonians, 2 Thessalonians has two thanksgivings (also 2:13-15), emphasizing Paul's gratefulness for the Thessalonians. Again, it is pluralized, indicating that the three missionaries participated in the letter's message. The reason they ought to thank God for their Christian siblings in Thessalonica is that their faith is growing abundantly, and their love for each other is increasing (v. 3). Therefore, the Pauline team boasts about the Thessalonians' perseverance and faith in persecutions and afflictions as they travel through the churches of God (v. 4).

Judgment on their Adversaries (1:5–11)

Paul contrasts the destiny of the adversaries causing them suffering with that of the Thessalonians. The suffering they are experiencing is evidence that they will be considered worthy of the kingdom of God for which they suffer (v. 5). They will experience his relief (v. 7). Those afflicting them, on the other hand, will face God's recompense—affliction (v. 6). This will happen when Jesus the Lord is revealed from heaven with his mighty angels, in blazing fire. He will inflict vengeance on those who do not know God and who do not obey the gospel of Jesus. Their punishment will be eternal destruction and being shut out of the presence of Christ the Lord and the glory of his might (vv. 7-9). This passage is Paul's most powerful statement about the fate of unbelievers in his letters. Scholars debate whether it is eternal torment in fire, eternal separation from God, eternal separation from all that is good (solitary confinement), conditional immortality, or annihilationism. Whatever is in view, it will be eternal and involve destruction and will happen when Jesus comes to be glorified in his faithful saints and to be marveled at among all who have believed because the gospel was believed by the Thessalonians and others (v. 10).

Prayer for Effective Faith that God is Glorified (1:11–12)

Paul shifts to prayer for the Thessalonians as he will at the end of each chapter. Paul states that he and his coworkers always pray for them that God will make them worthy of his calling and powerfully fulfill every resolve they have to do good works that derive from their faith (v. 11). This is so that the name of Jesus the Lord of believers will be glorified in the Thessalonians, and they in him, according to the grace of God and Christ (v. 12).

Events Preceding the Coming of the Lord (2:1–12)

Some in the early church seemed to promote the idea that the day of the Lord was imminent or had already occurred. The readers are not to be alarmed at such suggestions, whether from a spiritual revelation, a letter supposedly from Paul, or a spoken message (2:1-2).

Paul now reminds them of things he has told them before (v. 5) concerning the times and seasons—things he did not elaborate on in 1 Thessalonians (see 1 Thess 5:1). The Thessalonians are not to be deceived by false predictions of the return of Christ. Certain things must happen. First, a rebellion must occur, and a hostile figure will emerge. He is described as a man of lawlessness and the son of destruction. He will oppose everything claiming to be god or object of worship, exalt himself over them, and seat himself in God's temple as God (vv. 3-4). It is debated whether this is a religious figure, a political figure, whether it relates only to the Roman Empire, or a regime that rules the world. Many consider it aligns with the abomination that causes desolation (Mark 13:14), the beast (Rev 13), and an antichrist (1 John 2:18). The all-encompassing nature of the description makes the latter idea probable but not certain.

Still, vv. 6-7 indicate he is being restrained for the present. The nature of the restrainer is also debated as it is a thing in v. 6 and a being in v. 7. Something evil or Satan could be the restraining power. At the same time, most consider it a positive power or being, such as God, an angel, God's power, the Spirit specifically, the church, or even Paul. Most likely, it is God through his power in some way. Whatever is in view, the restrainer will be removed. Then, the lawless one will be revealed (v. 8). Jesus will kill him with his breath and render him nothing as he comes (see Ch. 1). When the lawless one does come, he will have evil power. He will perform false signs and wonders, wickedly deceive the perishing (not believers) who refuse to believe the truth (the gospel), and be saved (vv. 9-10). Because of their refusal, God sends them a delusion to consign them in their belief in what is false (v. 11) so that those who reject the truth and enjoy unrighteousness will be condemned (v. 12).

Thanksgiving 2 (2:13–15)

The second thanksgiving to God is again stated as something Paul and his coworkers should do. He addresses them as brothers and sisters loved by those who chose them as the first fruits to be saved.

This points to the future harvest of converts that will flood in since the gospel's first days. Their salvation comes through their sanctification by the Spirit and faith in the truth of the gospel (v. 13). They have been called through the gospel so that they may obtain the glory of Christ (v. 14). Their salvation, election, and glorification are the basis on which they are to stand firm and hold fast to the traditions that they received from the Pauline team through spoken word or letter (v. 15).

Prayer for Comfort and Establishment in Good Work and Word (2:16–17)

As Paul does at the end of each chapter, he prays a blessing over the Thessalonians. He prays that the Lord Jesus Christ and God their Father, who loves believers and gifts them eternal comfort and good hope through his grace, may comfort the hearts of the Thessalonians and establish them in all good work and word.

Prayer Request, Assurance, and Paul's Prayer (3:1–5)

Paul begins with one of his many requests that his churches pray for him. He prays that the Word of the Lord will speed ahead and be honored as it did in Thessalonica (cf. Ps 147:15). The second request is that Paul and his team be delivered from evil people, alluding to opponents in Corinth, where he writes. This prayer is required because not all people have faith (v. 2). Paul then assures the Thessalonians—even though some do not have faith, the Lord (Jesus) is faithful. As such, he will establish the Thessalonians and guard them against the evil one (v. 3). Paul next expresses his confidence in the Thessalonians, a conviction rooted in the Lord (Jesus) concerning them—they are doing and will continue to do what Paul commands them to do (v. 4). Paul shifts to prayer mode, praying that the Lord will direct their hearts to the love God has for them (subjective genitive) and the perseverance generated in believers by Christ (v. 5).

Keep Away from the Disorderly and Idle Members of the Church (3:6–12)

Mention was made of idle and disorderly Thessalonians (1 Thess 5:14) who were disruptive and did not earn their living (1 Thess 4:11). The problem has grown in the interim between letters. Paul asserts himself, commanding the Thessalonians in the name of Jesus to keep away from those Christians who are disorderly and who reject the Pauline tradition of earning one's own living (v. 6). In vv. 7-9, he reminds them to imitate his well-established pattern whereby he and his team earn their living while doing God's gospel work. He and his team had the right to receive payment but chose not to be a burden and instead gave themselves as an example to be emulated (vv. 8–9). His basic premise is that Christians unwilling to work should not be fed. The setting for this is unclear. Were they Christians expecting Christ's imminent return, or who believed that he had already returned and, as a result, were choosing not to work? Were they gospel workers demanding support? Were they effectively bludgers, relying on the patronage of the wealthy in the church? Whoever they were, they were disruptive, idle, refusing to work, and busybodies (v. 11). Paul commands and encourages such people in Christ to do their work quietly and earn their living (v. 12).

Final Instructions (3:13–15)

He concludes the letter urging the Thessalonians never to tire of doing good (v. 13, cf. Gal 6:9). Where people reject the instructions in the letter (especially concerning the return of Christ and idle disruption), that person is to be noted, and marginalized so that he is ashamed (v. 14). This is not ex-communication, but a way of warning him as a brother in the Lord (v. 15).

Final Prayer Blessing, Greeting, Signature, and Grace (3:16)

Every chapter ends in prayer, and this is no exception. Paul prays that the Lord of peace grants the Thessalonian believers peace at all times and in every way. He ends by praying that they experience the Lord's presence with them (v. 16). He writes his greeting with his own hand as a mark of authenticity (v. 17). He prays for the readers to experience the grace of God (v. 18).

Conclusion

The Thessalonian letters are refreshing in their warmth. They are full of blessings, assurances, and prayers that we can read and pray with Paul for ourselves and others. They give invaluable material on the events leading up to the return of Christ, the return itself, eternal life, and the destruction of evil and the ungodly (which is an act of grace and deliverance for God's people). We are also encouraged to be self-supporting Christians, working hard, living quiet lives, and participating in ministry with our gifts. The letters urge Christians to be strong in the faith, love others, be mission-minded, and persevere in suffering.

Part 2: The Corinthian Letters

Introduction

The two letters to the Corinthians are substantial, and this discussion will barely introduce the material.[3] They are especially valuable as many of the issues covered are of substantial importance for Christian life today. 1 Corinthians is written to a group of young Christians who are very worldly, stuck in many of the sins of their Greco-Roman context. Paul's responses speak to a range of ethical and other problems found in charismatic and Pentecostal churches today. 2 Corinthians deals with the problem of false teaching and the maligning of Paul and his team. Money is a critical issue, with Paul wanting to raise funds for poor Christians in Jerusalem (a commendable act) but experiencing criticism and false accusations from hyper-faith prosperity teachers (who are also Judaizers). The digital age has opened the door to many false ideas and teachers who can quickly and cheaply popularize their views. Money and prosperity teaching are ongoing problems. We need to listen very carefully to the words of Paul as he deals with them—they are as relevant now as they were then.

We read the account of the planting of the Corinthian church in Acts 18. The city had been rebuilt by Julius Caesar after its destruction in the Roman-Greek wars about a century earlier. It was an important trade center with two ports, between which boats were dragged to travel east and west from Achaia (Nero wanted to build a canal; there is one now built-in modern times). It was wealthy, and people came to it from the empire to make money and gain honor. It was also historically famous for sexual immorality and

---

3. For a fuller discussion, see Keown, *Discovering*, 2:137–202 (Chs. 4–5).

rhetoric. Although there were many Jews in the city, it was Greco-Roman to the core.

Paul came to the city and linked up with two Christians already there (who had no doubt begun the work of sharing the gospel), Priscilla and Aquila. Paul joined them in their tentmaking business and, especially after the arrival of Silas and Timothy, shared the gospel with Jews, proselytes, and God-worshiping Gentiles in the synagogue. As always, he did not last long in the synagogue and established the church next door in the home of Titius Justus, a God-worshiping Gentile (Acts 18:7). Two synagogue leaders joined the church as well—Crispus and Sosthenes (Acts 18:8, 17, cf. 1 Cor 1:14). The work flourished, and the gospel spread radically.

Tracking the movements of Paul and others to and from Corinth is important to understand the letters. After his first coming, Paul left the city for Ephesus and then to Jerusalem and Syrian Antioch. Later, he returned to Ephesus and stayed for over two years (Acts 18:18-19:10). While traveling, the firebrand evangelist Apollos came to Corinth and made converts and a significant impact. Peter must also have gone through to the city in the interim.

By the time Paul got to Ephesus on his third Antiochian mission, the Corinthians had developed factions around the three missionaries—Paul, Apollos, and Peter (1:11-12). These preferences grew out of their love of rhetoric and desire to gain honor through aligning with and financially supporting speakers.

At some point in Ephesus, Paul must have received news of sexual immorality among the immature Corinthians. He wrote a letter warning them not to associate with such unethical Christians. This letter was misunderstood as a command to stay away from unethical non-Christians (5:9-13).

Paul next wrote 1 Corinthians after news from Chloe's household (1 Cor 1:11) and through a letter enquiring about things (1 Cor 7:1),[4]

---

4. The formula *peri de*, "now concerning ..." features through 1 Cor 7-16 indicating those things raised in the letter: 1) Celibacy and

perhaps delivered by Sosthenes (1 Cor 1:1) or others mentioned in Ch. 16 (16:17). After this, at some point, Paul had visited Corinth (an event not mentioned by Luke in Acts). The visit had gone badly, with Paul humiliated in public (2 Cor 2:1–11; 13:2). Having returned to Ephesus on his third Antiochian mission in which he raised funds for the Jerusalem Christians in poverty, Paul then rethought the travel plans he had made in 1 Corinthians 16. He initially wanted to stay in Ephesus until Pentecost, the year of writing, and then travel through Macedonia to Corinth (1 Cor 16:5–9). Then, he must have changed his plan, wanting to come to Corinth first, to Macedonia from Corinth, then back to Corinth, and on to Jerusalem (2 Cor 1:15–16). Then, when he left Corinth, he went to Macedonia first to find Titus, for whom he was greatly concerned (2 Cor 2:13). He wrote 2 Corinthians from Macedonia from Philippi, Thessalonica, or Berea. The main reasons for writing include asking the Corinthians to give generously to the collection, to defend himself against charges that he is dishonest and a peddler of the gospel, to instruct them on restoring the person who humiliated him, and to vigorously attack the false teachers and accusers who are distorting the gospel and denigrating him. Both letters are passionate, powerful, and invaluable for understanding the church, its mission, and how to respond to false teaching.

marriage (7:1); 2) Virgins and marriage (7:25); 3) Eating food offered to idols (8:1); 4) Spiritual matters (12:1); 5) The collection for the saints (16:1); 6) Apollos (16:12).

1 Corinthians

Authorship, Integrity, and Date

1 Corinthians is a long sixteen-chapter letter in which Paul writes with passion and conviction to deal with various ethical matters among the Corinthians. The matters result from a flawed understanding of life in Christ. The Corinthians were young Christians who syncretized the gospel to their former lives in the Greco-Roman world. They are like contemporary Christians who believe in Jesus but have not worked through the implications of the faith for their relationship to contemporary issues like elitism, charismatic speakers, hedonism, marriage, sexuality, and an obsession with the spiritual gift of tongues. These false ideas were due to their inability to grasp who Jesus is, the work of the Spirit, and eschatology.

While the Pauline authorship of 1 Corinthians has not been seriously questioned due to its abrupt shifts of topics, some see it as a compilation of multiple letters of Paul to the city stitched together into one volume. Few, if any, take this seriously today. Instead, the shifts of focus result from the many issues in the church. Scholars debate whether there is one underlying issue with unity as a popular idea; however, the syncretism to typical Greco-Roman ideas seems to be the core issue, even though one of the crucial issues is unity. Many scholars hold that the Corinthians had an over-realized eschatology like Hymenaeus and Philetus of Ephesus, who held that the resurrection had already occurred (2 Tim 2:17-18). However, more likely, the Corinthians had absorbed the Greco-Roman ideas of ethics and an exclusively spiritual resurrection which Paul corrects.

The letter is dated between AD 53 and 55, meaning the church is three to five years old at the time of writing. The problems in the letter reflect classic issues at play when the Christian gospel collides with a city steeped in Greco-Roman culture. The Corinthians are addressed throughout as Christians, but they are immature and need to grow in their understanding of God, Christ, the gospel, and the ethical life God wants from his people. These are the key issues.

Through the Letter

Unity (1:1–4:21)

After the initial greeting, thanksgiving, and assurance, Paul launches the letter. The first matter is division reported to him from Chloe's household. The church has become divided based on their preference for different Christian preachers, Paul, Cephas (Peter), and Apollos. As noted, Corinth was famous as a destination for rhetoricians to ply their trade, and the locals were enamored with speaking skills. They also liked to bestow material gifts on their favored preachers; however, this was used to gain political advantage. While there may have been a group who also followed Christ, it is more likely that "I follow Christ" is the beginning of Paul's response to the problem. By ending the sequence with Christ, he draws the Corinthians away from attention on their favored speakers to a focus on Christ and Christ alone.

Paul's response indicates that the problem is not due to the failings of the three missionaries. The issue is the Corinthian infatuation with one over the other. Based on Luke's description of the Alexandrian Apollos as a brilliant speaker in Acts 18:24-28, many were drawn to his dynamic oratory. Cephas' supporters were probably Jewish or those who honored him as one of the Twelve. Paul's support came from those who enjoyed his simple gospel approach in which he presented Christ and him crucified without rhetorical flamboyance. Sadly, by attaching themselves to Cephas and Apollos, many had anti-Pauline attitudes, despite Paul having established the church.

From 1:10 to 4:21, Paul challenges them with argument after argument to get them to denounce their factionalism, their favoring of one preacher over another, their demeaning of others, and their political games. He called them to remember the gospel that saved them—a gospel of a crucified Messiah—that is true wisdom (not flowery rhetoric). He drew their focus to Christ and him crucified and the emulation of Christ's example (cruciformity). He reminded them that true spirituality is exhibited through people whose minds are conformed to Christ. The preachers they emulate are merely servants, doing God's work, subject to God's judgment and not theirs. He parodies their rejection of the call of the gospel to suffering and humility and invites them to emulate his example.

Sexual Immorality and Pagan Litigation (5:1–6:18)

In Chapters 5-6, the attention shifts to the problems of sexual immorality and taking brother and sister Christians to the Roman courts over matters that should be dealt with within the church. The ethics of the gospel were being violated in the direction of Roman culture, where sexual immorality was rife and in which court litigation to gain honor and cause shame was common. Paul will have none of it. In ch. 5, the issue is incest, and Paul calls for them to excommunicate the offending party and cease taking pride in such behavior. In 6:1-8, he urges them to deal with insignificant disagreements within the church. In 6:9-21, he calls the Corinthians to the sexual ethics of God whereby believers renounce the sins of their culture, live out of their statues as washed, sanctified, and justified believers, live out of God's creational sexual ethics, and as temples of the Spirit, be holy.

Marriage and Singleness (7:1–40)

Chapter 7 deals with two issues. First, some in the church were desisting from sexual relationships within marriage as part of their devotion to God. In 7:1-24, Paul urges them not to do so and gives valuable instruction on marriage, divorce, and family. Second, he deals with the question of being promised in marriage to a young woman, encouraging singleness but endorsing marriage. Quite what he means by the "present distress" 7:26 is highly debated, with some thinking he is referring to the imminent coming of Christ or an issue they were facing. Whatever the issue is, the chapter adds to our understanding of marriage and divorce, sexual relations in marriage, and singleness.

Food Sacrificed to Idols—Love Over Liberty (8:1–11:1)

Chapters 8 to 10 form a chiasm. The focus of the passage is love over liberty. The question at hand is eating food sacrificed to idols. Roman cities were full of temples to various deities. A critical question for early Christians was whether they should eat meat sacrificed to idols away from the temple and whether they could participate in temple feasts. In these chapters, Paul sees no issue with eating meat sacrificed to idols. However, when another person is offended by this, the Christian should not eat as he wants nothing to hinder another person's salvation. He places love over liberty. Where attending temple feasts is concerned, Paul is crystal clear—Christians should stay away as pagan religion is demonic, and believers participate in Christ and remember him in their exclusive feast—the Lord's Supper. Chapter 9 is double-edged.

On the one hand, despite it being appropriate for a preacher to receive their living from preaching the gospel, Paul asserts his freedom not to receive such a living so as not to burden others. On the other hand, he shows how he renounces his freedom to receive such a living for the gospel's sake. He demonstrates to the Corinthians how they should place the gospel over their freedom.

Clothing and Communion (11:2–34)

Chapter 11 deals with two matters related to worship. First, in a passage in which the details are debated, Paul tells the women of the Corinthian church to dress in a culturally appropriate manner as they come to worship, prophesy, and pray publicly. Some may have considered their freedom in Christ meant they did not have to dress in such a way. Second, he challenges their abuse of the Lord's Supper. The church was divided at this critical moment of weekly worship in which Christ's death is remembered and proclaimed. Some were eating and drinking ahead of others, likely the wealthy elite, and Paul calls them to task, warning them that God will judge such a violation of Christ's body. He gives strict instructions concerning the appropriate way to remember Christ's death. These are critical for the church today.

Spiritual Matters (12:1–14:40)

Chapters 12–14 focus on spiritual matters, primarily spiritual gifts. The underlying issue is whether tongues are the defining mark of receiving the Spirit. The passage forms a chiasm with chs. 12 and 14 focusing on the gifts, and ch. 13 highlighting the need for them to be exercised with love.

The first part of the chiasm in Ch. 12 indicates that the defining mark of receiving the Spirit is not tongues but is seen where a believer would not countenance cursing Christ but instead willingly and sincerely confesses Jesus as Lord (vv. 1–3). Paul then outlines the gifts, their source, and their purpose (vv. 4–11). He ensures that Corinthians understand that not all speak in tongues, that there are multiple gifts distributed as God wills, and that the presence and contribution of all gifts are equally important to the church—a diversity of manifestations of the Spirit in Christ's one body (vv. 12–31).

Chapter 13 shows that love must be the motivator of all gifts (vv. 1–3), defines love with actions that flow from it (vv. 4–7), and speaks of the permanence of love compared to gifts and other virtues of God (vv. 8–13).

Chapter 14 returns to the central matter at hand, tongues. He tells them that those obsessed with speaking gifts (rhetoric and tongues) should seek the greatest speaking gift that bestows the most benefit (love) to others—prophecy. He rejects the speaking of tongues in public gatherings unless they are interpreted and so become prophetic and beneficial (vv. -25). He endorses the use of prophecy but gives careful instructions for using interpreted tongues and prophecy in gathered worship (vv. 25–40).

Resurrection (15:1–58)

Chapter 15 alerts readers to one of the letter's underlying issues: the resurrection. While the Corinthians believe in Christ's resurrection, they are influenced by Greek ideas that see ongoing life as spiritual rather than corporeal (v. 11). Christians believe God raises the whole person, body included, not merely ongoing spiritual life. Throughout the chapter, Paul reminds them that the gospel they believe in includes the resurrection of Jesus and that of believers. First, he urges the Corinthians to hold fast to this doctrine (vv. 1–2). He next gives a neat list of resurrection appearances to indicate that the resurrection is founded on reliable evidence (vv. 3–11). In vv. 12–19, Paul shows that the Christian life is futile if Christ has not been raised. If Christ is not raised, we will not be raised, and our faith is worthless. He outlines the ultimate resurrection of all believers, the end of death, and the restoration of the cosmos (vv. 20–28).

In the remainder of the chapter, he then discusses what kind of resurrection body believers will have and how this will happen. The resurrection of believers will be bodily. The body of dust will be transformed into a body fully infused and animated by God's Spirit (spiritual body). The present mortal body is likened to a seed (our present Adamic body of dust) that must die to be raised immortal and imperishable (vv. 21–49). This metamorphosis will come to pass at the Consummation when in a flash, we will be transformed (vv. 50–54). The hopes of Hosea and Isaiah will be fulfilled (vv. 54–55; Hos 13:14; Isa 25:8). Knowing that the law is completed in Christ, sin is dealt with, and death is overcome, the Corinthians should be motivated to stand firm and serve God with all they have, for such work is not in vain (v. 58).

The Jerusalem Collection and Conclusion (16:1–24)

Chapter 16 gives instructions for the Jerusalem Collection Paul is taking up on the journey and has a range of other exhortations, greetings, prayers, and assurances.

2 Corinthians

Again, there is little debate that Paul is the writer of 2 Corinthians. However, many scholars are convinced that 2 Corinthians is a composite epistle, including three of Paul's letters sent at various times. Many break it up in this way: 1) 1:1–6:13; 7:2–13:14; 2) 6:14–7:1; 3) 10–13. Those that read it this way produce complex explanations for this, diverse settings for each letter, and their work becomes complicated by such details. Many scholars reject this analysis, seeing the letter as one unit. Most hold that the shifts indicate different matters being addressed. Others, including myself, hold that the letter is original in this form, written from Macedonia sometime in AD 56. It is, then, written one to three years after 1 Corinthians and after a difficult visit to Corinth, where Paul was humiliated.

I hold there is one main issue Paul deals with in the letter. After writing 1 Corinthians, Jewish false teachers came to Corinth, spreading malicious ideas about Paul. They accused Paul and his team of using the Jerusalem Collection as a pretext for getting material gain, i.e., being peddlers of the gospel. They also appear to have little time for Paul's emphasis on suffering in Christ, being triumphalists majoring in the miraculous, visions, and other claims. They may also have carried with them letters of endorsement from Judean leaders and questioned the apostolic credentials of Paul. With 1 Corinthians indicating that there were factions in Corinth and some anti-Paulinism, a fascination with spiritual power and gifts, and an immature church, they may have found fertile ground for their ideas. If this is correct, the letter can be seen clearly to have these parts.

Through the Letter

Greeting, Situation, and Defense of Travel Plans (1:1–7:16)

Prescript (1:1–2)

2 Corinthians starts with a typical Pauline greeting with Timothy named as co-sender. The use of "we" throughout may indicate he is a co-author, Paul's amanuensis for the letter, courier, or merely a co-signatory. The church and saints of Corinth and Achaia are greeted, indicating that the false teacher's poison is spreading. He adds his usual grace and peace greeting.

Blessing (1:3–11)

Paul usually begins with thanksgiving and prayer. Here, he declares a blessing of God for his comfort in suffering and requests they pray for his team.

He declares God blessed for his comfort in suffering that overflows to the Corinthians (vv. 3-7). He tells the Corinthians of the severe suffering to the point of death that he and his team experienced in Asia Minor and God's deliverance (vv. 8-10). The suffering is not specified, but many scholars speculate that Paul spent time in prison there. Some hold that he wrote some prison epistles during this time; however, the early church does not confirm this view. He concludes the section by implicitly requesting their prayers, which will see them delivered again (v. 11).

In 1:12-2:17, he defends his changes of mind concerning his travel plans, explaining that he went to Macedonia and not directly to Corinth because of his deep concern for Titus. He ends the introductory section declaring that he and his team are not peddlers of the gospel, unlike others (2:17). We see in this section three of their criticisms of Paul—his obsession with suffering and weakness, his changes of mind concerning travel plans, and that he and his group are ripping off churches in the guise of the Jerusalem Council (or skimming off the top).

Paul's Defense (3:1–7:16)

Then, from 2 Corinthians 3 to the end of Ch. 7, Paul launches his team's long and detailed defense (apologia). It is a brilliant and complex section, dripping with irony and power, in which he turns his opponent's criticism on their head. Speaking in the plural, he calls the Corinthians away from them to the perspective of the gospel they preached there, which is affirmed in the letter. This is all indirect, but he will go on the attack against them directly in Chs. 10-12.

2 Corinthians 3:1–3 indicates his opponents carry genuine or fake letters of recommendation from esteemed early Christians. Paul pushes back, reminding the Corinthians that he planted them, so *they* are his group's letter of recommendation (he does not need others). In the face of his Judaizing opponents' desire to bring new Christians under the law of Moses, he creatively describes the superior glory of the new covenant, the age of the Spirit, and the ministry of reconciliation over the Mosaic era (3:4–18).

In 2 Corinthians 4:1–5:10, Paul defends the integrity of their ministry and attributes spiritual blindness (including his opponents) to Satan. He will indicate in ch. 11 that these false emissaries serve the evil one, not God. He expounds his theology of suffering in which Christians participate in the sufferings of Christ in mortal bodies but are empowered from within by God's light, Spirit, and power, as they eagerly await their renewed bodies received in the consummation.

2 Corinthians 5:11–6:2 reminds them of the motivation for ministry, the nature of their ministry of reconciliation, and summons them to be reconciled to God and remember God's grace to them, for today is the day of salvation.

2 Corinthians 6:3–13 returns to the juxtaposition of suffering and struggle with the weapons of God that empower ministry. Again, he calls them to come back to the Pauline fold and away from the false teachers. While 2 Cor 6:14–7:1 is often ripped out of context and applied to marriage or Christians avoiding evil, the passage, including the quotation from Lev 26:12, targets the false teachers. The Corinthians are not to be yoked to them. As God's temple, they must separate themselves from the teachers. They are to purify themselves of their unclean, defiling, false gospel. He builds on that, boldly urging them to return to him for he loves them, is proud of them, and has acted with integrity toward them (7:2–4).

In 2 Corinthians 7:5, Paul effectively picks his narrative ended in 2:17, narrating what happened when they came from Asia Minor to Macedonia. Doing this, he shows that the *apologia* of 2:18–7:4 was an enormous "aside" to get the Corinthians to turn away from the malicious and demonically motivated false teachers to Paul's group and the gospel. 2 Corinthians 7:5–17 tells of continued suffering, his longing for them, his letter, explains the travel movements of Titus and himself, and prepares the way for the appeal for their contribution to the Jerusalem Collection in chs. 8 and 9.

Giving to the Jerusalem Collection (8:1–9:15)

In chapters 8 and 9, Paul appeals to the Corinthians to ignore the malice of the false teachers and give lavishly to the collection. First, he does so by commending the Macedonians who gave out of poverty and persecution—he hopes this will cause the more prosperous Corinthian church to respond in kind (8:1–5). Then, with Christ's self-giving central (8:9), he encourages them to give generously out of their abundance, not to make themselves poor, but that the Judean Christians may be cared for in their time of need (as would happen in reverse, 8:6–15). After mentioning his team's movements (8:16–24), in chapter 9, Paul reminds them that God gives lavishly and loves it when we respond in the same way to others. Indeed, he has made the Corinthians rich, not to bask in their wealth but to bless others who are poor. He assures them that God will continue to bless them and that if they give, it will overflow into a rich chorus of praise and thanksgiving to God. He ends by blessing God.

Paul's Appeal to the Corinthians and Attack on the False Teachers (11:1–13:10)

At the beginning of 2 Corinthians 10, there is a marked shift in the letter's tone. This change does not indicate a different letter but that Paul is bringing his appeal to its climax with irony and intent. He appeals urgently with irony, bitter sarcasm, vehemence, and creativity. Indeed, it is one of the most brilliant parts of the NT in which we get to discern more of their critique of Paul and his work and hear Paul's brilliant responses. Such a passage can be difficult for modern Christians, who see it as unloving and bitter. However, we need to remember that this is the first-century Greco-Roman world, the gospel was just getting started, and the church could easily be lost with false teaching. Paul is also addressing people he believes are demonically motivated false Christians. His powerful rebuke is because the salvation of the Corinthians was at stake (s.a. Galatians; Phil 3).

He begins with a defense of criticism of his seeming weakness when present and boldness by letter (another aspect of Paul's supposed flakiness). He warns that he is the same person with the same intent in all situations and, as such, they should be aware he does so to avoid having to do it in person but will discipline them if required (10:1–11).

He shifts to his opponents, stating that he will compare himself with them but will boast about the Lord and what the Lord has done in him in his sphere of influence (10:12–18). Chapter 11 begins with Paul expressing his zealousness for the Corinthians. He critiques the Corinthian preparedness to yield to the false gospel of the false teachers (11:1–4). He states that he is not inferior to his opponents, that his speech is knowledgeable, and defends his pattern of self-support so as not to be a burden on the Corinthians (11:5–9). He states that he boasts because he loves the Corinthians and to stop the false teachers from penetrating the church (11:10–12). In v. 13, we see how he really feels—they are "*false* apostles" and "deceitful workers." They disguise themselves as Christ's apostles and servants of righteousness, just as Satan disguises himself as an angel of light. They will face judgment (11:13–16).

Then Paul ramps up his boasting despite considering it foolishness. He does so not to inflate the Corinthians' view of him but to draw them away from these evil workers (11:16–21). He boasts that he has the same Jewish heritage as these wannabes (11:22). Against their claims of being servants of Christ, Paul defends his life of service to Christ against their claims—he has suffered far more than any of them. In his catalog of suffering, we see the anguish Paul has endured up to his point in his ministry (11:23-33).

He changes tack in 12:1-4 to address their claims to spiritual experience. He speaks of himself in the third person and tells the Corinthians of his extraordinary heavenly vision. Not considering this vision what matters most, he shifts his boast to his apparent weakness and the mysterious thorn in the flesh. This affliction is variously understood as persecutors, a psychological issue, or a physical ailment. The latter is preferable, as it seems to be something used by his opponents against him. One possibility is that he had a visible disability that was not healed, and they used that to critique his apostolic credentials and apparent lack of faith. Whatever the thorn is, Paul explains it is a gift from God through Satan to keep him humble so that God's power can be seen in his weakness. As such, he delights in it (12:5-10).

Paul next restates that he is boasting in a foolish way to help the Corinthian see he is not inferior to these "super-apostles"—an ironic tag that they may use of themselves (v. 11). He has done the signs and wonders expected of an apostle (v. 12). He has not been a financial burden on the Corinthians as they are in receiving support (implied), but out of love for them as their parent has provided for them (vv. 13-15). He has not taken advantage of them, just as Titus did not when among them, i.e., he and his team are not peddlers of the gospel (vv. 16-18). He expresses his fear and grief that when he comes for the third time, he will find them a broken and sinful church, and he will again be humiliated (12:19-13:1). Paul warns that he will come and demonstrate that God is speaking in him through God's power (13:1-4).

In 13:5-10, Paul concludes his appeal by calling them to examine themselves and recognize that he and his team are qualified in Christ. He writes that they will sort themselves out so that he does not have to act with authority against them when he comes.

Final Instructions, Greetings, and Blessing (11:1–13:10)

Paul ends the letter abruptly by his own standards with injunctions to be restored, unified, and peaceful in the God of love and peace. He adds a short greeting and grace (13:11-13).

Conclusion

1 and 2 Corinthians are astonishingly relevant to church life today. The church today is fragmented into denominations, and these denominations and churches are also inwardly divided, in many instances, because of people's preferences (e.g., modes of baptism, worship music). Differing views of sexuality and marriage are tearing the world church apart. Idolatry, seen (e.g., other religious expressions) and unseen (e.g., materialism), is a significant challenge. Since the rise of the Pentecostal and charismatic movements, spiritual gifts have continued to be contentious. Many Christians do not fully grasp the corporeal nature of the resurrection. Money is a significant issue, especially in the materialistic and consumptive western world. Many churches demand tithes, failing to see that this places people under the law. Prominent preachers expect financial support, and prosperity teaching is rampant. 1 and 2 Corinthians address all these things and should be obligatory study for any Christian leader. Through them, we are guided to unity, cruciformity, exclusive worship of our Triune God, sexual holiness, faithful marriage, celibate singleness, a correct understanding of gift expression through love, care for the poor, and financial integrity.

Part 3: Galatians and Romans

Introduction

This chapter focuses on two books written eight to ten years apart.[5] They are paired in this book because they both address the question of the inclusion of Gentiles, the place of Jewish law, and righteousness and justification by faith. Galatians was written earlier and is a dynamic, hard-hitting, earnest appeal to new churches to hold firm to the gospel of justification by grace through faith. Romans is a more extensive later letter covering similar ground but also drawing out many more implications of a correct understanding of the inclusion of Gentiles in the church. It ensures the unity of the church at the Empire's center and the ongoing mission to the nations. I will briefly discuss each in turn.

Galatians

Background Matters

Galatians is an undisputed letter of Paul supported by the brothers and sisters in the church in Syrian Antioch (1:1). Its date and recipients are in dispute. Many consider Gal 2:1–10 correlates with the Jerusalem Council Acts 15, written in the early to mid-50s to churches in the whole Galatian region or north Galatia. Others

---

5. For a fuller discussion, see Keown, *Discovering*, 2:203–18, 98–136 (Chs. 3, 6).

who correlate 2:1-10 with Paul's second visit to Jerusalem in Acts 11:27-30 see Galatians as Paul's first letter. It was written before the Jerusalem Council (AD 49) to the churches planted in Paul's first Antiochian mission (Acts 13-14). It is then dated in AD 47-48.

Either way, it addresses a church on the verge of yielding to the message of the Judaizers. These teachers accept Jesus but maintain that Gentile converts must become Jews (Judaize) to be saved and yield to Mosaic law to be included in God's people (Acts 15:1). Paul had preached that it is by grace that a person is justified. The only required response is genuine faith in God and his Son. Nothing else is required. To demand that they Judaize also introduces the problem of a superior culture in the church (Judaism) and a works salvation. Both are disastrous, for, in Christ Jesus, social barriers are swept up into the oneness of God's people, and works can justify no one in any way.

Through the Letter

Prescript and Problem Stated (1:1–10)

Paul's prescript has the usual things: sender, recipients, and blessing. However, he adds that his apostleship is from God and Christ (beginning his defense) and that God raised Christ, who, by God's will, gave himself for sins to rescue believers from the present age. The implication is that Christ's death and resurrection are sufficient to deal with sin—coming under the law is unnecessary. There is no thanksgiving and blessing, but the problem is clearly identified—false teachers are throwing the Galatians into confusion with a false gospel demanding faith and law observance for justification and inclusion.

Paul's Narrative Defending his Apostleship and Gospel (1:11–2:14)

The first part of Paul's defense is a long narrative reminding the Galatians that his gospel and call to be an apostle is from God. His gospel is consistent with that of the Jerusalem Apostles. The Jerusalem leaders also vindicate his apostleship and mission to the Gentiles, alongside their own call to the Jewish people. The passage gives invaluable information that expands our knowledge of Paul's missional movements in Acts.

The first point is that his gospel came from God and not people, as God revealed Jesus to him as he went about his persecution of Christians. Having seen Jesus for over three years in Arabia, God reformed Paul inwardly and reframed his understanding of salvation history (1:11-17). He then went to Jerusalem, where he met Peter and James (Jesus' brother). He then traveled to Syria and Cilicia but remained unknown in Judea, aside from a few in Jerusalem (1:18-24).

Galatians 2:1-10 describes a trip to Jerusalem, which can be either Acts 11:27-30 (as I prefer) or Acts 15. Either way, his gospel and mission to the Gentiles were approved. Then, Peter came to Antioch, and Paul challenged him as he withdrew from table fellowship with Gentiles to dine with the Jews separately. Peter's decision had the effect of compelling Gentiles to become Jews to be included at the Jewish table. Seeing the danger, Paul challenged Peter publicly because of his passion for the gospel of justification by faith, not law observance (2:11-14).

The narrative establishes Paul as a genuine apostle. It also confirms that his gospel is consistent with that of the Jerusalem leaders. They endorse him and his mission. Consequently, the Galatians should reject the false teachers with their false Jewish gospel.

The Proposition—Justification by Faith and Not Law (2:15–16)

Here, Paul states the core of his argument. Even though Jewish Christians are not Gentile sinners, they are still sinners who are incapable of keeping the law for justification. Hence, all Jewish Christians know that the law of Moses cannot justify them. Justification is by nothing other than faith in Jesus Christ.[6] The Galatians are, therefore, fools to leave "the faith" and go into a religion of works for salvation.

Arguments Supporting the Proposition (2:17–5:12)

Crucified with Christ (2:17–21)

From 2:17, with dazzling skill, drawing on an arsenal of biblical and theological arguments, Paul seeks to convince the Galatians of the integrity of the gospel they received and pull them away from the poison of the Judaizers. In the first section following the proposition, Paul deals with the foolish idea that Christ is a servant of sin (v. 17). He states that rebuilding Judaism in its old Mosaic form

---

6. Some scholars translate the genitive construct pisteōs Iēsou Christou as the "faith of Jesus Christ" or the "faithfulness of Jesus Christ." This is possible but even if this is the case, Paul makes clear that believers must also believe in what follows—"so we also have believed in Christ Jesus." Taking it subjectively as the faith or faithfulness of Jesus Christ is another way of saying that Jesus' work completely fulfils what is needed to justify those who believe in Jesus and God (see also 3:22; Rom 3:22, 26; Phil 3:9 where the same kind of genitive construct is debated). Other scholars see it as both-and (a plenary genitive) whereby it refers to both Christ's faith or faithfulness and ours.

only further reveals transgression of the law (v. 18). Memorably, he describes the effect of the cross—now crucified in Christ, he now lives by faith in him (vv. 19-20). Unlike the Judaizers, he does not invalidate God's grace, which is what their theology of justification by law does (v. 21).

The Spirit Received by Faith (3:1–5)

The focus in 3:1-5 is the Galatians' experience of the Spirit. They received the Spirit by believing the gospel, not by observing the law; consequently, they should not turn from faith to law. Paul next reaches into the Abrahamic story (as he does similarly in Rom 4) and other OT texts to support his arguments for justification by faith and not law.

Abraham the Father of Faith (3:6–18)

In 3:6-18, he clearly states that just as Abraham believed in God and was justified by faith. It is the same now—justification is through faith in Jesus. The blessings and promises to Abraham for the nations are coming to fulfillment in his descendant, Jesus, for those who believe—this includes the Spirit. He has taken the curse of human failure to live out God's law on himself. Jesus doing this is good because only flawless living of the whole law without exception brings the declaration of innocence by God. No one can do this. The covenant of Abraham stands and is being fulfilled in his seed, Jesus. The inheritance is passed on not through law, which came after Abraham, but through the promises being fulfilled in Christ.

The Law and Faith (3:19–29)

In 3:19-29, while endorsing the law as good, he explains that rather than bring justification, it imprisoned people. It functioned like a Roman *paidagōgos*, a tutor to discipline and protect Israel until the coming of faith in Christ. The law illuminates' sin and, by doing so, increases peoples' awareness of it and further imprisons them. Now Sinai and the law are transcended and subsumed into Christ, and faith in Christ is what matters. But now that faith has come, believers are released from the guardianship of the law and are children of God clothed in Christ. Whereas the law created social barriers between Jews and Gentiles, now these and other social boundaries are subsumed in Christ—believers are one people without favoritism. They are descendants of Abraham, his family, and heirs of the promises given to him.

The Spirit of Adoption (4:1–7)

Paul continues with the family motif in 4:1-7—believers are no longer slaves to the law and its principles but are adopted children of God with full inheritance rights because Christ redeems them. As such, they have received the Spirit who fuses them with other believers in Christ under God's fatherhood.

Do Not Return to False Religion (4:8–11)

In 4:8-9, he warns them that to heed the Judaizers is to again come under a false religion with its flawed theology and spiritual forces, just as they were previously pagans. Concerned that they are yielding to the Judaizers' demand to observe the Jewish calendar and other requirements, he fears for them and that his work with them was wasted (vv. 10-11). Paul urges them to imitate his example and do him no wrong (4:12).

Recalling Paul's First Visit (4:12–20)

He then reminds them of his visit to them, when they welcomed him despite sickness as if he were Jesus (4:13-15). He asks how they can now treat him as an enemy while yielding to the false teachers. Recalling his nurture of them as a mother with her infant, he ponders whether he must give birth to them again! He expresses his profound perplexity concerning them (4:18-20).

Hagar and Sarah (4:21–31)

In 4:21-31, he returns to the Abrahamic narrative, this time creating an allegory in which Hagar represents the Mosaic covenant and its bondage to slavery (now that Christ has come) and the Abrahamic covenant, which is fulfilled in Christ. Hagar represents slavery to the law, Mount Sinai, present-day Jerusalem, Mt Zion, its temple, and Mosaic law. Ishmael represents her children born into slavery to the law. Sarah corresponds to freedom, the Jerusalem above where Christ is enthroned, promise, and the Spirit, while Isaac represents believers in the freedom of God in Christ. Just as Sarah cast out Hagar, the Galatians must cast out the Judaizers who seek to enslave God's free people to the law.

Freedom to Love (5:1–6)

In Galatians 5:1-12, Paul makes his final direct plea. The Galatians, freed in Christ from law and sin and its devastating consequences, must not yield to the false gospel of the Judaizers and become enslaved to sin. To do so means Christ profits them nothing, as no one can keep the whole law as required; they would be cut off from the Christ who took the curse of the law and died for their sins, and they would fall from grace. They must continue in faith, living by the

Spirit, and awaiting the hope of final justification. Meanwhile, what matters is not circumcision but faith working out in love (5:1-6).

Remove the Judaizers (5:7–12)

In 5:7-12, he likens their Christian lives to a race, but as they run, the Judaizers cut in on them (a wordplay on circumcision and athletics). They must not let this happen. As he does in 1 Cor 5, he likens the church to a batch of dough leavened by yeast—the yeast being negative here (as at Passover), false teaching will infect the whole church. He expresses confidence they will do the right thing and deal with the offenders. Frustrated that they accuse him of preaching circumcision at times and not others, he expresses his wish that they cut their phalluses off (not just the foreskin, but like the Galli—priests of Cybele who castrated themselves!) This appeal has another possible meaning—they should cut themselves off from the church.

Living By the Spirit, Not the Flesh (5:13–6:10)

From 5:13-6:9, Paul answers the obvious question: "if we don't live by the law, how do we live the life God wants from us?" "If the culture of the kingdom is not Jewish as per the OT, what is it?" "If the law is good, has it been completely dissolved? How do we live to please God?"

Two things dominate his answer—love and the Spirit. Their freedom in Christ is not a freedom to live as they want, in their lusts and desires, but a freedom to live as human beings were created to live (to serve others in love). He goes to the law and singles out the command to "love your neighbor as yourself"—this is the central command of the Christian life. They must love one another and not destroy each other (5:13-15).

Galatians 5:16-6:9 posits two ways of living—the flesh and its lusts or the Spirit and its fruit. Having received the Spirit (3:2, 5; 4:5-6), the Galatians are to live by the Spirit. Law has no power to generate obedience; it enslaves people in their impotence to obey God fully. The solution is the Spirit poured into the believer. The believer is then to live (lit. walk) by the Spirit, be led by the Spirit, keep in step with the Spirit, and sow to please the Spirit. Still, creatures of flesh and desire are to put to death the deeds of the flesh that reap destruction. Paul outlines two lists—one that gives fifteen desires typical of humans living in the fallen world of Galatia (and generally). These are to be repudiated. The other is a list of virtues the Spirit generates in believers, Spirit-fruit. The Galatians are to crucify the desires of the flesh and, by the Spirit, produce the virtues of God. The power to do so is the Spirit. Supremely, they are to love others. Paul adds further aspects of this Spirit-filled life in Gal 6, including humbly restoring those who sin, bearing the burdens of others, and self-examination before God.

As such, the questions are answered: "if we don't live by the law, how do we live the life God wants from us?"—by the Spirit. "If the culture of the kingdom is not Jewish as per the OT, what is it?"—it is the culture of Christ that binds us together, clothes us, and is produced by yielding to the Spirit of Christ.

"If the law is good, has it been completely dissolved? How do we live to please God?"—by the Spirit, we live the life the law envisaged, a law now inscribed on our hearts by the Spirit, and that issues forth from us as we yield to him.

Postscript and Benediction (6:11–18)

The letter ends with Paul's autograph and a final appeal to live as new creations of God who have crucified the flesh and its desires and live cruciform lives. He pronounces a blessing on Israel (the church or Israel by descent), urges that no one trouble him as he bears the stigmata of Jesus on his body, and pronounces a grace, as he does in almost all his letters.

Romans

Background Matters

The authorship of Romans is not in question. However, it is the only letter we know was undoubtedly penned by an amanuensis, Tertius (Rom 16:22). It is the final letter before Paul's travels to Jerusalem to be imprisoned (15:28–32). Romans 16 indicates it was written from Corinth (16:1, 23), on the eve of his trip sometime in AD 56–58.

Paul indicates he wrote the letter for various reasons. He asks the Romans to pray for the delivery of the Jerusalem Collection to that city (15:28–32). He wants to come to Rome and teach and preach there (1:11–16). From Rome, having completed missional work from Israel through Anatolia, Macedonia, Greece, and Illyricum in the western Balkans, he wants to take the gospel west to Spain (and perhaps through Gaul [France] en route, 15:19–27). He writes to prepare the way for coming to Rome and onto Spain with the gospel.

The emphasis on justification by faith and not the law in the letter indicates he also wants to draw the Jews and Gentiles in the Roman church to greater unity in the gospel of grace through faith. These divisions may have been exacerbated by the Claudian Edict of AD 49 when Jews were expelled from the city (e.g., Priscilla and Aquila, Acts 18:2). In the same year, the Jerusalem Council ruled that new Gentile converts did not need to be circumcised and come under the law. Paul and Silas took the letter with them on the second Antiochian trip, likely delivered to Rome by Gentiles (perhaps Luke and others). From AD 49 to 54, the mission to the Gentiles would have accelerated now that the obligation to Judaize was removed. When the Jews returned, the church would have been Gentile in flavor. Paul may address differences between the returning Jews and burgeoning Gentile leadership and church.

Furthermore, he addresses differences of opinion in the church over what is eaten and holy days in Rom 14–15, suggesting there is ethnic contention in the church, so unity is paramount to Paul. Such unity will ensure the gospel of grace and faith can radiate from the capital of the largest Empire in world history to the ends of the earth north, east, south, and west. With all these things in mind, Paul writes Romans.

Through the Letter

Prescript and Letter Theme (1:1–17)

The letter begins with Paul asserting his apostleship and its divine origin. He moves straight to the gospel (indicating its importance as a theme) with its focus on Christ, the Messiah, the one declared God's Son by his resurrection from the dead. He then greets the Romans and prays with thanksgiving for the proclamation of their faith in the world by themselves and others.

He tells them of his longing and prayers that he can come to the city so that they can be encouraged together and that he can be the conduit for God to impart spiritual gifts. He also wants to preach in the city, win converts, and strengthen Roman Christians.

In 1:16–17, Paul states the theme of the letter—the gospel. He is not ashamed of the gospel of a crucified Messiah, even though it is highly shameful in Roman and Jewish contexts. He asserts that in the gospel, God's righteousness is revealed. So, within the wider framework of the gospel, he singles out righteousness as the central theme he will develop in the letter. As a righteous King and Judge, the declaration of righteousness over humankind is by faith and faith alone. He supports this with a citation from Habakkuk 2:4, showing that this is not a new idea—it is found in the prophets. (Later, he will find it in Genesis with Abraham.) As such, one is not justified by faith in God plus observance of the law (as Judaizers argue); it is by faith and always has been.

All People—Jews and Gentiles—Have Sinned (1:18–3:20, 23)

After declaring the central theme of the gospel and the main subtheme, he will develop righteousness/justification. Paul asserts that the wrath of God is revealed against all humankind because all people and peoples, without exception, are under sin. As such, they are destined for destruction unless saved by God.

In 1:18–25, Paul states the premise and problem—all humans are under God's wrath, and the central problem is their idolatry. They have rejected God in favor of false divinities they worship. The upshot is that God has handed humankind over to their depravity and its consequences. Then, in 1:26–32, Paul catalogs a list of the sins that characterize the Roman world and shows that the Gentiles are under sin. Romans 2:1–5 focuses on the sin of presuming that one is better than others who do these things, indicating Paul's target has shifted subtly from the Gentiles to the election presumption of the Jews who consider the Gentiles sinful but fail to perceive their own failure. In Romans 2:6–16, Paul states the basic principles of God's judgment—as he is without prejudice, Jews and Gentiles alike will face the wrath of God based on their works. Those who sin under the law will be judged on that basis. Those who do not know God's law will be judged against the law inscribed on their hearts, which they fail to uphold.

Romans 2:17–24 targets Jewish hypocrisy in their boast that they are instructed by the law when they fail to live up to it and, consequently, blaspheme God's name. He continues with his Jewish focus in Romans 2:25–29. What matters is not physical circumcision but circumcision of the heart by the Spirit. As Moses and Jeremiah said previously,[7] a true Jew has not been physically circumcised but one whose heart is circumcised. Such people believe in God and receive his praise.

Paul's condemnation of the Jews in their hypocrisy raises the

---

7. See also Deut 10:16; 30:6; Jer 4:4; 9:25.

question of whether there is any value in being a Jew and circumcision. Paul answers—yes!—Jews have been entrusted with God's oracles, which are the revelation of God and his righteousness (3:1-2). He defends the righteousness of God despite all people being sinners. He roundly repudiates the idea being spread by Paul's opponents that doing evil is a clever idea as it leads to good (forgiveness).

In 3:9-18, Paul pushes on with his relentless condemnation of all humankind (himself included)—while Jews have the oracles of God, in terms of sin, they have no advantage—Jews and Gentiles are under sin (3:9). He then proves this with five OT texts that aver human sin (3:10-18).[8] He draws the section together by asserting that because no flesh can be declared righteous before him and because from the law comes a recognition of what sin is and our own sinfulness, the correct response to the law is to be silent before God to whom all people are accountable (3:19-20). He will summarize the section more crisply in 3:22-23: "There is no distinction, for all [Jew and Gentile alike] have sinned and fall short of the glory of God."

Righteousness by Faith in Christ Jesus

Having demonstrated universal sinfulness, Paul gives the solution. God's righteousness has been revealed—he is righteous, he acts righteously, and he has revealed that he declares righteous those who have faith (justification by faith). The principle of justification by faith was always in the Scriptures (3:21, e.g., Hab 2:4; Gen 15:6) but had become obscured by the demand for legal observance. The declaration, "justified, pardoned, acquitted, not guilty," is declared not when a person obeys the law (implausible) but when they believe

---

8. In order, Pss 14:1-3; 5:9 (also 140:3); 10:7; Isa 59:7-8; Ps 36:1.

in Jesus Christ.[9] They are justified because of God's grace through Christ's redemptive and atoning death—he is the mercy seat (vv. 24-25). Christ's death means God, in his patience, passes over previously committed sins, demonstrating his justice and that he justifies based on faith (v. 26). This is the same for Jews and Gentiles. Any works, including the Jewish law, do not justify them. Jews and Gentiles alike are justified by faith (vv. 27-30). Yet, the law is not nullified but is upheld. It reveals sin. The law is the basis of God's righteous judgment. The law reveals God's desire for human worship and ethics. It is fulfilled in Christ, the sinless one. It includes the principle of faith, namely, Abraham! It tells of the greatest virtue of all—love!

It Has Always Been Faith—Evidence, Abraham (4:1–25)

In Chapter Four of Romans, quite brilliantly, Paul uses the Abrahamic story (found in the Torah) to demonstrate his claim that the law testifies to the principle of justification by faith. He argues that Abraham, the father of the Israelite people, was not justified by works but by faith. His key text is Genesis 15:6, the first mention of faith in the Bible: "And Abraham believed God, and it was credited to him for righteousness." His justification came because of grace, not his work. Paul next turns to the Davidic Psalms to reinforce the point. David implicitly confirms the principle of justification by faith when speaking of God's pure grace in forgiving peoples' lawless deeds and sins (4:5-8; Ps 32:1-2).

Paul then proves that this blessing of forgiveness and justification by faith is for the Gentiles and Jews—Abraham was justified by faith when he was uncircumcised! Only then was he circumcised and his righteousness sealed. Consequently, Abraham is the father of all who believe, Jews and Gentiles.

---

9. Or "the faithfulness of Jesus Christ" (see the earlier note).

In Jewish thought, the Abrahamic blessing was his inheritance of the entire world cf. Gen 17:5).[10] Paul states that as law produces wrath and reveals transgression in all people, the promise of the inheritance of the world is not received by law observance but by grace to the faithful (4:13–17). Romans 4:18–22 narrates aspects of Abraham's life in which he did not waver in his faith in God; hence, he is justified by faith. Finally, Paul applies this to Christians—this was written for the sake of all who believe in Jesus, who was handed over because of *our* trespass and was raised for our justification (4:23–25).

Reconciled to God (5:1–11)

By the end of Romans 4, Paul has answered the question, "on what basis is a person justified before God?" The answer is faith in God; now that he has come, faith in Jesus. In Romans 5–8, Paul focuses on a range of concomitants and consequences of justification by faith. The passage is an outstanding and equally important exposition of the outcomes of the work of God in Jesus. Believers are reconciled to God. The failure of Adam has been entirely undone by Jesus, the new Adam. As he has died for their sins and they are crucified in him, they are dead to sin and are alive to God. Their life vocation is to serve righteousness. Believers are released from the law to live by the Spirit. They have hope and are loved.

Starting with the statement, "therefore, since we have been justified by faith," Paul begins to unwrap the consequential

---

10. This is the logical result of God's promise that the nations would be blessed through him and his seed, that he would have a multitude of descendants and the father of many nations, and the removal of evil from the world. All that will be left on earth are those justified by faith in Jesus, his seed. All believing humankind will be justified by faith in Christ.

theological truths and ethical expectations in the gospel of Jesus Christ. First, in 5:1-11, Paul tells believers that through Christ, they are no longer under wrath (implied) but have peace with God; they are reconciled to him. As such, they now have access to his grace. They then boast in the hope of the glory of God they previously fell short of (3:23). Believers also boast in their sufferings as they participate in Christ's redemptive mission in a hostile world. Such suffering generates endurance, character, and hope. This hope will not end in disappointment or shame, for God has poured his love into hearts through the Spirit (5:1-5).

Next, in Romans 5:6-11, Paul speaks of the cross as a demonstration of God's love that sees believers justified, saved from God's wrath into Christ's life, and reconciled to God. They, thus, boast in God through Jesus.

Jesus the New Adam (5:12–21)

Paul now adds to his picture of sin and its thralldom by explaining that Adam's sin has caused death to spread to all people because they all sin—hence, they die. He then contrasts Adam and Christ, the new Adam. Due to Adam's sin, even though sin was not accounted for in the same way before the law, death reigned. It did so because of Adam's trespass, sin, and disobedience, which condemned all who followed and also sinned. Law had the effect of increasing awareness of sin.

Christ is the new Adam, a type of him in that as Adam was the first human, Jesus is the first of a new humanity. He brought the gift of eternal life by God's abundant grace that multiplied to those with faith. Whereas the disobedient Adam brought guilt and shame, the fully obedient Christ brought justification and reigning life. While law reveals and increases sin (awareness of it), the grace of the new Adam overwhelms sin. As such, grace reigns "through righteousness to eternal life through Jesus Christ our Lord" (v. 21).

Dead to Sin, Alive to God, Slaves of Righteousness (6:1–23)

Romans 6 builds around ideas being spread by opponents of Paul, who argue for law observance for new Gentile believers. They first distort the idea that where there is sin, grace abounds more; they twist this to argue Paul's logic leads to the conclusion we should continue to sin (as they think people will do without the law's protection), as this would see grace increase. Paul repudiates this as believers who have died in Christ have died to sin in him. This death to sin is symbolized in water baptism, which enacts a believer's death with Christ, burial, and resurrection to new life. This new life is patterned on the sinless life of Christ. As the body of sin is dealt with, and now believers will be in his resurrection. Those crucified in Christ are no longer enslaved to do so; they are freed from it. As those in Christ, dead and resurrected, they are dead to sin and alive to God in Christ. The natural consequence of this is not sinning more to enhance grace but repudiating sin, refusing to obey the desires of their fleshly body—using all they have and are for righteousness before God (6:1-11)

The second question in 6:15 is linked to the first in 6:1, should new believers sin because they are not under the law's tutelage but are under grace? Again, the answer is a resounding, "no way!" Paul expresses profound thanks (grace) to God because they are no longer slaves of sin but of God and his righteousness. They are free from sin and can now aspire to live righteously because they are in Christ (as he will say soon, they have received the Spirit). Rather than bear fruit from sin for eternal death, they bear fruit for God and live sanctified lives that culminate in eternal life (6:12-23).

Released from the Law (7:1–8:4)

Here, Paul's focus shifts from slavery to sin to the law. Using the analogy of marriage and divorce, Paul explains that just as a woman is freed from her husband when he dies, so believers are freed from the law as they have died to it. This analogy implies believers are now bound as in "a marriage" to Christ, who died for them and rose from the dead. They now bear fruit to God, not the flesh to death (7:1–5). They are released from the law not to live sinfully but to serve God in the Spirit's newness and not by the old patterns of the law (7:6).

Paul then posits an expected question—does the believer's release from the law indicate it is sinful? Again, the answer is, "no way!" Law exposes sin by making people aware of what sin is. Then, knowing the law only includes rules for living the life of God but no power to generate obedience, and because humans are universally sinful, the law produces sin (or, better, the awareness of it). Desire springs to life when a law restricting a behavior is made known—it has an inverse effect because of human sin. Knowing one must not covet, from the law, strangely leads to more covetousness (7:7–11). Still, this does not lead to the conclusion the law is sinful or evil; instead, "the law is holy, and the commandment is holy and righteous and good" (7:12).

Paul's words in Romans 7:13–24 are variously understood as his vexation while living as a Jew trying to live up to the law, a general statement of the struggle of believers, or Paul's new perspective looking back on his life as a Jew now that he is a Christian. The first view is unlikely, as Jews delighted in the law (e.g., Ps 119), and Paul himself saw himself as blameless in Jewish legal terms and violently defended it (Phil 3:6, cf. Gal 1:13–14). The second view has merit because the cognitive dissonance Paul describes here does apply to Christians who seek to live by the law (and so they should not do so). The third view is best—now that he has become a believer and reflected on how the law functions, he sees that this is the struggle people have. The law shows them the life they must live, they want to live it, but they cannot live up to it. This is because of their sin! Where a Christian Judaizes or becomes bound to any oppressive church system of law, this also becomes their experience.

In the passage, he takes readers on a journey of what happens when they seek to please God via the law. He does so by first posing another opponent's question and answering it: did what is good (the law) produce death? Again, the answer is, "no way!" (7:13). The problem is not the law but sin. In Adam, all people sin. Sin is a power under which all people are subjugated. Sin produces death. The law amplifies the awareness of sin. The law is spiritual, but humans cannot live up to it. When a person delights in the law, they find they cannot and experience cognitive dissonance. Their failure is because sin indwells their fleshly beings. So even with a genuine desire to live by the law, people still commit evil acts because they are permeated by sin. There is then a war in the inner being of the law-loving person, and while they rejoice in the law inwardly, they remain captive to sinning (7:14–23). All this leads Paul to cry out about his wretchedness and yearning to be rescued from his body of death (v. 24).

He answers with gratitude to God through Jesus (the solution to the plight), anticipating what will come in 8:1–4 and reflecting on what he has written thus far about God's redemption in Christ. In v. 25b, he summarizes the plight of the person bound by law: the mind is enslaved to God's law, but the flesh is enslaved to sin.

Paul now lands fully on the solution to the cognitive dissonance created by law. For those who are in Christ, there is no condemnation. They are free from it because the "law of the Spirit of life in Christ Jesus has set them free from the law of sin and death." "Law" in the first instance in 8:2 is used in the sense of "principle"—Christ's death for sin means a believer is declared righteous and, as a receptacle declared holy, receives the Spirit, and their end is eternal life and not death. Whereas the law was powerless to liberate people from sin, God achieved this liberation through Jesus. He came as a fully fleshly human, fulfilling the righteousness required to be saved through the law, and rose from the dead, having condemned sin. Now, the law is fulfilled in believers who are in him, the one who fulfilled the law. They live according to the Spirit who empowers their lives, not by the flesh and its desires.

Living by the Spirit (8:5–17)

Having twice hinted at life in the Spirit earlier (5:5; 7:6) and landing on believers living by the Spirit in v. 4, Paul extrapolates concerning living by the Spirit and not the flesh. While believers remain "in the flesh" (2 Cor 10:3; Phil 1:22, 24) and are subject to bodily lusts and desires, they are now recipients of the Spirit and are to live by it.

In 8:5–8, Paul contrasts life in the flesh with life in the Spirit. Those without the Spirit live by the flesh. They cannot live by the law and please God. They are compelled to seek the things of the flesh, are in enmity with God, and will reap death. Contrastingly, those in the Spirit seek the things of the Spirit and experience God's life and peace.

Romans 8:9–11 assures the Romans that they are recipients of the Spirit. Christ dwells in them, and they belong to him. So, they will be raised from the dead through God's Spirit. Their bodies are dead because of sin, but the Spirit is life because of righteousness.

Paul, in 8:12–18, draws out the consequence of being God's people, in Christ, having received the Spirit. They are now obligated to live by the Spirit who produces eternal life, not the flesh that yields eternal death. By the Spirit's power, they are now to put to death the misdemeanors of the flesh. They do this by being led by the Spirit as is fitting for children of God. They are his children through God's adoption by the Spirit, who generates in them the cry, "Abba, Father!" This glorious status as children of the Creator and siblings of Jesus is inwardly confirmed by the Spirit, who gives witness to the believer's spirit. As children, they will share in the inheritance of the cosmos with Christ. The path to this inheritance of the world is suffering in and with Christ as they participate in his people and mission to proclaim the *euangelion* of God to the world.

Hope in Suffering (8:18–40)

Mention of ongoing suffering raises the question, "what hope is there in this world, wracked with sin, suffering, and inevitable death?" The rest of Romans 8 addresses this question.

First, there is the eschatological hope of future revealed glory that dwarfs present suffering (despite it seeming to be overwhelming at times, v. 18).[11] This glory involves the creation, subjected as it is to decay and death in which it writhes like a woman in intense labor, being liberated into the fullness of God's resurrection life (8:19-23). Believers participate in this groaning but look forward eagerly and wait patiently for their final state—full bodily adoption and redemption. Into this hope, they were saved (8:23-25).

Second, the Spirit in believers joins in their groanings, interceding for them to God according to God's perfect will. The Spirit is God's presence in us, leading us and praying for us to our heavenly father that we will have God's victory and endure present suffering to the end (8:26-27).

Third, God is in total control. Not only do all things work together for the good of those God loves and has called according to his purpose, but his people were foreknown and predestined to be more and more like Jesus the new Adam, God's Son, and God's perfect image. Indeed, they were predestined, called, declared righteous, and glorified in him (8:28-29).

After stressing the hope of creation's future eschatological liberation, the Spirit's role in praying for us, and the assurance of God's complete sovereignty over all things, Paul asks a series of questions. The first question leads into the passage, and the others have obvious answers that give hope. As God is for believers, who can be against them—no one! And if they do, God will deal with

---

11. As I write these words, I have two family members in different NZ hospitals whose lives are precariously poised. All believers should imbibe Romans 8:17-40 as it builds hope even in despair.

them (cf. 12:19). The God who was prepared to sacrifice his own Son will give all things to his people. As God justifies, no one can bring charges against a believer. Nor can anyone condemn his people, for Christ died, was raised, reigns at God's right hand, and with the Spirit, intercedes for believers. Furthermore, no being or thing, however demonic, powerful, and hurtful, can separate God's people from his love in Christ (8:30–40).

The Place of Israel in the Purposes of God (9:1–11:36)

Having declared the gospel of justification by faith and many other associated realities brought to pass through God's redemption in Christ, Paul shifts to the question of the place of Israel in God's purposes. The primary debate in these chapters is what Paul means by "all Israel" in 11:26. Options include all Israelites from all time, all tribes of Israel, all faithful Israelites, all Israelites at the time of Christ's return, or the church, including faithful Jews and Gentiles. Getting lost in this debate obscures the passage's brilliance as Paul defends God's justice and declares that there remains hope for Israel if her people accept the gospel of their Messiah, Jesus Christ. Furthermore, all believers should hear in the passage God's call to continue to proclaim Christ to Israel as to all the nations so that this can happen.

In Romans 9:1–5, Paul shows his love and grief for his people. He prays that he could be accursed to save them (which, in fact, Christ has done). Earlier in 3:1, he mentioned the privilege of being entrusted with God's Word. Now he lists other advantages that flow from their relationship with God. These advantages include their adoption, God's guidance guiding them by his glory that filled the tabernacle and the temple, the covenants, the law, the temple and its system, the promises of God, the patriarchs, and the Christ (who Paul declares and blesses as God over all things).

Paul next defends God's faithfulness to his Word—history shows that not all those in Israel were, in fact, Israel—it is those who had circumcised hearts by faith (Rom 2:25-29; 4:1-12). Paul then shows how God has acted in history to establish his people by his choice—Isaac instead of Ishmael, Jacob instead of Esau. As such, he asks whether God is unjust and repudiates the idea, as God is merciful and compassionate as he wills and hardens (as in the case of Pharaoh in Egypt) as he desires. Romans indicates he does so where he finds faith. He likens God to a potter and humans pots God crafts. As the potter, he has the right to make as he wills vessels for destruction and his affection (9:6-22).

Those who are to be his recipients of grace include not only Jews but Gentiles, as the prophets expected (9:23-26). It will also include a remnant of Israel, with many others rejecting God's choices (as they did in history and are now doing with Christ having come, 9:27-28). In 9:30-33, he makes clear that Israel's problem is unbelief, their rejection of Jesus, the cornerstone, who has for them become a stone of stumbling. On the contrary, many Gentiles are receiving justification by faith.

Romans 10:1-12 contrasts the two paths to righteousness before God. Israel persists in pursuing righteousness through the law. God has acted in history, and now it is evident that justification is by faith in Christ. Paul begins praying again that zealous Israel will see Christ as their salvation and turn from seeking righteousness by the law to faith. The period of the law and its requirements have ended in Christ's perfect life and death. Now, all that is required is faith in him. Paul next unlocks what is required for salvation—believe the gospel, confess that Jesus is Lord, and believe in his resurrection. Those who do this are justified and saved and will never experience shame before God. This promise applies to Jews and Gentiles alike. All who call on his name will be saved.

In Romans 10:14-21, Paul asks a series of questions with the overall purpose—has Israel heard the Word of Christ, the gospel? He does so by showing the process of mission: people are sent—they preach—others hear—and believe. Faith is generated in the called as the gospel is heard. The person then calls on God's name. Paul next gives a series of OT texts which he appropriates for the present to demonstrate that, as in the past, Israel has heard the gospel and rejected it, while others have accepted it.[12] He ends by quoting Isa 65:2—all day long, God holds his hands out to Israel, even in their disobedience and resistance. We see here that there is hope for Israel if they turn to Christ.

Paul cuts to the chase in Romans 11. He asks whether God has rejected his people, which he repudiates, "no way!" First, he himself is an Israelite, a child of Abraham, a Benjaminite—he is evidence God has not rejected Israel (11:1). Second, at the time of Elijah, when the bereft prophet felt he was the only faithful one left, God revealed 7000 others—a remnant of God's people (11:2-4). In the present, there is again a remnant of the faithful in Israel—the Jews of the early church—chosen by grace, not works but, as implied, through faith (11:5-6). He explains Israel's rejection as a hardening due to God sending a spirit of stupor on them, causing them to be blind to the gospel (11:7-10).

Scholars interpret the following passage (vv. 11-12) differently. Some see here the certainty of Israel's future salvation, despite their stumbling over Jesus. They argue that, as God purposed, their stumbling allowed salvation to come to the Gentiles. Still, they will ultimately be jealous and turn to God in fullness (with different ideas of fullness depending on their view, see at the beginning of the section). Others believe Paul is speaking of a hoped-for outcome—he *hopes* they will become jealous and the fullness of Israel will be saved by faith.

Verses 13-24 warn Gentile readers not to become arrogant now that salvation has come to them. He likens the people of faith to a batch of dough and then an olive tree. Gentiles have been grafted into the tree, and from which the Jewish people, in their unbelief, have been broken off. He warns the Gentiles that they too can be broken off in unbelief and gives hope for Israel—her people can be grafted in if they turn and believe.

---

12. Ps 19:4; Deut 32:21; Isa 65:1.

In 11:25, Paul sees the day when the full number of Gentiles comes into God's people—this is Paul's way of speaking of the day when the gospel has reached the ends of the earth, all nations, and the mission is complete. In Mark 13:10 and Matt 24:14, the consummation then comes.

He also envisages all Israel being saved. As discussed, this is interpreted differently depending on one's reading of the passage. Whatever is meant by "all Israel," Paul ends the section in vv. 26b–27, seeing Jesus as Israel's deliverer from Zion who restores Israel (Isa 27:9) and the basis of a new covenant in which Israel's sins are forgiven (Jer 31:33–34). As such, Israel-in-rejection-of-Jesus are enemies but remain chosen and loved by God. Verse 29 is also debated, with some seeing evidence of Israel's salvation despite their rejection of Christ and others interpreting it as God's favor to Israel despite their rejection and loss. Just as the Gentiles have received God's mercy despite their disobedience, God will show mercy to Israel (vv. 30–32). Again, this is absolute for some scholars—all Israelites (as understood in each case) are saved. For others, the principle of justification dominating Romans means this must refer to those who turn from unbelief to belief. Whatever Paul has in mind, he ends with a magnificent doxology glorifying God for the superiority of his wisdom over human ponderings (11:33–36).

Being God's People in a Dark World (12:1–13:14)

The "therefore" (*oun*) at 12:1 is critical—what follows is an inference drawn from Paul's eleven-chapter exposition of God's mercies in the gospel. He delineates how people should live, considering this gospel of grace through faith.

Verses 1–2 give an overall summary—they are to emulate Christ's self-offering by worshiping God by giving their lives over in complete service to him. At the same time, they are to be increasingly conformed to thinking and acting in line with the ethics of God, rejecting the patterns of this fallen age. Doing this will enable them to discern God's will and live it.

Verses 3-8 focus on living humbly and authentically. They do so by recognizing the gifts they have received through faith and God's grace and exercising them with a determined effort to build up Christ's body. They are to encourage others to do the same.

What follows in vv. 9-21 is a series of behaviors appropriate to God's people. The critical virtue is sincere love, which should shape their relationships with all people. Other right attitudes and actions include clinging to goodness, not evil, esteeming others above themselves, zeal, spiritual fervor, service, joy, hope, patience, patience, prayer, sharing with the needy, hospitality, empathy, unity, humility, and egalitarianism. Where unbelievers are concerned, they are to bless their persecutors, repay evil with good, seek to live good lives, live peacefully with others as able, show hospitality to them, and leave revenge to God.

Romans 13:1-7 focuses on relations to the State. They envisage submission, even under the rule of an autocratic, all-powerful, ruthless Roman Emperor. Such an injunction is difficult for some Christians today but is consistent with other passages in the NT (Tit 3:1; 1 Pet 2:13-17). This submission is not absolute, for Jesus is Lord. Still, where the State does not demand idolatry and a violation of the gospel's core, believers should be compliant, subservient citizens. They do so partly because, for Paul, the State is an agent of God's cosmic rule. Knowing this should lead all Christians to pay the required taxes (as Jesus endorsed, Mark 12:17).

More important is the love command, which fulfills all laws, including the core of the Torah, the ten commandments (13:8-10). Paul ends the section urging the Romans not to partake in the false behaviors of the age and its lusts and desires but to be clothed in Christ.

The Strong Deferring to the Weak (14:1–15:13)

This passage leads many contemporary scholars to see Romans as a letter that articulates many aspects of Paul's gospel and addresses issues in the Roman church. The passage speaks of two groups in the church, one that has no issue with eating anything and others that eat only selected food (14:1-3). There are also differences of opinion in the church on keeping holy days (14:5). There are different ideas about the issues in this passage, such as Paul describing a hypothetical scenario. Most likely, it is about differences based on cultural preferences (Jew and Gentile) in the church, without it being a full Judaizing issue. This perspective makes sense—while Jews and Gentile sympathizers may not insist that adhering to the Jewish law is required for justification and inclusion, there may still be cultural elitism among the Romans. That this is a Jew-Gentile issue is confirmed in the use of clean and unclean language in v. 14.

Whatever the exact problem, Paul speaks of the two as the strong (who realize such things are unimportant and believers can eat what they like, and no day is holier than another) and the weak (who believe these things are significant). Paul urges the strong to accept the weak without arguing over such trivialities (14:1). He illustrates that those with eating differences must not treat those who differ with contempt nor judge one another (14:2-4). He urges people to make up their own minds on these things and live by their convictions and gratitude before the Lord Jesus Christ—for whom they live (14:5-9).

There is clearly judgmentalism concerning these non-essential things in the Roman church as Paul asks why they judge and look down on one another in v. 10. They must not do this and leave it to God who judges all people (14:10-13; Isa 45:23, cf. Phil 2:10-11). They must behave in a way that in no way causes another Christian to stumble—accept and stop judging one another (14:13).

In vv. 14-18, Paul personalizes things in the first person siding with the strong who hold no food is unclean. However, if another person holds such a conviction, they should live according to it (without imposing it on others and vice versa). Furthermore, if a Christian finds their choices regarding eating and special days cause another Christian to stumble, they should not eat—love trumps liberty (v. 15, cf. 1 Cor 8; 10:23-11:1). The bigger things of the kingdom—righteousness, peace, and joy—are what matters, not what people eat. Nevertheless, each should live to their own conscience before the Lord and receive his and people's approval (14:15-18). Paul sums it up by reiterating what he has said and encouraging them to live in a way that leads to peace and mutual upbuilding (14:19). Whatever their views on what they should eat and drink, they must live to their conscience before God and not cause another Christian to stumble (14:20-22a). Such a person who lives from faithful decisions on trivial things is blessed (14:22b-23).

Paul sums things up neatly in 15:1: "We who are strong ought to bear with the failings of the weak and not to please ourselves." For Paul, it is a general principle to seek to please our neighbors in non-essential matters, as Christ did (15:2-3). Paul shifts slightly to stress the importance of the Scriptures for present encouragement and prays that the God who gives endurance and encouragement will bless the Romans with unity of thought in sync with Christ's mindset and that they will glorify God and Christ (15:4-6).

He returns to the matter of accepting one another as Christ accepts believers, despite our failings and differences (15:7). He sees Christ as a servant of the Jews to confirm the promises to Abraham and his kin so that the Gentiles may join Jews glorifying God. Again, this stresses the need for unity between Jews and Gentiles in the church, despite cultural differences (15:8). He then lists a catena of OT verses that predict Gentiles praising God and Jesus (the root of Jesse who gives hope to the nations, Isa 11:10; Rev 5:5) with the Jews (in order, 2 Sam 22:50; Ps 18:49; Deut 32:43; Ps 117:1). He ends the section calling for unity despite minor differences with a prayer for hope, joy, peace, and faith by the Spirit (15:13).

Paul's Ministry Plans (15:14–33)

Here, Paul gives his ministry plans infused with essential information about his missional approach. By the time he wrote Romans in AD 56–58, Paul asserts that he has completed the work of evangelizing the region from Jerusalem to the western Balkans. This confidence means he has planted the faith sufficiently for it to spread into the hinterlands through local gospel workers (15:19, cf. 1 Thess 1:8). Now, he wants to go to regions that have not received the gospel. His focus is Spain, the western "end of the world" (15:24). He may intend to go through southern Gaul on the way, where it can spread north and then into Germany and Britain. On the trip, with contributing church representatives, he carried monetary contributions from Galatia (1 Cor 16:1), Macedonia, and Achaia. His priority before heading west is to deliver these to Jerusalem (15:26-28, 30-32). He asks them to pray that the gifts are well received, then travel to Rome for ministry (15:28, 32; 1:10–15), and then west to Spain (v. 28).

Aspects of Paul's missional approach are highlighted in this section. First, he is confident the Romans will be faithful to his ideas and share them knowledgeably (15:14). Paul trusts that God, by his Spirit, will use his words to correct others (s.a. Gal 5:10; Phil 3:14). Second, he sees his ministry as priestly service of Christ to the Gentiles, who are an acceptable holy offering to God (15:16). Third, he is proud in Christ of what God has done in and through him in his ministry of bringing Gentiles to obedience (15:17–18). His ministry included verbal communication, good deeds (like the Collection), and miracles from Jerusalem to Illyricum (15:18–19). Fourth, he recognizes that the gospel must go to unreached people groups and wants to be used in this regard to complete the mission to the world (15:20–21). Presumably, he then expects Christ will return (cf. 11:25). Fifth, he wants to use Rome as a base to push the gospel further west, as he did from Syrian Antioch into Anatolia, Macedonia, and Achaia. The Romans can offer support through prayer, finance, and people (15:22–24). Sixth, Paul's care for poor Christians is as critical as preaching and planting churches (15:25–26). He sees the Gentiles giving materially to the Jews as appropriate in that Jews brought them spiritual blessings through the gospel (15:27). Seventh, he recognizes the need for prayer support for the mission (15:30–32). Finally, he recognizes that God's will trumps everything—still, he states his desires (15:32–33).

Final Instructions, Further Greetings, and Benediction (16:1–27)

Romans 16 includes a commendation of Phoebe, likely the letter courier, a deacon of the Cenchreaen church, and a patron to Paul and other Christians. Then, many other Romans greet them, indicating Paul has many friends and coworkers in the city.[13] One of the stand-out features of the chapter is the many women (Phoebe, Prisca, Mary, Junia, Tryphena, Tryphosa, Persis, and Julia). Their language suggests women *worked* with Paul in his mission (also adding to the possibility that the limitation passages in 1 Cor 14:34–35 and 1 Tim 2:11-15 are not to be read universally). Of particular note are Phoebe (above) and Prisca, who, with Aquila, risked their necks to save Paul and have a church in their home, and Junia, who may have formed an apostolic partnership with her husband, Andronicus. Others include Herodian (probably from the famous Herod family), Rufus, and his mother (maybe the family of Simon of Cyrene).

Paul gives his final instructions, including watching out for false

---

13. Some earlier scholars doubted that Paul would know so many people and suggested that Romans ended at the end of Ch. 15, and that the version we have was sent to Ephesus (especially because of the mention of Prisca and Aquila). However, this is roundly rejected today.

teachers, his confidence in the Romans obeying his letter, and the future end of Satan (vv. 17–20). The final greetings indicate Timothy, Lucius (some think this is Luke, but the spelling is different), and Jason (of Thessalonica?). We have evidence in v. 22 that Paul used a scribe (Tertius). The names Gaius and Erastus indicate he is in Corinth (1 Cor 1:14; 2 Tim 4:20). Erastus is the Corinth city treasurer, so we mention an early politician who converted. He may be behind the famous Erastus inscription.[14]

Conclusion

Romans and Galatians are invaluable to the Christian faith. In them, Paul emphatically teaches that forgiveness and justification are received based on God's grace. It is received by people who sincerely believe in God and his Son as supreme and savior. Nothing can be added to what is required to be a Christian. Christ's work completes what is required. All we must do is believe in him and his Father. Any Christian sect, cult, denomination, church, or person who adds to this is apostate.

Furthermore, the two letters roundly state that every person from every nation and culture is equal before God and treated without prejudice. All are sinners and destined for death and eternal destruction. However, Christ's perfect obedience satisfies the requirements of God, and everyone is the same on the same basis—faith in him and his Father. As such, Gentile converts did not need to be circumcised, adhere to Jewish boundary markers, or observe the law to be included in God's people. Israel's culture is not a superior culture to which others must conform. As such,

---

14. Many hold the view it is the same person. See, e.g., Leon Morris, *The Epistle to the Romans*, PNTC (Grand Rapids, MI; Eerdmans, 1988), 544.

contemporary Christians, churches, and denominations must work fervently to remove all vestiges of cultural arrogance, whether it is racial, ethnic, or the culture of a church or denomination. In Christ Jesus, there is neither Jew nor Greek (or any other ethnic category), neither slave nor free (or any other status category), and neither male and female. Christianity must reflect our God, who does not show favoritism (Rom 2:11; Gal 2:6).

11. The Prison Letters of Paul

Introduction

The prison letters of Paul are those which indicate that they were written when Paul was in prison. These include Ephesians (3:1), Philippians (1:7), Colossians (4:3), Philemon (23), and the Pastoral Letters, 1 Timothy, 2 Timothy (1:8), and Titus.[1] The early church agreed that Paul wrote the three Lycus Valley letters (Ephesians, Colossians, and Philemon) and Philippians from Rome. However, some scholars in the historical-critical period question whether Paul wrote Ephesians and Colossians at all. Some also ponder whether they were written from another imprisonment, with Ephesus favored (and a few Caesarea Maritima). Many scholars agree that the Pastoral Epistles were written by someone other than Paul after his death, so it is unclear where they originated. Others accept Pauline authorship and usually place these in Paul's final Roman imprisonment. These six letters will be briefly considered in the following material, whatever the rights and wrongs of these details.

---

1. Paul's imprisonment is not explicitly stated in 1 Timothy and Titus; hence, they may have been written when Paul was not in prison. Most consider that the common ideas in the two letters and the relationship of 1 Timothy to Titus indicate that Paul was in prison at the time. Also, Tychicus is with Paul at the time of the writing of Titus (3:12). He delivered the letters of Ephesians and Colossians, as tradition holds, from Rome (below). Tradition holds Paul was in Roman imprisonment.

Part 1: Ephesians, Colossians, and Philemon

In this chapter, I will first discuss three letters written to churches or people in the valley of the Lycus River.[2] The first two are Ephesians and Colossians, which scholars often join together.[3] Some see them as non-Pauline letters written by the same author, assuming Paul's name after his death. Others see them as genuine letters of Paul, written to the same area of Asia Minor with a similar flavor.

Ephesians

Ephesians is a lovely letter covering various aspects of the Christian faith. Its authorship was never questioned in the church up until the historical-critical period. It was assumed to have been a letter of Paul, written from Rome during the imprisonment referred to in Acts 28:30–31; hence, ca. AD 60–61. However, some critical scholars have argued that Paul did not write it because of differences in vocabulary, theology (e.g., a realized eschatology, cosmic Christ), and tone. Still, many passionately defend the early church's view (as I do). Some manuscripts lack the words "in Ephesus" in Eph 1:1, and so some hold that it was initially a general letter rather than written to a specific church. This view also developed because, in the letter, Paul does not deal with specific issues like false teaching. As such, some even think Paul wrote Ephesians from Ephesus to the churches of Asia Minor. An increasing number of contemporary

---

2. "Lycus R. (Ionia) 22 - Λύκος," *Topos Text*, https://topostext.org/place/379291WLyc.
3. For a fuller discussion, see Keown, *Discovering*, 2:219–47, 266–88 (Chs. 7, 9).

scholars hold that Ephesians is a letter of Paul, and most hold it was sent to Ephesus.

As Ephesus was the capital of Asia Minor, it was probably written to be circulated to the other churches of Asia Minor (see the seven churches in Revelation 2-3 plus Colossae, which was not yet destroyed by an earthquake that came in AD 60-61). There are clear resonances with Colossians, including the same letter-courier, Tychicus (Eph 6:21-22; Col 4:12). As Onesimus is mentioned in both Colossians and Philemon, we can deduce that the three letters were delivered with the same group including Tychicus and Onesimus to the Lycus Valley churches (Col 4:9; Phlm 10).

Biblical students must not allow such historical matters to blur the beauty of Ephesians. It is exquisitely written and is invaluable for theology, worship, church relationships, and mission. It has an extremely high Christology that considers Jesus the Christ and Lord over the church and the universe. It gives a high view of the present status of those "in Christ" as already raised and seated at the right hand of God. Rather than pointing to a different author, this theology is likely developed for the context because Ephesus was a center of magic and the occult. By portraying Jesus so highly and speaking of the Christian life as spiritual warfare, the readers are comforted that he is in control and is sovereign over inimical forces. They have nothing to fear. The letter gives brief and contextually relevant instructions for Christian living in Asia Minor in the 60s ad. It is also replete with extraordinarily rich prayers to God for the Ephesians—prayers we can appropriate for those we love in the Lord.

Greeting, Blessing, and Prayer (1:1–23)

The greeting includes the same dynamics as others: sender Paul, his divinely gifted apostleship, the recipients—saints and the faithful in

Ephesus (remembering some do not include this)—and Paul's usual grace and peace prayer.

Usually, Paul next gives a thanksgiving for his converts. Here, as in 2 Corinthians 1, he pronounces a blessing to God. The passage contains powerful theological concepts that greatly encourage readers—spiritual blessings, election, sanctification, love, predestination, adoption, grace, redemption, Christ's death, forgiveness, reconciliation, conversion, the gospel, salvation, and the Spirit. God is bringing all these things to pass through Christ, who is mentioned thirteen times as Lord, Jesus, Christ, and the beloved. Noteworthy is "his blood," meaning his redemptive sacrificial death and participation in him (ten times).

In vv. 15–23, Paul continues, speaking of his ongoing prayer for the Ephesians to experience yet more of God in Christ by the Spirit. He tells the Ephesians he has heard good news from emissaries concerning their faith and love. Paul sends a stream of gratitude to God and prays for them, even though they have received the Spirit, that they experience the Spirit of wisdom and revelation afresh. He prays for them to know Christ more deeply, the hope of God's calling, the riches of their inheritance, and the greatness of his power expressed in Christ. He describes this power as one that raised him from the dead and set him above every spiritual and temporal power and his fullness that fills everything in every way.

Salvation and Inclusion (2:1–22)

Ephesians 2 can be neatly divided into two parts. Part one focuses on the individual conversions of the Ephesians from lives of darkness, sin, and death to salvation. Part two emphasizes that those saved by grace through faith are included together in Christ as one people without prejudice and favor.

The first half of the chapter itself can be divided into two. In Ephesians 2:1–3, Paul crisply summarizes the perilous state of the

Ephesians before their conversion (and all people who are not yet in Christ)—dead in sin, living by the world's false patterns, under Satan's rule and power, living by the desires of the flesh, and children of wrath (indicating their destiny—destruction).

In 2:4-10, signaled by "but God …," Paul waxes lyrical about God's glorious salvation. It is premised on his mercy and love (v. 4). Formerly dead, they are made alive in Christ. Previously under wrath, they are saved by grace. Once living by the world's ways, they are now raised and seated with Christ in the heavenlies (vv. 5-6). This special status with Christ beside God is so that God's grace and kindness in Christ is shown to all (v. 7). Ephesians 2:8-9 is the crispest statement of the gospel of grace through faith in Scripture. Salvation is not earned by works done so that a person can boast, but it is the gift of God. Verse 10 is crucial as it tells readers that while works do not save them, they are saved to do works God prepares for them. Paul does not have a works theology where salvation is concerned. However, he expects the saved to do good works by the power of the Spirit.

Part two of Chapter 2 is also neatly divided into two parts. In 2:11-12, Paul describes the state of the Gentiles before conversion—they were the uncircumcision, separated from God in Christ, not included in Israel, estranged from the covenants, and without hope and God. The second part also begins with "but now …." The believing Gentile Ephesians are now in Christ. Through his death (blood), they are now living at peace with God and other believers. Jews and Gentiles are now one; the old divisions are gone. The law is abolished, and now the two are one new person at peace, reconciled to God. This situation came to pass through his preaching and person. As one people in him, they now have open access to the throne room of God in and by one Spirit. They are one people; none are strangers and foreigners, they are all citizens, saints, and part of God's family—a temple of God built on the foundation of the ministries of the apostles and prophets in the church, and Christ holding it all together. Now, through God's ongoing mission, the church is growing into a holy temple into which new converts are integrated. All are together being built up as the temple of the Spirit.

Paul's Mission and Prayer for the Ephesians (3:1–21)

The first thirteen verses focus on Paul's role as the apostle to the Gentiles, presently in prison. This section focuses on his ministry of proclaiming the revealed mystery of the gospel to the Gentiles. Equal to Jewish believers, they are fellow heirs and members of Christ's body, partakers in the promises of God in Christ. In the gospel and his ministry, as purposed and effected through Christ, the creator God's wisdom is revealed to the spiritual powers through his people, the church. Now, whereas no one could freely enter God's presence in the Holy of Holies, all believers can boldly and confidently approach God through faith. With such a glorious gospel, ministry, Christ, and God, the Ephesians should not be discouraged by his sufferings; instead, they should see them as their glory.

The second half of the chapter is one of the most glorious prayers in Scripture. Paul prays to God that he may inwardly strengthen the Ephesians, who are established in his love, with power through his Spirit and that Christ may give them a fresh experience of his indwelling presence. He wants them to know the full extent of Christ[4] and his incomprehensible love so that they are filled with God. The prayer ends with a petition for God's action among and through them and a doxology.

4. The Greek does not specify what it is Paul prays for them to understand fully (breadth, length, height, depth). Options include God's power, wisdom, the mystery of the gospel, love, and, as I take it, Christ himself. Love features in the next clause.

Living as a Christian (4:1–6:20)

As in Romans 12:1, "therefore" (*oun*) signals Paul drawing inferences from the profoundly theological material thus far. He shifts from theological musings to paraenesis or exhortation concerning the Christian life.

The emphasis in 4:1-6 is unity and oneness. The Ephesians are to live up to their high calling to be seated at the right hand of God in Christ, exhibiting humility, gentleness, patience, love, unity, and peace in the Spirit. To highlight unity, Paul reels off a string of seven things of which there is one—body (church), Spirit, hope, Lord (Jesus), faith, baptism (water), and God and Father—who is over, through, and in all things.

Having stressed unity, Paul speaks of the diversity of gifts of grace in the body of Christ distributed by God in Christ, who came to earth and has now ascended to fill the cosmos (4:7-10). He next specifies five[5] notable charismatic functions in the church—apostles, prophets, evangelists, pastors, and teachers. He explains their role: 1) to equip the saints for the work of the ministry;[6] 2) to build up the body of Christ to unity and maturity

---

5. Some hold there are four. The Greek reads, "And he gave some, on the one hand (*men*) to be apostles, and (*de*) others to be prophets, and (*de*) others to be evangelists, and (*de*) others to be pastors and (*kai*) teachers. As the final clause follows *kai*, it could be translated as "pastors who teach." See the discussion in Frank Thielman, *Ephesians*, BECNT (Grand Rapids, MI: Baker Academic, 2010), 275, who suggests five are in view and *kai* is used because it is the last in the list.
6. The Greek can mean that Paul has in view that these leaders both equip the saints for maturity, so they do the work of ministry (not the saints). However, it is better to read it as meaning the leaders equip the saints for ministry (Thielman, *Ephesians*, 277-79).

in Christ; 3) to safeguard the church from false teaching; and 4) to ensure the growth of the church in Christ until it is functioning and growing in love (maturity and converts).

From Eph 4:17 through to 6:18, Paul expounds on aspects of God's life for believers. First, they are not to live as they did as Gentiles in their licentious sin. Instead, they are to "take off" their old lives and be renewed (clothed) creations in Christ, exhibiting righteousness and holiness (4:17–24).

They must set aside false behaviors like lying, anger, stealing, rotten speech, and so grieving the Spirit. Instead, they are to speak the truth, hold back when angry, work with their own hands, and be kind, compassionate, and forgiving as God is in Christ (4:24–32). They must imitate God and the love of his self-giving Son and offer themselves as sacrifices to God (cf. Rom 12:1). Vices that are fitting for those destined for destruction are to be put aside—sexual immorality, idolatrous greed, filthy and foolish talk—as well as those who tempt them into those spaces. Rather, they should give thanks and live to please God (5:1–6).

In 5:7–17, Paul contrasts living as children of darkness with living by God's light. They are to shine in goodness, righteousness, and truth. In 5:18–20, they are to live as people of God's wisdom, not the false wisdom of this evil world. Paul strikes a contrast between being drunk on alcoholic beverages and being filled with the Spirit—they are to be filled and worship God together with praise and thanksgiving.

This Spirit-filled live spills over into family life. In Eph 5:21, the people submit to other church members out of reverence for Christ. This submission is then worked out concerning family relations. The passage is carefully structured with instructions to those in the family structure who culturally submit (*wives* to husbands, *children* to parents, *slaves* to masters). Each part then lands on the leading male of the house (husband/father/master), envisaging men submitting to their wives by loving them sacrificially, raising the children in the Lord, and treating slaves like the slaves respond to them. The point of the passage is not to reinforce patriarchal patterns in the home but rather to paint a picture of the home where all serve all in love. In so doing, they emulate the example of God and Christ (5:1).

Then, finally, in 6:10-20, Paul ensures the Ephesians know the nature of the war they are in, their role in it, and how to win. It is a spiritual war, unlike the wars of the world waged between armies with swords, shields, and spears. It is fought with the spiritual forces of evil (6:11-12). It is won by being strong and mighty in God's strength, putting on the armor of God's attributes to enable them to withstand these evil forces—the truth (gospel and our fidelity), righteousness (by faith and lives embodying righteousness by the Spirit), the good news (prepared to share it at all times), faith (initial and ongoing life by faith), salvation (assurance but not arrogance), and the Word of God (for defense against false teaching, and to promote the gospel). Finally, they must always be prayerful, including praying for those on the frontline of the mission, like Paul.

Conclusion and Final Prayer (6:21–24)

Ephesians has a brief conclusion in which Paul endorses the letter-courier Tychicus and his role in encouraging them and explaining the letter and other things concerning Paul's situation. He ends with a brief blessing of peace and grace.

Colossians

Colossians has a similar feel to Ephesians and is clearly from the same author. Some agree with the traditional view that it is Paul, while others see it as a student of Pauline theology after his death. The reasons are the same as for Ephesians, with some differences in theology (realized eschatology) and a cosmic Christ who is the head of all churches (cosmic ecclesiology). People studying Colossians must negotiate the debate over authorship. Still, the early church tradition was unanimous that it is Paul's letter, and the differences could relate to different purposes or a different secretary. Colossae was also destroyed in an earthquake sometime in AD 60–61. A letter from after that date would be easily seen to be pseudonymous. This date fits nicely with Paul's imprisonment in Rome when he wrote Ephesians (above) and Philemon (Acts 28:30–31).

However, while the early church was in no doubt that Paul wrote Colossians from Roman prison, some contemporary scholars consider it likely Paul wrote it from Ephesus. They note that Paul suffered immensely in Ephesus at times, which may have included prison (1 Cor 15:31–32; 2 Cor 1:8–10). Advocates for Rome note that there is no explicit evidence Paul was in prison in Ephesus, despite these passages, and consider the early church's view more likely. Wherever Paul is, the letter was delivered by Tychicus, as evidenced by what is said of him in Col 4:7–9, which suggests he took both Ephesians and Colossians on the same trip.

Whatever the exact background, Colossians is an intriguing letter in several ways. Whereas Ephesians has no clear background issue, the Colossian church faced false views that Paul wrote to counteract. These include deceitful philosophical ideas and human traditions (Col 2:8); Jewish concerns like the Sabbath, festivals, and eating clean food (2:16); and the worship of angels. The focus on the deity and fullness of Christ in the letter points to a heresy that diminishes him below his rightful place as Lord of the cosmos. Some consider the heresy a protognostic blending of Jewish and Greco-Roman ideas.

In the letter, Paul ensures that the Colossians are reminded of their formation, the supremacy of Christ, the problems with heresy, and the virtues God wants from his people.

Greeting, Thanksgiving, and Prayer (1:1–23)

Paul begins, as is typical, with his name and his apostleship. This time, he names Timothy as co-sender and perhaps amanuensis. The recipients are the saints and faithful Christian brothers and sisters in the Colossae, a key city in the Lycus Valley inland from Ephesus and within a few kilometers of Hierapolis and Laodicea. Paul gives an abbreviated version of his usual grace and peace greeting.

As in nine of his other letters, the prescript is followed by the thanksgiving. His thanksgiving is pluralized, probably including Timothy and other coworkers. He thanks God in prayer for their faith in Christ and their love for other believers throughout the world. His reason is the hope God has reserved for them in heaven that they heard about in the gospel of truth. This gospel has reached them and is blossoming throughout the world as it is among them due to the work of their own Epaphras, a faithful fellow slave and minister in Christ from the Pauline group. He is likely one of those in Paul's evangelistic team trained at the Hall of Tyrannus and who evangelized Asia Minor in two years. He visited Colossae and returned, telling Paul and his team of their love generated by God's Spirit (1:3–8).

As he does in many of his letters, Paul turns to intercession in 1:9–14. He reports his team's ceaseless prayers for them since he heard of their faith and love. His prayer report focuses on God and what he has done for them in Christ, a counter to the heretical diminishing of Jesus. He and his team pray that they will be filled with the fullness of wisdom and spiritually insightful knowledge of God's will. He prays that this will lead to them living in a manner that pleases Christ the Lord in every way and that as the gospel blossoms among them, they will overflow in good works and divine understanding. He asks that God empower them with joyful and patient perseverance. He hopes this will result in a chorus of thanksgiving to God through whom they are qualified to inherit all things with other believers. He has rescued them from the dominion of darkness, and now they are citizens of Christ's kingdom. In Christ, who God loves, the Colossians have redemption and the forgiveness of sins.

Colossians 1:15-20 is one of the passages in Paul that may have been a preexisting hymn or a hymn or piece of exalted prose Paul himself wrote. It is a neat unit but integrated into Paul's prayer in which he shifts from prayer to exalting Christ. He probably extols Christ in this way because the heretical teachers are reducing him to the status of an angel (as in some cults today, such as the Jehovah's Witnesses). Hence, the section ensures that the Colossians understand the fullness of who Jesus is—God the Son.

In the hymnic piece, the first half (vv. 15-17) focuses on Christ's cosmic rule. Christ is the image of the invisible God, calling to mind his identity as the new Adam, God's true and faithful image bearer. In calling him the firstborn over creation, Paul is not saying he is created but preeminent over creation. He is preeminent because God created all things—seen and unseen, spiritual and physical—through him. He is not only the instrument for God's creation but rules all powers, political and spiritual. The universe was created through him and for him. He preexists all things, and he sustains them.

The second half (vv. 18-20) emphasizes his lordship over the church, his body, of which he is the head. As the first to be raised from the dead, he is the beginning of God's renewed humanity and is first in everything in God's people. In v. 19, Paul states his divinity—God's fullness dwells in him. And, through Christ, in v. 20, God's purpose is to reconcile all things to him by making peace through his redemptive death.

In vv. 21-23, after his glorious "aside" on Christ, Paul returns to address the Colossians again. Before their conversion, they were alienated from God, enemies in attitude and deed. Now, they are reconciled by Christ's redemptive death, to be presented holy before him. Verse 23 stresses the need for perseverance in the gospel, not shifting to the false teaching of the apostates. Paul speaks of the gospel having been proclaimed in all creation under heaven. Saying this does not imply that the message has been fully preached in the world but that Christ has come. God has spoken once and for all in his life, death, resurrection, and exaltation. Now that glorious gospel must spread through the world. Hence, Paul ministers in the gospel to that end.

Paul's Ministry (1:24–2:5)

The focus of this section is Paul's ministry in the gospel. First, he speaks of his participation in the ministry of Christ in his suffering for the gospel to build God's church (v. 24). His ministry is to proclaim the Word, which is a mystery now revealed, and which Paul is preaching to the Gentiles (vv. 25-27). The gospel is Christ, the "hope of glory," which he proclaims so that people may believe and be mature in him. Paul works at this by God's power (vv. 28-29). Colossians 2 continues the theme of Paul's ministry and his struggle for the Colossians, the Laodiceans, and others evangelized by the likes of Epaphras. He ministers that they may be encouraged, unified in love, and know the fullness of Christ—"in whom all the treasures of wisdom and knowledge are hidden" (2:3).

In v. 4, Paul begins to shift to deal more directly with the apostasy prevalent in Colossae—he writes so that they are not deceived with persuasive speech. While absent from them, he is present with them in spirit, rejoicing at their orderliness and perseverance in the faith.

Counteracting the Heresy (2:6–23)

Having warned them not to be deceived, Paul urges them to continue to live in Christ, in whom they are firmly rooted. They are to be built up and established in their faith. They are to abound in gratitude (2:6-7).

Colossians 2:8 is a direct warning not to be captured by the false gospel based on philosophy, empty deceit, and human tradition that is premised on the *stoicheia*—forces that inhabit the false ideology of the teachers (cf. Gal 4:3, 8). Having warned them, Paul again exalts Christ (indicating that the heretics are diminishing him).

God's fullness dwells in Christ's body, and believers are filled with God in him. He is supreme over every ruler, spiritual or temporal. They have experienced the circumcision of their hearts, been buried with him in baptism, and raised with him through faith. Although previously dead in sins and uncircumcision as Gentiles, they are now alive in him, forgiven, and freed from the law, which is nailed to the cross in Christ. He has disarmed all evil forces, triumphing over them in his death and resurrection (2:9–14).

In 2:15–19, because of the work of Christ and their participation in him (therefore), they must reject the false teachers. They judge people based on what they eat and drink and their participation in the Jewish calendar, including the Sabbath (v. 16). This interest in food and holy days indicates a Judaizing aspect to the false teachers. Such things merely foreshadow Christ who has come. They, then, must not allow anyone to condemn them concerning participation in such things. They must not worship angels, get sidetracked into a concern for spiritual visions, become arrogant in their fleshly minds, and fail to hold fast to Christ, who holds his body together and grows it in God.

Colossians 2:20–23 challenges them not to return to such false principles, which are demonic, get obsessed with what perishable things they can touch and eat, and get caught up in human commandments and teachings. These things appear to be wise, but are self-made religious ideas, a false asceticism, and have little value in stopping the indulgence of the flesh. Undoubtedly, the heresy involves the Jewish law and the demand to live up to its demand for proper eating, holy days, and ritual purity. Such ephemeral concerns should not preoccupy a person in Christ.

Living the Heavenly Life (3:1–4:6)

As he does in Romans and Ephesians, having written with profound theology, Paul shifts to what life looks like for those in Christ. In 3:1-5a, as those who have died in Christ and are raised in Christ who is at the right hand of God in heaven, and whose lives are now hidden in the resurrected and exalted Christ, the Colossians are to set their minds on the things of God's reign and not of earth.

Ultimately, Christ will be revealed (the second coming), and they will be revealed with him in glory. In the meantime, they are to put to death that which is earthly in them. They are to kill off their past earthly preoccupations—sexual and other bodily passions, idolatrous greed, false speech, and all that is evil. Because of such things, God's wrath is coming on disobedient humankind (3:5b-8). They are to remove falsehood, take off their old selves, and be clothed in their new selves, renewed in knowledge in accordance with Christ, the image of God. Old racial and social divisions are demolished in this renewed humanity. Christ has come for all people (3:9-11).

Colossians 3:12-14 focuses on the virtues that should replace the old vices in God's holy and loved elect: affection, compassion, kindness, humility, gentleness, patience, tolerance, forgiveness, and especially love. They are to be unified with the peace of Christ, be grateful, allow the Word to indwell them richly, and worship together with praise and thanksgiving in song (3:15-17).

Colossians 3:18-4:1 is a mini-version of Ephesians 5:22-6:9, in which Paul addresses the socially "weaker" household members, reinforcing the cultural imperative to be submissive (wives to husbands, children to parents, slaves to masters). As in Ephesians, he addresses the paterfamilias, the father, urging them to act counterculturally toward the "weaker" family members. They are to love their wives, not embitter their children and treat slaves justly and fairly. The upshot is an appeal for mutual service within the Christian family.

In Colossians 4:2–4, the focus is prayer in a general sense and always with thanksgiving and prayer for Paul to have the opportunity to preach the Word (*logos*) and to do it clearly and well. We are encouraged to pray for those at the frontline of God's gospel mission.

Colossians 4:5–6 encourages the Colossians in their mission—they are to act wisely toward those from outside the church. Their gospel speech (*logos*) is to be full of grace, seasoned with salt (flavorsome), and then they will know how to answer those who enquire concerning the faith.

Paul's Plans, Greetings, and Instructions (4:7–18)

In Colossians 4:7–17, Paul ends with travel plans, greetings, and instructions. First, he mentions the coming of his beloved and faithful fellow-gospel worker and slave, Tychicus. His mention first suggests he is the letter courier who will encourage them, add more details to the letter, and return with news of the Colossians (vv. 7–8). Second, he mentions Onesimus of Philemon-fame, who is now a faithful and beloved brother in Christ who will add further information. The cross-reference places Philemon and his church in Colossae.

Paul then sends greetings from his Jewish coworkers, Aristarchus (in prison with him),[7] Mark (showing he and Paul reconciled after the split in Acts 15:36–41), and Jesus Justus (4:10–12). Then he adds information concerning another blessed coworker (slave of Christ), Epaphras, who planted the church and prays fervently for them, the Laodiceans, and Hierapolians (4:13–14, cf. 1:7; Phlm 23). Other greetings come from Luke, who wrote Luke-Acts (we learn that he is a doctor), Demas (v. 14, cf. Phlm 24, who later deserted Paul and

---

7. Acts 19:29; 20:4; 27:2; Phlm 24.

perhaps the Lord, 2 Tim 4:10). Paul greets the Laodiceans and those in the home of Nympha, a wealthy Colossian woman house church leader (v. 15). He instructs that the letter be also read in Laodicea, showing that his letters were not just read in one community of faith. Paul encourages Archippus, a key figure in Philemon's church and maybe his son, to complete his ministry (v. 17, cf. Phlm 2).

This passage is invaluable for our understanding of the early church. First, we learn more about Paul's coworkers. Second, the cross-references to Philemon, who is clearly in Colossae and shows that Colossians should be treated as an authentic letter as Philemon's authorship is not questioned. Third, we have two Gospel writers with Paul in Rome (Luke and Mark), and 1 Peter 5:13 confirms this. Hence, we do not need a long gap between the writing of Mark and Luke-Acts who used Mark.

Final Greeting and Benediction

Paul signs the letter writing the greetings with his hand, asks them to remember him in prison (i.e., pray for him), and as he usually does always, ends with a grace blessing.

Philemon

Here I will discuss Philemon in some detail.[8] Doing this will give an idea of how we might approach a letter of the NT. Philemon has been chosen as it is a short letter (335 Greek words, 25 verses) which we can briefly examine with some detail. In so doing, a clearer understanding of how to interpret the NT letters can be gleaned.

Scholars enquiring into NT letters take nothing for granted. They

---

8. For a fuller discussion, see Keown, *Discovering*, 2:352– 400 (Ch. 13).

ask a standard range of questions such as, "who wrote it?" (authorship); "when and where was it written?" (setting and date); "to whom was it written?" (recipients); "what is its structure?" (rhetorical form and structure); and "what is its message?" (purpose and themes). Inquiry into such things helps us understand the story behind the letter. We understand it first in its historical and social setting. Then we can apply what we learn to today's world.

Introductory Matters

Philemon is one of Paul's captivity (prison) letters and one of four written to an individual. It has the form found in many of Paul's letters: 1) Writer/sender—recipients—greeting; 2) thanksgiving and intercession; 3) letter body; 4) final greetings and blessing.

Authorship

While some scholars have challenged Paul's authorship, this is rare, and Philemon is recognized as one of the seven undisputed letters of Paul. Careful readers will note that Timothy is also named in v. 1. This is not uncommon as some of Paul's letters have others named alongside Paul in the prescript. Timothy may then be a co-writer, a co-sender, or Paul's amanuensis, who penned it on his behalf. Scholars consider which of these is most likely, with most seeing him as a co-sender and possibly amanuensis.

Date and Setting

Paul is in prison but does not name the city or date (vv. 1, 9, 10, 13, 23). The NT gives three possibilities.

1. Caesarea Maritima (c. AD 58–59): Few consider this possibility.
2. Ephesus (c. AD 52–55): Some believe this is the best because it is close to Colossae (160 km/100 mi); Paul's statements of suffering in Ephesus make it likely he spent some time in prison in Ephesus;[9] the imprisonment of Epaphras adds to this hypothesis (Phlm 24, cf. Col 1:7; 4:12); an earthquake destroyed Colossae in the early 60s.
3. Rome (c. 60–61): The traditional view is early in Paul's two-year Roman imprisonment (Acts 28:30) and before the earthquake; there is no concrete evidence Paul was ever in prison in Ephesus; Phlm 9 suggests Paul is an older man; co-workers with Paul fit Rome better than Ephesus.

While I prefer Rome, where Paul was at the time of writing does not significantly affect interpretation.

Recipients

These are named in vv. 1–2: Philemon, Paul's "beloved co-worker;" "Apphia," who is "our sister;" Archippus, as "our fellow-soldier;" and the church in "your (singular) house." Apphia may be Philemon's wife (or Archippus'). Her naming and designation "sister" may indicate she is one of the church leaders. "Your house" is likely Philemon's home, as he is named first. He is wealthy, owning a home with a guest room (vv. 1, 22), has slaves (v. 16), and hosts a church (v. 1). He is also generous in his love and benefaction toward other Christians (vv. 5–6) and Paul (vv. 7, 17–20, 22). Archippus is mentioned in Col 4:17 as a fellow soldier engaged in mission. There are numerous cross-references to Colossians which indicate that they live in Colossae, a city in the Lycus Valley in Asia Minor, inland from Ephesus near

---

9. 1 Cor 15:32; 16:8; 2 Cor 1:3–11; 4:7–5:10; 6:3–10; 11:16–29, esp. 2 Cor 11:23; also 1 Clem 5:6.

Hierapolis and Laodicea (compare esp. Phlm 1, 24 with Col 4:7–17). It is likely that Colossians, Ephesians, and Philemon were written at about the same time and sent with the same courier, Tychicus (Eph 6:21; Col 4:7). Philemon is clearly the primary person being addressed, the owner of Onesimus the slave, and the host of the church.

The Occasion

Using mirror reading, the story behind the letters becomes clear. Paul is in prison. The occasion of the letter is found in vv. 8–20. One of Philemon's slaves, Onesimus, has left Philemon and come to Paul in prison and has become a Christian (v. 10). He was formerly not much use to Philemon but is now a changed man, useful to Paul and his owner. (Interestingly, his name means "useful one," v. 11). Paul is sending him back to Philemon. The reason for the letter is to urge lovingly (not command) Philemon to receive him back not as a slave but as "a beloved brother," just as he would receive Paul if he were to come (vv. 12–17). Paul also offers to pay any costs incurred through Onesimus' flight (v. 18). Paul then expresses confidence Philemon will do what he asks (v. 21) and also asks him to prepare a room for his visit (v. 22).

There are three main views on why Onesimus came to Paul:

1. Support for Paul: Some consider Philemon sent Onesimus to Paul to help him. However, this is ridiculous as Onesimus is described as useless, and if Philemon sent him to help Paul, this is more of an act of sabotage.
2. Friend of the Master (*Amicus Domini* Hypothesis): In the Roman world, a slave could leave a master to find a "friend of the master" (*amicus domini*) to resolve a dispute between master and slave. Paul would be ideal for such reconciliation.
3. A Runaway Slave (Fugitive): The traditional view has been that Onesimus ran away from Philemon. He is then a kind of

"prodigal slave." He fled to Rome because it was crowded, sought out Paul, who he knew of from Philemon, and became a Christian. Paul is sending him back as a Christian and is asking Philemon to have mercy on him.

The most likely one of these is the third option which was the unanimous view of the early interpreters living in the Greco-Roman world.

The Social Setting

Some background issues, especially regarding slavery, help interpretation. Being a slave was tough in the ancient world. Slaves were owned. They had no freedom. Slaves in the Roman world were considered inferior family members and lived within the master's home. Some experienced severe suffering. They did all the work required by the master. Some were educated and did important work like medicine, architecture, and teaching; some were even philosophers. They could buy their freedom or could be manumitted. They often ran away when poorly treated, escaping overseas, hiding in big cities, and seeking asylum in temples. If they did run away, they could be punished; Philemon was legally allowed to mistreat or kill Onesimus; it was his choice. The types of punishment could include Onesimus being resold, scourged, branded, cut, made to wear an iron collar, crucified, thrown to beasts, forced to become a gladiator, or killed by some other means. Often this was done in public. A warrant for Onesimus' arrest would have been issued.

Paul was also in potential danger if he retained Onesimus, for he would be guilty of harboring a slave. He was already under light custody in his own rental accommodation, and the last thing he needed was to be found guilty of harboring a slave! However, with the owner's consent, he could assist a slave and purchase their freedom (peculium). With the letter, Paul may have intended that Philemon set Onesimus free.

The Form and Structure of the Letter

Some scholars treat Philemon as deliberative rhetoric in which the writer seeks to persuade readers to their point of view (e.g., Witherington).[10] This perspective has not found widespread support. Most break down the letter in this way:

1. Letter Opening: Phlm 1–7

    a. Prescript: Phlm 1–3
        i. Author/senders: Phlm 1a–b
        ii. Recipients: Phlm 1c–2
  2. Greeting: Phlm 3
  3. Thanksgiving and Prayer: Phlm 4–5
    a. Thanksgiving: Phlm 4–5
    b. Prayer: Phlm 6
    c. Assurance: Phlm 7
  3. Letter Appeal: Receive Onesimus back as a brother: Phlm 8–21[11]
    a. Appeal to receive back Onesimus: Phlm 8–17
    b. Promise to pay costs: Phlm 18–20
    c. Statement of confidence: Phlm 21[12]

---

10. Ben Witherington III, *The Letters to Philemon, the Colossians, and the Ephesians: A Socio-Rhetorical Commentary on the Captivity Epistles* (Grand Rapids, MI: Eerdmans, 2007), 3, 51.
11. Scholars disagree on whether Paul's appeal ends in v. 20, v. 21, or b. 22. I see v. 21 as the concluding statement and v. 22 as the beginning of his conclusion, which often includes travel plans.
12. Some consider this the end of the body, e.g., James D. G. Dunn, *The*

3. Letter Closing: Phlm 22–25
   a. Travel plans: Phlm 22
   b. Greetings: Phlm 23–24
   c. Salutation: Phlm 25

Comments on Each Section

Here, I suggest you have Philemon handy and read it verse by verse with these ideas in mind. These are short notes and questions.

Letter Opening (Phlm 1–7)

Prescript (vv. 1–3)

We see the usual pattern: writer/sender; recipient. Notably, in v. 1, Paul does not describe himself as an apostle. As the letter plays out, we see Paul pull back from exerting his apostolic authority, preferring to make his appeal based on love. Neither does Paul describe himself as a prisoner of Rome but as a prisoner of Christ Jesus. He may be in prison under the Romans, but his Lord is in control, and he is there for him. Timothy is named as either co-author, co-sender, or Paul's secretary. Apphia may be Philemon's or Archippus' wife. She is likely a leader of the church. Archippus is a gospel worker, as the term "fellow soldier" indicates (cf. Phil

---

Epistles to the Colossians and to Philemon: A Commentary on the Greek Text, NIGTC (Grand Rapids, MI; Carlisle: Eerdmans; Paternoster Press, 1996), 309; Douglas J. Moo, *The Letters to the Colossians and to Philemon*, PNTC (Grand Rapids, MI: Eerdmans, 2008), 397.

2:25). Colossians 4:17 also refers to his ministry. They have a church that meets in their house. We here see the rich acting as patrons to the church. It is another indicator that the early church was a house movement (as in underground church situations). Their church would be comprised of a group of up to 30 people. The church in Colossae was made up of house churches. The city would have been destroyed in the earthquake soon after receiving the letter.

Paul uses his standard greeting found in eight of his letters. His prayers for grace and peace ask God for his full blessings to be bestowed on the recipients. Grace and peace would include sufficient income to meet needs, good health, unity, perseverance, joy, and life in all its fullness. Importantly, the source is God and his Son, and the Spirit's work is implied.

Thanksgiving and Prayer (vv. 4–7)

In vv. 4–5, we see the usual thanksgiving of Paul using *eucharisteō*, "I give thanks" (see Rom; 1 Cor; Phil; 1 Thess; 2 Thess). There are also other thanksgivings in Ephesians and the Pastorals. This prayer indicates Paul's passionate life of intercession. He prays continually (1 Thess 5:17). He also remembers people when he prays, a vital facet of interceding for others. Verse 5 gives the reason for his prayer. Philemon is a notable example of living out the two great commandments (Mark 12:29–31): love for God and for people. He is clearly a generous man who loves Jesus.

Paul switches to prayer in v. 6, as he often does in his thanksgiving. Prayer begins with gratitude for what God has done; only then do we pray for more. "The sharing of your faith" is not about evangelism, as the older NIV translation suggests. It speaks of sharing what he has with others. "Sharing" is *koinōnia*, a great word in the NT for defining the extremely close relationship and partnership experienced by those whom God loves. Philemon is generous (v. 5). Paul prays that Philemon's work in supporting others may become more effective and christologically knowledgeable. The work he has in mind will be explained in what follows—receive Onesimus back.

Addressing him as "brother," in v. 7, Paul expresses the joy and encouragement he has experienced from Philemon. He has experienced this because Philemon has refreshed the hearts of other believers (saints). Some see this as flattery. This idea is flawed, as Paul renounces such duplicity (1 Thess 2:5). Instead, Paul seeks to win Philemon to his point of view. We see here how generous Philemon is. For wealthy Christians, he is an example. He provides refreshment leading to joy and comfort. The word for comfort is *paraklēsis* which can also be translated as "encouragement," which fits well here. Philemon is what we all should be—a source of joy and encouragement to others.

Appeal to receive back Onesimus (Phlm 8–17)

Paul's Confidence (v. 8)

In v. 8, Paul states his confidence that Philemon will do what is right. What stands out is Paul's pastoral approach.

Paul's Appeal from Love (v. 9)

Even though he knows he has the authority to command Philemon as the apostle to the Gentiles, he chooses not to. Instead, he makes his appeal out of love. Paul's approach is an example of outstanding pastoral leadership. He wants Philemon's willing response, not something coerced with threat and fear.

While the term *presbytēs* can mean "ambassador," the term tells us that Paul is elderly at this point. In the Roman world, this means he is over 50. If this is in Rome in the early-60s, he is probably somewhere in his mid-50s or 60s. Paul's age suggests Rome as the point of origin. Paul restates that he is a prisoner for Jesus Christ (as in v. 1).

The Appeal for Onesimus (vv. 10–17)

Verse 10 begins the body of the letter and states his purpose—it is an appeal on behalf of Onesimus. He is described as Paul's child, indicating he became a Christian under Paul (cf. 1 Cor 4:15; 1 Thess 2:11). Verses 11-13 is a parenthetical note concerning Onesimus. Verse 11 stresses Onesimus' transformation from a previously useless slave to someone useful to both Philemon and Paul.

Paul, here, uses a clever play on words. Onesimus means "useful." Yet, he was, up until his conversion, "useless" (*achrēstos*). Now he is what his name entails, "useful" (*euchrēstos*). *Chrēstos* sounds like *Christos* (Christ) and was even used for Christ in some instances. Paul may also have chosen the words because of their possible double meaning.

In v. 12, Paul describes Onesimus: "my very heart." The Greek for "heart" here is *splanchnon*, a term related to the guts, speaking of deep affection and compassion. The related verb is used in the Synoptic Gospels of Jesus' deep compassion for the despairing crowds of people who came to him for healing and hope (e.g., Matt 9:36; 14:14; 15:32). Paul uses it in Phil 1:8 of his yearning for the Philippians with "the affection of Christ Jesus." He used it earlier in Phlm 7 ("*hearts* of the saints") and will use it again in v. 20: "refresh my *heart*." The verse shows how close Paul and Onesimus have become. Paul's commendation is confirmed in Col 4:9, where Onesimus is a "faithful and beloved brother."

In v. 13, Paul tells Philemon that he would have liked to keep Onesimus with him so that he could serve with him in the gospel on behalf of Philemon. One can imagine their surprise to hear that the useless runaway Onesimus is now a Christian who worked in mission with Paul. His transformation shows that God can really change people. However, for Paul to retain Onesimus without Philemon's consent would be illegal (as Philemon owned Onesimus). So, he resolved to do nothing without Philemon's consent. Paul did not want Philemon to feel compelled to do his bidding but wanted his consent. As earlier, we see Paul's tactful pastoral approach.

In v. 15, Paul spins Onesimus' flight from Philemon in positive terms. While they were separated for a short time, this has produced good—Philemon can now have him back permanently. "Have him back forever" speaks of the eternal relationship Onesimus and Philemon will now have now that they are both Christians.

Verse 16 is explosive and potentially speaks of Paul wanting Philemon to set Onesimus free from slavery. Whether this is correct, Paul wants him to treat him as a much-loved brother, not a slave. In v. 17, he goes further—welcome him back as you would welcome me. For Philemon, after Jesus, Paul is the most crucial person in the world, leading him to Christ (v. 19). He is saying to welcome him back as Christian royalty! He is to welcome him as if he were the great apostle to the Gentiles himself! Doing this is a hint at the end of slavery. Considering v. 22, he asks Philemon not to take Onesimus back into the slave's quarters but to house him in a guest room reserved for dignitaries.

Some consider "in the flesh" to indicate Onesimus is Philemon's brother and Paul is mediating a matter of sibling rivalry. Instead, "in the flesh" means brothers in Christ in this world, and "in the Lord" speaks of eternal brotherhood.

Promise to pay costs (Phlm 18–20)

In vv. 18–19, Paul effectively writes a blank cheque for Philemon for any costs incurred. His doing this also suggests Onesimus has wronged Philemon. For a slave, time spent away from his master without permission was an act of theft. We see an interesting parallel in the NT with the Prodigal Son, who effectively ripped off his father and was welcomed home. Onesimus is the prodigal slave.

Paul, then, is like the Good Samaritan who offers to pay the costs for the injured man (Luke 10:35). He is also like Christ, who paid the price for our sins. With Philemon's wealth and generosity, it is unlikely Paul would have ended up paying anything.

In v. 20, the benefit Paul wants is not something for himself, but that he accepts back Philemon. Is it not interesting that Paul sees him paying the costs of Onesimus as producing benefit? "Refresh my heart" is not general but speaks of Paul being refreshed in his heart through Philemon accepting Onesimus back. Paul speaks as a father handing over his son to Philemon, effectively saying, "Please look after my boy." It also makes us think of God sending his Son to the world.

Statement of confidence (v. 21)

Paul ends with a statement of his confidence in Philemon. By doing this, Paul makes his final subtle appeal.

Letter Closing (Phlm 22–25)

Travel Plans (v. 22)

In asking Philemon to prepare a room for him, Paul shows his confidence that he will be released. This assurance fits with Phil 1:24–26, where despite facing death, Paul somehow *knows* he will get out of prison in Rome (or Ephesus). It shows that while Paul was a tentmaker providing for himself, he was willing to accept patronage in certain circumstances. It also shows that Philemon was wealthy, with a large house, including guest rooms. He also implicitly asks Philemon to pray for him. Such prayer requests are found in most letters. There is also a subtle nudge—"I am coming soon to see if you have obeyed the letter."

Greetings (vv. 23–24)

As he usually does at the end of a letter, he sends greetings from those with him. Those named are some of Paul's key co-workers, and it adds to our picture of the early church and its key figures.

Epaphras planted the Colossian church (Col 1:7), was a prayer warrior for them, may have also planted the Hierapolis and Laodicean churches (Col 4:12–13), and was in prison with Paul, as this verse testifies. He is also a prisoner of Christ Jesus, not the Romans. God is in control.

Seeing Mark's name here and in Col 4:10 tells us that Paul and Mark were reconciled after the big schism earlier (Acts 15:36–41). From Jerusalem and a relative of Barnabas (Acts 12:12, 25), Mark is one of Paul's few Jewish co-workers. He is traditionally the writer of Mark's Gospel. He is called Peter's son in 1 Pet 5:12, showing their close relationship. Indeed, as we have seen, he wrote down Peter's Gospel in Mark at the time of Peter's death (see Ch. 2).

We also see Luke's name. He is a doctor (Col 4:14) and Paul's traveling companion, as evidenced by the "we passages." He wrote Luke-Acts, and so in this verse, are named two of the great writers of the NT. He is in Rome with Paul, which indicates that he was in the right place to gather material for his work.

Aristarchus is mentioned as a traveling companion of Paul (Acts 19:29; 20:4) and was on the ship to Rome with Paul (Acts 27:2). He is a Macedonian from Thessalonica, no doubt converted on Paul's visit to the city (Acts 17).

Demas is also mentioned in Col 4:14 and is a Gentile co-worker. He deserted Paul near the apostle's death and may have fallen from faith as Paul says he was "in love with the present age" (2 Tim 4:10).

Salutation (vv. 25)

Paul usually starts with a statement of grace and ends with one. He does so here. He asks that the grace of Christ be with the spirit of the readers. This is a prayer that they experience God's gracious spiritual benefits in their inner beings.

Leadership, Culture, and Ethics in Philemon

Paul's letter to Philemon is very instructive regarding leadership, culture, and ethics.

Philemon: Leadership

We see the art of a wise leader in how Paul handles this situation.

Paul's Leadership

Paul is very diplomatic in the letter. As the apostle to the Gentiles and Philemon's father in the faith, he has the authority and courage to tell Philemon what to do (vv. 8, 14). Yet he does not exert that authority or exercise his boldness. Instead, with great love and affection, he seeks to get Philemon to respond to what is right. While his words can be seen as flattery, they are genuine. He calls Philemon a beloved co-worker, showing that he loves him and sees him as one of the team (v. 1). He honors all the good work he has done for himself and others. Philemon is not only using his house for a church but being lavishly generous, which has refreshed the hearts and lives of many Christians (vv. 4-7). Paul's language is full of love and affection, showing that he is not afraid to express emotion toward Philemon (v. 12).

He uses family language through the letter drawing Philemon into realizing their oneness in the family of God (v. 1, 2, 3, 7, 10, 16, 20). Seeing churches as families is a beautiful way to move toward the intimate unity God wants for his church. He uses clever plays on words as he describes the situation (v. 11).

The way he interprets his situation as imprisonment for Christ rather than for the Romans, and the manner in which he sees the good in such a difficult situation, shows that he sees the world through what God is doing rather than what appears to be the case. God is in control even if things seem dire. God works out his purposes even in the bleakest situations (vv. 1, 9, 15-16, 23).

His preparedness to count the financial cost of Onesimus' flight speaks of Paul's material generosity (vv. 18-19). This offer is astonishing when we consider Paul is not out working at this time; he is in prison. Ministry brings great financial sacrifice as we give up income to pursue God's call and as we sacrifice wealth in the service of our ministries. Yet, for Paul, this is no issue.

All that matters is the reconciliation of the two parties. Jesus said, "Blessed are the peacemakers" (Matt 5:9). Paul gives a brilliant example of reconciliation; he acts as the mediator between two conflicting Christian parties. He receives Onesimus and counsels him, including leading him to Christ. He then acts as a mediator with the one wronged, another Christian, Philemon. Paul seeks to bring peace where there is conflict. In Christian leadership, conflict resolution is one of the essential skills to develop. Paul shows us how here as he lovingly brings unity between the men.

Paul knows he needs support and refreshment, even if he does provide for himself. He welcomes Philemon's refreshment and accepts his hospitality (Phlm 7, 20-21). To be a successful minister of the gospel means we must allow people to care for us and provide for us to be sustained in our mission. Paul is unafraid to do this. However, he does not impose himself without gratitude.

Other Lessons About Leadership

Philemon and Onesimus

We can also learn some things about leadership from Philemon and Onesimus. Onesimus shows us that God can take a useless criminal, a runaway slave, and turn him into a Christian minister. In Col 4:9, he has become "our faithful and beloved brother" who is granted, with Tychicus, the honor of reporting to the Colossian church Paul's situation in Rome. He is to be taken back as a brother and apostle (v. 16). This is fantastic!

Philemon and Apphia

Philemon and Apphia are also pictured as great and generous Christian leaders. Philemon and Apphia, like Priscilla and Aquila and Andronicus and Junia (Rom 16:3-7), are probably a wealthy Asian Roman couple who host the church. They then are preparing to use their wealth and home for God's cause (vv. 1-2). They are full of love and faith, and to share their love and wealth, refreshing the hearts of other Christians and traveling missionaries like Paul and his team (vv. 3-7, 20, 22). Paul may write the letter to get what he wants to be done, but he does so confident of the right outcome (v. 21).

The Coworkers—Team Ministry

The mention of his co-workers in v. 23 reminds us of Paul's team philosophy. Those named are brilliant people. Epaphras planted as many as three churches in the Lycus Valley (Col 1:7; 4:12-13). Mark was also a traveling missionary working with Paul, Barnabas, and became a special friend of Peter (1 Pet 5:13). Luke too was terrific—a doctor who traveled extensively with Paul and wrote the epic Luke-

Acts saga telling the story of the origins of the Christian movement. The Thessalonian, Aristarchus, was a traveling companion of Paul who accompanied the Jerusalem Collection and traveled to Rome with Paul (Acts 19:29; 20:4; 27:2). Seeing these luminaries named together shows how brilliant people can work together without being threatened, needing to outdo one another, or caught up in envy and rivalry. Not that Paul was perfect. His breakup with Barnabas and Mark is legendary (Acts 15:36–41). Yet, they were reconciled by this point in Rome. Mark's links to Peter also show that there was unity between Paul and Peter, something also reflected in Peter's positive view of Paul's letters in 2 Pet 3.

Philemon: Culture

Mention has been made of Galatians 3:28, a text in which Paul succinctly states the social implications of the coming of Christ—in Christ Jesus, the great social divisions between Jews and Gentiles, men and women, and slaves and free find their consummation.

Philemon focuses on the ancient social division between slaves and freed people. Slavery was normative until 1833, when it was outlawed in the British Empire and at the end of the Civil War in the US in 1865. The story of William Wilberforce's campaign to see it end in Great Britain is well-known through the movie *Amazing Grace*.

Paul's letter to Philemon is one of the seeds of Scripture on which the movement formed. In this letter, he asks Philemon to receive back his formerly useless slave as a brother, welcoming him as he would welcome Paul, the apostle. Receiving back a slave that could be punished severely is astonishing.

We see here the cultural revolution that Christianity is designed to be. Great divisions no longer plague us as they have in the past. At the foot of the cross, all humankind, male and female, adult and child, Jew and Gentile, Pakeha and Māori, slave and free, rich and poor, kneel together as one without prejudice.

Our challenge as leaders is to build this kind of culture in the organizations and churches in which we work. While leaders are needed to bring order from chaos and move organizations toward God's purposes, there is no real status differentiation before God. Slaves can be co-workers and preachers (e.g., Onesimus, Col 4:9; Phlm 16). Women are equally able to do the required work of the gospel as men—it is a matter of gifts, call, and Christian character.

Where there are hierarchies, the leaders must work extra hard to ensure that while these exist, the "strong" are deeply concerned for the "weak." The organization's values should be those central to the gospel: honoring one another, humility, service, love, selflessness, sacrifice for others (especially for the vulnerable), gentleness, kindness, partnership, and the like (see further below).

The culture must be one of partnership and collaboration, as between Paul and Philemon; Philemon, Apphia, and Archippus; Paul and the co-workers of Phlm 24; and if Philemon hears Paul, between Paul, Philemon, and Onesimus. In this way, Christianity has the power to explode, which is not possible without such unity.

In NZ, we see something of this in the transformation of the All Blacks after Graham Henry took over the team in 2004. The team of leaders included three of the best coaches in the world: Graham Henry, Wayne Smith, and Steve Hansen. Yet, they laid their egos aside, dropped the players whose egos got in the way, and set about rebuilding the team's culture. They also set up a leadership group among the players, removing the top-down "do what I say" type of leadership and replacing it with a collaborative form of leadership led as much by the players as the coaches, who worked as a collective, along with a range of other coaches and supports staff. They began winning almost everything. They had a terrible setback at the 2007 World Cup. Yet, the NZRFU kept faith in the team. They won most tournaments from 2007 on, and in 2011 they won the RWC. Then, Steve Hansen took over, and the collective culture continued. They continued to win and won the 2015 RWC.

To me, these men were using tried-and-true methods of the gospel (even if they did not realize it). These include team leadership, establishing a culture of participation and collaboration, laying aside egos for the cause, forming a family culture, being authentic with each other, unity, and focusing on the cause. For Christians, to "win" means to be faithful to God's call to worship, love one another, and graciously share God's Word with unbelievers. Doing these things will yield results if we persevere, for the gospel is the power of God for salvation.

Philemon: Ethics

Cultures are based on shared values, ethics, and virtues. Philemon is full of them.

Love

Love is the supreme virtue that sums up all virtues. There is a lot of love language in Philemon. Philemon is beloved (v. 1), as is Onesimus (v. 16). God is thanked for Philemon's love toward Christ and all the saints (v. 5). Paul directly thanks him for the joy and comfort he has received through him and for the way he has refreshed the hearts of other believers (v. 7). Philemon embodies the twin commands of God to love him with everything and to love others (Luke 10:27). Paul also exemplifies love as he appeals to Philemon not from a position of dominance, but for *agapē*'s sake (v. 9). Paul's love for Onesimus is also apparent. He is his very heart!—he loves him deep in his gut! (v. 12).

Grace

Grace means "unmerited favor." In Christian thought, grace is God's generous kindness expressed toward humankind, especially in and through Christ. Paul begins and ends his letters with grace (Phlm 3, 25). The source of this lavish grace is God the Father and Jesus.

Joy

Joy is the second fruit of the Spirit (Gal 5:22). It is not merely happiness but something more profound, something not affected by a surface situation but which wells in the heart despite adverse circumstances. Paul is facing the struggles of a first-century Roman prison but casts his mind back to the joy he has received from Philemon (Phlm 7). Where the freedom of the Spirit is found, despite our responsibilities as God's people to please God and further his mission, there should be a mutual experience of joy.

Encouragement

As noted earlier, the Greek for "comfort" in Phlm 7 (*paraklēsis*) can be translated as "encouragement." Philemon provided Paul with joy and encouragement. *Paraklēsis* is also a spiritual gift in Romans 12:8, a gift Philemon has clearly received (as had Timothy, 1 Tim 4:13). God is the God of *paraklēsis* in Rom 15:5 and 2 Cor 1:3 (s.a. 2 Thess 2:16). We receive encouragement in Christ (Phil 2:1). True NT prophecy has the effect of *paraklēsis* (1 Cor 14:3). Whether we have the gift or not, we are to be a source of encouragement and comfort to others (see also 2 Cor 1:3–7).

Non-Coercion

Absolute authority gives people the power to compel people to do their bidding. A Christian value is that we wish people to respond with goodness, not from compulsion but of their own accord (Phlm 14). This attitude is seen in Jesus. Although he is equal to God, he "emptied *himself*," "humbled *himself*," and "gave *himself*" willingly for the world.[13] We see this value expressed in Christian giving, with each person giving without reluctance or compulsion. They give from the heart, "for God loves a cheerful giver" (2 Cor 9:7). The sign of an excellent Christian culture is one in which people want to participate and contribute. Paul's whole letter is designed to see this at a new level from Philemon.

Sacrificial Generous Self-giving

We see the value of self-giving and sacrifice powerfully in Philemon. First, Philemon and Apphia are models of self-giving as they use their home for the church and lavish generosity on Paul and the saints refreshing their hearts (Phlm 2, 5, 7).

Paul demonstrates self-giving in sending Onesimus back, a man he has come to love as a brother and co-worker, who is his very heart. He would have loved to have kept Onesimus with him to continue the gospel mission he and his co-workers were doing in Rome. However, as God was prepared to send his heart and Son Jesus to save the world, Paul willingly sent Onesimus back (Phlm 12–13). He knew to keep Onesimus without Philemon's consent was legally wrong, even if the ends justified the means (v. 14).

Hope

The language of hope is not explicitly used in Phlm. However, v. 15 calls to mind the hope of Romans 8:28, where Paul expresses his confidence that all things work for the good of God's loved and called people. Paul understood that while suffering is horrendous, it is temporary. Even though pressures and pain buffet us, the light of God dwells in us—jars of clay by his Spirit. This truth is powerfully

---

13. See Gal 1:3; 2:20; Eph 5:2; Phil 2:7, 8; 1 Tim 2:6; Tit 2:4.

expressed in 2 Cor 4–5. We have the light of the gospel in our beings, though we are frail, broken, and vulnerable (2 Cor 4:1–7). Because of the internal power of God in us, the Spirit, we are afflicted, crushed, persecuted, struck down, yet not defeated. We experience the sufferings that come to all humankind and those specific to Christians, yet the burning cauldron of God's presence is in us, sustaining us (2 Cor 4:8–12). Hence, we do not lose heart even if our outward bodies are failing us because God inwardly renews us daily (2 Cor 4:16). Further, we are earning an eternal weight of glory that makes our suffering pale into insignificance—eternal bodies and life with God forever (2 Cor 4:16–5:10). The presence of the Spirit and our certain futures give us hope. An authentic Christian community is founded on faith, expressed in love, and optimistic in hope.

Egalitarianism

In Philemon, an apostle writes to a group of church leaders about a slave, yet all participants in the letter form one family in Christ. There is no hierarchy of demand. The ancient world was full of hierarchies and pecking orders. We still see this today, especially in autocratic states and businesses. Christianity flattens the structures of the world. Egalitarianism can sometimes be frustrating for leaders who find it hard to get things done as quickly as they like. Consultation can annoy others who want leaders to get on with it. A hierarchical world often feels ordered and safe. Christianity is more daring. It invites all to participate, encouraging the priesthood of all believers. Inclusivism creates processes that mean it takes longer to get things done. But when there is synergy and people function from the kingdom's values, lead as servants, and do their God-given part, the church can explode with a power seen nowhere else in the world. The kingdom envisages the young and old, rich and poor, slave and free, and men and women from all cultures coming together with the common cause of the kingdom. Such possibilities should excite us in a multicultural city like my home city, Auckland, where the fields are ripe for the harvest (John 4:35) and plentiful, but the workers are few (Matt 9:36). Who knows what is possible?

Partnership

Paul uses *koinō–* language in the letter. He describes Philemon's generosity toward others as his "partnership (*koinōnia*) in the faith" (v. 7). He describes himself as Philemon's partner (*koinōnos*) in v. 18. He speaks of Timothy as a brother (Phlm 1).

He uses *syn* (with) language to emphasize partnership. Philemon is his "beloved co-worker (*synergos*)," working together for the gospel (v. 1). Archippus is his "fellow soldier," contending in the spiritual war for the world as a tightly knit army (*systratiōtēs*, cf. Eph 6:10–17). Epaphras is Paul's "fellow prisoner" (*synaichmalōtos*) "in Christ Jesus," speaking of a three-way bond between Paul, Epaphras, and Jesus (Phlm 23). Mark, Aristarchus, Demas, and Luke are Paul's "co-workers" (*synergos*), laboring together for the gospel (Phlm 24).

Father and Son dwell in an intimate partnership, extending grace and peace to the church (Phlm 3). There is a lovely partnership in prayer as Paul prays for Philemon (Phlm 4, 6), and through the prayers of Philemon, Apphia, Archippus, and the others in the church, he will be released to come to them (Phlm 22). There is a delightful father and son gospel partnership between Paul and Onesimus in Rome, cut short by Paul's need to send him home (Phlm 10–13). This ministry time must end because Onesimus must return to Philemon to continue the master-slave partnership, but in a wholly reframed way—master and slave serving together as brothers in the gospel in the Lycus Valley (Phlm 11–16). There is a partnership between all the Christians involved as they work "in Christ Jesus" (v. 8, 20) and "in the Lord" (v. 20). A financial partnership in the gospel is implied with Philemon blessing Paul and others lavishly (Phlm 4–7, 20, 22) and Paul's offer to repay what is owed by Onesimus (Phlm 19).

Hospitality

Hospitality, whereby we welcome and care for each other, is an essential Christian virtue. God and Christ are the ultimate hosts, inviting us into the Godhead so that we are "in Christ Jesus" (Phlm 8, 16, 20, 23). Hospitality is seen through Philemon and Apphia, who host a church (Phlm 1). They also provide for other saints and Paul himself (Phlm 4–7, 22). Despite his humble situation in imprisonment in his rented accommodation, Paul has hosted Onesimus as a father with a son and has led him to Christ (Phlm 10). Philemon is also to host Onesimus, not as a slave, but as a beloved brother and as if he were the apostle Paul himself. The letter implies Philemon is to house him in his guestroom set apart for the likes of Paul rather than the slave's quarters (Phlm 22). As the prodigal slave comes home, as does the Father in the Prodigal Son, he is to dress him in his best robe, place a ring on his finger and shoes on his feet, kill the fattened calf, and party (Luke 15:22–32). As the angels in heaven rejoice when one sinner is saved, Philemon's whanau and church are to party like it is 1999 for the lost sheep who has come home, for the coin that was lost but now is found (Luke 15:7).

Part 2: Philippians

Philippians is a brilliant little letter in which we see Paul's deep pastoral concern for his converts. It is often seen as a letter full of joy without a significant issue in the church; however, that is misguided. As we will see, the letter indicates a range of issues. Still, joy beams through the letter as we read it. We begin looking at introductory matters, followed by a quick skim through the letter.[14]

---

14. Students who are interested can consult my commentary for

Background Matters

The authorship of Philippians is uncontested, and it is considered one of the undisputed letters of Paul as it is seen as consistent in style and theology with others. In other words, Paul wrote it (Phil 1:1). Paul also names Timothy in the prescript because he was present when the church was evangelized (Acts 16:1–40), he plans to send him to Philippi (2:19, 23), and he will mention Timothy as an example to the Philippians (2:19–24). Timothy may have been Paul's scribe, and most scholars think he is a co-sender rather than a co-author.

The date and provenance are disputed. Paul is obviously in prison (1:7, 13–14, 17). From early writers until the mid-nineteenth century, Christians agreed he wrote it in Rome sometime in the 60s. However, in recent scholarship, two other theories have been posited. A few scholars have proposed his imprisonment in Caesarea Maritima as the place of writing sometime in AD 58–59. A good portion of other modern scholars holds he wrote it in Ephesus sometime AD 52–55, around the same time as 1 and 2 Corinthians, Romans, and perhaps Galatians. Those in favor of Ephesus highlight the great distance from Rome to Philippi (1283 km) and his great suffering in the city (esp. 2 Cor 1:8–11). Traditionalists hold that the early church is more likely to know where he wrote it and that there is no actual evidence Paul was imprisoned in Ephesus. I side with the traditionalists, as my commentary defends. However, it is essential to note that good evangelicals have different views, and the letter is not specific—it doesn't affect the meaning of the sacredness of the text. In my view, Paul wrote the letter after his situation in

concentrated detailed work. Mark J. Keown, Philippians, EEC, 2 vols. (Bellingham, WA: Lexham, 2018). For a concentrated shorter analysis, see Mark J. Keown, "Philippians." https://www.thegospelcoalition.org/commentary/philippians/.

Rome deteriorated compared to the "easy" imprisonment of Acts 28:30-31, which we can date AD 60-61. He was about to go to trial, and the outcome was uncertain, although Paul was strangely confident (1:19-26). So, a date around AD 62-63 in Rome seems appropriate. People also debate whether he got out of prison or whether Philippians is his last letter. I believe he did; however, we can't be sure.

Another matter of debate is the integrity of the letter. Some recent scholars have argued that Philippians is made up of three of Paul's letters to Philippi fused into one. Part 1 includes Ch. 1-2; Part 2, 3:1-4:2 or 9; and Part 3, 4:10-20. For them, it is a composite letter (as some view 2 Corinthians). However, most contemporary scholars are siding against this view, noting that the letter has themes and language found throughout each part of the letter, complicating interpretation unnecessarily.

The recipients are the Christians of Philippi. Philippi was not the capital of Macedonia but a town of about 10,000-15,000 people, which the Romans highly loved. Their favored status was because one of the great wars in the Roman civil wars, the Battle of Philippi, happened on the plains beside the town. They supported Octavian, who eventually became Emperor Augustus, and as a result, were afforded the privilege of being a colony. Many retired Roman soldiers were given land, and it was a very Roman town, and many of its inhabitants were proud of it. It is unique among the towns Paul visited in that there was no synagogue, only a place of prayer. This all female gathering outside the town indicates there were few, if any, Jews and Jewish men in the town. The only person we are sure of is Lydia, a woman from Asia Minor who was a businesswoman who traded fine purple for the elite and a gentile God-worshiper. The town's Roman orientation is seen in inscriptions and the charges brought against Paul and Silas in Acts 16:21.

We read of Paul's evangelization of the town in Acts 16 on his second Antiochian mission. He was directed away from further evangelization in Asia Minor to Macedonia in a vision from God. He, Timothy, Silas, Luke, and any unnamed others traveled from Troas to Neapolis, the port of Philippi, about sixteen km southwest on the Aegean Sea. He traveled to Philippi and evangelized a group of women by the river Zygakti and Lydia was converted. Later, Paul exorcised a demon from a girl with a Pythia Spirit, who brought messages from the god Apollos. He and Silas we then imprisoned for offending Roman customs after being flogged. A great earthquake set them loose, but instead of fleeing, they stayed and led the Roman Jailor to the Lord with his family. Philippians mentions a few others, including a brave leader Epaphroditus, two women, Syntyche and Euodia, and Clement (who reputedly became Bishop of Rome years later, 2:25; 4:2–3).

The letter indicates that the Philippian church was a special church for Paul. They uniquely supported Paul financially in his mission (4:10–19). They participated in the gospel in other ways, including prayer (1:19), suffering (1:29–30), and gospel proclamation (4:2–3). Paul speaks glowingly of the church throughout the letter.

The main issue raised in the letter is the matter of unity. The matter of unity is hinted at indirectly throughout the letter (e.g., 1:12–18a) or with injunctions (1:27–2:4; 2:14–16), with much of its message aimed at ensuring the Philippian church did not become another Corinth. Indeed, every part stresses partnership in the gospel, love, unity, and other vital themes. It climaxes in 4:2–3 with Paul urging two church women to unite in their thinking in the Lord. These two women, Euodia and Syntyche, must have been significant for Paul to be so concerned. Perhaps they were overseers or deacons, who Paul singles out in his prescript as recipients of the letter with all the church. Paul is not merely urging unity but unity in the Lord and the gospel. These evangelists must stop arguing and come together in the Lord to shine like lights in the world as they allow their gentleness to be seen by all (4:4) and hold forth the word of life (2:15–16).

The other matters the letter addresses include the need to continue to share the gospel despite opposition (1:12–30; 2:12–18), perseverance in suffering (1:28–30), joy (mentioned 16 times in the letter), right thinking in the Lord (esp. the Greek *phroneō*, "think" mentioned ten times), standing firm against false teachers (3:2–21), and Paul's gratitude for their financial support (4:10–20). One of the core ideas in the letter is citizenship, which would have appealed to people who loved their Roman identity. The Philippians are to continue to live as citizens worthy of the gospel (1:27) as they await their savior from heaven, Jesus (3:20). Another important theme is hope, as Paul mentions, again and again, their future expectation of salvation, the prize of eternal life, their transformation to bodies of glory, when Jesus returns.

The central theological passage in the letter is the so-called "Christ-hymn" in 2:6–11. It may have been an early church hymn or a composition of Paul that tells the story of the preexistent divine Son's coming to earth to die on the cross and be exalted as Lord and God. It also summons people to emulate his example of humble servanthood in life and mission. He is the supreme example of what it means to be a Christian. Other examples dot the letter, which I will highlight in the overview, including especially Paul himself, Timothy, and Epaphroditus, among others.

Overview of the Letter

Prescript (1:1–2)

Paul begins naming himself and Timothy. They are a team, unified in the mission of God—so right from the start, Paul stresses unity in mission. He does not then say "apostle of Christ Jesus" or something similar as in so many letters, but states that they are "slaves of Christ Jesus." The preference for "slaves" indicates Paul is not exerting apostolic authority but is calling the Philippians (and us) to take up the same posture toward each other and the world. He addresses the letter to "all the saints (or holy people) in Christ Jesus," reminding them of their identity and status as God's holy people. He locates them in Philippi and, uniquely in his letters, singles out the church's key leaders—the overseers (elders) and deacons. Christian leaders should sit up and take note of Philippians in particular. He adds his usual greeting blending the Greek "grace" with the Hebrew "peace." This prayer is to the only true source of these things, God and Jesus. God is labeled "Father," meaning now, for the Philippians, Yahweh transcends Jupiter/Zeus and all other so-called deities. He names Jesus "the Lord Jesus Christ." At the time of Philippians, Nero ruled in Rome and held Paul prisoner (he would kill him a few years hence). But for Paul's team and the Philippians, Jesus is Lord! He is also Israel's Messiah who came to save the world.

Thanksgiving and Prayer (1:3–11)

The warmth Paul feels for the Philippians is seen in him beginning the letter with thanksgiving to God (as he does in many letters). He gives thanks for *all* of them *every* time he remembers them, and he does so with joy (vv. 3–4). Verse 5 gives the reason—because of their "fellowship/participation in the gospel" from the day they became Christians (v. 5). The letter expounds on the many ways they partnered with Paul, including the things mentioned in the introduction. Verse 6 is traditionally seen as referring to their salvation—God will bring it to completion at the consummation (the day of Christ Jesus). Many scholars, including myself, argue that the good work is the work of mission—God will bring the partnership of the gospel to completion. Either way, it is a note of assurance. Grace in v. 7 is similarly debated—it can be the grace of salvation or Paul's missional grace. Either way, Paul knows it is right to feel good about the Philippians because they share with him in grace. So, he has them in his heart because they share with him in his mission of the defense and establishment of the gospel in the Roman world. So desirous for them is he that he calls God to the dock as his witness to testify to his deep affection for them (v. 8). The term for affection is splagchnon from the same Greek root that gives us the word for Jesus' great "gut compassion" on the crowds in his ministry (e.g., Matt 14:14). Paul feels gut love for his longed-for ones in Philippi. Notable here is Paul's use of the language of partnership and love throughout the thanksgiving is already summoning them to unity.

The prayer in 1:9-11 is focused on love—Paul wants them to overflow with rivers of love. This love is not to be scattered around willy-nilly; it is a discriminating and insightful love that will enable them to know the best course of action in any situation. Knowing that they are becoming disunified, this first calls them to love one another. However, it means more than that—they are to love God, love one another, love Paul and his team, and love the lost. Paul wants them to do this so they will be filled with the righteous fruit of the Spirit that flows from being declared righteous by faith in Christ. Then, they will be blameless and pure, confident as they stand before God on the day of Christ's return and the judgment. This fruit comes from Christ and brings glory to God.

The Gospel's Advance (1:12–18a)

Rather than launch into a direct appeal to the Philippians, Paul starts the letter proper with a report on his situation. He does this for two reasons. First, they no doubt were very concerned for Paul, having heard of his imprisonment and forthcoming trial. Second, Paul uses his situation to challenge them to continue the gospel mission in unity rhetorically. The passage runs from 1:12-26 and is broken into two parts.

In part one (1:12-18a), Paul does not dwell on his own suffering but on the gospel's progress. This passage shows his priorities—the gospel, the gospel, the gospel. In vv. 12-14, he tells them the good news that despite his horrible situation in prison, where he no doubt faced extreme hardship and danger, the gospel is advancing like a military invasion. If this is Rome, as I suspect, it is penetrating the heart of Nero's court as soldiers and others involved in his situation have come to know why he is in prison—Christ! Equally exciting, in v. 14, he explains that most Christians at his point of imprisonment have become fired up to share the gospel fearlessly. Christ is using his situation to inspire others to evangelize—this is excellent news for the evangelistically active Philippians.

However, vv. 15-18a indicate that there are two groups within these preachers—the well-motivated and the poorly motivated. Both groups preach Christ, and so are authentic Christians, not false teachers. However, one group is motivated by attitudes like envy, rivalry, and selfish ambition and wants to cause Paul to suffer in prison. They are likely led by some who do not like Paul and are jealous of his impact and standing. They may be Romans who returned after Claudius' edict subsided and had lost power in the church. The others are exemplary—they preach Christ out of goodwill toward Paul and others, out of love, and they recognize that Paul is in prison because he is appointed to defend God's gospel in the Roman world. Paul wants the Philippians to emulate the well-motivated evangelizers and not share the gospel to advance their own status. Despite these two groups, Paul rejoices because whether they are well motivated or not, Christ is being preached. In the end, that is what matters. This passage is good news for us because the gospel is advanced despite our weaknesses, disunity, and failings if we preach Christ.

In the second part of the passage, 1:19-26, Paul focuses more on himself and the Philippians. He not only rejoices that the gospel is preached but because he knows that his situation will turn out for his salvation. "Salvation" is a play on words here. It can either mean "deliverance" (in that he gets out of prison) or eternal salvation. Paul means both. Whatever happens, it will turn out for his release, and if not, and he is killed, he will be saved anyway. He is confident because of the prayers of the Philippians and, more importantly, the help (or the supply of) the Spirit of Jesus. Verse 19 speaks of partnership in mission—we pray for each other, God acts by his Spirit, and his purposes are achieved.

Because of their prayers and the Spirit, in v. 20, Paul is confident that at his coming trial before Nero, he will be full of courage to boldly give witness to Jesus so that Christ is glorified in his speech and, if need be, in his death. That is because for Paul, ongoing life is being in Christ and Christ working in and through him, but to die is to gain even more (1:21). Ongoing earthly fleshly life will mean more ministry, more converts, more disciples mature in the faith (1:22a). Still, Paul is torn as to whether he wants to die or live (v. 22b). Indeed, he will not make known to the Philippians what he will choose, showing he believes he has power over his situation. In v. 23, he ponders life and death and is torn between the two. He desires to die and be with Christ, which is the greatest thing. Yet, in v. 24, it is way better for the Philippians (and his other converts) that he remains. As such, in v. 25, he states his knowledge (to this point withheld) that he will remain and continue with them so that they progress and rejoice even more in the faith (v. 25). There is rich debate over why Paul speaks as he does here. Perhaps he had a word from God; perhaps he had been told he would be released; perhaps he had an escape plan. Who knows? He will remain so they can boast more and more about Jesus because of his return to them. Through this passage, Paul shows the struggle of being a Christian in ministry and great suffering. He chooses life and ongoing ministry and is an example to us all.

Live as Citizens Worthy of the Gospel (1:27–30)

Philippians 1:27-2:18 is a unit with Philippians 1:27-2:4 and 2:12-18 forming a frame around the Christ-hymn in 2:5-11. The framing passages give the essence of the appeal to the Philippians, restated twice differently. The center gives Christ as the supreme example they are to emulate—Jesus!

It begins in 1:27-30 with the first command of the letter. English translations err by not stressing citizenship, which lies at the heart of the appeal. The core command is "Only live as citizens worthy of the gospel of Christ." The Romans cherished citizenship and despised slavery. Here, Paul is speaking about heavenly citizenship, a theme he will return to in 3:20. They are to live as citizens of heaven on earth by the life of the gospel. They are to do it whether Paul is with them or not. In what follows in 1:27c–2:4, Paul will describe their activity and the appropriate attitudes they are to embody as they live out their citizenship. First, he uses athletic and military language to describe how they will fulfill their duty as citizens. Like a Roman army standing and moving in perfect unison and unity, they are to "stand firm in one Spirit." The Spirit here can be their oneness, or the Holy Spirit, which binds them together (cf. 2:1; 4:1). Like athletes and soldiers, they will contend as one soul together for the faith of the gospel. This standing means ongoing unified missional contention, whether defending the gospel or advancing it (as Paul is doing in Rome). In v. 28, he stresses they are to do this courageously like those fearlessly sharing the gospel in Rome (1:14). While their opponents are real, they are not to be intimated by them. He encourages them in v. 28 that their ongoing contention for the gospel and their opponents' ongoing opposition function as a sign of their mutual destinies—salvation for the Christians. For the opponents,

In v. 29, Paul reminds them that they should not be surprised at their suffering; it is granted to believers as a package to believe in Jesus for salvation and to suffer for him. Verse 30 tells us the nature of their suffering—as Paul experienced yesteryear in Philippi and presently in Rome, they are being opposed by local Macedonians. Indeed, some may be going to prison as he is.

The Attitudes of the Heavenly Citizen (2:1–4)

In Philippians 2:1–4, Paul shifts from what they are to do to their attitudes as they do it. In v. 1, he reminds them of what they have in Christ—encouragement, comfort from love, the fellowship of the Spirit, affection, and compassion. This grace-laden unity is what they experience, what should shape their existence, and what should flow from them into the world. Because they have these things, Paul appeals to them to "make my joy complete" in v. 2a. How? By four things in v. 2b: 1) having the same mindset, 2) embodying the same love, 3) being bound with the same soul, and 4) having the one mindset. This verse is an appeal to unity in the gospel. Verse 3 warns them away from the selfish ambition of the falsely motivated preachers in his setting (1:17) and seeking empty glory for themselves (this is the way of the world). Instead, clothed in humility (as is Jesus, see v. 8), they are to esteem others above themselves and look out for the interests of others, and not only their own needs and wants.

Have the Mindset of Christ (2:5–11)

Some think this passage is the center of Paul's thought and ethics and is undoubtedly foundational to his cruciform perspective. It begins with Paul shifting their attention to Jesus—they are to have the mindset Jesus had when he left preexistent glory in heaven to come to earth to serve and die the worst of all Roman deaths—that of a slave and a criminal, a cross! If the Philippians get this—their unity will be assured.

The hymn traces the movement of Jesus in his incarnation, life of service, death, resurrection, and glorification as Lord of the world. It begins with Jesus existing as the invisible God in very form with full divine majesty (equality with God). However, although he could have come to earth and forced the world to submit like a glorious ancient Emperor, he did not use his status and power for such a Satanic purpose.

Instead, in v 7, he emptied himself. This metaphor does not mean he was no longer divine or did not have his divine attributes;

instead, it means he poured himself out for the world in service and death to save it. He did this by taking the form of the lowest of the law, a slave. He was still in the form of God, but he clothed himself in the form of God's Servant, a slave to all. He did this assuming human likeness—the new Adam. Whereas Adam failed, this man did not. He humbled himself by becoming obedient in every moment of his life to the point of death as the sinless one who fulfilled God's law in every way. He took this all the way to the most humiliating death imaginable for a Roman—crucifixion! This movement is Christ's descent from being the greatest and most gloriously honored Being in the Cosmos beside God, his Father, to the lowest—naked on a cross, butchered mercilessly as a slave or thief, killed and paraded before the world in humiliation.

Notably, perhaps intentionally for dramatic effect, Paul jumps past the burial, resurrection, and ascension to Jesus the exalted Lord in v. 9. Therefore! God exalted him! From the lowest of the low to the highest of the high. God gave him the name above all names, which can only be "God," the only name that cannot be trumped. God humbles himself in this regard, and we see the partnership of the gospel at its essence.

His purpose and the result are that every being in the cosmos will bow the knee to Jesus and confess that he is Lord. This declaration is the fulfillment of the vision of Isa 45:23, where the world bows to Yahweh—now it is Jesus! He is "God with us!" Not only is he Lord, but also Savior (3:20). This passage declares the mission—to go to the world and tell them Jesus is Lord and Savior. Many will willingly bow and confess—they will be glorified. Many will reject and be enemies of the cross—they will bow and then be destroyed.

Work Out Your Salvation (2:12–18)

Paul begins this section with "therefore," alerting readers that what follows is how we should respond to the Christ hymn and its implicit appeal to emulate Jesus. We are to be ever obedient, as the Philippians have been from the first. They and we are to "work out our own salvation." Verse 12 does not appeal to "work for our salvation" as if we can gain it through good works. Instead, if we believe, we are saved and are to work that salvation out by following the instructions of Paul in the letter and the whole Bible. We do it with "fear and trembling," which speaks of knowing who our God is—we should always relate to him with reverence, awe, and a knowledge that he can be a consuming fire (as Hebrews warns us, 10:29, cf. Exod 24:17).

However, we cannot do this in our own strength. Verse 13 tells readers that God supplies the strength, working in them to will and act according to his good purpose. In v. 14, Paul applies more directly to their situation of disunity and what it means for them to work out their salvation obediently. They are not to grumble like Israel in the wilderness. Nor are they to argue with each other, which is likely one of their issues. If they put those vices behind them, they will be blameless and innocent children of God in their fallen and corrupted culture. They will shine like lights in the world (cf. Matt 5:16) or stars in the universe.

It is debated whether Paul means "hold fast" or "hold forth" the word of life in v. 16a. I have argued forcefully for "hold forth," which is a lovely metaphor used in the Roman world of offering food or drink, pushing forward sword (Eph 6:17), and so on. Either way, Paul means "the gospel." And, of course, believers should both hold the word and offer it to others. This effort is all so Paul can be confident before God at the judgment.

In v. 17, Paul gives us a hint of his suffering, which he describes as being poured out as a drink offering (libation). As Paul is confident of release (1:19, 25), this does not refer to his death but his life of service. He is being poured out on the sacrifice and service of the faith of the Philippians. The drink offering was the secondary offering, so by saying it this way, Paul highlights their suffering and service—a beautiful image of partnership in the gospel. In 2:17b-18, Paul uses joy language four times to invite them to rejoice with him as he rejoices over them. We see the juxtaposition of suffering and joy—the paradox of being a Christian.

Travel Plans and Two Great Examples (2:19–30)

In Philippians 2:19-30, Paul cleverly does two things. First, he tells them his plans to send Timothy and Epaphroditus to them. Second, he gives them two more examples to emulate by commending their service for the gospel and their unity with Paul. Paul, in this passage, is like God sending Jesus to the world to save it as he sacrificially gives up two of his best workers to go to Philippi to ensure they are okay.

He starts expressing his hope to send Timothy depending on how his trial goes (v. 19). He then commends him for his uniqueness in his concern for others and the interest of Jesus and partnering with Paul in the gospel (vv. 21-22). After repeating his hope of sending him (v. 23), Paul tells them he hopes to come soon (1:24, recalling 1:19-26).

He then tells them he is sending Epaphroditus, who will no doubt carry the letter to them. He commends him powerfully with five descriptors. He is Paul's brother, a coworker (gospel minister), and a fellow soldier (another term for gospel worker). Again, they are partners, and Paul is subtly appealing to the Philippians to put aside their disagreements. Epaphroditus is also "your *apostolos* and servant to my need." Scholars discuss whether Paul means "messenger" or he means "apostle" (as I argue). Either way, he is their gospel worker, and he has shown them the way in what he has done.

He has brought Paul financial support from the Philippians and nearly died doing so. Paul assures them of Epaphroditus' love, concern for them, and his merciful recovery that spared him great grief (2:26-27). His reason for sending them is that they may rejoice at his return and welcome them home with honor for his courageous service in bringing the gift (vv. 28-29). The Philippians are comforted that their man has recovered and come home and that Paul has received the help he needs. They are also challenged to emulate Epaphroditus' service and unity in the gospel with Paul and Timothy.

Warning Against the Judaizers (3:1–14)

In this section, Paul does three things. First, he warns them of the false teachers demanding that gentiles obey the law of Moses for salvation and inclusion. If we are right to date Philippians in the early 60s, this shows that despite the Jerusalem Council, Judaizers were still active in the church. By warning the Philippians, Paul shows that there are limits on Christian inclusion—where the gospel is being irrevocably corrupted, people are to be rejected. Secondly, the way he puffs up his resume and then writes it off as rubbish or excrement is an intentional mirroring of Jesus—the greatest Being aside from God in the universe, and yet who emptied himself for the world. What matters is not us; it is Jesus! He is Paul's everything, and he is ours. Third, it implicitly urges the Philippians to emulate Paul's attitude, something he will directly say as he moves into the next section.

In v. 1, Paul calls the readers to rejoice in the Lord (recalling 2:18 and anticipating 4:4). Their joy is not in suffering or false teachers, but the Lord—he is the basis for joy whatever is going on in our lives. Paul tells them that it is no bother to remind them again of the Judaizers—this safeguards them.

Verse 2 is a stunning description of the Judaizers using the same Greek verb *blepete*, "watch out for," three times in a row. First, they are to watch out for these people who consider the gentiles (including the Philippians) dogs are themselves dogs. Second, they are to watch out for them as they are workers of evil, hinting at their demonic power. Third, they are to watch out for those who demand circumcision (*peritomē*) but are, in fact, mutilators (*katatomē*). They are no different from the Galli of Galatia, who castrated themselves to become priests of Cybele.

Paul responds to the three descriptors of the Judaizers, with four to define Christians. The Philippians should take no notice of their poison because they and all Christians are now the "circumcision," the renewed people of God, including faithful Jews and gentiles across the world. They worship in and by the Spirit. They boast in and about Jesus the Messiah. And they do not place their confidence in the flesh as these foolish Judaizers do (v. 3).

In vv. 4-6, Paul shifts to himself. If a person in the world could be confident before God and claim righteousness through the law (as these Judaizers demand), it is him. He has more extraordinary claims than any other Jews, reflected in his seven-fold resume. He is a true Jew—circumcised on the eighth day, an Israelite from the favored tribe of Benjamin, a full-blown Hebrew in every way, and an honored member of the strictest sect in Israel, the Pharisees (vv. 4-5, cf. 2 Cor 11:22). Moreover, it was he who led the way persecuting the church zealous for the traditions of his nation (cf. Gal 1:13-14). He was blameless in his commitment to be righteous by the law (v. 6).

He then mirrors Christ's self-abnegation by writing these seemingly eternally profitable things off as loss and dung. They pale into nothingness compared with the most extraordinary thing of all—knowing Christ Jesus my Lord, for whom he has given up all these things (vv. 7-8). He has done so to gain Christ and be found in him, not through righteousness gained through his own effort to obey the law, but through faith in Christ (vv. 8-9).[15]

He did this for five reasons: 1) so he would truly know Jesus, 2) he

---

15. Or "the faith of Christ," or "the faithfulness of Christ." Here, I believe it is "faith in Christ," as Paul is stressing what he did to become a Christian—he believed in Jesus instead of "doing the law" for righteousness.

would know the power of the Spirit through whom God raised him from the dead, 3) he would experience the fullness of suffering in, for, and with Christ, 4) that he would be conformed to Christ's death, and 5) that he would attain to the resurrection from the dead. This five-fold description should motivate all Christians to emulate Paul, who emulates Christ, who is the image of God (cf. Rom 8:29; 1 Cor 11:1).

Still, in vv. 12-14, Paul stresses to the Philippians that he is not there yet! He hasn't received all that God promises him in Christ in the age to come; he is not yet perfect. Instead, like a great athlete racing for the Olympic gold and wreath, he presses on toward that call of God when the day comes. He is confident because God has taken hold of him in Christ. But Paul does not rest on his laurels—the one thing that matters to him is to keep running until he gets there. The Philippians are to do the same.

Imitate Paul and Others Like Jesus (3:15–17)

Paul makes explicit what is implicit—his desire for them to emulate his attitude, which will heal any rifts among them and ensure the gospel is untarnished and can continue to spread through the gentile world. The mature Philippians should listen and agree. Still, if they don't, Paul is confident God will reveal the rightness of Paul's instructions (v. 15). They are to live up to what they have attained in Christ—righteousness by faith and not law (v. 16). They are to join together and imitate Paul. Furthermore, they are to closely watch Christians who follow the way of the cross, as do Timothy, Epaphroditus, and others who follow their lead.

Warnings of Other Enemies (3:18–19)

The warning of "enemies of the cross" may be Judaizers who Paul parodies. Alternatively, it is a general warning against all who oppose the message of a crucified Messiah. Or, as I have argued, it warns them of gentiles who persecute Christians and live licentious debauched lives. Whoever is in view, Paul tearfully repeats earlier warnings that many in the world oppose God and his crucified Son. In v. 19, Paul gives a fourfold description of them: 1) their end is eternal destruction, 2) they worship their god—their earthly appetites (the Greek can be stomach or genitals), 3) their glory is in their shameful lifestyles that will end in eternal shame; and 4) their focus is on the things of the world, stuff, materialism, consumerism—not the things of God. These people are to be rejected because they are idolatrous consumers who do not know God.

Our Citizenship and Hope (3:20–21)

If the enemies will end in eternal destruction and shame, it is not so for the Philippians. Their citizenship is in heaven (1:27), where their names are inscribed in the book of life (4:3). They are then citizens of heaven left on earth to represent God and establish his reign forming colonies of righteousness into which the world is invited. But we are not deserted but have hope. Our hope is the future coming of our Savior, the Lord Jesus Christ (v. 20). Paul assures them of what will then happen. When the Savior comes at his Parousia, he who is in the form of God (2:6), took on the form of a slave and died on a cross (2:7–8), who was raised to Godness (2:9), will conform us, who have taken on his slave-form in service for our lives, transforming our bodies of humiliation, into bodies of glory—just like his! (v. 21a). How do we know? Because he has the power to bring all things under his feet (Ps 110:1), he must be able to transform us into eternal beings with him forever in the twinkling of an eye.

Appeal for Unity (4:1–3)

Paul now gets direct to the contending groups in the church led by Euodia and Syntyche. But before he does, we see his skill as a pastor in his six-fold commendation of the Philippians. The first five head the verse: 1) my beloved, 2) my brothers and sisters, 3) my greatly desired ones, 4) my joy, 5) and crown. These assure the Philippians of his love for them and their status as God's children and heaven's citizens. He then echoes 1:27 by urging them to be like Roman soldiers in tight unison at war and "stand firm in the Lord." There is no room for division and disunity in the Roman army, let alone God's people. He then finishes the verse with a repetition of the first term: 6) beloved. Note how twice they are "beloved"—the Philippians are loved by God and Paul—they must love one another as must we.

Paul then gets direct. Using the language of appeal, not demand, and echoing 1:27 and 2:2, he urges Euodia and Syntyche to be of one mind in Christ the Lord (v. 2). In v. 3, he asks a loyal partner in the gospel to help them. Scholars discuss who this helper might be, Luke? Epaphroditus? Lydia? Who knows? This person is to act as a mediator bringing reconciliation (blessed are the peacemakers, Matt 5:3). Paul then commends the two women, showing that he esteems highly as does God and that their rupture is not extreme (yet!). They are evangelistic coworkers who worked with Paul in partnership and with other Philippians like Clement. Such people's names are in the book of life—not because of their service, but their faith. Their service, however, is a sign of assurance that their names are listed in God's sacred scroll of citizens destined for eternal life.

Living as Citizens (4:4–9)

This section brings home five right attitudes and actions that will cement unity. When put together with the things said in 1:12-18; 27-2:4; 2:14, we get a rich list of appropriate Christian virtue.

First, they are to always rejoice in the Lord, whatever happens (4:4). Second, they are to let their gentleness (reasonableness, tolerance, temperateness) be evident to all people, including the lost (4:5). Third, because the Lord is near to hear our prayer (cf. Ps 144:18), and alleviate all anxiety, they are to pray in and about everything, so that they will experience God guarding them by saturating their minds and hearts with peace (4:6-7). Fourth, they are to focus their attention and shape their thinking with things that are true, honorable, right, pure, pleasing, commendable, virtuous, and praiseworthy. These are the things of God and goodness in his world (4:8). Fifth, and finally, they are to put into practice what Paul has shown them in his teaching, passing on of tradition, and his actions they have observed. If they do this, they will experience that peace of God that comes through prayer and righteousness (v. 9).

Paul's Joy at Their Support (4:10–19)

In the final section, being careful not to give them the impression they are obligated to send him more financial support, Paul expresses his joy and gratitude for sending him gifts. He is joyful for their thought for him and their recent gift (v. 10). Not that he needs more because he has learned the secret of being content whether well-supplied or impoverished—he can do all things through the one who strengthens him (vv. 11-13). We must reflect on these verses, as contentment and not consumerism is God's way, and because we can cope in times of suffering through God's strength. We can note that v. 13 is often misused as if God can strengthen us for all things, like sports victories and more. No, this is about God's strength in suffering and deprivation—we can get through such things because God is with us in Christ by the Spirit.

In vv. 14-18, Paul speaks of their gift sent with the brave Epaphroditus (cf. 2:25-30). They did well in partnering with Paul in his material privation by sending the gifts (v. 14). Indeed, the Philippians are the church that is most generous to mission in the NT (a lesson for our churches today). From the day Paul left Philippi, even in the next city, Thessalonica (Acts 17), they sent him gifts (vv. 15-16). Paul's acceptance of their gifts shows that while Paul was determined to provide for his own needs through his tentmaking when evangelizing a place, he would accept gifts when he left (to show he is not a peddler of the gospel, cf. 2 Cor 2:17). They sent him gifts again and again. In vv. 17-18, he carefully ensures they do not hear his words as an appeal for more—he has enough because of what they sent with Epaphroditus. He describes the gifts in sacrificial terms and as pleasing to God. We are also encouraged to give to God's mission—making such sacrifices pleases God.

Verse 19 restates passages like Matthew 6:19-34, assuring Christians who seek first God's kingdom that God will supply our needs through his riches in glory in Christ Jesus. Notably, he supplies our "needs," not our "wants"—this verse is not prosperity theology. He ends the body of the letter with a doxology ascribing to God the Father eternal glory.

Superscript (4:20–23)

Paul ends the letter as he usually does, but with brevity. He sends his own greetings and those of the believers with him to the believers of Philippi and Macedonia. Notably, in v. 22, he sends greetings from those of Caesar's household. While this can refer to slaves in the service of Nero, more likely, this confirms that the gospel is spreading in the emperor's inner sanctum, as hinted at in 1:12-13.

This greeting is wonderfully reassuring, showing that even though the Apostle to the gentiles is imprisoned, the gospel cannot be bound (2 Tim 2:9), and it is penetrating the heart of the Roman Empire. One day it will become the empire's state religion. He began the letter with grace, and he ends with it, praying that Christ's grace would be with their spirits (v. 23).

Philippians is a stunning, rich, and encouraging letter that urges us to emulate the example of Christ in our mission, attitudes, and speech. Let us whose names are written in the book of life hear its message and be citizens of heaven on earth who walk in the pattern laid down by our Savior, Paul, Timothy, Epaphroditus, the well-motivated Romans of Ch. 1, and Euodia, Syntyche, and Clement in earlier days. If we do, the gospel's advance will be accelerated, Jesus will return, and we will receive our prize!

Part 3: The Pastoral Epistles

Here, I will briefly consider the three letters dubbed by scholars "the Pastoral Epistles."[16] They are labeled like this because Paul writes them to coworkers charged with dealing with issues in particular churches—Timothy in Ephesus and Titus in Crete. They are also considered a unit because of their common language, theology, terminology, church structures (e.g., elders), and the issue of false teaching besetting both churches. While they are all considered prison letters by many, Titus was written before Paul's final imprisonment from Nicopolis (Tit 3:12), and it is unclear where 1

---

16. For a fuller discussion, see Keown, *Discovering*, 2:331–51 (Ch. 12).

Timothy was penned. If authentic, 2 Timothy is undoubtedly Paul's final letter from his last Roman imprisonment.

There is an ongoing debate concerning whether these are Paul's genuine letters or whether someone penned them after his death. There are reasonable reasons for asking this question, as the Greek vocabulary and theological ideas used and emphasized in the letters sometimes differ from those in the undisputed letters. For example, Christ's return is labeled an *epiphaneia*, "appearance," whereas, in the other Paulines, it usually is a *parousia*, "coming." Other examples are God and Christ both being called "Savior" and the mention of elders and deacons in 1 Timothy 3 and Titus 1.

Others (me included) find no basis for the claims that these are not authentically Pauline. If so, all the autobiographical material concerning Paul and the details of Timothy and Titus are spurious, which seems fanciful. Further, while there are differences in vocabulary and theological ideas at places, Paul elsewhere does use the same ideas of God, Christ, and the church, but not that often. As amanuenses were given different degrees of freedom, it might be that Paul gave instructions to an amanuensis who wrote on his behalf rather than dictation. A different writer with more freedom could account for the differences (e.g., Luke). Moreover, on close examination, the theology of the letters is consistent with Paul's other ones.

As such, Those rejecting Paul's authorship must produce reasons why an unknown would produce false letters. The Pastorals do not present another gospel, and it is hard to see what motive an unknown later person would have to produce letters that lack anything notably different from Paul's earlier letters. Finally, there seems little reason to suppose that people centuries later removed culturally and geographically from the days of the early church would know better concerning authorship than the early Christians. With these and other factors in mind, we can be confident Paul is behind the Pastoral letters.

If the tradition is to be trusted, these were written during the mid to late 60s before Paul's death (AD 65–67). Those who accept these traditions postulate that Paul went on another trip after his imprisonment in Rome, mentioned in the Lycus Valley letters and Philippians (Acts 28). The trip can be pieced together with data from the Pastorals and other hints in the other letters, including his possibly going to Spain and also Crete, Ephesus, Colossae, and Miletus in Asia Minor, Philippi in Macedonia, Corinth in Achaia, and Nicopolis in Epirus (see Tit 3; 2 Tim 4).

On this journey, Paul left Titus in Crete and Timothy in Ephesus to deal with false teachers and the churches' issues. Titus appears to have been written while he was in Nicopolis in the province of Epirus to the west of Greece before Paul went to Rome for his final imprisonment and death (ca. AD 65–67). Those who reject Paul's authorship date them anywhere from AD 70 to the early second century, and the point of origin is uncertain.

The recipients are two of Paul's key coworkers. Timothy pops up all over Paul's letters and Acts as his righthand man after joining him in south Galatia on his second Antiochian mission (Acts 16:1–4). He was a preacher, emissary, co-sender, and perhaps writer or amanuensis for some letters, assistant, pastor, and teacher. Paul highly regards him, as the letters show.

Titus is mentioned less often. He features in Galatians 2 and through 2 Corinthians. If Galatians was Paul's first letter, then he was with Paul throughout much of his career, from his trip from Antioch to Jerusalem (Acts 11:28–30; Gal 2:1–10), through his third Antiochian mission in which he collected funds (2 Cor), and then traveled with Paul on his final journey. After remaining in Crete, he went to Dalmatia in the northern Balkans (2 Tim 4:10).

Titus

The letter of Titus has invaluable material concerning Christian leadership, participation in God's people across ages and stages,

Christian submission to the state, and some helpful material on salvation and ethics.

Prescript (1:1–4)

As always, Paul begins 1:1-4 by naming himself. As he does elsewhere, he describes himself as a slave (Rom 1:1; Phil 1:1) and an apostle (as he does commonly). His ministry purpose is stated as establishing the faith and truth of God that accords with godliness and gives hope of the promise of eternal life. This hope has now been disclosed in God's Word, now entrusted to Paul by God the Savior. While he describes his ministry differently from the undisputed letters, it is consistent with what is said in those letters. He writes to Titus, who he describes as a genuine child in the common faith. His greeting is a reworking of his usual grace and peace.

The Appointment of Appropriate Elders (1:5–9)

Titus 1:5-16 tells us that Paul left Titus behind in Crete as he moved on to other locales in his final mission. His task was clearly stated as appointing elders to oversee[17] the churches across the island. These would no doubt lead the church after Titus then left.

As in 1 Timothy 3, the requirements are stated in vv. 5-9. Those appointed are to be Christians without serious blame, married with one wife and believing children, not involved in un-Christian

---

17. Two terms are used interchangeably here, *presbyteros* (presbyter, elder) and *episkopos* (overseer), which explains a key aspect of their task—to oversee the church.

dissipation, nor people who rebel against authority. They are trustworthy Christians, compliant, not prone to sharp anger, not addicted to wine, not violent nor greedy, and not peddlers of the gospel for material gain. Instead, they are hospitable, lovers of good, wise, fair, devout, self-controlled, gospel-centered, and capable of instructing others. Notably, no age range is given. While it appears that Paul wants these people to be married men, there is no direct prohibition of others in the role. Consequently, whether others can fill this role remains debated in the modern church. If one holds that others can fill the role, we can surmise that anyone not married would need to demonstrate the kind of character and faith that Paul otherwise endorses here.

Warning of Rebellious Judaizers (1:10–16)

Verses 10 to 16 have a dual effect. The passage highlights those unsuitable for eldership and summons Titus and others who hear the letter to leave behind the vices he mentions. Verse 10 indicates that the church is infiltrated by difficult people who are rebellious, speak foolishly and deceptively, and a good number are Jewish (vv. 10, 14). This likely indicates Judaizers and those who wish to impose Judaism and other ideas on the church members. Titus is urged to silence them, as they are destroying families with their false teachings and demands for financial support. The citation in v. 12 comes from Epimenides, a Cretan poet from the sixth-century bc. Paul uses the quote to show that these false teachers are importing their cultural baggage into the church with their lying, evil, and gluttonous greed. As they have received the gospel, they should be ridding themselves of such sin, so Titus is encouraged to challenge them vigorously to bring them back to the faith and stop focusing on Jewish myth and law. Paul ends the section contrasting appropriate Christian purity with the defiled thoughts of these opponents. They are hypocrites who claim to know God but are detestable, disobedient, and whose deeds deny God. Sometimes a leader must challenge the thinking and behavior of members of the church who are causing division. Confronting people like this is never easy, but it has to be done to save the church.

Teaching People Across Age, Stage, and Status (2:1–15)

Titus 2 includes Paul's instructions concerning how four groups in the church should live. Titus is to pass on this to them. Verses 1 and 15 frame the section and sum up what is to be done—he is to authoritatively speak what is fitting for the sound instruction and correction of those in the Cretan church to bring the church back to a healthy state.

First, older men are to be even-tempered, worthy of respect, self-controlled, faithful to the gospel, and characterized by love and perseverance (v. 2). Second, older women should be holy and pure, not involved in slander, not big alcohol drinkers, and good teachers to encourage younger women in their marriages and parenting. The women are to exhibit self-control, be busy in the home, be good, and be submissive to their husbands, so the Word is not slandered. Such a command can sound patriarchal to a modern reader, but this was an era before modern birth control methods in which a woman's role was in the home, and there were few other options. Furthermore, as we read more broadly in Paul's letters and Acts, we see that husbands are to respond with sacrificial love. Women were encouraged to learn and be involved in mission and church life.

Third, younger men are also to be self-controlled, doers of charitable deeds, sound in teaching the gospel with dignity, and in so doing, putting opponents from the false teachers to shame.

Fourth, as Paul says elsewhere, slaves should be subject to masters and please them in work and speech, not steal, and be faithful to God and his Word. Doing this will ensure that God's teaching in everything is represented well. As with patriarchy, slavery offends contemporary westerners. The logic of the gospel allowing no favoritism leads us to a fully egalitarian understanding of humankind. The church, in its wisdom, has worked these things out over the centuries. Now many churches and denominations stand against slavery and other forms of oppression.

Verses 11 to 14 give the basis for the life he wants the distinct groups of people to live. God's grace has come and brought his salvation. God is training Christians as his saved people so they are no longer ungodly people living by worldly desires but will be righteous, godly, and self-controlled. They do this anticipating the blessed hope of the return of the "great God and Savior Jesus Christ"—a passage showing that Paul endorses Christ's divinity. Verse 14 focuses on his self-giving to redeem humankind from lawlessness and purify people who are zealous to do good deeds. These verses give a brilliant basis for ethical behavior—because of God's grace and wonderful salvation, his people are to live righteous and godly lives that please him.

Instructions Concerning the World (3:1–3)

Chapter 3 adds other things Titus should pass on to the Cretan Christians. First, in line with Romans 13 and 1 Peter 2:13-17, he reminds them to be subject to the rulers and authorities of the age. Such injunctions are remarkable, as Nero was, at the time, an unhinged megalomaniac. Despite this, believers must be compliant citizens without violating their prior commitment to God and his Son. Although there are times to stand against the government for those in need, generally speaking, the NT vision for Christians is that they are not revolutionaries in a hostile world. Instead, they are always prepared for good work, reject malicious speech, and are peaceful, gentle, and courteous. Such attitudes are fundamental to the Christian mission in a hostile world.

Verse 3 contrasts the virtuous life in 3:1-2 with their former lives as "brute beasts" of Crete. Before becoming God's people, they were foolish, disobedient to God, deceived by false gods and religious ideologies, wicked, envious, appalling, and full of hate. They are no longer to live like this.

Salvation from God (3:4–7)

Verses 4 to 7 are one of the best descriptions of the heart of Paul's understanding of the gospel in the Pauline corpus, making it highly likely that he is the author. Despite their terrible sinfulness, God's kindness, love, and mercy toward humankind became manifest in Christ. So, God, through Christ, saves us. This salvation is not given based on what people have done, whether observing Mosaic law (as the Judaizers and Jews require) or seeking perfection of good works in any religious system, Christian or otherwise. It is gifted purely because of God's mercy. Those who accept God's grace by faith are washed through the regenerating and renewing work of the Spirit, which has been poured into believers through Jesus Christ, their savior. As such, believers are justified by God's grace and heirs to the hope of everlasting life.

Final Instructions (3:8–11)

Paul rounds things off in 3:8-14 with final instructions that the Cretan faithful insist on concerning this gospel of mercy and encourage the faithful to respond to the gospel with good works that are good and beneficial to all. They are to avoid debates about the law, which are useless and fruitless. Where someone persists in being divisive on such things or others, they are to be rejected after two warnings to the contrary. Paul sees anyone who does not heed the caution as perverted (lit. "turned aside"), sinful, and self-condemned. The first converts in Crete agreed to the gospel of grace through faith fourteen to sixteen years previously. They should know better than to abandon it. Little wonder Paul was losing patience with Judaizers and their sympathizers.

Travel Plans, Greetings, and Grace (3:12–15)

In 3:12–15, Paul ends Titus with travel plans. Paul is in Nicopolis with Artemas and Tychicus (see Eph 6; Col 4). Titus is to rush to him in Nicopolis from Crete. Zenas, a lawyer, will visit Titus with Apollos (see Acts 18–19; 1 Cor 1–4). They likely delivered the letter from Paul to Titus. The apostle ends the letter by stressing the need for honorable deeds, gives greetings, and ends with a prayer for grace.

1 Timothy

As discussed, the authorship of this letter is disputed. However, I believe this is a letter from Paul to Timothy. Clues as to when and where it was written are sparse. It is not written from Ephesus but after Paul had left Ephesus for Macedonia (1:3). Hence, it could have been written from any point on Paul's potential fourth journey (see the locations above) or from Rome as tradition holds. It could be dated on Paul's third Antiochian collection mission, as he traveled from Ephesus to Macedonia (2 Cor 2:13; 7:5). However, there is no mention of the Jerusalem Collection, and a later date seems likely. The letter, like Titus, is addressed to the individual in its title, Timothy, with instructions concerning sorting out a problem with false teachers in the Ephesus church. Again, there is a Jewish dimension to their distortion of the gospel. Women appear to be among their victims, accounting for Paul's gender-limiting instructions; they are divisive and argumentative, and there is evidence of peddling the gospel.

Prescript (1:1–2)

As he commonly does, Paul names himself and describes himself as an apostle appointed by God and Christ. The recipient is Timothy, who, for Paul, is his genuine son. He gives a variant of his usual greeting adding mercy to grace and peace. Timothy is mentioned twenty-four times in the NT. Luke records that he was a promising disciple who joined Paul on his second Antiochian mission in Lystra. Paul circumcised him, presumably because his mother was Jewish, and to enable him to share Christ in synagogues with him. According to Acts, he traveled with Paul, remaining in Macedonia and then rejoining him in Corinth (Acts 17:14–15; 18:5). Paul sent him to Macedonia from Ephesus (Acts 19:22). He rejoined Paul in Macedonia and traveled with the Jerusalem Collection group to Jerusalem (Acts 20:4). Timothy is not referenced after this in Acts.

In the letters, we learn that Timothy preached the gospel with Paul and Silas in Corinth (2 Cor 1:19). He also traveled to Thessalonica to establish and encourage the suffering church. He returned with the good news of their faith, love, and endurance (1 Thess 3:2, 6). On Paul's next journey, he was sent by Paul from Ephesus to Corinth and reinforced Pauline teaching to them (1 Cor 4:17; 16:10). Described as a coworker, he was with Paul in Corinth when he wrote Romans (Rom 16:21). Timothy is a co-sender and perhaps amanuensis for six letters (2 Cor 1:1; Phil 1:1; Col 1:1; 1 Thess 1:1; 2 Thess 1:1). Paul planned to send him ahead of him to Philippi from Rome (Phil 2:19). Both 1 and 2 Timothy were addressed to him (1 Tim 1:2, 18; 6:20; 2 Tim 1:2). At some point, probably in the 60s, he was in prison and released and was known to the writer of Hebrews (13:23). The address "my true child" confirm that he was a genuine man who served as Paul's number two faithfully to the end of Paul's life.

Challenge the False Teachers (1:3–11)

The letter body begins in 1:3-11 with Paul urging Timothy to stop the false teaching of a group of spurious teachers. They have deviated from Paul's instructions concerning purity, love, and sincere faith to teach false doctrine and are concerned with myths, genealogies, and speculations rather than God's plan by faith. They have a Jewish orientation teaching the law but not understanding it correctly. The law exposes people's transgressions. Paul lists a range of sins common to the Ephesus context. These violate the ethics of the gospel and include sexual immorality and slave trafficking, among others.

Thanksgiving and Doxology (1:12–17)

As he often does in letters to churches, Paul gives thanks. This thanksgiving runs from 1:12-17 and is personal. Paul expresses gratitude to Christ the Lord for his grace, strength, appointment to ministry, and mercy despite his former blasphemy, persecution, violence, ignorance, and unbelief. A feature of the Pastorals is Paul's mention of trustworthy sayings—one of which is that Christ came to save sinners, of whom Paul is at the forefront (as he had tried to destroy Christ's church). Now he has experienced mercy, so Christ's patience is revealed. The example of Christ's patience with Paul gives hope to other sinful people who believe in him and will receive eternal life. As he often does, he ends the thanksgiving with a doxology declaring that the immortal, invisible, and God, the King of the Ages, be glorified and honored forever.

Fight For the Faith Before False Ideas (1:18–20)

1 Timothy 1:18-20 is a passionate appeal from Paul to his child Timothy to fight the good fight for the gospel against those who have shipwrecked their faith and have been excommunicated into the realm of Satan to be taught not to blaspheme. Here, as in other biblical passages, Satan is God's agent to discipline believers (Job 1:6-2:7; Luke 22:31). Similarly, in 1 Cor 5:5, Paul commands the Corinthians to hand over a sexually immoral believer so that he will be saved. Excommunication is never merely to punish an offender. Expulsion from the church is the last resort after a careful three-step warning process and opportunity to repent (Matt 18:15-20; Tit 3:10). Its purpose is not punitive. Instead, it is done in the hope that the offender will be restored and so that the gospel and church are not corrupted.

Let the Men Pray (2:1–8)

1 Timothy 2:1-8 is framed with injunctions to the church's men to pray. Timothy and the Ephesians are to pray for rulers so that they may live without disrupting the social order. Doing this pleases God because his real purpose is to save people. Prayer is possible because there is one God and one mediator—Christ, who gave himself as a ransom to save the world at the right time. Through him, people have open access to the throne room of God. For this salvation, Paul was appointed a herald and apostle to teach the Gentiles in faith and truth. Because of this, men are to be prayerful without angry contention.

Let the Women Be Godly Learners (2:9–15)

1 Timothy 2:9–15 is contentious because of its seeming limitation of women; yet, in the first century, it is wonderfully liberating and subversive. Furthermore, its seeming limitations are likely due to the disruption in the church caused by false teachers.

The previous passage focused on men, but this passage centers on women. They should dress humbly and without expensive ornamentation, as is appropriate for godly women. They are also to be characterized by appropriate godly virtuous deeds. They are to learn in quietness and submission. Interestingly, it is unclear what they are to submit to, and as such, we cannot assume it is men—equally, it could be the church, the gospel, or God himself. In v. 12, Paul expresses his personal opinion—he does not permit a woman to teach or dominate a man.[18]

The word for dominate is *authenteō*, found only here in the NT. In broader literature, it is most often used for murder. So then, it is a powerful term indicating authoritative and coercive domination.[19] Instead, women should be people who do not create disturbances. Paul justifies this from the creation-fall narrative, where Adam was created before Eve, and Eve (not Paul) was deceived. Paul's use of the pre-fall narrative leads some to see this as a universal imperative. Others disagree, seeing this as a local issue related to the Ephesian women's vulnerability to false teaching (further below). Paul then states she is saved through bearing children if she continues to be a woman of faith, love, holiness, and self-control. There are different approaches in contemporary Christianity to this passage.

For some, Paul's teaching here is a universal command that rules

---

18. Compare with 1 Cor 7:12, where Paul gives his personal opinion in distinction with the Lord's command.
19. See, e.g., Appian, *Bell. civ.* 1:115; 3:16; Apollonius, *Argon.* 4:479; Aeschylus, *Eum.* 212; Euripides, *Her.* 839, 1359; Herodotus, *Hist.* 1.117.

out women leading churches or preaching and teaching men, endorses their role in raising children, and limits their teaching to other females. Others reject this as a cultural issue that need not apply today. Yet others, including this writer, see it as Paul's personal, specific command to the Ephesus church in which women were involved in coercive false teaching due to their being deceived. Paul placed limits on women only here and in 1 Cor 14:34-35. His injunction in 1 Corinthians 14 follows his earlier statement allowing women to pray and prophesy in church (1 Cor 11:5). As such, many scholars consider that the Corinthian prohibition is specific to the misuse of tongues in the church. If that is the case, 1 Tim 2 is the only passage limiting women's ministry in the NT. Notably, in eleven letters, Paul does not limit women. There are no gender limits on the spiritual gift lists, and many women worked with Paul (including Priscilla, mentioned in 2 Tim 4:19, seven times NT). Luke tells us that, with Aquila, she taught Apollos (Acts 18:26).[20] As Paul rejects salvation by works, the emphasis in the final verse falls on continuing to walk in faith rather than raising children as a means of salvation.

Appointing Elders (3:1-7)

Akin to Tit 1:5-9, in 1 Timothy 3:1-13, Paul advises Timothy concerning the appointment of elders and deacons. Paul endorses the elder role as good and urges him to choose overseers with

20. Romans 16 mentions the work of Phoebe (vv. 1-2), Priscilla (vv. 3-5), Junia (v. 7, Persis, Tryphena, and Tryphosa (v. 9), Julia, and Nereus' sister (v. 15). Others mentioned are Chloe (1 Cor 1:10), Euodia and Syntyche (Phil 4:2-3), Nympha (Col 4:15), and Apphia (Phlm 1). Lydia is mentioned in Acts 16. Women were required for the evangelism to other women in a world bifurcated along gender lines.

specific credentials. They must not be recent, spiritually vulnerable converts. They must be blameless, faithfully married, temperate, self-controlled, respectable, hospitable, skilled teachers, not excessive drinkers, non-violent, gentle, peaceable, and not materialists. They must be men who manage their families and children well (such people will manage God's church well). They must be credible witnesses outside the church. As in Titus, this may limit eldership to married men; however, this is not explicitly stated. If other people are proposed for leadership, they must be people of similar integrity.

Appointing Deacons (3:8–13)

Deacons must be honorable, sincere, not big drinkers, not corrupt, strong in the faith, well tested, beyond reproach, faithfully married, and who manage their families well. Vv. 11-13 could focus on their wives or on women who are deacons. In favor of this is Phoebe being entitled a deacon in Rom 16:1.[21] Additionally, Paul says nothing about the elders' wives in the previous section and Titus 1. These female deacons or wives must also be honorable, speak appropriately of others, even-tempered, and trustworthy. Those who serve well in these roles will receive divine honor.

Paul, the Church, and Christ (3:14–16)

1 Timothy 3 ends with a statement of Paul's desire to come, and if

---

21. Although some scholars disagree, most scholars consider the use of the masculine *diakonos* for Phoebe indicates she was a deacon of the Cenchreaen church.

not, that readers conduct themselves appropriately in God's church. He describes the church as God's household, the pillar and mainstay of truth, and adds a hymnic piece telling the story of Christ.

In 1 Timothy 4:1–5, Paul warns against false teachers who desert the faith, spread ideas from demons, are hypocrites and liars, have no conscience, and forbid marriage and eating particular foods that can be legitimately eaten with gratitude to God. The mention of food suggests that the false teachers were imposing asceticism and Jewish food laws.

Leadership Instructions (4:1–6)

1 Timothy 4:6–16 is an excellent passage for pastors. It includes a series of instructions for Timothy in his leadership role. He is to teach others what is in the letter and reject myths circulated by older women (indicating their involvement in the false teaching). He must take care of himself physically and spiritually. He should endure and stand firm in suffering, hoping in God and Christ. Despite his youth,[22] he is to be an example in speech, conduct, love, faith, and holiness. He should read, teach, and exhort from the Word to strengthen the church. He must continue to exercise his spiritual gift received through the elders. If he does these things well, he will save himself and his hearers.

---

22. I. Howard Marshall and Philip H. Towner, *A Critical and Exegetical Commentary on the Pastoral Epistles*, ICC (London; New York: T&T Clark International, 2004), 239. This likely means he was under 40.

Pastoring People of Various Ages and Especially Widows (5:1–16)

In 1 Timothy 5:1-2, Paul advises young Timothy on how best to lead others in the church. It emphasizes that the church is the family of God. Older men should be treated gently and with the respect afforded to fathers. Younger men are to be approached as brothers, older women as mothers, and younger women as sisters.

Widows were especially vulnerable financially in the ancient world. So, Paul gives detailed instructions in 1 Tim 5:3-16, ensuring they are cared for by the church (showing his commitment to social justice and care for the needy within the body of Christ (cf. Acts 6:1-3; Jas 1:27).

Timothy must ensure those cared for are genuine widows. Those in this category are not sexually immoral and do not have families to care for them (if so, the family *must* care for them). They must be faithful, prayerful Christians who are over sixty. They must have been faithfully married and good mothers. They should be devoted to doing good deeds, showing hospitality, and serving other needy Christians. Younger widows are to avoid sexual immorality, idleness, and idle speech. They are to be encouraged to get married and raise a family.

Verse 15 shows again that women were especially deceived in this church. The other believing women are to help them and support the church's worthy widows in need. We are not told what the church is to do for the widows, but it probably meant support for the bare essentials of food, clothing, and secure lodgings.

Further Instructions for Elders (5:17–20)

1 Timothy 5:17-20 instructs that elders who serve well, especially the church's preachers and teachers, must be doubly honored. The

quotes from Deut 25:3 and Luke 10:7 (cf. 1 Cor 9:9, 14) indicate that elders received financial support. Paul elsewhere defends this principle (1 Cor 9:1-14). Yet he preferred to support himself in ministry. No doubt, being self-sufficient was also an option for elders. As Jewish law requires, any accusation against elders must be verified by two to three witnesses (Deut 19:15).

Further Instructions (5:20–6:2)

Paul gives another list of bullet point instructions in 1 Timothy 5:20-6:2. Timothy is to admonish the sinful before the church, take care in laying on of hands, avoid sin, remain pure, and drink a little wine as he is vulnerable to sickness through the ancient unclean water (alcohol purifies the water).

After giving Timothy advice to distinguish the sinful from the good, in 6:1-2, Paul's protégé must encourage the slaves to treat their masters (even if they are unbelievers) with honor. Doing this will ensure God's name is not slandered. Those with believing and loving masters are not to disrespect other slaves who do not but focus on serving their masters. We see how slavery was a fixed institution in the first century, and the church's approach was to ensure slaves and masters conducted themselves in accordance with the gospel. Later in its history, the church would lead the western world to end slavery.

Dealing with the False Teachers (6:3–10)

Paul began the letter with instructions on dealing with false teachers; he ends with further guidelines. Those who teach doctrine contrary to Christ and God are written off as arrogant, ignorant, controversial, and pedantic disputers who generate envy, strife, slander, evil suspicions, and depraved and false wrangling. They also peddle the gospel (cf. 2 Cor 2:17). Paul endorses godliness and contentment, which brings spiritual gain. People are born and die with nothing and should be content with having the basics—food and clothing. Those who seek wealth will be trapped in ruin and destruction because the love of money is a root of all kinds of evil that causes people to go astray from the faith and experience pain.

Further Instructions (6:11–14)

Unlike these money-grabbing false teachers, in the sight of God and Jesus, Paul commands Timothy, as a man of God, to repudiate these things and pursue righteousness, godliness, faith, love, patient endurance, and gentleness. He is to fight the battle of faith and hold tightly to eternal life, as he has from the beginning. He is to be without reproach until the return of Christ (or his death).

Doxology (6:15–16)

In vv. 15–16, Paul lands on another of his powerful statements of worship toward God. He describes God with a series of powerful titles. He is the Blessed and Only Sovereign, the King of kings, the Lord of lords, the only Immortal One, He Who dwells in unapproachable light, and He Whom no human being has seen nor can see. He ascribes to him honor and eternal power. No wonder he ends with "amen."

Instructions to the Wealthy (6:17–19)

Whereas earlier in the chapter, Paul renounced those who preach a false gospel for money, in Ephesians 5:17–19, he instructs the wealthy members of the Ephesus church to avoid pride. Rather than putting their hope in uncertain temporal riches (that can come and go), they must place their pride and hope in God, who provides for all people. Echoing Jesus in Luke's Gospel, they are to use their wealth to be generous and do good works for those in need.[23] By doing this, they store up heavenly treasure and will receive true life (eternal life).

Final Instructions and Grace (6:20–21)

He ends with a final instruction to Timothy to guard the gospel and avoid the pointless debates of the false teachers that lead people astray. As usual, he ends with a grace blessing.

2 Timothy

2 Timothy, as with the other Pastorals, is considered pseudonymous by many scholars. However, 2 Timothy bears the hallmarks of a letter from Paul. It is a moving letter from Paul in Rome on the eve of his final trial and death. It is the last of his letters, written sometime between AD 65 and 67, around the same time as 2 Peter. There is a strong tradition that soon after these letters, Paul and Peter were executed at the hand of Caesar Nero.

---

23. Luke 12:33; 14:13, 21; 18:22; 19:8.

Prescript (1:1–2)

Paul begins in 2 Tim 1:1-2 with his name and describes himself as an apostle of Jesus Christ by God's will. His purpose is to declare the promise of life in Christ—clearly, he has eternal life in mind. The recipient is Timothy, his beloved child. As Paul tells the Philippians, Timothy has character proven in ministry, and as a son alongside his father, he served with Paul in the gospel (Phil 2:22). As usual, he adds a prayer for grace and peace, to which he adds mercy.

Thanksgiving (1:3–7)

The thanksgiving that follows in 2 Tim 1:3-7 is directed to God, who he serves with a clear conscience, as did the faithful in Israel's past. Again, we observe his persistent prayer life for those who serve under him. He prays for Timothy constantly, day and night. Showing his intimate pastoral heart, he speaks of his tearful longing to see Timothy so that he might be filled with joy. Whether or not Paul did see him again depends on whether Timothy made it to Rome (4:21).

He next thanks God for Timothy's sincere faith, passed onto him from his grandmother Lois and mother Eunice. He became a Christian through these amazing women, one or both of whom were probably converted on Paul's first Antiochian mission to Derbe and Lystra (Acts 14:6-21). We see the importance of grandparents and parents passing on the faith to their descendants.

Continue to Persevere in Faith and Ministry (1:6–14)

Having stated his confidence in Timothy's faith (v. 5), Paul urges him to continue to kindle his spiritual gift received through the hands of other Christians, probably the elders (1 Tim 4:14). What gift is in view is unclear. Still, it is likely a ministry gift like leadership and preaching. The gift comes from the Spirit, who generates power, love, and self-discipline instead of timidity. Some postulate that Timothy was timid; however, the way he is described in other letters as a courageous, faithful minister of the gospel makes that unlikely. This appeal urges Timothy not to lapse into timidity. He must continue to serve God by the Spirit faithfully.

2 Timothy 1:8-14 includes an appeal not to be ashamed of the gospel (testimony about our Lord) or of Paul, in his suffering. The gospel of a crucified Messiah and Paul's imprisonment could be considered shameful in the ancient world. Not for Timothy—he is urged to suffer with Paul by God's power. God is then described as the one who saved and called Christians according to his purpose and grace in Christ, and not a person's works (showing that the theology of salvation by grace through faith, here, lines up with Paul's other letters). The grace of God in Christ was predestined (before time began) and is now revealed in the appearance of Jesus Christ, the Savior. He is described as the one who "abolished death and brought to light life and immortality through the gospel" (v. 11). It was for this gospel that Paul was appointed herald, apostle, and teacher, and for this gospel that he suffers. Still, as he says in Rom 1:16, he is not ashamed of the gospel or its source because he knows God and his Son and has been entrusted by them to guard this gospel. So, as Paul has done, Timothy must hold fast to the teaching Paul has given him and the "faith and love that are in Christ Jesus" (v. 13) by the Spirit.

Deserters in Asia Minor (1:15–18)

Paul now tells Timothy that he has been made aware of the mass desertion of Asian Christians, including Phygelus and Hermogenes (two otherwise unknown Asian Christians). Paul has been made aware of this by the faithful Onesiphorus. He is a faithful believer who had provided refreshment for Paul in Ephesus and is now doing so again in Rome. Paul prays a blessing over him and sends greetings to his family 2 Tim 4:19).

Ministry Instructions to Timothy (2:1–7)

2 Timothy 2:1-7 urges Timothy to be strong in the grace that is in Christ. He is to pass on what Paul has taught him to other faithful people with teaching skills, ensuring the church has strong leadership. Like a good soldier and hardworking farmer, he is to work hard, suffer for the gospel, and receive his living from that work.

Remember Jesus (2:8–13)

Essential to his ministry is remembering Jesus—resurrected, David's descendant (and so the Messiah). It is for him that Paul is bound. Yet, Timothy and modern readers are assured—God's Word can never be bound and will continue to multiply through the world (as history shows). Because he knows this, Paul continues to endure suffering so that others can be saved. Verses 11 to 13 are a poem, creed, or early church hymn Paul cites as trustworthy to assure Timothy—believers have died in him and live in him now (by the Spirit) and, ultimately, forever. If they endure in faith, they will reign over creation with him. However, if they deny him (speaking of complete abandonment), he will deny them (so they are encouraged to endure). Yet, if they are unfaithful to him, he is unchanging in his faithfulness which is integral to who he is. As such, Timothy, and those reading today, are urged to endure in our faith.

Instructions for Ministry (2:14–26)

In 2:14–19, Timothy is to remind such people of the gospel, to stop needless debates about minutiae that destroys relationships and people. Such pointless chatter produces ungodliness and spreads like a deadly infection into heresy. Poisonous speech like that is so destructive comes from two locals that Paul names: Hymenaeus and Philetus. These people claim that the general resurrection has occurred and disturbed people with their views. Such an idea leads to the false notion that you can do what you like (e.g., immorality, drunkenness) with your bodies now that you are raised. Conversely, Timothy must hold fast to the future bodily resurrection (implied) and determinedly present himself by working in a manner pleasing to God.

Doing this includes preaching the orthodox message accurately (v. 15). He is to stand firm on the solid foundation of God and Christ (the Lord). This foundation is inscribed with two statements. The first states that God knows his people. The second urges those who confess the name of the Lord to turn away from wickedness (v. 19). Timothy is to preach in such a way that hearers are assured of God's intimate concern and urged to live righteously.

Verses 20–21 illustrate the need for living righteously by imagining the church as a house (cf. temple of God) with valuable and less valued vessels, and Timothy should cleanse himself (and encourage his hearers to do the same), so they can be used for honorable, productive work for Christ (the Master). In context, this refers to rejecting unproductive chatter and false theology.

Paul often puts lists of virtues and vices into his letters. He does so in vv. 22–23. As slaves of Christ the Lord, he and his hearers are to pursue righteousness, faith, love, peace, a pure heart, kindness to all, and tolerance. He and his hearers are to avoid youthful desires (cf. 1 Tim 4:12) and unhelpful controversies that produce quarrels. He is to teach those who are harsh effectively and correctly so that they repent, change their mindsets, and escape the devil's snare.

Troubles for the Church in the Last Days (3:1–9)

The period of the "last days" in the NT is not the final period leading to the return of Christ but the time from the resurrection to his second coming. What Paul describes here is not general but what will happen in churches, as verse 4 makes plain. They are already facing such things in the Ephesus church, and what Timothy is trying to correct. The things listed are common throughout the church's history to the present.

The types of things that will be experienced include a range of vices: love of self and money, arrogance, malicious speech, disobedient children, ungratefulness, unholiness, hardheartedness, conflict, a lack of self-control, savageness, wickedness, treachery, recklessness, hedonism, and nominalism. Such divisive and sinful so-called Christians are to be avoided. Those who live like this corrupt the church by taking captive the vulnerable and uneducated (such as the first-century women of Ephesus) and leading them into desire, sin, and false gospels. Jannes and Jambres are not otherwise named in the Bible, but in Jewish tradition, were the Egyptian sorcerers who opposed Moses. Like these evil sorcerers, false teachers oppose the gospel, corrupt people's minds, and disqualify themselves from faith and salvation. Paul ends positively—they will be exposed to the church, as the two Egyptian magicians were by God's power in the Exodus. All false gospels are destined to die; God will ensure they do.

Final Instructions to Timothy (3:10–4:5)

Here, Paul gives his final instructions to his protégé. Paul reminds Timothy that he is closely acquainted with the Apostle's teaching, way of life, purpose, faith, patience, love, endurance, persecutions, and sufferings in South Galatia where he met Paul (Acts 16:1–4) and the many times God rescued him (vv. 10-11). Indeed, Paul reminds Timothy that such suffering is typical for those who live godly lives in Christ Jesus (modern readers, be warned, v. 12). This is because evil people and imposters will emerge who go ever deeper into their deception (v. 13).

In contrast, in vv. 14-16, Timothy is to continue to hold with conviction the things he has learned from Paul. He is to hold firm to the inspired Word of God that he learned from his childhood through his grandmother and mother. They bring wisdom for salvation through faith in Christ Jesus. The Scriptures have this power because they are God-breathed and valuable for being equipped and prepared for all forms of ministry.

As such, Paul urges Timothy to preach the Word in the sight of God and Jesus, who will judge all people at Christ's coming. He is to be ready to share God's Word whether or not the harvest is in season. He must challenge, correct, and encourage with patience and careful instruction (4:1-2). Again, Paul warns of tough times when hearers surround themselves with those who preach a false gospel they prefer (vv. 3-4). In the face of this, Timothy is to be self-controlled, endure hardship with patience, continue preaching the gospel, and fulfill his ministry.

Paul's Impending Death (4:6-8)

In a few verses and in a very moving way, Paul gives context to what he has just said. He envisages himself as a drink offering poured out, speaking of his ministry of service and his soon-to-be-spilled blood (cf. Phil 2:17). His death is imminent. He is confident he has fought, run well, and been faithful in his service to the Lord. He knows that salvation (the crown of righteousness) awaits him and that Christ (the Lord) will give it to him. Others are encouraged to assume Paul's attitude as they face imminent death—this is for "all who have loved his appearing" (v. 8).

Paul's Situation, Instructions, and Confidence (4:9–18)

Paul urges Timothy to come to him quickly from Ephesus through Troas, where he is to get his scrolls and cloak from Carpus (indicating he is cold in prison). We learn that Demas has deserted him for Thessalonica and may have fallen away, as he is described as being in love with "the present age." Crescens has also gone to Galatia, although it is uncertain whether he has also fallen away. Titus has gone to Dalmatia in the northern Balkans.

Only Luke, the writer of the Gospels and Acts, is with Paul. Mark also has left Rome and is either in Ephesus or Troas, described as useful for Paul's ministry. The references in Col 4:10 and Phlm 24 show that he and Paul were thoroughly reconciled after falling out (Acts 15:36–41). Again, we have two gospel writers' lives intersecting. 1 Peter 5:13 confirms Mark came to Rome and was connected to Peter.

Tychicus has again gone to Ephesus, as he did with the letter of Ephesians and Colossians (and Philemon?) earlier (Eph 6:21; Col 4:7). Paul has suffered at the hands of Alexander the metalworker (cf. 1 Tim 1:20). He may have testified against him in Rome.

Finally, Paul refers to his previous trial in which he was alone without support, suggesting no one spoke in his defense. However, Christ the Lord got him through and enabled him to share the gospel before Nero, the lion. Paul ends the section with a prayer stating his confidence that Christ will rescue and save him for his heavenly kingdom. So, he pronounces a doxology.

Final Greetings and Benediction (4:19–22)

Paul sends greetings to Prisca and Aquila, and Onesiphorus. He also explains that Erastus remained in Corinth (cf. Acts 19:22; Rom 16:23) and that he left sick Trophimus in Miletus (Acts 20:4; 21:29)—we see the reality of human suffering and a non-triumphalist gospel here (cf. Gal 4:13–14; Phil 2:26–30). He wants Timothy in Rome by winter (it is too dangerous to travel by sea during that period). He sends greetings from the otherwise unknown Eubulus, Pudens, Linus, Claudia, and all the Christians in that context. He ends with a grace blessing as always.

Conclusion

The Pastoral Epistles are a superb repository of instruction for anyone in church ministry. They give clear guidance concerning dealing with false teachers who can invade the church anytime. When they infiltrate the church, God's leaders remain faithful to the gospel and are brilliant examples of holding to it and living by its ethics. They refuse to participate in the vices of their age. They know the Word intimately and profoundly and can identify where it is being corrupted, and they challenge it with patient pastoral instruction. We learn about structuring the church with elders and deacons. They will lead the church and preserve the gospel. We are also warned against the dangers of money that lead God's faithful people astray.

Young leaders are urged to stand firm in the gospel rather than allow themselves to be put down for their age and show maturity beyond their years. The importance of prayer is stressed, as is the need to care for those in need, such as widows. The heart of it all is Jesus, the mediator, sent from God to save us according to God's mercy and grace, not through our efforts. Yet, knowing we are saved, we are encouraged to flourish in him with godly lives and good works. We must submit to the government without compromising the gospel and refuse to live as our sinful, unbelieving neighbors live. In Paul's final letter, we are reminded that salvation awaits us and will be amazing. In the meantime, we must be faithful and preach the Word in and out of season.

12. Hebrews

Part 1: Background

Hebrews is the longest of the non-Pauline epistles and an excellent resource for understanding the OT as read through the lens of Christ by a believer.[1] The central theme of the letter is that Jesus is the culmination of God's speech to the world and the fulfillment of the hopes of Judaism.

Authorship and Date

Many in the early church considered Paul had written the letter to the Hebrews. However, today, few, if any, scholars hold the view that Paul directly wrote it. This conclusion is based on the differences between Hebrews and the Pauline letters, the lack of an ascription naming Paul (as in his other letters), and Heb 2:3, which clearly states that the author was converted by first-generation preachers of the gospel. There is a lot of debate about who did write it, with options including Apollos, Barnabas, Luke (perhaps on behalf of Paul), Clement of Rome, Priscilla, Aquila, Titus, and Silas (to name a few). Origen said, "God alone knows," and this is perhaps the best response.

---

1. For a fuller discussion, see Mark J. Keown, *Discovering the New Testament: An Introduction to Its Background, Theology, and Themes: General Letters & Revelation*, Vol. III (Bellingham, WA: Lexham Press, 2022), 1–62.

The main clues to the setting and date are: 1) Heb 13:24: "Those from *Italy* send you their greetings;" and 2) the reference to Timothy being with the author (Heb 13:23). These hints suggest that Hebrews was written when Timothy was in Rome with Paul, before or after Paul left for Philippi (Phil 2:19) and Ephesus (1 and 2 Tim). The most likely date is AD 60–62 (cf. Acts 28:30–31; Phil 1:12–13). Alternatively, it may have been written when Timothy returned to Rome with Paul's parchments (2 Tim 4:9, 21), i.e., after AD 64.

Core Issue: People Turning to Judaism

The problem in the letter is identified in Heb 10:32–39, where the author refers to their readers' falling away from their initial faith in the face of persecution. They appear to be Jewish Christians abandoning Christianity for some form of the Jewish faith. This desertion could relate to the pressure Christians came under in Rome around the time leading into and during the Neronian persecution. The author seeks to convince them not to fall away by presenting Christ as "better by far" and warning of harsh consequences if they fall away. Alternatively, these are Christians anywhere in the empire turning from Christ to Judaism.

Major Features

The Superiority of Christ

The key theme in Hebrews is the superiority of Christ as God's final revelation (Heb 1:1–4). It begins with a beautiful hymnic statement of the divine Christ as God's final Word to the world who saves and who now reigns (Heb 1:1–4). Two main threads follow this:

1) The superiority of Christ over Judaism.

2) Warnings not to fall away and encouragements to persevere. These warnings and encouragements include constant references to OT examples of believers who struggled.

A High Christology

Hebrews has a very high Christology as the author constantly seeks to demonstrate Jesus' superiority to all that has come before. Jesus is seen as:

1. Superior to the angels because he is God the Son (Heb 1:5–14).
2. The fulfillment of humanity's role to rule over creation, i.e., Jesus is greater than Adam (Heb 2:5–18).
3. Jesus is greater than Moses (Heb 3:1–6).
4. Jesus is the great high priest in the order of Melchizedek (Heb 4:14–5:10, s.a. Gen 14:17–24; Ps 110:4).
5. The certainty of God's promise is based on Jesus, the great high priest (Heb 6:13–20).
6. A high priest superior to the Levitical priests (Heb 7:1–28).
7. A high priest of a superior covenant (Heb 8:1–13).
8. A high priest of the heavenly sanctuary (Heb 9:1–28).
9. The supreme once-for-all sacrifice superior to Jewish sacrifices (Heb 10:1–19).

One can see the importance of Jesus as the high priest. The author finds in Psalm 110 not only Jesus' kingship but his high priesthood. He is both the priest and the sacrifice the priest makes for the sins of the world. He also becomes the entry point to God's heavenly kingdom.

Warnings

Throughout Hebrews, there is a series of warnings not to fall away, along with encouragement to persevere. These punctuate the teaching on the superiority of Christ:

1. First warning: do not drift away from the truth (Heb 2:1–4).
2. Second warning and encouragement: against unbelief in the same way Israel drifted into unbelief in the wilderness (Heb 3:7–4:13).
3. Third warning against falling away (Heb 5:11–6:12).
4. Fourth warning against falling away, an encouragement to persevere, and a reminder of past commitment (Heb 10:19–39).
5. A fifth and final warning against rejecting God's grace (Heb 12:14–29).

Perseverance

After Heb 11, there is a shift away from a concern for the superiority of Christ to encouragement to persevere. These are linked to the warnings above, often leading to a summons to endure. These include:

1. The nature of true faith (Heb 11:1–40).
2. The supreme example of Jesus (Heb 12:1–4).
3. Endure hardship as the discipline of the Lord (Heb 12:5–11).
4. Exhortations to right living (Heb 13:1–19).
5. Benediction, final exhortations, and greetings (Heb 13:20–25).

Can a Believer Fall Away?

The main theological controversy from Hebrews is whether a believer can fall away (6:3–8). Most contemporary scholars argue that the author warns against genuine believers falling away as they return to Judaism or some variant thereof. These warnings should serve as a reminder of the dangers of turning from Christ.

Understanding the OT

Finally, we can say that Hebrews is the best book in the NT to grasp how the coming of Christ has transformed the institutions of Israel. Now that Christ, God's final Word, has come, everything, including the covenant, temple, sacrifice system, and priesthood, is fulfilled and transformed because Christ has come.

Part 2: A Brief Journey Through Hebrews 1–7

The Prescript (Heb 1:1–4)

Hebrews lacks the usual prescript (author … recipients … prayer). Instead, the author does not state who they are, preferring to focus everything on Jesus. AH[2] begins powerfully affirming that God has

---

2. I am using AH (the Author of Hebrews) for the author as there is a possibility it is a woman.

spoken many times in the past through the prophets, vindicating the Old Testament as God's Word (remembering that Moses was seen as a prophet, as was David). But now, God has spoken in the last days (beginning at the resurrection) through his Son, Jesus. Jesus is then described powerfully as the heir of all things, the conduit through whom God created the world, the radiance of God's glory, the exact imprint of his character and being, the sustainer of the universe (by his Word), the one who made purification for sins (his death), and his exaltation to God's right hand (assuming his resurrection and ascension). As the Lord (Adonai) who fulfills Ps 110:1, he is superior to all the angels.

Christ's Superiority to the Angels (1:5–2:9)

Hebrews 1:5–2:9 is a long passage that forms a chiasm with part A (1:5–14) correlating with part A2 (2:5–9). In the center, part B is the first warning passage and summons to persevere.

Part A1—Christ Superiority Over Angels Part 1 (1:5–14)

AH then puts together a catena of OT texts to demonstrate Christ's superiority over the angels. This interest in angels may suggest that some in the church, as in Colossae (Col 2:18), saw Christ as less than the divine Son of God and as a super-angel. In quick succession, he cites seven OT passages.[3] He shows that no angel has ever been declared God's Son. Jesus is God's begotten Son and

---

3. Ps 2:7; 2 Sam 7:14; Deut 32:43 [LXX], Pss 104:4; 45:6–7; 105:25–27; 110:1.

God his Father. Hence, he is superior. God has commanded that the angels worship him. Angels are spirits, flames of fire, and God's ministers. Yet God has declared Jesus King forever, a King who holds the scepter of uprightness loves righteousness, hates wickedness, and is the anointed sovereign. He also laid the foundation of the world and formed the heavens. While they will wear out and then be transformed by God, Christ remains the same eternal one. God has never said to the angels that they will sit at his right hand until God crushes his enemies under his feet, but this he said to this Son. He concludes by clearly stating what angels are—ministering spirits sent to serve God's people who will inherit eternal life.

Part B—Appeal and Warning Passage 1: Do Not Neglect God's Salvation (2:1–4)

Because Jesus is superior to the angels, God's Son, his very being, his Word, creator, sustainer, and more, the readers must give closer attention to the gospel they have heard and not be led astray by false ideas that will shipwreck their faith. The message declared by angels likely refers to the giving of the law (cf. Gal 3:19), which proved reliable for centuries to sustain Israel. Transgressions and disobedience are revealed through the law, and God's just response is appropriate. But now that God has spoken in Christ and purified believers from sin, there will be no escape for those who have heard the gospel of salvation and neglected it. This message was first declared by the Lord (Christ). It was passed on to AH and others by those who heard him (indicating that the author is not one of the Twelve and those with Jesus in his ministry). God testified to the integrity of the ministries of Christ and the first generation of missionaries by signs, wonders, miracles, and gifts of the Spirit distributed as God willed. We see here the close correlation between the theology of AH and Paul.

Part A2: Jesus, not the Angels, Rules the Cosmos (2:5–9)

Having given his first appeal with a warning to the readers, AH returns to Jesus' superiority to the angels, laying the foundation for what will follow concerning his ministry.

It was not to angels that God has subjected the renewed world coming to pass, but to God's Son. In support, AH cites Ps 8:4–6, initially referring to Adam as a son of man. With Jesus' identification of himself as Daniel's Son of Man, the passage speaks of Jesus as a human *and* transcendent figure who rules the world (Dan 7:13–14, also 1 En. 37–71). The passage applied to Jesus speaks of his being human, becoming lower than the angels in his earthly state and death, and his subsequent crowning with glory, honor, and absolute sovereignty over God's creation (everything). His unopposed reign has not fully come to pass as people and spiritual forces resist God. However, Jesus, who was lower than the angels and then crowned with glory and honor, suffered and died by God's grace for everyone.

The Founder of Salvation and High Priest (2:10–18)

The passage could be read as continuing the previous through to the end of the chapter. However, the theme of angels is left behind, and AH speaks of what this Son of God and Man, superior to the angels, has done.

He is not only the one for whom and by whom all things were created, but he has brought many sons and daughters to glory through his work. He is the founder of salvation completed[4] through suffering. He sanctifies his people and is unashamed to call them brothers and sisters. He then cites another catena of OT passages emphasizing the Messiah's praise of God among brothers and sisters who have placed their trust in him (vv. 12–13; Ps 22:22; Ps 18:2; Isa 8:18).[5]

What follows in vv. 14–18 is a neat summary of the effect of Christ's work and climaxes on his high priesthood. First, Christ was fully human and suffered, as indeed do all people. Second, through his death, he overcame the devil, who has the power of death. AH here hints at the end of death (1 Cor 15:26). As such, he delivers people enslaved to the fear of death. Angels are again mentioned in v. 16, showing this passage continues earlier themes. Christ did not suffer and die to help angels but Abraham's children. These children are faithful Jews and Gentiles who believe in God and his Son. Verse 17 states the logical need for Christ to be fully human so that he might be a merciful and faithful high priest serving God. His humanity is required because a priest is a mediator who represents other humans before God. In his death, he atoned for the sins of the people.[6] Verse 18 indicates that Christ suffered the fullness of human temptation and can help similarly tempted people (as all are).

---

4. The term here can be "perfected," but as Christ is perfect, it speaks of the completion of his priestly ministry through his suffering.
5. The use of Ps 22:22 is likely chosen because the Psalm narrates the death of the Messiah, his resurrection, and his subsequent praise to God amongst other believers.
6. The term used for atonement can mean propitiation (aversion of God's wrath), expiation (cleansing), or atoning.

Christ's Superiority Over Moses and Joshua (3:1–4:13)

Moses is a critical figure for Israel who led Israel from Egypt to the land with Joshua. Here, AH indicates how the ministry of the Son and the High Priest is superior to their work. Those Christians considering desertion of Christ are returning to a people heavily shaped by Moses and his teaching; hence, this is an important counter to them doing so.

Christ's Superiority Over Moses (3:1–6)

In Heb 3:1-6, the writer first assures the readers of their status in Christ—they are holy brothers and sisters and share in the call from heaven. He urges them to consider Jesus and outlines his superiority over Moses. Jesus is the apostle and high priest of a believer's confession; Moses is neither. While Moses was faithful in leading God's people (God's house), Jesus is worthy of greater glory as he is not merely the leader of God's people but the house itself, built by God. Moses was faithful over Israel (cf. Num 12:7), but as a servant,[7] testifying to things that were to be spoken in the future. These things have now happened, and Christ is faithful to God's house as his Son and heir. The final sentence assures readers they are his house, his temple. It also warns them with the condition that they hold fast in confidence, boasting of the hope embedded in the gospel.

---

7. The Greek for servant here is unusual, *therapōn*, "one who renders devoted service, esp. as an attendant in a cultic setting, attendant, aide, servant" (BDAG 453).

Appeal and Warning Passage 2: Ensure You Enter God's Rest (3:7–4:13)

After laying out the condition of their participation in God's temple (hold fast ...), in vv. 7–11, AH cites Ps 95:7–11. The original passage warns Israel not to be hardhearted like the generation that failed to enter the promised land but died in the wilderness. The way he introduces the citation indicates AH believes the Scriptures are sourced in the Spirit (inspired, cf. 10:15). The "Sabbath" rest AH has in mind, however, is eternal rest. The rebellious generation came under the judgment of God, and readers are warned of eternal wrath if they do not heed AH's appeal.

AH moves from the citation to applying it. The readers (brothers and sisters) should not turn from Christ to evil, unbelief, and fall away from God. Instead, they are to exhort one another daily, so they do not become hardened by sin's deceitfulness. Verse 14 restates v. 6—they together share in Christ if they hold to their original confidence to their deaths (the end).

In vv. 15-19, AH focuses on Ps 95:7-8 and further explains that the wilderness generation heard God's voice and rebelled. And so, they failed to enter God's rest in the land but died in the wilderness. They failed to do so because of disobedience and unbelief. The implication is that the present readers must heed God's voice to enter God's rest.

Hebrews 4 carries on the theme of entering God's rest and is a sustained appeal to them to hear God's voice and obey (unlike the wilderness generation). The readers have heard the good news and believe it. They need to ensure they are not like the first generation of Israelites fleeing Egypt who failed to believe God's Word during the Exodus deliverance and received no benefit from the promised land. They must remain faithful. Christians have heard the Word, believed what was heard, and entered God's eternal rest. But those who do not do so will fail to enter a wrathful God's rest (4:3; Ps 95:11). Verses 3-4 connect AH's ideas to creation where God rested on the seventh day (Gen 2:2). In v. 5, he again cites Ps 95:11, indicating that he is applying "rest" here to Christians to participating in God's eternal Sabbath rest.

Continuing the appeal, in v. 6-7, he again cites Ps 95:7-8, warning them not to harden their hearts to God's voice heard in the gospel and AH's letter. He states that they must act "today" as God appoints a day when he acts in his wrath against such disobedience.

In v. 8, AH focuses on the Conquest and Joshua's failure to subdue God's enemies and bring God's rest in the land or eternally (Josh 13:13; 17:13). Hence, God has spoken of future rest, a Sabbath rest for God's people in which they rest from their works as did God at creation (vv. 9-10). The new Joshua, the Son of God, has brought people into God's eternal Sabbath rest.

Verse 11 drives home the appeal to remain obedient to God's Word and enter God's rest. Verses 12-13 speak of the power of God's Word, which created the cosmos, formed Israel, and led the people. God's Word, through the prophets, anticipated the age that has come in Christ. Jesus preached this Word, as do his followers. This Word will see believers enter God's rest. That Word is dynamic, alive, piercing people inwardly and exposing the thoughts of every living creature (cf. Isa 55:8-11; Eph 6:17). It is implied that they obey the gospel to enter God's rest.

The High Priesthood of Jesus (4:14–5:10)

Having made his second passionate warning and appeal, AH focuses on the theme introduced in 2:17; 3:1; 4:14-16—the high priesthood of Jesus. The earlier mentions may have led readers to think AH sees Jesus as a replacement for the Aaronic high priest in Jerusalem. He will ensure this is not the case by aligning Jesus with the mysterious OT figure, Melchizedek.

He begins in vv. 14-16 by continuing his appeal to stand fast in their confession, confident obedience, and faithfulness to the gospel (indicating that this can be seen as a continuation of the previous). His appeal concerns what Jesus has done (based on things he wrote earlier about Jesus' suffering, atoning death, and exaltation). He is the Son of God who has passed through the heavens, indicating his ascension.

AH now describes Christ's priestly ministry. He can sympathize with human weakness, as he experienced the fullness of human temptation but was without sin.[8] As he has fully experienced human temptation and overcame it, we can confidently approach him at any time in prayer for our temptations and testing. He is seated at the right hand of God's throne, where God's grace and mercy flow.

Hebrews 5:1-4 describes the role of the Aaronic high priest. That person is chosen from among Aaron's descendants and makes the appropriate sacrifices for Israel's sins. The priest can deal graciously with sinners, as he, too, is prone to the same things. As he is also a sinner, he is required to offer sacrifices for himself and his people. Still, the Aaronic high priest is not self-appointed but called by God.

In vv. 5-6, AH turns his focus on Christ, who did not appoint himself but was appointed by God: first, as God's Son (Ps 2:7); second, as a priest after the order of Melchizedek (Ps 110:4). Melchizedek appears in Genesis 14:18-20. His name means "king of righteousness," anticipating Christ. After a military victory, Abraham returns and meets the king of Sodom in the Valley of the King (Shaveh).[9] Melchizedek, the king of Salem (Jerusalem), a priest of God Most High, brought out bread and wine (anticipating communion) and blessed Abraham for his victory. Abraham then tithed to him. In Ps 110:1, the Davidic Son of God is also the priest

---

8. Taken on face value, this indicates Jesus experiencing the full gambit of desires that lead to the sins in the many vice lists of the NT; that is astonishing. What is more amazing is that he did so without yielding to them.
9. The valley lies at the meeting point of the Kidron Valley and the Valley of Hinnom, south of Jerusalem (2 Sam 18:18).

after the order of Melchizedek, i.e., King and priest over Jerusalem. Jesus is King and priest over the new Zion, its people (believers), and the whole cosmos.

Verses 7 to 10 speak of Jesus' intercessory ministry of fervent, tearful prayer to God, who saved him from death and was heard because of his reverence. He learned obedience through his suffering (he was never disobedient, his understanding of obedience grew with the obstacles). He was made perfect (in his sinless obedience). He became "the source of eternal salvation to all who obey him" (5:9). He did this, having been designated by God the Melchizedekian high priest.

Appeal and Warning Passage 3: Do Not Fall Away but Go Deeper into God (5:11–6:12)

Having established Jesus' credentials and status as the high priest of Jerusalem who has brought salvation and to whom access is always open, AH now cuts to the chase with a warning passage with real bite.

Verses 11–14 focus on the readers' potential failure and what AH wants from them. Having been Christians for some time, they ought to have moved on from the basics of the faith to be mature enough to teach them to others rather than having to go through them again. Sadly, their hearing is dulled; they are infant Christians drinking milk rather than mature, discerning Christians who can pass on the faith to others.

In Heb 6:1-3, AH is more specific, listing what he thinks are the foundational principles: repentance, faith, baptisms, laying on of hands, resurrection, and eternal judgment. He urges the readers to move on to mature confidence in these things. Verse 3 indicates he is confident that this can happen.

Verses 4 to 6 clearly warn against falling away, yet they are controversial due to the presuppositions people bring to the text from their theological tradition. Here, AH warns readers that there is no possibility of restoration for those who have had a full and rich conversion experience but have fallen away. The description is of a Christian who has experienced the gift of salvation, shared in the Spirit, and tasted the goodness of God's Word and the powers of the age to come. Such a person has had a full and rich conversion experience. If that person falls away, they cannot come to repentance, as they would have re-crucified Christ causing themselves harm and bringing shame to Christ. Verses 7 and 8 illustrate the impossibility of re-repentance in such instances with a well-fed and watered plant that formerly produced crops showing it is blessed by God but is now bearing thorns and thistles and is then burned. This passage seems to warn of eternal destruction to those who fall away.

Whether this speaks of the possibility of losing one's salvation is debated. Some hold such a person was not entirely a Christian in the first place. Others hold this is a person who is a Christian but ceases to be in a saved state. While it is true that no one is fully saved until their life is completed, and so no one is fully saved yet, the passage portrays someone with a complete and rich experience of God in Christ by the Spirit, and so supports that one can fall away. Another view is that this is hypothetical, which remains a possibility as in v. 9, Paul is confident that the readers will heed and continue to salvation.

Whichever is correct, the readers are warned to hold fast to their faith. In vv. 9–12 AH states his confidence that they (his beloved) will continue to salvation and that they will continue to serve the saints and receive God's reward. He urges them to continue to the end. AH desires that they persevere with eagerness, fully assured of the hope in the gospel, and not become sluggish. Instead, they should imitate "those who through faith and patience inherit the promises," i.e., faithful believers from the OT and the early church.

The Certainty of God's Promise (6:13–20)

As with Paul (Rom 4; Gal 3) and James (Jas 2), mention of imitation and promises draw AH's attention to Abraham—undoubtedly one of the key OT figures in the NT. He begins by mentioning the promise of God to Abraham to bless and multiply him (Gen 22:17)—which is being fulfilled in Christ. Abraham's example is stressed—he waited patiently and obtained the promise of a nation, a land, a great name, an heir, and many nations. Verse 16 refers to the human practice of swearing an oath to something or someone greater than themselves to confirm a promise. As there is nothing greater for God to make an oath to, God guaranteed it with his own oath. Based on God's incapacity to lie, two unchangeable things guarantee the certainty of God's decisions here—his promise and oath. Because of God's guarantee, believers who have fled to him for refuge have powerful encouragement to hold fast to the hope set before them in the gospel. Verses 19 and 20 indicate the certainty of God's promise and oath—Christ. Although sometimes believers feel buffeted by the wind and tossed about on waves, we have Christ as a sure and unmoving anchor of the soul within the holy of holies (inner place beyond the curtain). This sacred space was only open to the Aaronic high priest on the Day of Atonement and with the appropriate sacrifices and rituals. Now Jesus has entered the most holy place, the forerunner of believers, now anchored as the "high priest forever after the order of Melchizedek" (v. 20).

Melchizedek (and so Jesus) is Superior to Abraham (7:1–28)

AH now explains why Jesus is superior to Abraham, his forebear. In Heb 7, AH devotes substantial space to demonstrating Melchizedek's superiority to Abraham and Christ's status as God's final Word and ruler over all humankind. Establishing Christ's superiority over Abraham is essential. Like Moses, Abraham is central to God's promises in the OT. Anyone who deserts Christianity for Judaism does so, at least partly because of their high view of him.

Melchizedek Superior to Abraḥam (7:1–10)

In Heb 7:1-10, the story of Gen 14:17-20 is narrated with an eye on his argument that Jesus is supreme. AH first states Melchizedek is the king of Salem (Jerusalem, Zion). Priest of the Most High God—indicating he is authentically a man of God and prefigures Christ who rules the heavenly Zion and is a Melchizedekian priest (v. 1). He draws on Gen 14 concerning Melchizedek blessing Abraham and his response of giving him a tenth of the proceeds of war. To ensure readers make the connection from Jesus to Melchizedek, he explains that his name means king of righteousness, king of Salem, and king of peace (all now Jesus). AH also postulates that because he appeared from nowhere and disappeared immediately from the biblical narrative, his origins are unknown (without father, mother, genealogy, beginning, or end). As such, he bears a similar form to Jesus, who is a priest forever.

In vv. 4–7, AH restates that Abraham tithed to him and uses this as a basis to argue for Melchizedek's superiority. Levitical priests take tithes from the people and are descended from the great patriarch Abraham. Abraham, then is greater than the Levitical priests. However, Melchizedek received Abraham's tithes, showing Abraham's inferiority to this figure. Melchizedek's superiority is also demonstrated because the tithes received by the one who lives (Melchizedek, anticipating Jesus) were paid not only by Abraham but by Levi and his descendants. They were within Abraham yet to be born (vv. 8–10).

The Superiority of the Melchizedekian High Priest to the Levites (7:11–28)

Earlier, AH showed how Jesus brings eternal rest, whereas Moses and Joshua failed. Here, he demonstrates how Christ's priesthood completes what is impossible for the Levitical priests—absolute atonement.

Using a question, AH states that if perfection before God were possible through the Levitical priesthood and the law, there would be no need for another high priest (v. 11). He clarifies in v. 12 that if a new high priest is inaugurated then the law changes as well (for it is from the law and under it that priest is appointed). Verses 13–14 reinforce that Jesus is not a Levite, he is from the tribe of Judah, and the law does not allow him to be the Levitical HP. Although a Judean, Christ has not become the high priest through Israel's law but through his complete fulfillment of the law (an indestructible life). He transcends and fulfills the law and has become its arbiter (vv. 15–16). His doing so fulfills Ps 110:4 (v. 17). So, the law is set aside because of its inability to bring redemption, for the law is impotent other than telling us right and wrong (vv. 18–19). However, in Christ, the Melchizedekian high priest, a better hope has come through which we can draw near to God—him! (v. 19). Furthermore, the God who cannot lie (6:18) has sworn an oath in Ps 110:4 stating Jesus is Melchizedekian high priest forever. As such, Jesus is the guarantor of a superior covenant that does not just give laws to be upheld but opens the way to the inner sanctum of God for those who hold fast to their confession (v. 22).

AH returns to the matter of the Levitical priests in v. 23. Because they died, there have been many priests. However, as Jesus is raised to eternal life and is a priest forever, he is superior. Unlike the Levitical priests who made repeated sacrifices that temporarily dealt with sin but did not remove the problem of sin and death, he is always able to save those "who draw near to God through him" as he lives to intercede for them (vv. 24–25). As is right, he is the required high priest—holy, innocent, undefiled, separated from sinners, and exalted in the heavens (v. 26). He does not need to bring sacrifices daily for himself and others; instead, as the high priest, he has offered himself as the once for all sacrifice for sin.

The law then that sees sinful men appointed as high priests is superseded. Now, by God's word of oath in Ps 110:4, which came after the law, he has appointed a Son and priest made perfect forever, and through whom we too are made complete—if we persevere.

Part 3: A Brief Journey Through Hebrews 8–13

Jesus, High Priest of a Better Covenant (8:1–13)

Part 2 ended with AH declaring that Jesus is our high priest, appointed by God, superior to the Levites, who has sacrificed himself to deal with sins now and forever. AH continues in Hebrews 8:1-2, ruminating on Jesus as the high priest. As he has said from the beginning of the letter, Jesus is seated at God's right hand in heaven. He ministers as the high priest in the holy places of heaven where God is worshiped. He likens it to the tabernacle, although this does not demand a replica of the tabernacle in heaven. AH is clearly thinking figuratively. The heavenly sanctuary where God and Christ are enthroned is God's creation (unlike the tabernacle and temple).

In v. 3, he explains that the high priest makes the appropriate sacrifices for sin to God. That sacrifice is Jesus himself. If Jesus were on earth, he would not be a priest (he is a Judean, not a Levite), and these Levitical priests offer gifts expected by the law (v. 4). Such gifts are a copy and shadow of what Christ is doing in the heavens (the effect of his offering of himself for sin).

In vv. 5-6, AH contrasts Moses erecting the tent according to God's requirements with Jesus' ministry. His ministry is superior, as indeed is the new covenant, based on superior (eternal) promises. Indeed, if the Sinai covenant (first) had been able to do this, there would be no need for the new covenant (v. 7).

Evidence that this second covenant was always planned to eclipse the first inferior faulty one is Jer 31:31-34, where the prophet prophesies that in coming days, God will establish a new covenant with Israel and Judah (remembering Jesus is from Judah). It will be different from Sinai, which Israel failed to uphold.

This new covenant will not be premised on law inscribed on slabs of stone, but it will be in their minds and hearts, and they will walk in a saving relationship with God. Teachers will no longer be required, for each one will know God, and he will forgive their sins (vv. 8-12). Here, AH neatly describes the covenant that has come into effect through Christ, who died for their sins and sent the Spirit into the hearts of believers. As such, the new covenant has rendered the old obsolete and will soon vanish.

Entering the Holy Place (9:1–28)

Chapter nine again contrasts the superior Jesus and covenant with the inferior patterns of the old covenant. The focus is on the holy places of the temple, both on earth and in heaven.

The Holy Place in the Old Covenant (9:1–10)

The first part of the chapter focuses on the earthly rituals of entry into the Jerusalem Temple's sanctums to maintain Israel in its relationship with God. This discussion will set up the contrast with

Jesus entering the heavenly sanctums and bringing eternal redemption.

AH outlines aspects of Israel's worship in the temple in vv. 1–5. The focus is the tabernacle (tent). There were clear rules for worship in the first (Sinai) covenant. Holy items such as the lampstands, table, and bread of presence were found in the holy place. Then, behind the second veil was the most holy place, with holy items, including the golden altar of incense, the golden ark of the covenant containing manna, Aaron's budded staff, and the tablets with the Ten Commandments. The top of the lid was the mercy seat, overshadowed by glorious cherubim.

Then, v. 6 describes the regular entry of priests into the first holy place to perform their religious duties. Verse 7 focuses on the Most Holy Place. Once a year, the high priest enters with blood shed to atone for his own sins and the unintentional sins of the people. For AH, these rules show that the Spirit is saying that the holy places are not yet open to all humankind while the structure is standing. That is, there is no entry into the holy places for people other than priests in this present age (noting that Christ inaugurates the new one). The sacrifices offered have no lasting effect on the inner beings of the worshiper; they deal with external ritual matters of the law (food, drink, washing, bodily regulations [e.g., circumcision, eunuchs, etc.]).

Jesus Entering the Heavenly Holy Place in the New Covenant (9:11–28)

The transition comes in v. 11, where AH turns again to the superior complete work of Christ. He is the high priest of the good things that have come through his redemptive work. Again, not necessarily speaking in literal terms as if there is a heavenly tabernacle that is a type of the earthly one, he has entered the superior and perfect inner sanctums of the heavenly tabernacle made by God. He entered once and for all into the holy and most holy places not by shedding animal blood but by his own blood, securing eternal redemption (not temporary cleansing, v. 12).

In vv. 13-14, working from the lesser to the greater argument, AH postulates that if sprinkled sacrificed animal blood mixed with ashes on the unclean can purify the flesh; how much more does the blood of Christ, who by the Spirit offered himself as an unblemished sacrifice to God, purify people internally from dead works to serve the living God.

Jesus is the mediator of a new covenant so that the called (believers) may receive the promised eternal inheritance. This inheritance is possible because Jesus' death as the sinless Son has fulfilled the requirements to deal with transgressions of the law required in the first covenant (v. 15).

AH appears to shift ideas when he says that a will requires the will-maker's death to come into effect (vv. 16-17). However, he is setting up a similar requirement that a covenant between God and humankind requires death. The requirement for blood is seen in the first (Sinai) covenant. When the law was declared, animals were sacrificed, and the blood was sprinkled over the book of the law and the people with an appropriate declaration (vv. 18-20). Then, when the tabernacle was built and its vessels made, and indeed everything related to fulfilling the law was created, blood was sprinkled for purification (v. 21). For "without the shedding of blood there is no forgiveness of sins" (v. 22).

Reasoning from the need to cleanse the holy things in the tabernacle, AH considers that better and more complete and efficacious sacrifices are required to do the same in the heavenly sanctuary. Now with Christ's sacrifice of himself, he has entered heaven itself, made by God, and he stands before God as high priest of God's church on behalf of its people. The tabernacle system required repeated sacrifices, including the high priest with animal blood, to atone for sin. In contrast, Christ entered as the high priest after becoming human, dying once and for all for sin by sacrificing himself. As such, unlike the earthly requirement for repeated sacrifices, Christ does not continually need to make sacrifices—which would mean perpetual suffering for all time.

Verse 27 states the human reality that all humans live, die once, and face judgment (ruling out reincarnation and post-mortem opportunities to hear the gospel). Christ, who has died once as well and bore the sins of many, will appear a second time (the second coming), not with the intent of dying for sin (which is complete), but to save those who early await him. The readers are, then, encouraged to persevere for that day.

Christ the Once For All Sacrifice For Sin (10:1–18)

AH continues the contrast between Christ and his redemptive death and Israel's sacrificial system. The law is a shadow of the good things to come for AH. He further expounds how the same sacrifices are made annually, yet never perfect the worshipers (10:1). If they could cleanse people wholly and inwardly, then they would not be repeated but would have ceased (10:2). As it is, they are made every year reminding people of their failure (10:3). This is so because the blood of slaughtered animals cannot deal with sin—they are temporary measures (10:4).

Verses 5-7 are a citation of Ps 40:6-8, and AH attributes them to Christ. The passage may be a genuine recollection of a saying of Christ or a theological reflection of what Christ or the pre-existent Christ declared as he came into the world. It is also a Psalm of David, Christ's ancestor, so the writer may consider that David's words are those of his descendant Jesus. The citation stresses that what God wants and takes pleasure in are not sacrifices and offerings burnt for him but a body prepared for him (i.e., Christ). He is the one who fulfills Ps 40:7—he came to do God's will as it is written of him in God's Word.

In vv. 8-10, AH expounds on aspects of the citation. The sacrifices in view are offered according to the law. However, when one came who did God's will (completely), he did away with the Sinai covenant and law to establish the new covenant. The basis of this is the offering of the body of Jesus once for all so that people are wholly sanctified in him (in a way the law could never do).

Verses 11-12 contrast the priests of Israel and Jesus. The Jewish priests offer sacrifices daily, yet they can never take away sins. In contrast, the high priest Christ offered a single sacrifice for all sins for all time. Having done so, he sat down at God's right hand as the Son of God and High Priest. Now, he waits for the time when all enemies are a footstool for his feet (Ps 110:1). By the one offering of himself, he has made complete and perfect those who are being sanctified. These people are those who believe in him.

In vv. 15-17, AH returns to the matter of Jeremiah's new covenant mentioned in 8:8-12 (Jer 31:31-34). Again, we see that he attributes the writing of the Scripture to the Spirit (v. 15, cf. 3:7). He cites Jer 31:33, which focuses on God's covenant with people whereby his laws are written on their hearts and minds. As such, an external law is not required, for God generates law-obedience from the inside out. He then quotes the next verse (Jer 31:34), which states that God will no longer remember their sins and lawless deeds in this covenant. This citation implies ultimate forgiveness and no need for further sacrifices for sin (10:18).

Appeal and Warning Passage 4: Persevere in Faith or Face Judgment (10:19-39)

Having expounded the superiority of Christ's high priesthood, his once for all sacrifice for sins, and the new covenant over Sinai and its law—the repeated daily sacrifices that do not deal with sin, and the Levitical priesthood who slave away day after day—AH again directly challenges the readers to continue to live by faith, hold fast to their confession, and walk in worship and goodness.

The passage breaks neatly into three sections. Part one is an appeal to persevere (vv. 19-25). This injunction is followed by a warning of wrath if they do not (vv. 26-31). The third section reminds them of their past faith and service, which is the basis of his appeal to them.

Let Us Persevere (10:19–25)

AH begins by stating the outcome of what Jesus, the high priest, has achieved for believers. The address "brothers and sisters" indicates they are not yet lost. As God's family in Christ, believers (we) can now confidently enter the holy places of the heavenly sanctuary by Christ's blood that deals with sin (v. 19). AH describes the path as a "new and living way" that Christ has opened for believers through the curtain that marks entry into these sacred spaces. Ripped asunder at his death, the curtain now comprises his flesh. Through him, believers can now enter the Holiest Place (v. 20, cf. Mark 15:38). He has created a path for all people to access God in worship, prayer, and ongoing relationship.

As God's children have this great priest who stands as leader over the temple/tabernacle (house) of God, all believers, including himself and readers (let us), should draw near in full assurance of faith (not works). As they have faith, their whole beings (inward and outward) are washed clean with pure water (perhaps he has the Spirit in mind here, and perhaps an allusion to water baptism) (vv. 21-22).

As such, he draws out three appropriate responses, all using the inclusive "let us." First, in v. 23, he urges all believers to hold fast to their initial confession of their hope without wavering. The basis is that the God who made these promises is faithful. Second, in v. 24, they should all carefully consider how to motivate each other to show love and do good to everyone they encounter (there is no object here). Third, they are not to neglect gathering to encourage one another. Sadly, he implies that some are withdrawing from fellowship. AH emphasizes the need for them to continue to do so as the day of the Lord (Christ's return and judgment) approaches (v. 25).

Warning of Judgment (10:26–31)

AH shifts from exhortations and assurances to a warning in v. 26. If believers (we) continue sinning deliberately, even though we have received the knowledge of the truth, then there is no sacrifice for sins. Here, AH warns us against abusing the grace of God with ongoing disobedience. What such people face is the fearful expectation of the first of God's judgment that will destroy his enemies (v. 27).

In v. 28, he refers to the Mosaic law whereby a person was put to death for a capital crime on the evidence of two or three witnesses (Deut 17:2–6). In that the new covenant trumps the old (as shown throughout Hebrews), much worse is expected for those who have once believed but then irrevocably turned away. Such a person has trampled the Son of God under their feet, profaned the blood of the covenant by which they were sanctified, and outraged God's Spirit (the Spirit of grace). The same debates rage over this as other warning passages in Hebrews—can a Christian fall away? Was that person really a Christian in the first place? Is this hypothetical? Whatever position one takes, it must be observed that this is not a Christian having a difficult day or doubts; this is a person who formerly believed but now repudiates Christ, his death for sin, and the Spirit. AH here is speaking of absolute apostasy.

Such a person faces God's vengeance. To make this point, AH strings together a catena of three OT passages. First, he cites Deut 32:35 (also cited by Paul in Rom 12:19), which states that vengeance belongs to God, and he will repay. He adds Deut 32:36, which declares that "the Lord will judge his people." Finally, he quotes

Isa 13:14, in which eighth-century Judeans are warned that it is a terrifying thing to fall into the hands of the living God (v. 31). Readers are directly warned that to fall away exposes them to the wrath and judgment of God.

Endure as You Did at the Beginning (10:32–39)

AH returns to appeal rather than a warning. He reminds readers of their past commitment to the faith and urges them to continue in this vein. Verses 32–34 indicate that the readers had previously been converted (enlightened) and faced severe persecution. Their experience included public reprimand, suffering, and the looting of their property. They also partnered with others suffering the same plight helping those in prison. They endured in such a way because they held hope for God's better eternal provision.

In v. 35, AH draws out the inference (therefore) from this—they must not throw away their initial confidence as it will bring immeasurable reward. They must endure in the will of God to receive what is promised (v. 36).

To reinforce the appeal, he cites two OT blended texts (vv. 37–38). First, Isa 26:20 assures them that Christ will come without delay. Second, Hab 2:4 states that God's righteous one will live by faith (cf. Rom 1:17; Gal 3:11). Unlike Paul's use of the text, AH adds the alternative—if the faithful, righteous one shrinks back, God takes no pleasure in him. As such, they are warned to continue in faith.

If it sounds like some may be lost, in v. 39, AH turns to state his confidence in them—believers (we) are not those who shrink back and are destroyed; instead, they are people of faith by which their souls are preserved.

The Requirement of Faith (11:1–40)

Having landed on faith toward the end of Heb 10, AH now devotes 40 verses to the theme. He describes faith, states its importance, and lists great OT saints who demonstrated faith (and so will be saved). This Faith Hall of Fame inspires readers to endure in faith and preserve their souls.

He begins with a crisp definition of faith in 11:1—"faith is the assurance of things hoped for, the conviction of things not seen." Faith then is premised on hope not yet seen. It is also based on the one they believe in—the utterly faithful God and his Son. In 11:6, without such faith, it is impossible to please God, as those who wish to draw near to him "must believe that he exists and that he rewards those who seek him."

Hebrews 11:2-38 lists those in the OT who demonstrated the faith that AH wants from his readers. The list includes supplementary information illuminating essential aspects of faith.

Verse 2 states the premise: the people of old received commendation *by faith*. This emphasis on faith shows that AH agrees with Paul's understanding that people in the past were justified by faith; case in point, Abraham—who also dominates this chapter (vv. 7-12, 17-19; Rom 4; Gal 3:6-9). Verse 3 shifts to believers trusting God, who created the cosmos *ex nihilo*.

In v. 4, the list begins with "by faith …" and continues this on. The list includes sixteen figures,[10] including two women (Sarah and Rahab). Seven are from Genesis, one from Exodus, one from the conquest (Rahab), four from Judges, one is a king, and the other is the final judge and prophet Samuel. There are two groups referenced—the people who crossed the Red Sea and the Prophets

---

10. Abel, Enoch, Noah, Abraham, Isaac, Jacob, Joseph, Moses, Rahab, Gideon, Barak, Samson, Jephthah, David, Samuel.

of Israel. One event is mentioned—the fall of Jericho, implying Joshua.

Throughout, the faith of those in each situation and subsequent actions commend them. Abel is commended for his faith and acceptable sacrifice (v. 4; Gen 4). Enoch did not see death but was taken by God due to his faith (v. 5; Gen 5:22-24). God warned Noah of the flood. Due to his reverent fear, he built the ark to save his family and condemned the world to destruction. He became an inheritor of righteousness from faith (v. 7; Gen 6-9).

In vv. 8-12, Abraham is highly commended for his obedience to God's call to go to a place he did not know and lived in the land of promise in tents as a foreigner with his sons, all the while looking forward to the city founded, designed, and built by God. Similarly, despite her age, due to faith, Sarah conceived, and despite Abraham's age, a myriad of descendants followed (Gen 12-25).

In the explanatory aside of verses 13-16, AH explains that these people died without receiving the promises but having seen them from afar and living as strangers and aliens on earth. They lived seeking a homeland and continued to desire a heavenly home, not returning home (as they could have). Due to their faith, God is unashamed to be called their God and has prepared for them a city.

Verses 17-19 return to Abraham, commending him for the faith demonstrated in his near offering of Isaac despite the promise of his offspring coming through his son. His preparedness to sacrifice Isaac demonstrated his faith in God to raise the dead (Gen 22).

Verses 20-22 commend Abraham's descendants, Isaac, Jacob, and Joseph. Isaac is commended for invoking blessings on Jacob and Esau and Jacob for blessing Joseph, and Joseph for seeing forward to the coming Exodus from Egypt to the land and his instructions for burial (Gen 26-50).

Five verses are dedicated to Moses (vv. 23-28). First, his parents are commended for hiding him despite the Pharaoh's demand he is killed. Then Moses is commended for refusing the trappings of Egyptian royalty and choosing maltreatment for his people over sin. As such, he preferred the reproach of Christ and future reward of greater value than Egyptian wealth. Readers are encouraged to resist wealth and pleasure for the gospel's sake. Moses is commended for standing up to Pharaoh due to his faith in the unseen God and keeping the Passover. Consequently, the Destroyer and the Exodus spared Israel's firstborn children and beasts (Exodus 1–15).

The people of Israel, despite all but two falling in the wilderness, are commended for crossing the Red Sea on dry land while the Egyptians drowned (v. 29). Joshua and Israel's army are commended for their obedience that brought down the walls of Jericho (v. 30; Joshua 6). Rahab is commended, despite her prostitution, for harboring the spies (v. 31; Joshua 2:1-3; 6:17-25).

At this point, in v. 32, AH indicates he could go on into Israel's subsequent history, listing four judges who delivered Israel (Gideon [Judg 6-8]; Barak [Judg 4-5]; Samson [Judg 12; 14-16], and Jephthah [Judg 11]), King David (1 Sam 16-24), and Samuel (1 Samuel). He then adds a group, the prophets. This group includes many people, including Elijah, Elisha, the literary prophets, and many others. Verses 33-38 draw out a range of the activities of the prophets. Clearly, AH could have gone on and on listing people of Israel's past with details of lives that demonstrated their faith. He concludes that all of these were commended for their faith and yet did not receive the fullness of God's promise (v. 39). Now, Christians live in the age of God's superior promises in the gospel, and these faithful saints of old will experience the same reward as we will (v 40).

Consider Jesus and Run with Perseverance (12:1–17)

AH brings home his appeal in this chapter. First, he invokes the image of the ancient games with crowds screaming as athletes circle the stadium. The readers are likened to athletes. The crowd surrounding them as they race includes a great cloud of witnesses, including the faithful of Heb 11 and the many OT saints and martyrs of the Christian era he does not name. With the crowd roaring on, the readers and AH himself (let us) must throw off anything holding them back, including sin, and run with endurance the race set before them (v. 1). They do so by fixing their eyes on Jesus, the founder, and perfector of their faith. They are to emulate his commitment to enduring the cross, despising its shame, and for the sake of the joy set before him completing his race. Now, he is seated at the right hand of God, and believers race toward him as he awaits them as they cross the finish line of death or when he returns (v. 2).

In v. 3, AH urges the readers to consider Jesus' endurance in the face of hostility aimed at him. They must do this so they do not become weary or fainthearted. Verse 4 indicates that while they are suffering, unlike Christ, they have not yet died for the faith. Verses 5-10, beginning with Prov 3:11-12, comfort them that their suffering is a positive sign that God, their loving Father, is disciplining them as his children. In v 11, he assures them that while now it is painful, it will yield the peaceful fruit of righteousness in them.

As God is disciplining them, they must rediscover their strength, continue toward their goal, and be healed of their spiritual lameness (vv. 12-13). They must strive for peace and holiness (v. 14). They are to see no one fails to obtain the grace of God by falling away, that no root of bitterness arises among them (v. 15), and that none are sexually immoral or unholy (v. 16). They are not to be like Esau who sold his birthright to Jacob for a meal and experienced rejection (vv. 16b-17).

Appeal and Warning Passage 5: The Glorious Destination and Final Warning (12:18–29)

Coming to the Heavenly Jerusalem (12:18–24)

Verses 18-24 paint an incredible picture of the destination to which readers are heading. Again, AH contrasts the Old Testament with the new work God is doing in Christ and God's people. In Exodus 19, Moses and Israel came to Mount Sinai. The scene is dramatically described as involving a mountain able to be touched, theophanic blazing fire, smoky darkness and gloom, trumpet blasts, a booming, terrifying voice, warnings to kill animals that touch the mountain, and a sight so terrifying that they tremble with fear (vv. 18-20).

Contemporary believers have come on a pilgrimage to a different mountain, Mount Zion. However, this is not the earthly Mt Zion and Jerusalem, but the heavenly Jerusalem, the city of the living God (v. 22, cf. Gal 4:25; Rev 3:12). The description is spinetingling, with myriads of angels gathered in celebration, the church of the Christ the eminent one enrolled in heaven, God who is judge, and the spirits of the righteous made perfect through Christ's redemptive death, and Jesus himself. He is described as "the mediator of a new covenant" (8:7-13). This covenant is premised on his sprinkled blood that recalls and supersedes Abel's blood (Gen 4:10). The verb "have come" (*proseuchomai*) in the perfect tense indicates that they *have come* and continue to come. They can freely approach God in the holiest place through Christ, the fleshly curtain, and because of his atoning death.

Warning—Do Not Refuse God (12:25–29)

In this passage, AH warns readers not to refuse God, who speaks through his Son and the Spirit in his letter. He returns yet again to Israel's story, calling to mind the fall of a generation of Israelites in the wilderness and exile. This generation of Christians is not to fail to heed God's Word as they did. If they disobey, they also will not escape his judgment. Using Haggai 2:6, he warns that God will shake the earth and heavens again and remove shakable and temporary things. This citation speaks of eschatological judgment.[11] Doing this will reveal what remains. Therefore, Christians (let us) should be thankful for receiving God's kingdom, which is eternal and unshakable. Furthermore, they should offer acceptable worship with reverence and awe. They must do this because God is a consuming fire—a terrifying image of his judgment (Deut 4:24).

Instructions for Christian Life (13:1–19)

Most of the last chapter is made up of ethical commands instructing readers concerning how to live as God's faithful people. A range of virtues is commended to them in vv. 1-5, including family love, hospitality to strangers (who may be angels), empathetic care for those in prison and otherwise mistreated, marital faithfulness (with a warning of God's judgment on the sexually immoral and adulterous), renouncing material greed and being content. The basis for their contentment is that just as God never forsook Joshua, He will never leave his Christian people (Josh 1:5). AH quotes Ps 118:6, in which God is Israel's helper, meaning he is with them to help them today. They need not fear human threats (v. 6).

---

11. It could possibly portend the fall of Jerusalem as well.

Further instructions flow in vv. 7-19 with asides commending Jesus. They are to remember their leaders who evangelized them and emulate their example. He adds a comment about Jesus' unchangingness. Consequently, the readers should emulate him and his faithfulness and not desert the faith. They are also to resist false teaching that emphasizes what one can eat and rely on grace. This mention of food indicates a Judaizing problem.

The mention of eating and grace leads AH to again compare the old and new covenant in Christ. Those who remain faithful to the old covenant and serve in Israel's cult while rejecting Jesus have no place at the altar (figuratively speaking) on which Christ was sacrificed. He next recalls the pattern of the bodies of the sacrifices being burned outside the camp (v. 11). Jesus also suffered outside the city gate to sanctify people with his blood. Jesus outside the camp may refer to his death at Golgotha outside Jerusalem (John 19:17-20). Alternatively, it speaks of his death outside the gates of the heavenly Zion. Either way, Golgotha is in view—Christians are to go to him in his crucified state and join in his suffering on behalf of God's gospel (v. 13). Believers have no permanent residence on earth but await the city that is to come (at the restoration of the cosmos), and as such, through the high priest who leads the heavenly worship, should offer a perpetual sacrifice of praise to God. They must also do good and share with others as a sacrifice that pleases God (v. 17). They should also obey and submit to their leaders, whose job is to joyfully keep watch over them, knowing God will judge their ministry (v. 18). Finally, they are to pray for AH and those with them that they have a clear conscience, a desire to act honorably, and that he can be restored to them soon.

Final Prayer (13:20–21)

The penultimate section is a powerful prayer to the God of peace and the resurrector of Jesus. Jesus is then described as the great shepherd of the sheep by his blood that ratified the eternal covenant established by God in and through him. The content of the prayer offered through Jesus Christ is that God equips them with everything they need to do his will and work. He ends by ascribing glory to Jesus Christ forever.

Final Appeal, Greetings, and Grace Blessing (13:22–25)

His final appeal is that they bear with his Word of exhortation (or encouragement). Some see here evidence that Barnabas, the son of encouragement, is AH (v. 22; Acts 4:36). He adds the good news of Timothy's release, indicating he spent time in prison. There is no record of this in the wider NT, so this could indicate a date for Hebrews after the deaths of Paul and Peter. He is coming with AH to the recipients. He sends greetings to the leaders and saints from Italy (probably indicating it was sent from Rome). Like Paul, he ends with a grace blessing.

Conclusion

Hebrews is an excellent literary work. No other NT book so fully informs us how we should read the OT in light of Christ's coming. For AH, he is not just the Son of God but the high priest of God's people. In him, all the institutions of Israel are swept up so that he fulfills what is required to bring God's redemption to humankind. He is not only God's exact imprint and radiance but rules the cosmos. He transcends the prophets as God's final Word, the angels, Moses, Joshua, and all the saints of old. He eclipses the priests of Israel as the high priest after the order of Melchizedek—the king of peace, righteousness, Jerusalem, and the world. He sacrificed himself for the world, an unblemished lamb who fulfilled the requirements of Sinai and dealt with sin absolutely and forever. Readers are urged not to desert him for Judaism, as Judaism continues in him. He rules in the heavenly Zion, and believers approach him there, enter God's presence through him, and God hears and responds to him. They are to remain faithful to their first confession of him, living in hope. They are to meet regularly to encourage each other, do good, show love, be faithful to the ethics of the gospel, be hospitable and generous, and offer praise continually.

13. The General or Catholic Epistles

Introduction

"The General Epistles" is a term used to describe the collection of seven letters that appear after the Paulines in the Bible. They are James, 1 & 2 Peter, 1, 2 & 3 John, and Jude. The General Epistles are also called the "catholic" epistles, formed from the term catholic (*katholikē*), meaning "universal" or "worldwide." The term originated in the late second century and was used by some third and fourth-century writers to describe these letters. They are called "general" because scholars consider them written for a wider audience rather than one specific church or individual.[1]

---

1. For a fuller discussion, see Keown, *Discovering*, 3:63–65.

Part 1: Letters from Jesus' Brothers

James

Authorship and Setting

The authorship of James is highly disputed.[2] However, as with the letters of Peter, Jude, and John, it is improbable that the early church would have accepted a pseudonymous work only supposedly written by the brother of Jesus, who was also a leading apostle. James had been converted after seeing the resurrected Christ (1 Cor 15:7) and became the leader of the Jerusalem Church in the early 40s (Acts 12:17; 15:13; 21:18, cf. Acts 1:13; Gal 2:12). Later church tradition says a considerable amount about him as James the Just. The letter of James must be dated before AD 62 when James was stoned to death by the Sanhedrin (see Josephus, *Ant.* 20.200). Some date it before the Jerusalem Council (the mid-40s), and so it represents James' pre-Council view. However, it was likely written between that time and James' death in AD 62. It probably originated from Jerusalem, James' and the Jerusalem church's base, and was written to scattered Jewish Christians throughout the Empire.

Style

It is written in excellent Greek with numerous imperatives (fifty-nine) and many analogies (e.g., tongues like ships' rudders or

---

2. For a fuller discussion, see Keown, *Discovering*, 3:65–107.

sparks). It reads like a series of sermonettes and has no one clear issue. It is jampacked with links to the OT and the Synoptic Gospels (e.g., the royal law in 2:8), and especially the Sermon on the Mount (e.g., Jas 5:8, cf. Matt 5:8). There are also many links to 1 John (e.g., Jas 1:17, cf. 1 John 1:5).

Purpose and Content

Its primary purpose is to encourage and instruct diaspora Jewish Christians in their faith:

1. Be encouraged in trials (e.g., Jas 1:2–3, 12; 5:7–12).
2. Seek God's wisdom (see Jas 1:5–8; 3:13–18).
3. Do not favor the rich (Jas 1:9–11; 2:1–12; 5:1–6).
4. Resist sin and temptation (Jas 1:13–16).
5. Repudiate contention, anger, slander, and poor speech (Jas 3:1–6; 4:1–2).
6. Resist nominalism and antinomianism[3] (Jas 1:22–27; 2:14–26).
7. Submit to God, repent, and renounce pride, greed, covetousness, and the world (Jas 4:1–12).
8. Rely on God's will and not human plans (Jas 4:13–17).
9. Make vows without swearing (Jas 5:12).
10. Faithful prayer (Jas 5:13–18).
11. Bring back the lost sheep (Jas 5:19–20).

---

3. Antinomian: "A term used to characterize believers in the early church who wrongly thought that salvation by faith in Jesus Christ freed them from all moral obligations and that they could sin with impunity (Gk *anti*, "against," *nomos*, "law"). The problem of antinomianism is addressed in such NT passages as Romans 6:1–11 and 1 John (cf. 1 Jn 1:9–10)," see Patzia & Petrotta, PDBS 12. It is thus the opposite extreme of legalism and Judaising.

Reconciling James and Paul

One issue is the supposed clash between James and Paul over works and faith. Luther had little time for James, once describing it as an "epistle of straw" that should be removed from the canon. The problem is that Paul preaches a gospel of salvation by grace without works (Eph 2:8-9; Rom 3:28; Gal 2:16) with Abraham as the role model of faith (Rom 4:1-3). On the other hand, James argues for a faith accompanied by works, and Abraham is used as his example (Jas 2:14-26). However, this is not such an issue when we realize that Paul is speaking of faith for entry into salvation and James is speaking of what authentic faith looks like; a faith springing forth in works, something that Paul heartily agrees with (e.g., Eph 2:10; Rom 6:14-23; Phil 2:12-13). Indeed, James affirms faith but emphasizes the need for good works. The most significant value of James is that it teaches us that authentic faith has content and is not just intellectual assent; it is a life lived in obedience to God, particularly in caring for the poor.

A Brief Overview of James

Prescript (1:1)

James begins with a simple prescript. He signs the letter with his name. He next identifies as a slave of God and Jesus, using his threefold name. James did not believe in his brother throughout his life (John 7:5). The letter confirms his conversion after seeing the resurrected Jesus (cf. Acts 1:14; 1 Cor 15:7). He is now honored to serve his brother, who he now knows is the Messiah and Lord of the world. He writes, almost certainly from Jerusalem to the twelve tribes of the diaspora (dispersion), which could mean diaspora Jews, diaspora Jewish Christians, or, as I prefer, all diaspora Christians.

His greeting is the standard Greek salutation—*chairein*, "joyful greetings."

Rejoice in Testing (1:2–4)

Like Paul in Rom 5:3–5, James urges readers to rejoice in tests (or temptations) as they produce perseverance. Enduring trials grow them into mature Christians. Beginning this shows that James knows the many challenges diaspora Christians face.

Pray for Wisdom (1:5–8)

The readers who lack wisdom should ask God for it as he gives generously and without favor. They should pray with faith and not doubt to receive it from the Lord.

Be Truly Humble (1:9–11)

James speaks in vv. 9-10 of the reversal that comes in the gospel—the lowly are raised, the rich brought down. Both groups should boast in this leveling of the playing field that comes in Christ. They should do so because they are here one minute and gone the next like a flower that withers under the sun. Such wilting will happen to the rich while pursuing more wealth. As the letter unfolds, it is clear James has heard of wealthy Christians refusing to use their wealth for the good of the poor—a key theme in the letter.

Do Not Yield to Temptations (1:12–18)

James pronounces a blessing on men who stand firm under

temptation (or trial). Such a person will receive the crown of life promised to God lovers, a figurative description of eternal life. The tempted are never to accuse God of being the one tempting, as God himself is never tempted and tempts no one. It could be that some hold that God is tempting them, rather than a person's weakness leading to temptation. He gives a neat description of the sequence of temptation to death: temptation springs from a person's desire, which grows into sin, which brings death.

Verses 16–18 reinforce the notion that God does not tempt people. They are not to be deceived into thinking he does. Instead, all perfect gifts come from him, who is unchangeable.

Heed the Word of Truth (1:18–25)

James confirms the importance of the gospel and Scriptures to believers. God has birthed believers through the Word of truth (the gospel) by his will. As such, believers are the firstfruits of his creatures that will populate the new humanity. With this in mind, beloved Christian family members are to be quick to hear, slow to speak, and slow to anger, as anger does not produce God's righteousness. They must put away wickedness and warmly welcome with humility, receive the Word of God, which saves them. Having received it, they are to do it. To fail to do so is self-deception. It is as foolish as looking in a mirror and immediately forgetting one's reflection. The Word of God, then, is likened to a mirror in which we see ourselves. Conversely, Christians who look into God's perfect law that brings freedom (the gospel) and persevere in it are blessed.

Be Truly Religious (1:26–27)

Here, James tells readers four things that characterize pure and undefiled Christian religion. Christians who are genuinely religious bridle their tongues (he will develop this in James 3), are not self-deceived, visit and support the needy such as orphans and widows in their time of affliction, and keep themselves unstained from the world.

Remove Prejudice from the Church (2:1– 7)

James 2:1-7 indicates that the churches had fallen prey to marginalizing the poor as they gathered. Such distinctions were prevalent in Jewish synagogue settings and the Greco-Roman world. James will have none of it. Christian churches should not treat the wealthy differently from the poor. Addressing them as siblings (and so equal in Christ), they are not to show partiality if they believe in Jesus, the Lord of glory. He gives a fictitious example of the warm welcome of a wealthy person and the marginalization of a poor person (vv. 2–3). James rejects such distinctions as evil (v. 4). James teaches them that God has chosen the poor to be rich in faith and heirs of God's kingdom promised to those who love him (v. 5). Such distinctions dishonor the poor and support rich oppressors who blaspheme the name of Christ (vv. 6–7).

Love Your Neighbor as Yourself (2:8–13)

No doubt this section reinforces the injunctions in the previous passage, but there is no connective, and it also transcends it into all of life. James summons the readers to live by the law of neighborly love (the second Great Commandment, cf. Mark 12:31). He calls it the royal law, indicating its supremacy over all laws. Showing partiality violates this law. He echoes Paul in stating that a person who fails at one point of the law has broken it all (v. 10). The readers are to live by love, recognize that they will be judged under the law of liberty, and yet anticipate and delight in God's mercy toward them. They must also show mercy to others (vv. 11–13).

Demonstrate Your Faith with Works (2:14–26)

James is aware of misinterpretations of Paul's theology of grace and faith. These are reflected at various points in the NT.[4] One problem is that Paul's theology of justification by grace and faith was misunderstood to imply Paul did not expect believers to produce good works. This interpretation is flawed because Paul has a rich theology of Christian works. However, they do not bring justification, salvation, merit, and a reason to boast before God. Yet, he still expected believers to live by the Spirit, doing works God has prepared for them (e.g., Gal 5:13–6:10; Eph 2:10).

James challenges such views by arguing that faith without works is not true faith. He illustrates this in numerous ways. When a believer sees a person in material need and does not help them, it is useless, and such a faith is dead (2:14–17). Faith is to be shown by works (v. 18). He implies in v. 19 that faith without works is demonic. He affirms that Abraham was justified by faith but illustrates that his faith produced works. Such works include Abraham's preparedness to offer Isaac to God (2:20–23; Gen 15:6; 22). He adds the example of Rahab's harboring of the spies as evidence that justification is not by faith alone—true faith produces works (vv. 24–25). His final example is that the body is dead when the spirit is absent, so faith without works is dead (v. 26).

---

4. Rom 3:8; 6:1, 15; Gal 2:17; 2 Pet 3:15–16. Some scholars argue Matthew is also targeting misunderstandings of Paul's theology.

Use the Tongue for Good and not Evil (3:1–12)

Having given instructions about appropriate speech in 1:19-20, 26, James hones in on the problem of inappropriate speech for Christians. He begins telling them that only a few should become teachers, as they face stricter judgment from God (v. 1). He then decries the idea that any Christian can perfectly subdue their bodies (v. 2). He then focuses on speech and how like a bridle is used to guide a horse, or a rudder is used to steer a ship, the tongue guides us (vv. 3-4). He then focuses on the smallness of the tongue, yet its power to destroy like a small fire lighting a forest fire (v. 5). The tongue used for evil (set on fire by hell) can set ablaze a world of unrighteousness, stain the whole body, and set on fire the entire course of life. While it is possible to tame any animal, the tongue, a restless evil full of deadly poison, cannot be tamed (vv. 7-8). The same tongue produces praise of God and the cursing of people made in his image (vv. 9-10). Christians cursing this way is as inappropriate as a spring producing fresh and salt water, a fig tree yielding olives, a grapevine producing figs, or a salt pond yielding fresh water (vv. 10-11). Clearly, James urges readers to tame their tongues and speak appropriately to God and others.

Seek God's Wisdom (3:13–18)

Here, James urges readers to seek and reflect on God's wisdom in their lives. The wise do good works humbly and are pure, peaceable, gentle, reasonable, merciful, impartial, sincere, and produce a harvest of good ethical fruit. They reject bitter jealousy, boasting, and falsehood. These things are earthly, spiritual, and demonic, producing disorder and corrupt practices.

Do Not Be Worldly but Draw Near to God (4:1–12)

The ethical tone of the previous passage carries on into James 4. Here, the contrast is between the patterns of the world and God. The readers are to repudiate the passions, desires, and covetousness that lead to quarrels, arguments, and "murder" (not literal) in the church. They desire other things, do not have them, and do not ask God for them, and when they do, they do so with false motives (vv. 1–3). They are thus adulterous idolaters who love the world and oppose God (v. 4).

Verses 5–6 warn them that God yearns for them zealously and gives grace, especially to the humble, while he opposes the proud (citing Prov 3:34 LXX). Verse 8 calls them away from worldliness to submit to God. They are to resist the devil (causing him to flee), purify themselves of false actions (hands) and thoughts (hearts), and stop being double-minded regarding the world and God.

Verse 9–10 appeals to repent of their worldliness with tears, mourning, and self-humbling before the Lord. Such a person, God will exalt. Verses 11–12 again raise the matter of false speech. They are not to be worldly and speak evil of one another, for this is judgmental and usurps the one lawgiver and judge—God.

Warnings to the Rich (4:13–5:6)

Earlier in Jas 1 and 2, being truly religious means caring for the needy, refusing to favor the rich over the poor, and demonstrating faith with care for the poor. Here, he turns more acutely to the wealthy business owners in the church.

Verses 13–17 lead to the direct and powerful challenge to the wealthy in 5:1–6. James challenges those who boast of their business organization and the subsequent profits they will make. He warns them that no one knows what tomorrow will bring, that our lives are a vaporous temporary mist, and that the Lord's will matters most.

He writes off such boasting as evil and the sinfulness of not using their wealth for good, despite knowing the good they should do.

Then, in 5:1–6, he calls for the rich to weep and howl at the miseries God will bring them. These will see their riches rot, their garments eaten by moths, the gold and silver corroded, and their flesh consumed (eternal destruction implied). This judgment is due to their hoarding of wealth. He decries them for oppressing and defrauding underpaid laborers whose cries God has heard. They live in luxury and self-indulgence, condemn and murder the righteous who cannot resist them, which serves to fatten them for God's slaughter.

Be Patient in Suffering (5:7–11)

James began referring to facing trials, and the penultimate section of the letter returns to this theme. They must establish their hearts with patience until Christ comes (the Lord, vv. 7, 8). He provides everyday analogies to make his point, as he often does. Readers are to emulate farmers who wait patiently for their crops to fruit after the rain. They are not to grumble to ensure they are not judged for doing so by Christ, the Judge, who stands at the door (v. 9). The prophets and Job are presented as the supreme examples of patience and perseverance in suffering. They know, too, that the Lord is compassionate and merciful and is working out his purposes, despite their suffering (v. 11).

Avoid Swearing Oaths (5:12)

In 5:12, he recalls the teaching of Jesus in Matt 5:34, warning them not to swear oaths but be true to their word, whether it is yes or no.

Be Faithful in Prayer (5:13–18)

He ends the letter body, urging them to pray. They are to intercede when suffering and sing praises when cheerful (v. 13). When someone is sick, the elders are to lay hands on them and anoint them with oil to see the Lord's healing. People are forgiven through confession and prayer when sin is committed (vv. 14-16). James believes that the prayer of a righteous person is powerful and effective, as in the case of Elijah, who stopped the rain for three and a half years and then, through prayer, caused rain to fall (vv. 16-17).

Bring Back Those Who Wander (5:19–20)

He does not have a clear letter ending with plans, greetings, and prayers. Instead, he ends by urging them (brothers) to bring back those who wander from the truth so that the person is saved and their sins covered over.

Conclusion

James is often demeaned as a letter because of its supposedly inferior theology to Paul. This attitude, to me, is unjustified. At times the NT stresses faith and, at other times, good works to ensure that people know that salvation is by faith and that those saved must produce good works. James is among those writings that stress the requirement that believers are virtuous. In particular, the rich are reminded to care for the poor and marginalized—something all Christians should do by habit. We are also reminded to embrace suffering, heed God's Word, be humble and impartial, speak constructively, pursue God's wisdom, and be prayerful.

Jude

As I did with Philemon as an example of a Pauline letter,[5] I am devoting more detail to Jude as an example of the General Epistles. The letter of Jude is noticeably short (one chapter, twenty-five verses, and 458 words long, NA 28). Only Philemon and 2 and 3 John are shorter. It has much in common with 2 Peter, leading to great speculation about the relationship between the two letters. Other aspects of the letter are also contentious, including its canonicity, authorship, date, and setting. Despite all these questions, it is a power-packed letter urging its recipients to contend for the faith against false teachers who compromise the gospel. Living in a world where the gospel is challenged in multiple ways, whether from within the church or without, we are encouraged to be faithful to God's Word.

Authorship

The letter is attributed to *Ioudas*, Jude or Judas, further described as a "brother of James" (Jude 1). Judas is a common name in the NT, used for some people we can quickly rule out as the author of the letter: Judah the son of Jacob from the OT,[6] Judas Iscariot,[7] and Judas the rebellious Galilean (Acts 5:37). Of NT figures named Judas (Judah, Jude, Theuddas, or Theudas), possible but unlikely candidates for the writing of the letter include Judas of Straight Street in Damascus (Acts 9:11), Judas Barsabbas (Acts 15:22, 27, 32),

---

5. For another discussion, see Keown, *Discovering*, 3:240–64 (Ch. 7).
6. Mentioned in the NT in Matt 1:2, 3; Luke 3:30, 33; cf. Matt 2:6; Heb 7:14; Rev 5:5.
7. E.g., Matt 10:4; Mark 3:19; Luke 6:16; John 6:71.

Judas the son of James, Judas the *brother* of Jesus, James, Joseph (Joses), and Simon (Matt 13:55; Mark 6:3).

Of these, some have argued that the writer is Judas Barsabbas of Acts 15, arguing that "brother of James" in v. 1 means "co-worker of James" (Ellis). Others prefer the Apostle Judas, the son of James, who may also have had a brother James which is possible as often a father's name was passed onto the son (Calvin). Early church history has a couple of others with James, who could be the author. One is Judas, the third bishop of Jerusalem, as proposed by Streeter (Eusebius, *Hist. eccl.* 3.34.5; Apost. Con. 7.46).

Yet another option is that the letter was written pseudonymously using the name. One suggestion is that the author is Thomas (also called Judas Thomas, Gos. Thom. 1) or his twin brother.

Yet, the overwhelming favorite is Judas, the brother of Jesus and James, the traditional position (Luke 6:16; Acts 1:13). Those who reject this note that the writer never describes himself as Jesus' brother. Instead, he is his slave (v. 1) and Jesus his master and Lord (Jude 1, 4).[8] Rejectors of Jude, the brother of Jesus and James, also argue that the Greek is very polished, which does not fit with the idea of a carpenter's brother. They also think the letter was written long after the gospel's initial spread (see Jude 3, 17).

Supporters of the traditional position note that the early church rejected pseudonymous works as they constructed the NT. They also argue that the only Jude in the early church we know to have a brother called James is Jude, the brother of Jesus. The idea that brother indicates "coworker" is possible, but the phrase "brother of" in the NT usually means literal brother. Decisively, no early church writer considered Judas Barsabbas as the author. The style of the letter cannot be used to determine authorship as amanuenses were

---

8. Jesus is also the one who cares for the called (v. 2), who saved the people from Egypt (v. 5), who the apostles belonged to (v. 17), whose mercy that leads to eternal life believers await (v. 21), and the one to whom he attributes praise (v. 25).

often used, and the style reflects that of the secretary, not the actual author. The claim that Jude 3 and 17 point to a later date is weak as Paul makes similar statements of prior proclamation in 1 Cor 15:1–3; Gal 1:9; Col 1:6–7.

Judas, the apostle, is unlikely, as while his father is named James, we have no evidence of a brother with that name. By far, the most well-known James in the early church is James, the brother of Jesus.

Early church tradition also argues in favor of Jude, the brother of James, and Jesus as the author. The letter may be referenced as early as AD 110 in Ignatius' letter to Smyrna ("love feast," see Jude 12; Ign. *Smyrn.* 9). The inclusion of Jude in the Muratorian Canon (ca. AD 170–200) suggests a well-known early church figure wrote it. Clement of Alexandria (ca. AD 150–215) describes Jude as "canonical Scripture" (Eusebius, *Hist. eccl.* 6.14.1, s.a. 6.13.6). Similarly, Origen (ca. AD 185–254) accepted Jude as "true, filled with healthful words of heavenly grace" (Origen, *Comm. Matt.* 10:17). While some questioned its authenticity, this was due to its use of 1 Enoch.

Davids sums up things nicely,

> [We] clearly have a Judas who had a brother James who was well known in the early Jesus movement, for James the brother of Jesus was the main leader of the Jesus movement in Jerusalem (and probably in all Palestine) from at least AD 44 (the latest date when Peter had to flee Jerusalem, although James was probably the leader long before this) to his martyrdom in a.d. 61.[9]

Who was Jude?

Jude was one of Jesus' younger brothers (Mark 6:3; Matt 13:55–56).

---

9. Peter H. Davids, *The Letters of 2 Peter and Jude*, PNTC (Grand Rapids, MI: Eerdmans, 2006), 10.

Like James and the other brothers, he rejected Jesus in his earthly life (John 7:5). Yet, after the resurrection, he is among the people of the first church undoubtedly due to the resurrection appearances, perhaps through his brother James meeting the risen Lord (Acts 1:14; 1 Cor 15:7). He was in the room at Pentecost (Acts 2:1-4). He is a missionary traveling with his wife, perhaps as far as Corinth (1 Cor 9:5). Eusebius claims that Julius Africanus wrote that Jesus' relatives spread the gospel through Judea (meaning Palestine) (Eusebius, *Eccl. hist.* 1.7.14).

Eusebius also records Hegesippus' account of his grandchildren (the second cousins of Jesus). After Domitian (AD 81-96) had ordered the killing of any Davidic descendants, Jude's relatives were also brought before Domitian as descendants of David (cf. Matt 1:1-18; Luke 3:23-38). This material suggests Jude was dead by the time of Domitian. Eusebius records that they governed churches and lived through the reign of Trajan (AD 98-117). The details confirm Jude was married and had a family that clashed with the Emperor.

Date

Little in the letter helps us know when Jude was written. Some would date it late in the century, along with 2 Peter, or even as late as AD 160, which is extremely unlikely. However, assuming the author is Jude, the brother of Jesus and that he died before the reign of Domitian, AD 81 is the upper limit for the letter. It must have been written after the resurrection of Christ in AD 30 or 33. There has been time for some extreme false teaching to emerge.

Further, Jude 3 and 17 may indicate a date sometime later in the period AD 33 to 81. However, nothing in the letter suggests the apostles are dead. Neither does "the faith" indicate a late date, as

Paul uses it in the undisputed letters.[10] If Jude used 2 Peter, then a later date would be appropriate. If Peter used Jude, an earlier date in the 50s to early 60s would be appropriate. However, if Jude and 2 Peter drew on independent traditions, this suggests a date anywhere from the 50s to 81. Finally, "brother of James" could suggest James is still alive, which would give a date before AD 62 when he was martyred. A date in the 50s to early 60s would seem appropriate.

Provenance

Again, there are no signals concerning the provenance. Most of our scant knowledge points to a location in Israel-Palestine, but Syria cannot be ruled out. Some have suggested Alexandria, as the letter appears to have been accepted early in Egypt and has excellent rhetoric. James' use of Hebrew and Aramaic sources suggests Palestine, where the brother of Jesus was based.

Recipients

To whom is Jude writing? Again, there is nothing explicit to indicate his recipients. The letter suggests that they are Christians in a context where the gospel is being gravely distorted in the direction of Greco-Roman licentiousness and ethical failure. Yet, on the other hand, Jude draws on Jewish apocalyptic, especially 1 Enoch (v. 14) and the Testament of Moses (v. 9), in his argument. It is likely that the recipients are familiar with Jewish tradition but are at the same time being lured into pagan sin.

---

10. 1 Cor 16:13; 2 Cor 13:5; Gal 1:23; Phil 1:25, 27; Phlm 5, s.a. Eph 4:13; Col 1:23; 2:7.

These thoughts suggest a context where the converts were Jewish and were being lured into licentious sin. Alternatively, they were Gentiles familiar with Jewish Greek writings but were syncretizing the gospel to the immorality of their culture. Most scholars opt for the former because the Jewish traditions point this way.

Yet, a reader of Jude does not need a great understanding of Jewish traditions outside the LXX to make sense of his appeal. So, either view remains plausible. Alternatively, we look for a situation where a considerable number of Jews and Gentiles are together in the same church, where Jewish traditions are shared and known, but where there is significant social pressure to syncretize the gospel to Greco-Roman licentiousness. Somewhere like Syrian Antioch would make sense. Although further from the likely point of writing, a situation like Corinth might work, especially as Paul had traveled there (1 Cor 1:12; 9:5). Then again, if Jude had traveled as far west as Corinth in Greece (Achaia), he had visited a wide range of contexts. As such, he could have written to a portion of Asia Minor or Macedonia. The similarity in tone with 2 Peter could suggest the former. Then again, the early reception of Jude in Egypt may suggest somewhere in north Africa, such as Alexandria. As such, scholars have suggested a range of recipients from Israel, Syria, Asia Minor, and Egypt. We simply do not know.

Genre

Jude is written in Hellenistic letter form. It begins with the usual letter opening (sender, recipients, greeting). The body of the letter is signaled by "beloved" in v. 3 and ends in v. 23. The letter's closing lacks any comments on writing, greetings, and travel plans but adds a doxology.

Some consider the body more of a homily than a letter and class it as an "epistolary sermon." It includes loose use of the Jewish technique of midrash seen in OT and apocalyptic texts and applying them to the contemporary situation (vv. 5–19).

Another approach taken is to read Jude as macro-chiasm. Osburn takes it this way:[11]

   A   Greeting: Jude 1–2
       B Introduction: Jude 3–4
          C Literary Warnings: Rebellion = Fate: Jude 5–7
             C2 Link Rebellion = Fate of Eschatological Enemies of God to Rebellion = Fate of Intruders: Jude 8–16
                D Apostolic Warnings: Jude 17–19
       B2 Concluding Appeal. Specific of "Contend" in Verse 4: Jude 20–23
   A2   Doxology: Jude 24–25

This construct fails to convince. First, the chiasm breaks down in vv. 17–19. Second, the verb "contend" (*epagōnizomai*) is not found in vv. 20–23. Third, the parallels lack specificity and are general.

Structure

The structure below draws out the core thematic threads that develop through the letter.

1. Letter Opening: Jude 1–2, including a) Sender: Jude 1a; b) Recipient: Jude 1b; c) Greeting: Jude 1c
2. Contend for the faith: Jude 3
3. The false teachers introduced: Jude 4
4. God's Judgment in Salvation-History: Jude 5–7, including a) Exodus: Jude 5; b) Fallen angels imprisoned: Jude 6; c) Sodom and Gomorrah: Jude 7

---

11. Carroll D. Osburn, "Discourse Analysis and Jewish Apocalyptic in the Epistle of Jude." In *Linguistics and New Testament Interpretation: Essays on Discourse Analysis*, ed. David A. Black (Nashville: Broadman, 1992), 287–319 (esp. p. 309).

5. Description of the False Teachers and Warnings from Jewish History: Jude 8-16, including a) Description: Jude 8; b) Michael, the Devil, and Moses: Jude 9; c) Description: Jude 10; d) Woe, Cain, Balaam, Korah: Jude 11; e) Description and fate: Jude 12-13; f) Enoch's prophecy: Jude 14-15; g) Description: Jude 16
6. Appeal to Live the Apostolic Faith: Jude 17-22 including a) Remember the Apostles' warning: Jude 17-18; b) Final description: Jude 19; c) Maintaining the faith: Jude 20-21; d) Mercy to those who are swayed: Jude 22-23
7. Letter Closing: Doxology: Jude 24-25

Relationship to 2 Peter

A quick read of 2 Peter and Jude shows many similarities between the two documents, especially between 2 Pet 2:1-18/Jude 4-13 and 2 Pet 3:1-3/Jude 16-18.

Four explanations have been made for the similarities:

1. The two letters have the same author.
2. Jude is dependent on 2 Peter (e.g., Luther).
3. 2 Peter is dependent on Jude (majority view).
4. A common source or sources.

A good case can be made for 1) to 3). However, while there are many similarities between Jude and 2 Peter, they are not as pronounced as the literary agreements between Matthew and Luke or their use of Mark's Gospel. There are substantial differences between the two letters. The view that best accounts for differences and similarities is that they used a common source that lists OT arguments against false teaching.

Jude utilizes the Exodus, Michael and the Devil, Cain, Korah, and Enoch, none of which are used in 2 Peter. Jude has a much-abbreviated reference to Sodom and Gomorrah. Jude does not cite Prov 26:11. Hence, rather than either 2 Peter drawing on Jude, vice versa, or the same author, the agreements and variances point to a source which could be Jesus, Peter, or another of the disciples.

There was perhaps a document with a catalog of examples of rebels and false teachers that they drew on. While the source is intriguing, the two letters should be analyzed in their own right. Each letter deserves the same level of treatment every NT letter receives without prior assumptions on authorship and sources.

Opponents

The key reason the letter is written is to deal with false teachers. Jude appeals to his readers to "contend for the faith that was delivered once for all to the saints" (v. 3). Certain people have snuck into the community (v. 4). They are ungodly. (vv. 6, 15). They pervert the grace of God in the direction of sensuality, perverting the gospel in the direction of sexual immorality and associated debauchery (v. 4).

As with the opponents in 2 Peter (2 Pet 2:1), they deny the lordship of Jesus Christ (v. 4). In the warning of vv. 5–7, sexual immorality is emphasized concerning Sodom and Gomorrah (v. 7).

In v. 8, they rely on their dreams, suggesting a pneumatic elevated view of spiritual experience as determinative. They value people's spiritual experiences, such as visions, dreams, and prophetic words, above the message of Jesus they received through the apostles. Overvaluing experience is a danger in churches with a charismatic or Pentecostal viewpoint.

They defile the flesh, reinforcing that they misuse their bodies and suggesting a Greek view of the body. They reject authority, including Christ (cf. v. 4).

As in 2 Pet 2:10, they blaspheme angels. The illustration of Michael's refusal to blaspheme the devil suggests demons are in mind (v. 9). They seek material gain (v. 11). They are participating in the Lord's Supper (love feasts), indicating that they consider themselves members of the believing community (v. 12).

The false teachers are described as shepherds, indicating they are leaders or believe themselves to be so (v. 12). They are not only ungodly (v. 15) but are grumblers like Israel in the wilderness. As grumblers and malcontents, they pursue their sinful desires (vv. 16, 18); they are boastfully arrogant and discriminate to gain an advantage. Thus, they are not only sexually immoral but also moaners, full of arrogance, and seek status.

Jude next describes the pseudo-teachers as "scoffers" who follow their ungodly passions (v. 18). They cause divisions. They are *psychikos*, indicating that they are unspiritual and worldly. They are devoid of the Holy Spirit, meaning they are not Christians but dead, worldly people (v. 19).

Although the response to the heresy draws on a range of Jewish traditions, the descriptors do not indicate a specifically Jewish or Judaizing heresy (e.g., circumcision, eating protocols, law). Instead, these sound like the issues faced by 2 Peter—people who syncretize the gospel to sins prevalent in the non-Jewish and non-Christian Greco-Roman world. They willingly engage in sexual and other impure behaviors. They seek status. They peddle their gospel.

The key is v. 4, where they pervert God's grace—suggesting abusing the grace of God by arguing that being under God's grace, they are free to do what they like (cf. Rom 3:8; 6:1, 15; 1 Cor 6:12; Phil 3:19; 2 Pet 2:2, 10, 12-14, 19). They may distort Paul's teaching (2 Pet 3:15-17).

A range of opponents is proposed in scholarship. Gnosticism was highly favored until more recently when it is generally agreed that Jude predates the development of Gnosticism in the mid-second century. Others consider them hyper-spiritual pneumatics who emphasize spiritual experience, and ecstatic visionaries who consider themselves spiritually superior.

The best solution is to avoid labeling them too specifically but instead to see them as a combination of those who are libertine morally and pneumatic spiritually. These teachers have a theology that views grace as a basis for doing as they see fit. They are arrogant self-professing Christians who dare to eat at the Lord's

Supper yet engage in debauched living. To an extreme level, their minds are not renewed, and they live by the patterns of their age (cf. Rom 12:1-2). Jude believes the teachers are not Christian and face certain destruction.

Jude's Response

After the prologue and launching his appeal (vv. 1-3), Jude names their problem in v. 4. They are ungodly people who are perverting the grace of God toward sensuality and a denial of Christ.

His response in vv. 5-7 is a reminder of the past acts of God in salvation and judgment. First, the Exodus is recalled. In v. 5, Jude attributes the Exodus to Jesus. His argument is similar to Paul's when he speaks of Christ as a rock that accompanied Israel in the wilderness (1 Cor 10:4). For Jude, God through Christ saved a people from Egypt while destroying the unbelievers. The implication is clear—Jesus will save the faithful of God, including those who heed the letter's warning. Conversely, the unrepentant false teachers will be destroyed.

In v. 6, Genesis 6:1-4 is in view—the angels or "sons of God" left eternity to engage in sexual immorality with human women and were confined to destruction (see also 2 Peter). This view draws on Jewish interpretations.[12] In v. 7, the destruction of Sodom and Gomorrah is invoked—they were destroyed by fire due to their engagement with "sexual immorality" and pursuing "other flesh" (that of angels—another jibe at the mockery of the false teachers toward "glorious ones"). Sodom and Gomorrah are a symbol of divine judgment and are common in Jewish and Christian writings.[13] Such destruction anticipates the final punishment of eternal fire

---

12. E.g., 1 En. 6-9, 86-88; Jub. 4:15, 22; 5:1; CD 2:17-19; T. Reub. 5:6-7.
13. See Isa 1:9; Jer 23:14; Hos 11:8; Amos 4:11; Zeph 2:9; Matt 10:15; 11:24; Mark 6:11; Luke 10:12; 17:29.

that awaits those who do not believe. In context, this speaks particularly of the eternal destruction of the false teachers.

Verse 8 details some of their false ideas—they rely on their dreams, defile the flesh, reject authority, and blaspheme glorious ones. Verse 9 focuses on the final of their false attitudes, their blasphemy of "glories" (*doxai*). "Glories" is used of angels in Qumran (1QH^a 10:8) and in apocalyptic and Gnostic literature (2 En. 22:7, 10; Asc. Isa. 9:32). This is because they participated in or embodied God's radiant glory. In context, fallen angels seem in view (see v. 9). As such, the heretics mock the demonic, claiming spiritual superiority over them.

Verse 9 draws on Jewish tradition. In the OT, Moses died and was buried (Deut 34:6). However, as his burial was not witnessed, there was speculation in Jewish literature over what happened at his death and burial. This verse draws on one tradition whereby the archangel Michael when disputing claims over Moses' body after his death, dared not blasphemously judge the leading fallen angel, the Devil. Michael is one of God's seven archangels (leading angels) in apocalyptic literature, also mentioned as a prince in Daniel (Dan 10:13, 21). In Revelation, he defeats the dragon and evil angels.[14] The language is legal, speaking of the Devil seeking to demonstrate his guilt and claim his body. While Michael could have stood in judgment over the Devil, he did not bring a blasphemous judgment against him. Instead, alluding to Zech 3:2, where Satan sought to condemn Joshua, but God vindicated Joshua and rebuked Satan, Michael called the Lord to rebuke him. Here Michael is an example to the believing recipients—rather than emulate the false teachers who dare to blaspheme demons, they must not do so. They are humbly to let the Lord rebuke them.

The origin of this story is unclear. It comes from either the Assumption of Moses or the Testament of Moses. However, this is uncertain as we do not have the original version. We know that the

---

14. Rev 12:7, s.a. 1QM 9:16; 1 En. 9:1; 10:11; 20:5; 24:6.

devil challenged Moses' claim of an honorable burial because he had killed the Egyptian. Michael then called on God to rebuke the Devil, and the Devil fled, enabling the completion of the burial. Scholars debate the precise nuance of the dispute, but what is clear is that readers should be humble and not overstep the mark where angels and demons are concerned. That is the Lord's business.

In v. 10, the false teachers are not named; they are "these people." They are not worthy of being named. They are slanderous, blaspheming the sacred. While they are people, they are nothing better than "unreasoning animals." They are corrupting themselves.

Verse 11 is a woe oracle—an interjection of their impending doom. The reason is that they have emulated three OT characters who symbolize sinful rebellion against God.

First, Jude compares them to Cain, who presented a flawed offering to God and murdered his brother (Gen 4:1–16, s.a. Heb 11:4; 1 John 3:12). These false teachers participate in the Lord's Supper yet are utterly corrupt and drink judgment on themselves (cf. 1 Cor 11:29). In seeking to corrupt others, and lead them astray from the gospel, they are effectively committing fratricide as those they corrupt face God's wrath with them.

Second, they followed Balaam's error. Balaam was a false prophet who was paid by Balak, the king of Moab, to curse Israel en route to the land. A donkey rebuked him.[15] These false teachers are false prophets of a false version of the Christian faith who seek material gain.

Third, they are like Korah, the great-grandson of Levi, who led a rebellion of 250 leaders against Moses and Aaron. The leaders and their families were swallowed up by God and taken to Sheol, and the rebels were destroyed by fire. After this, the complaint again broke out, and 14,700 died of a plague (Num 16:1–50). The false teachers are rebels like Korah challenging God and his leaders. They will be

---

15. Num 22–24; Deut 23:4–5; Neh 13:2; 2 Pet 2:15; Rev 2:14.

eternally destroyed by fire and in Sheol. The readers must not join their rebellion.

In vv. 12–13, Jude's description invokes their fallen state and urges the readers to have nothing to do with them. He describes them as "hidden reefs" or "blemishes" at their love feasts. The love feast was the gathering in which the Lord's Supper was taken (cf. 1 Cor 11:17–34; Acts 2:42, 46).

The same idea is found in Ignatius' letter to Smyrna: "It is not permissible either, to baptize or to hold a love (*agapē*) feast without a bishop" (Holmes, Ign. *Smyrn.* 8:2). It is a gathering of love between the triune God and his people. These people shipwreck the faith of others at these gatherings, or they stain them with their impurity. They "feast without fear," arrogantly believing themselves to be right with God when they are a disgrace before him. They are "shepherds who feed themselves," implying that they are leaders but ones who are self-absorbed. They are like those in Corinth who go ahead of others taking the choicest food and getting drunk, while others go hungry and thirsty (1 Cor 11:17–22). They are waterless clouds, meaning they are nothing, for a waterless cloud is not a cloud. They are swept by the winds, showing they lack a foundation and are lightweights (cf. Eph 4:14). They are dead like fallen trees that shed leaves and bear no fruit (cf. Mark 11:12–14, 20–25, and pars). Indeed, they are utterly dead (twice dead) and uprooted from the source of life, Jesus Christ. They are not only non-clouds blown by the wind. They are also like sea waves foaming up shame (Isa 57:20).

They are wandering stars that do not hold to their God-ordained movements. Stars were considered deities, implying that they were effectively demons. Further, the celestial bodies were used for guidance, especially at sea—they mislead people into eternal lostness. Their fate is named: "the gloom of utter darkness has been reserved forever." Jude's theology of eternal destruction involves eternal darkness. The warning is apparent—those who join them will experience eternal darkness.

Verses 14–15 draw on another non-canonical book, 1 Enoch 1:9. It reads, "Behold, he will arrive with ten million of the holy ones to execute judgment upon all. He will destroy the wicked ones and censure all flesh on account of everything that they have done, that which the sinners and the wicked ones committed against him" (Charlesworth). Jude describes Enoch as the seventh from Adam, counting inclusively. Enoch was described as one who "walked with God" and "was not, for God took him" (Gen 5:21-24). Tradition held that he did not die. Some apocalyptic writings are attributed to him, including 1 Enoch. These works are obviously pseudonymous. 1 Enoch 1-5 was written by the time of Jude, and so the mid-first century. Jude knew of the work, and so did his readers (or it would be redundant). Jude's use of it (along with the Assumption of Moses) shows his respect. However, citing it does not imply canonicity any more than the Greek poets Epimenides and Aratus Paul quotes should be included in the canon (Acts 17:28; Tit 1:9). Neither 1 Enoch nor the Assumption of Moses is canonical to Jews or Christians of any persuasion. Still, it shows the value of the Jewish apocryphal and apocalyptic writings—they state the truth even if they are not inspired. The point of the citation is clear: God is coming in judgment on the ungodly. In v. 16, their grumbling, discontent, sinfully lustful lives, arrogant boastfulness, and prejudice must be repudiated.

Verse 17 is a call to remember not OT Scriptures of doom but the predictions of Christ's apostles. This appeal implies that they have been taught these predictions. In v. 18, they are cited with a saying that is not found in any apostolic writings but should be seen as an example of early apostolic teaching (cf. 2 Pet 3:3): "In the end time there will be scoffers, following their own ungodly passions." These false teachers and those in 2 Peter fulfill this prophecy (as have many since). In v. 19, they are again described as divisive, worldly, and devoid of the Spirit.

In verses 20-23, Jude instructs them on how to live in the face of these challenges.[16] In v. 20, they first take responsibility for their

---

16. Verses 22-23 are textually difficult as there is a range of readings,

faith by building *themselves* up. Jude 20 is an important verse reminding us to be personally responsible to ensure that we grow in the faith. Second, they are to pray in the Spirit, speaking of being led by God and not the heresy of the false teachers. Third, they are to keep themselves in God's love rather than violate the love of Christ as the false teachers do at the *agapē* feasts. Fourth, they are to await Christ's mercy leading to eternal life, rather than live abusing his grace.

Where others waver or doubt, perhaps due to false teaching, they are to have mercy upon them, as Christ has had mercy on them. Where believers are being deceived and led astray by the likes of the false teachers, they are to "save" them by "snatching them out of the fire" (v. 23). This speaks of doing everything in our power to save them from the eternal destruction that awaits them. The final category of people is unclear. The best solution seems that these are those who are defiled by sin. They must show mercy to them, but with fear (of contamination), despising their "clothing" of sin. This requirement speaks of reaching out to those swept aside into deep sin, seeking to save them without being drawn into their sinful lifestyles.

The final doxology is a remarkable statement of assurance; God "is able to preserve you from stumbling and present you blameless before" him. As is fitting of a brother of Jesus, he ends with the glorification of God through Christ. All Christians should memorize this assurance to strengthen their faith.

meaning that it is unclear whether there are three classes of people or two in mind. Metzger, A *Textual Commentary*, 658–61. These do not greatly affect meaning, and I have gone with NA28 in this brief discussion.

Conclusion

Jude is a fascinating little book written by one of Jesus' brothers, who came to Christ after Christ's resurrection, perhaps due to his brother James' experiencing Christ's resurrection. He was at Pentecost and undoubtedly a key figure in the early church. His letter reminds us how important it is to preserve the gospel and that leaders sometimes have to deal with false teachers firmly. For the NT writers, judgment and eternal destruction are real, and we must take this seriously. Fascinatingly, Jude cites pseudepigraphal works that make us think about canonization and sacred scripture. We are warned against compromising our faith in the direction of the world. We must not be flippant about spiritual matters. It is possible to fall from faith, and we must work hard to maintain a strong relationship with God and Christ. We build ourselves up in our faith and pray in the Spirit. We are also urged to be missional, show mercy to doubters, and do our best to save others from the fires of eternal destruction. The final doxology should be read in worship regularly. It is superb.

Part Two: The Petrine Letters

There are two letters attributed to Peter in the NT. They are both highly contentious in terms of authorship, especially 2 Peter. I will look briefly at each in turn.

1 Peter

Authorship and Setting

The authorship of 1 Peter is challenged.[17] However, the arguments are not strong, and there is little reason to believe that the early church would have accepted a pseudonymous letter from the one who was viewed as "the rock of the church." The letter was probably written in Rome toward the end of Peter's life (the mid-60s). Silas (also Silvanus) probably penned it for him (1 Pet 5:13).

Recipients and Purpose

It was written to Anatolia churches, including Pontus, Galatia, Cappadocia, Asia Minor, and Bithynia. These are areas that Peter did not personally evangelize and was either evangelized by Paul or others unknown. It is possible that Peter had traveled through this area in the mid-50s after his visit to Corinth and that he had developed a bond with these churches.

He writes to encourage them under persecution and gives directions on how to live in this world. He calls believers foreigners and aliens, using the language of exile to describe them. There is a strong emphasis on living in relation to governing authorities. Peter encourages his readers to submit to authorities as much as they can without violating their allegiance to Christ and to give witness through their lives and words of their renewed life in Christ.

---

17. For a fuller discussion, see Keown, *Discovering*, 3:108–51 (Ch. 3).

A Brief Overview

Prescript (1:1–2)

The letter begins with the name Peter. He is clearly Simon, renamed Peter (the rock) by Jesus, who dominates the Gospels. He was one of Jesus' earliest disciples, a brother of Andrew, and was one of Jesus' inner circle, along with the Zebedee brothers. He was also often the spokesperson of the Twelve. Tradition holds that Mark's Gospel is a recording of his teaching by John Mark, who is described as his son in 1 Pet 5:13—indicating a close relationship. Acts 12 indicates they knew each other as well. Peter also dominates the first half of Acts and is the dominant leader in the first phase of Jerusalem Christianity.

After Agrippa I killed James, Peter left the city and traveled extensively. We can track his movements to Syrian Antioch (Gal 2:11-14) and Corinth (1 Cor 1:12), and this letter indicates he traveled through Anatolia and was known to the churches to which he writes. Tradition holds he died by crucifixion (upside down) at Nero's instigation sometime AD 65-67. He describes himself as an apostle of Jesus Christ, which is appropriate as he is one of the Twelve appointed by Christ (Mark 3:16 and parr.). He writes to those who are "elect exiles of the Dispersion" throughout Anatolia (mod. Turkey). These, then, are those elected by God (Christians) who are separated from their heavenly home on earth (exiles). Verse 2 describes them as those chosen according to God's foreknowledge and sanctified by the Spirit. Their purpose is obedience to Jesus and purity by the blood he has shed. Like Paul, he adds a blessing of grace and peace.

Blessed Be God for Our Glorious Salvation (1:3–12)

Paul begins 2 Corinthians and Ephesians with blessings to God, and

Peter does the same here. He blesses God and Christ. He does so because of God's mercy shown in Christ that has caused them to be born again into the hope of the resurrection of Jesus (v. 3). Christian readers are born again into an imperishable inheritance held in heaven for them by God (v. 4). Meanwhile, God is guarding them for salvation at the culmination of the age (v. 5). Despite suffering many trials that grieve them and test their precious imperishable faith, the readers rejoice (v. 6). Their perseverance will result in increased honor to Jesus at his coming (v. 7). The readers love Christ, believe in him, and rejoice greatly and gloriously. However, they have never seen him (v. 8). Because of their faith, they will receive the salvation of their souls (v. 9). This is the salvation premised on the sufferings of Jesus and his glorification that was revealed to the prophets by the Spirit (vv. 10–11). The things they anticipated and which angels long to see have now been announced to the readers through those who evangelized them by the Spirit from heaven (v. 12). Those who did this were probably Paul's coworkers when he was in Ephesus (Acts 19:9–10); like Epaphras (Col 1:7).

Instructions for Christian Life (1:13–4:19)

This passage is long with many detours. However, throughout, Peter instructs his readers on how they should live in the pagan Roman world of Asia Minor, considering the glorious salvation that is theirs in God.

Be Holy (1:13–19)

The "therefore" that starts this section indicates what follows are things they should infer from the glorious salvation with which the readers have been blessed. They are to be mentally prepared for action, sober-minded, and always hopeful in God's grace experienced through the revelation of Jesus in the gospel (v. 13). As

God's obedient children, they are not to be conformed to the lusts that dominated their former ignorant pagan lives (cf. Rom. 12:2). Rather, just as God is holy, they are to be holy (Lev 11:44). They have a God who judges each person's deeds justly. They also know that he has ransomed them by the blood of the unblemished Jesus from the futile life of their idolatrous and heathen lives of their ancestors. Knowing these things, they are to live as foreigners in an unholy world with reverence for God (vv. 18-19).

Born Again by the Word of Jesus (1:20–25)

The unblemished lamb Jesus was foreknown before creation but has been made known now for the sake of God's people who, through him, are believers in God who raised him from the dead to glory for this very purpose (vv. 20-21). Purified by obedience to the gospel (truth), they are to love each other earnestly and sincerely (v. 22). They do this because they have been born again through the imperishable, living, and abiding Word of God (v. 23). While people are like grass and flowers that wither and fall, the Word of the Lord (Jesus) preached to them remains forever (v. 25). Peter here endorses that Christians are to live by the Word of God, for it is by the Word they experienced God's salvation.

Put Away False Speech and Grow in Maturity (2:1–3)

As those born again by this Word, they are to put away their own false words—malice, deceit, hypocrisy, envy, and slander (1 Pet 2:1). They are to be hungry for more of that Word, like babies yearning for milk. In such a way, they will grow up into salvation now that they have tasted that the Lord is good (2:2-3).

Priests Declaring the Excellencies of God (2:4–10)

Peter draws on the image of the temple in this section. Jesus is likened to a living stone rejected by people but chosen and precious in God's sight (2:4). Those who come to him are living stones built together with Christ, the living stone into a spiritual house (temple). They are also a priesthood who, through Christ, offer spiritual sacrifices of service that are acceptable to God (2:5). To reinforce the idea, Peter cites three OT texts (Isa 28:16; Ps 118:22; Isa 8:14) that early Christians applied to Jesus (Rom 9:33; 10:11). He is the chosen and precious cornerstone laid in Zion by God, who is the object of belief, and will never shame those who trust in him (v. 6). However, for those who do not believe in him and disobey the Word (as destined to do), he is the stone rejected by the builders who, nevertheless, is the cornerstone (v. 7) and a stumbling stone of offense (v. 8).

The Anatolian recipients, however, have believed in him and, as such, are a chosen race, a royal priesthood, a holy nation, and people belonging to God—one of the most concise and brilliant summaries of Christian identity in the NT. Their purpose is to proclaim the excellencies of God who called them out of darkness into his marvelous light (v. 9). While previously, the diverse recipients were not united as one people but were divided by race, social class, and gender, and were objects of wrath (implied), now they belong to God having received mercy (v. 10).

As foreigners in a hostile world and exiles separated from their heavenly home, they are to abstain from the passions of the flesh that blight their souls. As they live among the Gentiles, they are to always live with honor even when treated as evildoers. They do this in the hope that unbelievers will see their virtuous deeds, take note, and glorify God when his Word is proclaimed to them (vv. 11–12).

Submit to Authorities (2:13–20)

1 Peter 2:13-17 sits alongside Romans 13:1-7 and Titus 3:1 as passages that should shape how Christians live in relation to the state and human authorities. In line with Paul in these passages, Peter urges them to be subject to human institutions; whether it is Caesar, or his appointed governors sent to punish the evil and praise the good (v. 13). For Peter, this is God's will. He hopes that their goodness will silence the ignorance of foolish people (vv. 14-15). They are to live as people freed by God but not to do evil. They are to be God's slaves in and for the world (v. 16). Verse 17 is a set of maxims summarizing how they are to live. They are to honor everyone, love their fellow believers, revere God, and give honor to Caesar. Domestic slaves are also to be subservient to their masters with respect even then their masters are not good or gentle (v. 18). For Peter, this is how all Christians mindful of God should behave when enduring unjust punishment (v. 19). It is creditable to suffer for doing good but not for evil (v. 20).

The Example of Christ (2:21–25)

Although this section flows out of the injunctions to domestic slaves, it applies more broadly to Christians living in any social situation where they are disparaged. Indeed, soon after 1 Peter, Peter died at the hands of Nero. The supreme example of perseverance and non-retaliation when suffering is Christ.

Suffering Christians are called to endure and respond with goodness. They are to do so because Christ suffered for the readers (and all Christians) in this same way. Believers must walk in his steps (v. 21). First, he did not sin, so while they can never live up to this supreme standard, they should resist sin. Second, they should emulate Christ's example of utter fidelity in his speech (v. 22). Third, he did not respond to malicious slander toward himself, so Christians should do the same. Fourth, they must imitate his example of trusting in God rather than threatening their opponents when they cause them suffering (v. 23).

Verse 24 is a crisp summary of Christ bearing the sins of humankind on the cross so that they might die to sin and live to righteousness. Again, they are exhorted not to sin. Verse 24b cites Isa 53:5 of the servant who heals people by his wounds. Jesus is the Servant through whom people experience healing. This healing is salvation when God acts as he wills to alleviate suffering in the present and finally and entirely at the eschaton. Verse 25 is an allusion to Isa 53:6 that sums up the human state—like straying sheep, we waver from God's ideals. Now, the readers (and all believers) have returned to Jesus, the Shepherd and overseer of our souls. Praise God.

Instructions to Wives and Husbands (3:1–7)

The theme of submission to authority launched in 2:13 continues, so this is another section under that heading. The backdrop is the ancient world in which it was unquestionable that wives were to submit to their husbands as slaves did to masters. The situation is not general; Peter is addressing the specific situation where a believing woman is married to a heathen person who has heard the gospel (Word) and refused to obey it. As this is the setting, and as the many other references to the submission of wives are interpreted variously, some hold that what is said applies specifically to an analogous situation. Others hold that this is a universal imperative.

In whatever way we apply this, Peter urges women married to unbelievers who have rejected the gospel to win them not with more gospel proclamation but with their respectful and pure conduct. Doing this includes being gentle and quiet and maintaining a modest appearance (which pleases God). Unlike the elite woman in the first-century Greco-Roman world who were drawn to the trappings of elaborate hairstyles and clothing (as many wealthy people are today). Verses 5–6 tell the women that this is how the holy woman of God adorned themselves in Israel's story. He illustrates his appeal by recalling Sarah's obedience to Abraham as her master (Lord, Gen 18:12). Those who do are Sarah's children and do not need to fear (cf. Gal 4:21–31).

As Paul does in Eph 5:22–33 and Col 3:18–19, Peter balances the injunctions to wives with instructions to the husbands to be understanding and honor their wives as weaker vessels as they inherit the grace of life (eternal salvation). Furthermore, their prayers will be unhindered if they treat their wives in such a way. The implication is that maltreatment of one's spouse can cause prayers to be unanswered by God. There is debate about what Peter means by "weaker vessels"—is this physical or about their social status? Is this universal, cultural, or purely contextual? Such questions are challenging and require analysis of the whole biblical data.

Suffer with Humility and Love (3:8–22)

The dominant theme in this section is suffering. When Peter wrote the letter, Christians were persecuted by Jews and Gentiles spasmodically outside of Italy. In Rome, Nero was beginning to persecute Christians. Verse 8 is a general appeal for all to show Christian unity, love, gentleness, and humility.

Verse 9 introduces the dominant issue—how to respond to persecution. First, Christians are not to retaliate to evil and abuse with the same. Instead, Christians are to bless persecutors as they are called to do so, and for which they will be rewarded (Luke 6:28; Rom 12:14).

Peter supports this in vv. 10-12 with Ps 34:12-16. In the Psalm, those seeking a good life do not speak evil but do good and pursue peace. Jesus (the Lord) is watching his people and listening to their prayers, but he opposes evildoers.

Verses 13-17 begin with Peter asking who will harm them if they are zealous for goodness. Yet, Peter is not naïve; he is aware that even if they do good, sometimes they will suffer (as across the empire and in Rome). If they do suffer for the sake of righteousness, they are blessed. They are not to be afraid or troubled but respond with honorific worship of Jesus (vv. 14-15a). They are always to be prepared to make a defense when asked by unbelievers to give a reason for the hope they have. Their defense must be made with gentleness, respect, and a clear conscience. Such a response will cause those who slander them to be put to shame (vv. 15b-16, cf. Rom 12:17-21). He concludes that it is better to suffer for doing good if that is God's will, not evil (v. 17).

As he did in 2:21-25, Peter goes to the example of Christ, again with fascinating details that have led to substantial debate. The utterly righteous Christ suffered once for sins to bring the righteous to God. He was put to death in the flesh but made alive in the spirit—a physical, spiritual body fully animated by the Spirit (cf. 1 Cor 15:44). In vv. 19-20, Peter explains that the risen Jesus went and proclaimed to the imprisoned spirits who had not previously obeyed during the days of Noah as he built the ark to save his family of eight through the flood. For some, this is evidence that Jesus preached in hell to those dead before Christ's incarnation. Others see this as Jesus' triumphal proclamation to the spirits of fallen angels, including those who cohabitated with humans (Gen 6:2; 2 Pet 2:4; Jude 6-7). The latter seems more likely, but one cannot rule out the former idea that supports the credal notion of Jesus' descent into hell.[18]

Whatever is meant, in v. 21, Peter likens the deliverance of Noah and his family to baptism (compare how Paul speaks of baptism and the Red Sea in 1 Cor 10:2). He reminds them of their water baptism that corresponds to the flood. They are saved not by removing external dirt but by being cleansed internally by God through Christ's resurrection. Verse 22 summarizes Jesus' status now—his

---

18. E.g., the Apostle's Creed: "He descended into hell." However, it is not included in the Nicaean Creed.

ascension, exaltation to God's right hand, and complete authority over all spiritual and temporal powers. Remembering that he earlier said believers are to yield to the governing authorities, this reminds us that our commitment to God and his Son trumps this when we are forced to do something that violates the core of the gospel.

Reject the Heathen Passions of the Flesh (4:1–11)

This new section divides neatly into two. The first half in vv. 1-6 focuses on rejecting the passions and lusts of their Gentile (heathen) world. The second half calls them to the virtues of life in God.

In v. 1, Peter carries on the theme of Christ, returning to his redemptive death in which he suffered "in the flesh." Readers are to emulate Christ and resist the desires of the flesh, rejecting its passions and so ceasing to sin, and live by the will of God (v. 2). Verse 3 reminds them of the passions that dominated their lives as Gentiles—sensuality, lusts, boozing and partying, orgies, and idolatry that violates the law of exclusive worship of God. They must continue to avoid such things, even though the Gentiles presently cannot understand why the believers no longer join them in such depravity and abuse them for doing so. However, they have done the right thing as they and all people will face God in judgment and, unlike the lost, will come through saved (implied). Verse 6 is another possible reference to Christ going to hell to preach to the dead. However, others believe this refers to people on earth who heard the gospel and will face judgment so that they, too, may live in a way to please God.

Verses 7 to 11 list appropriate behaviors for God's people as they await the end of the age. As it is approaching, they are to have self-control, be sober-minded (so their prayers are heard), love each other deeply (above all things—which covers over sin), and show each other hospitality without complaint (vv. 7-9). Verse 10 shows that Peter holds a similar understanding of spiritual gifts to Paul and the author of Hebrews[19]—as good stewards of God's grace, each member should use their gifts to serve other believers. Verse 11 urges them to speak carefully and wholeheartedly serve God so that he is glorified through Jesus Christ (and through them). Like Paul, he ends with a doxology (cf. Rom 11:36; Eph 3:21).

Rejoice in Suffering (4:12–19)

The theme of suffering dominated 3:8–22. Peter returns to the theme again, showing that Peter and the readers were facing severe challenges at the time. The readers should not be surprised that they are experiencing a fiery trial (v. 12). This does not necessarily mean literal burning for the readers, but this may allude to Nero's burning of Roman Christians (Tacitus, *Nero* 15.44). Such things test believers but are not unexpected in a hostile world (this applies today). Peter urges them to rejoice in these, not because they are good, but because in their suffering, they share in Christ's.

Further, they will rejoice when he is revealed as those who persevere receive their salvation (v. 13). He assures them that when they are insulted for Christ, they are blessed as God's glorious Spirit rests on them (v. 14). As he mentioned earlier in 3:13 and 17, they are not to suffer for doing evil things like murder and theft. Such things bring shame (implied). However, if they suffer as Christians, they should not be ashamed but give glory to God (v. 16).

Verse 17 could indicate that Peter views their suffering as God's judgment. However, it more likely points forward to eternal judgment when they face God, as will all people. They must continue to obey the gospel, as the outcome for those who do not is unimaginable. Verse 18 cites Proverbs 11:31 to reinforce their need to persevere and ponder the horrors awaiting the ungodly and sinful. Verse 19 concludes with a summary—those who suffer must

---

19. Rom 12:4–8; 1 Cor 12–14; Eph 4:11; Heb 2:4.

continue to do good and entrust themselves to their faithful Creator God.

Instructions to Elders and Their Flock (5:1–5)

In 5:1-4, Peter gives instructions to the presbyters of the church (elders), appointed to lead God's churches (Acts 14:23). In v. 1, he makes his appeal as a fellow elder, witness to Christ's sufferings, and partaker of future glory. He commands them to shepherd God's flock. The elder's role, then, is that of a shepherd who ensures their flock is protected from false teaching and fed with the Word (2:25).[20] They are to do so with careful oversight, willingly, not seeking material gain, eagerly, without dominating, and by being examples (5:2-3). If they do, when Jesus (the Great Shepherd) appears, they will receive their reward of eternal life (unfading crown of glory).

The church members are to be subject to the elders as their leaders. They are to be clothed in humility toward one another. Like James (Jas 4:6), Peter supports this notion with Prov 3:34 (LXX) that God gives grace to the humble while opposing the arrogant. As such, they are to humble themselves before God's mighty hand so he will exalt them at the appropriate time (vv. 5-6). He gives other instructions. They are to cast their anxieties on God as he cares for them and be sober-minded and watchful (v. 7). In one of the great texts concerning Satan/the devil in Scripture, he warns them that he is their adversary who prowls like a roaring lion seeking someone to devour (v. 8).[21] As such, readers are to resist the devil and stand firm in the faith while recognizing that Christians all over the world

---

20. The shepherd image is common in the NT applied to Jesus (Matt 9:36; John 10:2-16; Heb 13:20) and elders and overseers (Acts 20:28).
21. Some hold this is a veiled reference to Nero, the lion; however, this is unlikely.

are experiencing such suffering (v. 9). In v. 10, he assures them that after their suffering for a little while (compared to eternal glory, cf. Rom 8:18; 2 Cor 4:17), the God of all grace who called them to eternal glory in Christ will complete his work in them (restore, confirm, strengthen, establish). He concludes the letter with another cry of praise, declaring God's dominion forever (v. 11, cf. 4:11).

The Writer, Final Appeal, and Greetings (5:12–14)

He ends with a fascinating postscript. We learn Silvanus (Silas) is the amanuensis for the letter. He is described as a faithful brother. His faithfulness is confirmed in the wider NT as he was a Jerusalem NT prophet who delivered the letter from the Jerusalem Council and traveled with Paul extensively. We see strong links between Peter and Paul with the mention of Silas and Mark. The modern myth that early Christianity was irrevocably split between Pauline and Petrine Christianity is challenged by such cross-references. We learn the purpose of the letter; that they stand firm in the true grace of God (v. 12).

Verse 13 sees Peter describe Rome as Babylon, as was common in early Christian literature. The church in the city of God's chosen sends greetings, as does John Mark, who he describes as his son. This association adds credence to the tradition Mark's Gospel is more Peter's than Mark's. He urges them to greet each other with a kiss of love (otherwise, the holy kiss).[22] He finishes praying for peace (Shalom) for all who are "in Christ— a touch of Paul's theology.

---

22. Rom 16:16; 1 Cor 16:20; 2 Cor 13:12; 1 Thess 5:26. An embrace and cheek-to-cheek kiss.

Conclusion

Peter's first letter is an excellent resource for discipleship. It starts by reminding readers of the glorious blessings they experience in the gospel. Readers are then equipped for life as aliens and strangers in a world now foreign to them as God's people. They are to be holy and obedient to the Word that saved them. As they are priests, they are to offer appropriate spiritual sacrifices and proclaim God's excellencies in the church and world. The letter gives great guidance for living under oppressive rule, stressing the importance of emulating Christ's example. They are guided in giving witness to unbelieving spouses and when challenged concerning their faith. Believers are to reject the sins of their age and recognize suffering as a blessing. All Christian leaders should dwell on 1 Peter 5:15, and all Christians must persevere in resisting evil, suffering, and hope.

2 Peter

Authorship and Setting

The authorship of 2 Peter is hugely challenged, so much so that most scholars believe it is not the work of the apostle Peter.[23] Although there are significant differences between 1 and 2 Peter and similarities to Jude's work, it is improbable that the early church would accept a work in Peter's name written by someone else. It is most likely that Jude used Peter, Peter used Jude, or they used a common source (the view I prefer).

The date is hard to ascertain. Those who maintain it is pseudonymous argue that it must be later than Peter's death, so opt

---

23. For a fuller discussion, see Keown, *Discovering*, 3:152–91 (Ch. 4).

for a date in the 70s to 90s. Those who accept Petrine authorship date it before Peter's death (unsurprisingly), in AD 65–67. They also believe it was written from Rome, where Peter was incarcerated. His impending death is apparent in 2 Pet 1:12–13.

Recipients

It is written to "those who have obtained a faith equal in value to ours through the righteousness of our God and Savior Jesus Christ" (2 Pet 1:1). In 2 Pet 3:1, he mentions that this is his second letter to his recipients. As such, it is probably written to the same churches of Anatolia addressed in 1 Peter 1:1.

False Teaching

This time there is evidence of false teaching. The main reason for the letter is to call the readers to resist and reject them.

Some of the features of these false teachers and prophets from chapters 2 & 3 include:

1. Denying Christ (2 Pet 2:1).
2. Sexual immorality (2 Pet 2:2, 7, 13).
3. Greed and exploitation (2 Pet 2:3, 14).
4. Slandering celestial beings and angels (2 Pet 2:10–11).
5. Sin and seductiveness (2 Pet 2:14).
6. Boastfulness and empty words (2 Pet 2:18).
7. People who previously believed but have turned to heresy (2 Pet 2:20).
8. Repudiating and mocking the return of Christ and the establishment of the new heavens and earth (2 Pet 3:1–13).
9. Distorting Paul's teaching (2 Pet 3:15–16).

Identifying the exact set of ideas is challenging. It has some aspects of Greco-Roman perspectives (e.g., sexual immorality). The teaching seems to question aspects of eschatology in the wider NT, such as Christ's return.

Peter's Response

Peter's letter encourages his audience to trust in God's promises and add to their faith other character attributes, including self-control, perseverance, and love which will cause them to be effective for Christ (2 Pet 1:3–9). Knowing he will die soon (2 Pet 1:12–13), he writes to encourage them, reminding them that he is an eyewitness to Christ at his transfiguration (2 Pet 1:16–17) and that the inspired prophecies have been fulfilled (2 Pet 1:19–21).

Peter's rebuke of the false teachers is powerful. He uses powerful language to describe them and their judgment in 2 Pet 2:4–9. He recalls the judgment on the ungodly when the sons of God copulated with human women (Gen 6:1–4), at the flood (Gen 6:5–8:19), Sodom and Gomorrah (Gen 18), and Balaam (cf. Num 22). Just as these sinful people experienced God's wrath in history, these false teachers will also experience terrible suffering for all eternity (2 Pet 2:17).

Chapter 3 speaks of the coming judgment on the scoffers in the last days. Just as the world was purged with the flood at the time of Noah, and only he saw it coming, Christ will come unheralded, like a thief, and the world will be purged with fire (2 Pet 3:3–13). This passage recalls Jesus' teaching in Matt 24 and Luke 17, where judgment is likened to the flood. A new heaven and earth will supersede the earth. However, God wants everyone to be saved from this (2 Pet 3:9).

Believers should live holy and pleasing lives while they await this day (2 Pet 3:11, 14). Peter mentions the letters of his dear brother Paul which some distort but are actually Scriptures. This statement is radical as it places Paul's letters alongside the Scriptures of Israel. Peter finishes with a warning to not be deceived by the false teachers and fall from grace but instead grow in grace and knowledge in Christ (2 Pet 3:15–18).

A Brief Overview

Prescript (1:1–2)

Peter begins describing himself as Simeon, his original name that was simplified to Simon. Peter, of course, is his Greek name given to him by Jesus, meaning "rock." He describes himself as "a slave and apostle of Jesus Christ," combining a maligned and demeaning concept (slave) with a highly honorific title (apostle). By doing so, readers recognize that an apostle may be a leader, but their dream job is serving their Lord Jesus.

He addresses the letter in a way that affirms the readers as being of equal status by faith with the apostles. They received such an exalted identity "by the righteousness of our God and Savior Jesus Christ" gifted to all who believe—justification by faith (Rom 5:1; Gal 2:16).

His greeting includes Paul's favorite combo, grace (unmerited favor), and peace (with God and one another, Shalom). He asks God to multiply it to them with the knowledge of God and Jesus the Lord.

Cultivate Virtues that Confirm One's Calling (1:3–15)

Peter confirms to his readers that God and his Son's divine power have bestowed on them what is necessary for life and godliness. This power is experienced through knowing God, who calls Christians by his glory and virtuous character (v. 3). Through God's virtue, he has also granted believers the precious and great promises of the gospel. He has done this so that the readers (and all Christians) can share in God's divine nature—what a glorious statement of participation in God and his being! They partake in God's nature and have escaped the corruption of the world birthed by people's evil desires (v. 4).

Having escaped the world's corruption and become sharers in God's divine nature, believers are to diligently add to the faith that saves them a series of virtues that will enable them to live godly lives. These include excellence of character (imitating God, v. 3), knowledge, self-control, perseverance, godliness, brotherly affection, and love (vv. 5–7). This passage is crucial in understanding Christian ethics—their source is God, the virtues are named, and we are to pursue them diligently.

Verse 8 tells readers that if they increase in such things, they will not be useless and unproductive in their knowledge of their Lord Jesus Christ. Conversely, in v. 9, those who do not develop these things are blind, nearsighted, and have forgotten they have been cleansed from their former sins. Therefore, the Christian readers and members of God's family are even more zealous than ever to secure their calling and election. Their assurance is that those who develop these attributes will never stumble (v. 10). Indeed, the entrance into the eternal reign of Jesus Christ the Lord and Savior will be richly provided for them (v. 11).

Verse 12 states Peter's intention—to continually remind them of these things of the truth that they already know and in which they are established. Verses 13–14 indicate that Peter knows he will soon die, as Christ has made clear to him by personal revelation—as such, he knows it is right to stir up the readers regarding godly living and to ensure their entry into eternal life. Knowing he will die, he wants to leave behind the letter so they can remember what is required of them (v. 15).

Peter's Testimony (1:16–21)

Anticipating the critique of the false teachers that will dominate chs. 2 and 3, Peter affirms his proclamation about Jesus and the prophetic message of the gospel the readers have heard.

In vv. 16-18, Peter states emphatically that his message is not made up of "ingeniously concocted myths" but came via the disciples who walked with Jesus experiencing his ministry. They saw his power firsthand (v. 16). They were witnesses when he received God the Majestic Glory's honor and glory as he spoke from heaven at Jesus's baptism declaring him his beloved Son, in whom he is well pleased (Mark 1:11, vv. 17-18). Furthermore, they heard the same voice from heaven on the holy mountain—referring to his transfiguration (Mark 9:2-8).

Verses 19-21 shift from Jesus to the reliable prophetic Word of God, which may refer to the OT, but in context, may refer to the gospel, including the prophetic oracles, their fulfillment in Christ, and the message spoken to the readers. By the time of writing, the letters of Paul are considered Scripture (3:15-16), and it is possible Mark, Luke, and Acts were in circulation. Whatever he means, they are to pay attention to its message as God's light shining in a murky world until they experience his enlightenment in their hearts. He describes this beautifully as the day dawning and the morning star rising in their hearts (v. 19). Verses 20 and 21 indicate that the readers are to acknowledge that the prophetic words of Scripture came through the Spirit and not men (unlike the corrupt message of the false teachers). Peter here affirms the divine inspiration of Scripture.

The Fate of the Futile False Teachers (2:1–22)

This chapter is a blistering and brilliantly creative attack on the false teachers attacking the churches of Asia Minor. Peter recalls the OT era in which there were false prophets in Israel. Similarly, there will be false teachers in the Christian church. They bring heresies that cause destruction. They deny Christ ensuring swift destruction (v. 1). They are also licentious and cause people to revile the way of truth

(v. 2). They are greedy people who exploit the readers with false words. Yet, their condemnation and destruction are already awake and active (v. 3).

In verses 4 to 7, Peter lists OT examples of God's judgment on the wicked—God has not changed, and the false teachers will face him as well. First, he recalls angels who sinned against God and were imprisoned in Tartarus in chains of darkness to be kept for judgment. As in Jude 6, this likely refers to Gen 6:1-2 (v. 4). Second, Peter remembers the flood in which God destroyed the world of the ungodly while preserving Noah and seven others (Gen 6–9). He describes Noah as "a proclaimer of righteousness," anticipating the apostles to whom the readers should remain loyal (v. 5). Third, he reminds readers of the fiery destruction of Sodom and Gomorrah. They are supreme examples of the fate of the ungodly. However, God rescued righteous Lot despite his being worn out and tormented by the lawlessness and licentiousness of the inhabitants of the cities (vv. 6–8).

Verse 9 applies these three examples. The Lord knows how to save the godly (Noah, Lot) from trials. He also knows how to set apart the unrighteous—especially those who pursue fleshly, defiling lusts and despise authority—for punishment on the day of judgment. Knowing they will be destroyed, the readers are then to resist them, and God will rescue them as he did Lot and Noah.

Verses 10–22 describe the unrighteous. They are bold and arrogant, prepared to blaspheme majestic spiritual beings, which angels would never dare to do, despite their superior strength and power (vv. 10–11). They are like irrational animals that live by instinct to capture and kill. Consequently, they will be utterly destroyed as wages for their unrighteousness (vv. 12–13). They party decadently during the day and do so even when they feast with other Christians (v. 13). They are adulterous, sin continually, entice the unstable and vulnerable, and are greedy accursed children (v. 14). They have left the path of truth, following Balaam and his love for money that led him to curse Israel (v. 15; Num 22:5, 7). However, he also experienced

God's judgment for his lawlessness through a donkey who restrained the prophet's madness with a human voice.

They are waterless springs and mists driven by a fierce storm, destined for darkness (v. 17). They speak impressively, but their words are empty and merely entice the fleshly desires and licentiousness among those vulnerable to their error (v. 18). They falsely promise freedom when they are slaves of depravity (v. 19). As they are people who had escaped the corruption of the world through the knowledge of Jesus Christ the Lord and Savior and have again become entangled and have succumbed to such things, their final state will be worse than their previous state (v. 20). Peter pronounces that it would have been better for them to have never known the way of righteousness than turning away from it and turn back from the gospel (holy commandment) preached to them (v. 21). They fulfill Proverbs 26:11 and are like dogs returning to their vomit, or clean pigs wallowing in mud (v. 22).

The Day of the Lord is Coming! (3:1–13)

Verses 1–2 indicate Peter is writing his second letter to his beloved Christian family in the churches of Anatolia (1 Peter being the first). Both letters were written to stir their minds to remember the words proclaimed in the past by the holy prophets, the commandments of Jesus, the Lord, and Savior, through the apostles.

Verse 3 recalls 2:1, referring to the appearance of scoffers in the last days. They will follow their desires. They will also mock the promise of Christ's return as life goes on as it has since the creation—another feature of the false gospel of the heretics (v. 4).

Again, Peter turns to the flood to argue against them (cf. 2:5). These false teachers have not noticed that God, by his Word, destroyed the world he had created from water (vv. 5–6). Similarly, God has declared that the present heavens and earth are reserved for fire, kept for the day of judgment and the destruction of the ungodly (v. 7). Peter's meaning is debated. Some consider Peter is speaking of a literal fire that destroys the present world. Alternatively, fire is a metaphor for judgment; as the flood purified the world with water, this world will be purged by fire. If so, this refers to God's judgment and the destruction of the ungodly (as in the Flood). Therefore, God will not destroy the cosmos but renew it.

Either way, he pushes back against the scoffers. They fail to understand what God has said in his Word (Ps 90:4)—God's idea of time is not the same as that of people. For him, a day is like 1000 years and vice versa (v. 8). As such, the length of time is not at issue; God is faithful to his Word, however long it takes. He states this in v. 9—he is not delaying his promise according to such human machinations. Instead, he is patient toward humankind because he wants all to come to repentance and no one to perish. Again, scholars debate whether this is a general statement specific to the readers.

Whichever is correct, in v. 10, Peter asserts that the day of the Lord will come like a thief, and so suddenly and unexpectedly—a common NT motif.[24] Then, the heavens will disappear with a rushing noise, the celestial bodies will be destroyed by burning, and the earth and the deeds done on it will be disclosed. As this destruction is coming, people must be holy and godly as they wait and hasten the day's coming (vv. 11–12). Again, he asserts that the heavens will be destroyed by burning. The celestial bodies will melt in the extreme heat (v. 12). However, as Isa 65–66 portend, believers wait for the new heavens and new earth in which righteousness resides (v. 13). Again, scholars debate how this is to be understood—is it the destruction of the present universe and a new creation? Or is it the renewal of the cosmos by judgment and the destruction of evil?

---

24. See Matt 24:43; Luke 12:39; 1 Thess 5:2, 4; Rev 3:3; 16:15.

Final Instructions (3:14–18)

Peter ends his final letter with an appeal to his beloved Asian Christian family, urging them as they wait to give their everything to be at peace with God and each other and be spotless and unblemished in Christ (v. 14). They are to consider the patience of Christ in his not returning as salvation since people have opportunity to respond to the message. For Peter, this is the intent of Paul when he wrote his wise letters to the Asians (Ephesians, Colossians, Philemon, 1 Timothy, 2 Timothy) (v. 15). For Peter, Paul writes in this way in all his letters, speaking about such things including things difficult to understand. Sadly, others that Peter considers ignorant and unstable distort them and bring about their destruction (as they do all the Scriptures). This mention of Paul indicates that the false teachers are people like those who misappropriate Paul's ideas in Rome (Rom 3:8; 6:1, 15), Galatia (Gal 2:17), and Corinth (2 Cor 10–13). Peter's words warn us today to take care we interpret God's Word carefully and correctly.

As such, the beloved, knowing this, must guard themselves, so they do not lose their safe position in God by being led away by the error of such lawless people. Instead, as he began the letter, they must grow in the grace and knowledge of their Lord and Savior, Jesus Christ. His final written words are a doxology ascribing eternal glory to Christ.

Conclusion

Peter's last words should inspire us to stand firm in the authentic gospel handed down to us by the writers of Scripture. We should heed his Word and not distort Scripture, as people in his day were doing with Paul's letters. Instead, we are to be wary of false gospels, identify them, and reject them. The letter starts with some wonderful insights concerning our identity as people righteous before God and who participate in him. The following virtue list is an excellent summary of the progress we should want to make in God. The final chapter encourages us not to be impatient concerning Christ's return. God wants all to come to repentance, and Jesus will return when all have had that opportunity. In the meantime, we are to live holy lives that speed his coming. Then, we will live forever in the new heaven and earth purged of evil.

Part 3: The Johannine Letters

Background Issues

Authorship and Setting

The authorship of the three letters— traditionally attributed to John, the apostle—is highly disputed. Some consider them written by the elder John, mentioned in Papias. Many scholars see them as productions of a supposed "Johannine school" centered around the apostle John but not necessarily from his pen. As discussed concerning the authorship of John's Gospel, we must ask why the early church would have attributed them to the Apostle John without good reason.

They were written in Ephesus around the late 70s to 80s, after John's Gospel. 2 John and 3 John each have their own addressee, while 1 John does not have a specific recipient or recipients.

False Teaching

The letters of John focus on a heretical distortion of the Christian faith. The letters, and 1 John, in particular, suggest these features of the problem:

1. Some have left the community (1 John 2:18–19).
2. They deny Jesus is the Christ, the Messiah (1 John 2:22) and that he is God's Son (1 John 2:23; 4:14–15).
3. They are trying to lead the Christian recipients astray (1 John 2:26; 3:7).
4. They are false prophets (1 John 4:1) who do not acknowledge that Jesus came in the flesh (1 John 4:2, cf. 1 John 4:6; 2 John 7). Hence, they are docetic (Jesus was divine and not human).
5. They deny their sin (1 John 1:6–10).
6. The emphasis on love could imply that they are showing hate.

In summary, some false teachers or prophets are teaching that Jesus is not truly the Messiah because he is not truly a man (not of flesh), and they have broken away from the orthodox churches of the region.

There are different theories of which heresy this is:

1. *Gnosticism*: a movement based around secret knowledge and a duality between matter and Spirit. In Gnostic thought, Jesus only appeared to be human.
2. *Docetism*: a view that holds that Jesus appears to be a man but was not.
3. The *Heresy of Cerinthus*, who severed Jesus from the divine Christ. The Spirit/Christ came on Jesus at his baptism, leaving him to suffer on the cross.

While John is not addressing Gnosticism itself, John is likely opposing a docetic tendency and the first seeds of the Gnostic movement. Gnosticism flowered as a full-blown heresy half a century later.

1 John

1 John was written by John toward the end of his life (c. AD 90–100). He is an eyewitness who recalls walking with Christ, the Word of life (1 John 1:1–4).[25]

John's Response to the False Teaching

As noted above, 1 John has heresy in the background. The letter starts by emphasizing the reality of Jesus' incarnation. John declares that he saw, heard, and touched the human Jesus (1 John 1:1–4). He introduces the theme of light and darkness; true believers walk in the light forgiven by sin. False believers claim to be without sin. They should confess and be forgiven (1 John 1:5–10).

In chapter 2, John continues the theme of sin, urging his readers not to sin, but telling them that Jesus' death deals with sins (1 John 2:1–2). He urges obedience, perhaps challenging the false teachers (1 John 2:3–6). He states that this is not new but is the truth they initially heard (1 John 2:7–8). In 1 John 2:9–11, he introduces the idea of love, which is essential to the light. 1 John 2:12–14 is a poem urging all in the church to stay faithful to the truth. This love cannot be directed to the things of this world that are flawed and corrupted. Lust and boasting must be left behind because the world we know is passing away (1 John 2:15–17).

1 John 2:18–27 warns against the false teachers who are antichrists (see above). The believers know the truth and must not be deceived by these liars who deny the incarnation of Christ (1 John 2:20–27). As children, they must carry on in him, experiencing the love of God and not be led astray (1 John 2:28–3:10). The letter strongly emphasized that believers must love one another as Christ loved the

---

25. For a fuller discussion, see Keown, *Discovering*, 3:192–218 (Ch. 5).

world and that they must be obedient (1 John 3:11–24). In chapter 4, John again warns of false spirits and prophets. Believers must not listen to them (1 John 4:1–6). He again emphasizes love—for God is love (1 John 4:7–21).

In the last chapter, he urges faith, love, and obedience and stresses the reality of Christ's incarnation (1 John 5:1–12). He concludes the letter with a statement of confidence in prayer (1 John 5:13–15), the renunciation of sin (1 John 5:16–17), that Satan rules the world (1 John 5:19), and that Jesus is the true Son of God who has come. He is God and eternal life (1 John 5:20). Believers must avoid idolatry that challenges the exclusive worship of God and his Son.

A Brief Overview

Prescript (1:1–4)

Unusually for an NT letter, 1 John does not begin with a name (e.g., John) and a description (e.g., apostle), mention of the recipients, nor a greeting, thanksgiving, prayer, or blessing. Rather, recalling John 1:1–18, John begins by focusing on Jesus, the Word.

He is the "Word of life," from the beginning, heard, seen, and touched by the disciples (we) (v. 1). He is the life that was made manifest among them that they saw and of whom they testify. He is the eternal life, who was with the Father and who they proclaim to the readers (v. 2). They have seen and heard this life and proclaim it again to the readers with the purpose that they may have fellowship with them and with God the Father and Jesus Christ the Son (v. 3). He writes on their behalf that their joy may be complete (v. 4).

Walk in the Light (1:5–10)

This section focuses on the theme of light and draws a contrast between genuine people who acknowledge their sins and come to God for forgiveness and those who do not. The message Jesus gave them and that they have passed on is that God is pure light without darkness (v. 5). However, if someone claims to walk in a relationship with him yet walks in darkness, they lie and do not practice the truth (v. 6). This hints at the problem of false Christians behind the letter. However, if people walk in God's light, they are joined together in fellowship and cleansed by the blood of Jesus (v. 7). This walking in the light is not perfection or sinlessness. Indeed, if someone claims to have no sin, they are self-deceived, and the truth does not dwell in them (v. 8). But if someone acknowledges their sin and confesses them, God is faithful to forgive them of their sins and to cleanse them from all unrighteousness. This forgiveness is possible because of Christ's redemptive death. Those who say they have not sinned make him out to be a liar, and his Word does not dwell in them (v. 10).

Keep His Commandments (2:1–6)

Affectionately addressing readers as "my little children," John tells readers he writes so they will not sin. However, if anyone does, Jesus is their advocate (*paraklētos*) before the Father and the propitiation who averts God's wrath for the sins of the entire world (v. 2). Still, those who keep his commandments are those who truly know him (v. 3). Those who claim to know him but do not keep his commandments, are false. The truth is absent from them (v. 4). The love of God is perfected in those who keep his Word (v. 5). Those who walk in the pattern of his life abide (or remain) in him (v. 6).

The Old Commandment of Love (2:7–11)

Addressing them as "beloved," he reminds them of the new commandment to love one another (John 13:34–35), which is now an old commandment to them (v. 7, indicating that 1 John was written after the Gospel of John). The commandment is true in Christ and in readers because the darkness is passing away, and the true light (Jesus) already shines (v. 8). He draws out the implication of the old/new commandment. To claim to walk in the light but hate a fellow Christian is to be in the darkness (v. 9). Such a person is in the darkness and walks in it, not knowing where they are going because that person is blind (v. 11). The alternative that John endorses is that they love their siblings in God. If so, they abide in the light and, unlike the lost, will have no cause for stumbling (v. 10).

Victory for All the Family of God (2:12–14)

These verses are poetic or hymnic. In them, John addresses six distinct groups in the church, assuring them of their identity and status in God. Each of the six groups is addressed as the recipient of the writing. Little children are assured their sins are forgiven (v. 12); fathers that they know Jesus who is from the beginning twice (vv. 13a; 14a); young men that they have overcome the evil one twice (Satan, v. 13b) and that they are strong because God's Word abides in them (v. 14b); and children that they know the Father (v. 13c). The overall effect is that the church of believers can have confidence and assurance in God.

Do Not Love the World (2:15–17)

Readers are then instructed not to love the world or its things. Here, John speaks of the world's fallenness and sin. Where a person loves the world, God's love is absent from them (v. 15). All that is in the world—fleshly desire, lusts of the eye, and pride in this life—are from the world and not God the Father (v. 16). Moreover, the world is passing away with its desires. At the same time, those who do God's will abide forever (v. 17). Hence, readers are urged to pursue God's will, reject the desires that dominate the world, and abide with God forever.

Be For Christ and Not Against (2:18–29)

When John says it is the "last hour," he refers to the time between Christ's first and second comings. The readers know that an Antichrist and antichrists are coming. Even so, many antichrists have already made their presence known (v. 18). These are those who oppose Christ in the world and church.

Verse 19 speaks of a group who have left the church. Implied is that they are antichrists. They are not of God and his people, or they would have remained. Those who remain (you) are truly anointed by the Holy One, God, and have his knowledge (v. 20). He writes to them because they know the truth that is without a lie (not the schismatics, v. 21). Those who left are liars who deny Jesus is Israel's Messiah, God's anointed one, the Christ. Hence, they are antichrists who deny Father and Son (v. 22). Such a person who denies that Jesus is the Son and Christ is not in fellowship with the Father. On the contrary, those who confess Jesus is the Son and Messiah walk in fellowship with him (v. 23). The readers heard from the beginning that Jesus is the Son and Messiah and must allow that to remain in them, and if they do, they will abide in God the Father and the Son (v. 24). And they are then recipients of the promise God made; that they will receive eternal life (v. 25). Verse 26 makes plain John's intent in writing—to warn them against the deceivers. Yet, being anointed by God and his Son, they know the truth and require no teaching because the Spirit in them is teaching them as he abides in them (v. 27). So, as God's little children, they must abide in him so that they can be confident and unashamed when he comes (v. 28). They know that he is righteous and those who practice righteousness are born of him (v. 29).

Be Children of God (3:1–10)

As in John 8, John contrasts God's children with those not of him, who are children of the devil. God's love is shown in that believers (we) are called children of God. The world does not recognize this because they do not know him (hence, they do not recognize his own, v. 2). As God's beloved children now, what they will be at his appearance (coming) is not yet revealed. Still, they know when he does appear, they will be like him because they will see him as he is (v. 2). Those who hope in him purify themselves as he is pure (v. 3). Verse 4 warns against those who persistently sin and practice lawlessness (v. 4). The readers know that in him was no sin. He appeared to take away sins (v. 5). Those who abide in him, know him, and see him, do not persist in sin (v. 6).

Addressing them affectionately as "little children" and warning against deception, John contrasts two groups in vv. 7 and 8. The one who practices righteousness is righteous. Those who sin persistently are of the devil, as he has sinned from the beginning. Jesus came to destroy his works. As such, no one born of God persists in sin, for God's seed is in him. He cannot continue in persistent sin because he has been born of God (v. 9). For John, those who do not practice righteousness nor love their Christian sibling are children of the devil and not God (v. 10). Hence, readers must pursue righteousness and resist sin.

Love One Another (3:11–24)

John's letter is famous for its emphasis on love, which is most profound in chs. 3 and 4. This section forms a chiastic frame with 4:7–21 around the warning against false spirits and false teaching.

Here, John reiterates the message they have heard from the beginning—we should love one another (v. 11). He presents Cain as a negative example. He was from the evil one and murdered his brother Abel because his deeds were evil in contrast to the righteous deeds of his brother (v. 12). In vv. 13-14, John tells readers not to be surprised that their love for one another will see the world hate them even when they know that they have passed from death to life. For him, anyone who does not love does not abide in God and life, but in death (v. 14). So, to hate a brother or sister is an act of murder, and those who do this are not indwelt with eternal life (v. 15).

Verses 16-18 crystalize love for the reader. Love is known by Christ's laying down his life for us. So, believers should lay down their lives for their Christian brothers and sisters. Verse 17 asks readers if they see a sibling in need and do not reach out to help them, how can God's love abide in them? He concludes that as God's little children, they must not love merely in words but in action and truth (v. 18).

Readers are now given assurance. They can know they are walking in the truth in two ways. If their hearts condemn them, God is greater than their hearts and knows everything (vv. 19-20). On the other hand, if their hearts do not condemn them, they can have confidence before God (v 21). As such, they can confidently pray because they keep his commandments and please him (v. 22). Verse 23 specifies what commandments are in view—that they believe in the name of God's Son, Jesus Christ, and love one another as commanded by Christ. Those who keep these commandments abide in God, and God in the person by the Spirit (vv. 24).

Test the Spirits to See Who Is From God (4:1–6)

Again, addressing them as "beloved," John gives instructions on discerning false teaching and implies that it comes from evil spiritual forces. They are not to believe everything they hear but test the spiritual source of prophetic oracles. They must do this because false prophets have gone into the world (v. 1). He gives guidance on how to tell the difference in vv. 2-3. If the prophetic oracle is premised on the confession that Jesus Christ has come in the flesh, it is from God (v. 2). If not, it is the spirit of the antichrist that they were warned of and that has come (v. 3).

However, the little children of the Asian churches need not fear, for they are from God, and because he is greater than the devil who is in the world, they have overcome these spiritual forces seeking to seduce them (v. 4). Those who hold to the false teachings of the evil spirits are from the world, speak from the world, and the world heeds their message (v. 5). They do not listen to John and other authentic gospel preachers. However, true believers are from God and listen to John and other true proclaimers of the Word. They can distinguish between the Spirit of truth and the spirit of error (v. 6).

God Is Love (4:7–21)

John returns to love again in this passage that is in chiastic parallel to 3:11-24. The beloved Asian Christians are to love one another because love is from God. Hence, those who love are born of God and know him (v. 7). Those who do not show love are not from God because God is love—one of the most beautiful definitions of God in Scripture (v. 8). God's love has been made manifest among God's people in the sending of his only Son into the world that believers may live through him (v. 9). Love is seen not so much in our love for God but in God's love for us and the sending of his Son to be a propitiation for sins (averter of God's wrath, v. 10). In v. 11, John tells the beloved that if God loves us in this way, we ought to love one another. So, although no one has ever seen God the Father, where believers love one another, God abides in them, and his love is perfected in them.

Believers know they abide in God and he in them because he has gifted the Spirit to them (v. 13). John and other first-generation witnesses have seen and testify God the Father has sent Jesus his Son to be Savior of the world (v. 14). Where people confess Jesus is the Son of God, God abides in them, and they in God (v. 15). They have come to believe the love God has for them. He is love, and whoever abides in love, abides in him, and he in them (v. 16). His love is perfected in believers, so they are not afraid of judgment because they live in consistency with him in the world (v. 17). Indeed, there is no fear in love, it is cast out by perfect love, because fear is about punishment and does not flow from perfect love (v. 18). Verse 19 makes apparent that believers love because God first loved them (v. 19). And if someone says they have a love for God, but hates a sibling, that person is a liar. They are duplicitous because when a person does not love his sibling in Christ, who he has seen, he cannot love the unseen God (v. 20). So, he summarizes in v. 21 with Christ's command: whoever loves God must love his brother. The upshot of this is that God loves Christ and us, Christ loves God and us, and we who are believers are to love God, Jesus, and one another.

Overcome the World By Believing and Keeping His Commandments (5:1–5)

John restates much of what he has said here. Those who believe Jesus is the Messiah, God's Anointed, are born of God. Everyone who loves God the Father is born of him (v. 1). We know we love the children of God if we love God and obey his commandments (v. 2). Love for God is to keep his non-burdensome commandments (v. 3). Those who believe Jesus is the Christ, the born of God, overcome the world in its enmity to God (v. 4). The victory for this comes from faith (v. 4). More specifically, those who overcome the world do so by believing Jesus is the Son of God (v. 5).

The Three Witnesses to Jesus (5:6–12)

When John says Christ came by water and blood, he likely means his baptism in water and his death on the cross (v. 6).[26] Then came the Spirit's descent, and so he testifies as he is truth (v. 7). In v. 8, he puts the three together into the three witnesses: the Spirit (Pentecost), the water (Christ's baptism), and the blood (his death). They frame his ministry as Messiah and Son of God. Remembering the Jewish requirement of two or three witnesses (Deut 17:6), these three that agree Jesus is the Messiah, the Son of God, who came in the flesh, are sufficient for John.

In v. 9, John suggests that if we are prepared to believe human testimony where three agree, the testimony of God in Christ and his Spirit is greater and must be believed. As such, those who believe Jesus is the Son of God have God's testimony within them. The opposite is true—those who do not believe what God has testified in these three witnesses make God a liar by refusing to believe the witness he has given concerning his Son (v. 10). Verse 11 makes crystal clear the message and testimony—God has given us eternal life and this life is in his Son Jesus. So, John can say with supreme confidence in v. 12, "Whoever has the Son has life; whoever does not have the Son of God does not have life."

Postscript (5:13–21)

John does not end with greetings, signatures, and travel plans but continues unabated to the end of his letter appealing to readers to believe in Jesus.

John 20:30–31 clearly states the purpose of the Gospel—that readers will believe Jesus is the Messiah and Son of God. Here in 1 John, John tells readers that he writes to those who already believe in the name of the Son of God so that they may *know*

---

26. Alternatively, he means the blood and water that flowed from Jesus' side on the cross. However, the baptism and cross mark Christ's ministry in the Gospels, which is a better option.

that they have eternal life (v. 13). He tells them to be confident in prayer, knowing that God will hear our prayers when we ask in line with his will, and as he hears, we know he will grant our requests (vv. 14-15). Importantly, this confirms God's readiness to grant our prayer requests when they align with his will.

Verses 16-17 puzzle interpreters who ponder what is the sin that leads to death that John has in mind. While this could be the unforgivable sin against the Spirit in Mark 3:29, more likely, it is the sin of not believing in Jesus being the Christ and Son of God and perhaps, especially where a person previously believed and then deserted the faith (cf. Heb 6:1-8). Whatever is in John's mind, he urges readers to pray for those who fall into sins that are not this severe case of sin (almost all sin then), asking God to grant that person life (v. 16). Then he speaks of the sin that leads to death, which in John is the sin of unbelief and a consequent lack of love. The readers are not to pray in the same way for that person. Still, for John, those born of God will not persist in sin but will be protected by God from the evil one's touch (v. 18).

Verses 19 and 20 speak of the shared knowledge believers have. They are from God, while the world lies under the power of the evil one. However, we also know that the Son of God, Jesus the Christ, has come and given understanding, so believers know him who is true and are in him (God) and in his Son, Jesus Christ. Astoundingly, and yet consistent with the declarations of Christ's divinity in the Gospel, he declares Jesus is the true God and Eternal Life. He ends, in v. 21, telling readers with his affectionate "little children" to keep themselves from idols. In other words, do not worship anything other than God the Father and God the Son by God the Holy Spirit.

Conclusion

John's first letter reminds us that we are to hold firm to the truth that Jesus is the Christ, he is fully divine and human, and God the Son. Anything less is inadequate. At the same time, the letter calls us to resist sin yet reminds us of God's forgiveness and his love. One of its brilliant concepts is "abiding" or "remaining" in him, something we must do. No other NT writer so clearly tells us that God is love, that he loves us, and that we are to love him and his Son. God's victory over evil is announced in the letter, and again we are reminded to resist false teaching.

2 John

2 John is written by the "elder," the Apostle John, or another disciple and elder from the Johannine community (see also on the authorship of John).[27] It is unique because it is written to a woman and her children. We do not know who these people are. The letter expresses joy at their walking in the truth, reiterates the importance of love and obedience, warns against antichrists and false prophets who deny the reality of Christ's incarnation (above) and warns of the consequences of such denial, i.e., the rupture in the relationship with God. John says they should not welcome such false teachers. The letter concludes with John saying he desires to see them face to face rather than write using paper and ink.

3 John

While this short letter is attributed to the same author, the authorship of this letter remains an open question. This letter is also from "the elder," either John the disciple or another John, this time to Gaius, who is not likely to be the Gaius of Macedonia

---

27. For a fuller discussion on 2 and 3 John, see Keown, *Discovering*, 3:219–39 (Ch. 3).

or Corinth (cf. Acts 19:29; 20:4; Rom 16:23; 1 Cor1:14). He is clearly a believer. John prays for blessings. He commends Gaius' faith and his walking in the truth. Gaius is showing hospitality to visitors, and he is commended for it. John speaks of Diotrephes, who is not commended, for he is a gossiper and will not welcome the brothers. John urges Gaius to do good. He commends Demetrius. As in the previous letter, John ends by expressing his desire to see them in person rather than through writing.

14. Revelation

Part One: Background Issues

No NT book garners more intrigue than the *Apokalypsis* of John.[1] This interest is due to its fascinating symbolism, whether it should be read figuratively or literally, and whether its teaching points to the eschaton or its immediate context in first-century Rome. With these questions in mind, in this section, Revelation is introduced.

Place in the Canon

There was a lot of debate concerning the inclusion of Revelation in the Canon of Scripture. In the western churches of the Roman world, it was excluded by Marcion, who rejected any NT book with strong allusions to the OT. It was also rejected by Gaius (Rome at the beginning of the second century) and the sect called the Alogoi. In the eastern churches, the Egyptian Bishop Dionysius questioned its apostolic authorship to minimize its authority. His view influenced other Eastern thinkers, and the Council of Laodicea (AD 360) did not recognize Revelation as canonical.

However, there were also significant voices in the west and east that did support Revelation's authority. In the west, it may have been known to Ignatius (AD 110–117) and Barnabas (AD 135), and it was used by the author of the Shepherd of Hermas (ca. AD 150). It was accepted as authoritative by Papias (d. AD 130), Justin Martyr (mid-

---

1. For a fuller discussion, see Keown, *Discovering*, 3:265–374 (Ch. 8).

second century), and Irenaeus (AD 180). It is found in the Muratorian Canon at the end of the second century. In the east, Clement of Alexandria and Origen supported its authority. The majority wanted its inclusion.

Authorship

John writes Revelation (Rev 1:1, 4, 9; 22:8). Traditionally, this is John the Apostle, but as with many NT books, the identity of this John is questioned. The possibility of another author is supported by the style of the Greek, which is much inferior to the Gospel and John's letters. The ideas are also regarded to be quite different. However, a compelling case can be made for John the Apostle. The simple placement of the name "John" four times suggests he is well-known. John traditionally lived his later life in Ephesus and ministered to Asia Minor. His association with Asia fits with Revelation, sent to the area's seven churches. Different amanuenses can account for the diverse Greek for the Johannine writings. The different ideas are likely due to the different purposes and genres. The Gospel looks back and tells the story of Jesus. The letters are momentary communications to address specific issues. Revelation looks forward to events and focuses on history and its climax, the return of Christ. Concerning genre—Revelation is apocalyptic literature, 1–3 John are letters, and John's Gospel is a written affidavit concerning Jesus.

Date

The date is unclear. Some opt for an earlier date, not long after Nero died in AD 68. They see Nero as the prototype for the book. A myth of Nero's return (Nero Redivivus) circulated. Some consider that the beast is modeled on him. If this is the case, it is written in the 70s. The majority view, however, is that Emperor Domitian's persecution of Christians and Jews is a better setting. He ruled from AD 81 to 96, and this would place Revelation in this period.

Setting and Recipients

We know from Rev 1:9 that, at the time of writing, John was imprisoned for preaching the gospel on the island of Patmos, a small island around 50 km SE of Ephesus off the coast of Asia Minor (western Turkey). There is a cave on the island where he was supposedly imprisoned, although this is uncertain.

We also know who the recipients were, the seven churches of Revelation planted in the main urban centers of Asia Minor (remembering that Colossae was destroyed in the earthquake in AD 60–61 and not rebuilt): Ephesus, Smyrna, Pergamum, Thyatira, Sardis, Philadelphia, and Laodicea.[2]

Apocalyptic Genre

The key to understanding Revelation is to recognize its genre. Revelation is written as a letter with an epistolary prologue in Rev 1:4–8 in which the writer is identified as "John," the recipients are named "the seven churches in Asia," and a greeting and blessing are given.

However, while it is a letter, it is also labeled in Rev 1:1

---

[2]. For a map of the seven churches, see "The Seven Churches of Revelation," Net Bible, https://classic.net.bible.org/map.php?map=nt2.

as *Apokalypsis Iēsou Christou*, "the revelation of Jesus Christ." This clause identifies Revelation as an example of apocalyptic literature. Apocalyptic literature is found in Judaism and early Christianity from around 200 bc to 200 ad. There are many other examples in the Pseudepigrapha (e.g., Apocalypses of Abraham, Adam, Baruch, Ezra, among many others) and early Christian writings (e.g., The Shepherd of Hermas).

Apocalyptic literature is usually written in the first person, often using the name of a great saint (which may support it not being written by John) to people suffering great persecution. They often involve an angel or seer who takes the writer on a journey, giving them visions of heaven and things to happen on earth. They are full of symbolism, such as numbers (e.g., 666), fierce animals (beasts, dragons, locusts), and people (e.g., a harlot). They often involve cataclysmic events like wars, earthquakes, plagues, and other natural and supernaturally caused disasters. They usually revolve around a conflict between God with his angels and the Devil and his demons. The people of God are also swept up in this conflict, the children of light versus the children of evil. They are ramped-up good versus evil battles. They involve governments, politics, and war. They usually resolve into a cataclysmic victory of God and his angels, the vindication of the faithful, and the Shalom that God's people await.

Apocalypses are notoriously tricky to interpret because they are full of symbolism drawn from the context and cannot be interpreted literally with any certainty. They are like sci-fi or fantasy dramas that point to the realities behind their symbolism but are not necessarily to be taken directly.

The ideas and symbolism must first be understood in relation to the context. In the case of Revelation, written sometime under Roman rule, the Roman Empire and its Emperors loom behind it. It is also full of Old Testament allusions and imagery. It draws on some of Jesus' teaching. It has Greek ideas behind some of it. In many cases, there are multiple possibilities for interpretation that leave us looking at meanings that are probabilities more than certainties.

Bible readers who have not investigated the genre of Revelation and the idea of apocalyptic literature can get into trouble trying to interpret it literally and directly. With so many natural disasters and events, it is not difficult to associate contemporary historical situations with Revelation's diverse material. If they have not looked at the history of its interpretation, they do not realize that others have done this before and have all been wrong. We must think very carefully about the point each part of Revelation is making and not simply transport it directly to our world. However, as Scripture, it does have meaning and importance, and we need to read it carefully and consider its message.

Part Two: Revelation—Methods of Interpretation

The critical matter is the message of Revelation. What does Revelation mean? To what do the visions of John refer? What are we to learn from them? There are four main perspectives on Revelation.

The Preterist Approach

The View

Preterists read Revelation in its context and do not read it as a prophecy of future events. It is written to and for the first readers only. It is the most held view among biblical scholars today.

In this approach, the visions of John relate primarily to John's time and world. They grow out of and describe events happening then and are not to be read as futuristic. Hence, they are like other apocalypses which speak to the events happening at the time, usually times of terrible evil and persecution. They were written to encourage people in great suffering, reminding them of the impending triumph of God.

The purpose of Revelation, then, is to show the first readers how God will bring his judgment on those oppressing them in their world and how God is triumphing over the forces of their age and delivering them from their suffering. It is not to be taken literally and applied to history. So, Revelation is a prophecy of God's triumph *in the present*.

Those who take this view interpret the book against the Neronian persecution, the destruction of Jerusalem, the Domitian persecution, which was threatening the church in Asia, and the persecution of the wider church at the time. They rigorously apply the symbolism to that time only.

So, the beast is one of the Roman Emperors (Domitian or Nero), and the false prophet is the cult of Emperor worship. Revelation assures the readers of Christ's imminent return to destroy Rome and establish his earthly kingdom.

Assessment

There is an element of truth to this view. Revelation was written out of, and speaks into, a time of persecution. However, there are significant differences between Jewish apocalypses, which were to be interpreted against the contexts in which they were written. In particular, Revelation concerns salvation history from the OT to the NT. John employs a rich array of OT imagery to prophesy into the future. In addition, this view misunderstands the nature of OT prophecy. While the OT prophetic oracles related to their own day, they also had a futurist emphasis, e.g., they predicted the return from exile and the ultimate hope of the new heavens and new earth (Isa 65–66). It is doubtful that Revelation should be considered to have *no* futuristic dimension, whether general, symbolic, or specific. However, Revelation *must* first be understood in relation to its original setting. So, the descriptions of the future grow out of the present experience of John and his readers. For example, it is possible that the Fall of Jerusalem is a pattern for the culmination and that the historical event and some future catastrophes are in mind. If so, reading Revelation through a preterist lens helps discern the pattern.

The Historical Approach

The View

In this view, Revelation and its symbolism should be interpreted against the backdrop of actual historical events. In the Middle Ages, for example, there was a belief that the millennium was about to begin. To support this view, thinkers interpreted the events of Revelation as a sketch of *church history* from the time of Christ to their day. In this way of interpreting Revelation, events in church history correlate to the seals, trumpets, bowls, and other symbols. This approach was popular among the Reformers like Luther and Calvin, as it enabled them to interpret the beast in Revelation as the Catholic Church and Papacy. The historical approach has been used for various schemes, including those who accept a literal millennium (e.g., Isaac Newton) or those who do not (e.g., Luther) and postmillennialism.

Assessment

This view has little merit. Its problem is that each interpreter can make any symbol in Revelation correlate to anything they suppose in history, making the whole enterprise spurious. This kind of thing has happened in our time as people find a modern state (e.g., the new Roman Empire) or ruler (e.g., Trump, Putin) in Revelation. They are always proved wrong. On the other hand, if the events of Revelation are future-orientated, the symbols may have some legitimate general and repeated correlations in human history.

The Idealist or Symbolic Approach: The Symbolism is General, Not Specific.

The View

In this perspective, the symbolism in Revelation is not to be read literally and precisely but points to repeated events on earth in a general sense. Along with preterism, this is the most common view in biblical scholarship. So, the symbolism of Revelation is designed to help us understand God's person and plan in a general way; that is, Revelation does not give us specific incidents but the principles or ideals at work in history. The symbols then reflect spiritual powers in the world. Hence, Revelation is predictive generally but not specifically predictive, i.e., the message assures the readers that God will triumph without going into specifics. The things described are apocalyptic descriptions of suffering and struggle without necessarily correlating them to specific historical situations. However, all apocalyptic is based around a correlation between the symbols and historical events, so one would expect some correlation in Revelation.

Assessment

This approach is helpful because Revelation is highly symbolic, and this should be recognized. It also helps us to read Revelation non-chronologically, i.e., it can be understood as containing parallel rather than merely consecutive sections.

The Extreme Futurist Approach, i.e., Classical Dispensationalism

The View

In this view, the symbolism speaks of Israel, the Church, and the world's end. Until the mid to late twentieth century, it was popular to interpret Revelation through the lens of Classical Dispensationalism. This theology has two divine programs: one for Israel and one for the church. All the seals, trumpets, and bowls that belong to the Great Tribulation relate only to Israel and not the church (which has been raptured).

In chapters 2 and 3, the church is on earth. However, the word "church" never occurs again until 22:16. The twenty-four elders (Rev 4:4) are the church, raptured and rewarded. The rapture occurs at 4:1 when John is taken up to heaven. The 144,000 people of God on earth who remain are Jews, 12,000 from each of the twelve tribes (Rev 7:1–8). They proclaim the "gospel of the kingdom" during the tribulation and win many Gentiles to God (Rev 7:9–17). The Beast is the head of the restored Roman Empire or another contemporary imperium (cf. Dan 9:27). The final seven years begin with a covenant between the Beast (antichrist) and Israel that will be broken after three and a half years (forty-two months). Then the Beast will turn on the Jews. The great conflict in Revelation is between the antichrist and Israel, not the antichrist and the church. Chapters 4–19 have to do with the tribulation period, and chapters 2 and 3 alone are for the church and the church age. The seven churches represent seven successive periods of church history; the final period (Laodicea) is one of apostasy and spiritual apathy. Chapter 19 to the end speaks of the events that will occur beginning with Jesus' return. There will be a millennium, final conflict, judgment, and the new heavens and earth.

Assessment

This view remains popular among many Christians because of the *Left Behind* books and movies that have popularized it, especially in the USA. However, to a large degree, this extreme futurist view died out in the mid to late twentieth century in scholarship, even among many classical dispensational scholars. It is undoubtedly a flawed view, as Rev 4:1 says nothing about a rapture. Instead, the church remains on earth and experiences a period of extreme suffering, something consistent with the rest of the NT.[3]

The Moderate Futurist Approach

The View

Some do not accept the Classical Dispensational perspective but believe that the symbolism of Revelation speaks to a yet unfulfilled future in a general and sweeping way. It is a variant of the symbolic

---

3. E.g., Mark 13 and parr.; 1 Thess 5; 2 Thess 2; 2 Peter 3.

view, considering how the symbols relate to the final days. This view is sometimes called a *consistent* futurist approach, which holds everything from chs. 4–22 in Revelation finds its fulfillment in the last days of human history. Adherents reject seeing a secret rapture in 4:1 and consider the events foreseen in chs. 4–22 concern all humanity, Christian or otherwise. Revelation thus depicts the consummation of God's redemptive purposes involving salvation and judgment.

One variation of this is a more *moderate futurist approach* that believes that *some* of the events in these chapters, particularly the earlier ones, take place in history before the end. This blends the idealist and futurist viewpoints removing the ideas of dispensationalism. Often such a view will reject the idea of a secret rapture. Rather, events on earth will become increasingly dire, leading to Christ's return. They leave room for a millennium after Christ's return or before he returns (postmillennialism or amillennialism).[4]

Assessment

This view faces the problems of which events should be taken literally and which ones should not. It is not clear what aspects of Revelation point to the present and the long-term future. It is, however, a reasonable view because Revelation's final events are

---

4. Put simply, postmillennialists hold we are in the millennium now and expect the world to get better and better until the Kingdom is consummated. Christ's return is minimalized. Amillennialism similarly argues we are in the millennium now, and it will consummate with Jesus' return. Most agree there will be a period of horrific strife before Jesus' return, although some would disagree.

futuristic and tied to the end of the age—Christ's return, the millennium, eternal judgment, and the new heavens and earth.

Conclusion

It is probably best to take an eclectic approach and include dimensions of the preterist, idealist, and moderate futurist views when approaching the interpretation of Revelation.

The seven churches of Asia are most likely actual churches with real problems addressed by John, albeit in a stereotypical form. They do not refer to eras in history but are actual words from God to John for these churches. Taking the letters in this way is supported by specific places (e.g., Ephesus, Smyrna), names (e.g., Antipas), groups (e.g., Nicolaitans, Jews), and situations described. For example, the reference to the lukewarmness of the Laodiceans fits our understanding of the water supply in the town. Whereas the water at Hierapolis was warm and healing and at Colossae cool and refreshing, the water at Laodicea was undrinkable and useless. The description of Pergamum as Satan's throne fits with the importance of the Temple of Zeus or Asklepios to this city.

In ch. 4–22, John describes, in highly symbolic terms, the events surrounding the end of the age when God will establish his kingdom and evil will be defeated. The backdrop is life in the persecuted church under the tyranny of Rome and the Emperor Cult (preterist). That being the case, the vision of the future is to be interpreted through a first-century lens so that the situation of the churches at the time gives the first layer of meaning to the symbols used. While the orientation is the future, the message appeals to the first readers, giving them great encouragement as they face struggles and persecution, particularly the assurance of God's ultimate victory over evil and the vindication of his people (generally futurist).

However, reading history in Revelation remains highly

contentious, and I would take a conservative and tentative general line in seeking to interpret events. For example, when considering the millennium, there seem to be two options that can work. First, that one takes a post-tribulation premillennialist approach, with Jesus returning and restoring his world in an interim millennial period. Second, that one takes the amillennial position, seeing the millennium as concurrent with history, with Jesus returning at some point to complete the restoration work.

Frankly, anyone who wants to interpret Revelation cannot do it without the aid of excellent commentaries.[5] Each verse is a literal repository of links and connections that require assistance in understanding.

Part Three: Textual Analysis of the Beast of Revelation 13

A beneficial book to enable readers to come to grips with the different ways scholars interpret Revelation is Steve Gregg's *Revelation, Four Views: A Parallel Commentary* which reads each passage demonstrating the different approaches to the text.[6] Here I will summarize the different approaches to the mark of the beast to illustrate how the four approaches interpret the idea (Rev 13:16–18). Doing this is vital because of all the symbols in Revelation, the mark

---

5. Examples include Grant R. Osborne, *Revelation*, BECNT (Grand Rapids, MI: Baker Academic, 2002); Leon Morris, *The Revelation of St. John*, TNTC (Grand Rapids: Eerdmans, 1969); Robert H. Mounce, *The Book of Revelation*, NICNT (Grand Rapids, MI: Eerdmans, 1997).

6. Steve Gregg, *Revelation, Four Views: A Parallel Commentary* (Nashville, TN: T. Nelson Publishers, 1997).

of the beast is arguably the most contentious. Closely considering this can help us read the whole book.

In Revelation 13:16–18, a second beast working on behalf of the first causes everyone to receive a mark on the right hand or forehead, without which no one can buy or sell. The number of this beast is 666, and the reader is challenged to interpret this. It needs to be remembered when interpreting this that the letters of the Greek, Hebrew, and Latin alphabets also served as numbers.

Preterism

Many *Preterists* identify the beast with Nero. Caesar Nero in Hebrew is *Nrwn Osr* (pronounced "*Nerōn Kaiser*") which includes seven Hebrew letters adding up to 666 (50, 200, 6, 50, 100, 60, and 200). The number, then, is a code used to refer to him while avoiding the Roman authorities. The ban on trading is the economic boycott of Christians by Nero. Christians should not yield to his rule. For some, the beast is not a future figure but Nero. If so, Revelation was written before his death in AD 68. An alternative is that it is Nero returned or points to an Emperor like him (e.g., Domitian) or another future Nero-like ruler. Whatever the precise meaning, Revelation tells the story of his eventual defeat and God's victory.

Idealistic (or Symbolic, Spiritual)

The *spiritual* (*symbolic or ideal*) interpretation does not consider the mark literal any more than the "seal" in 7:3 or the 'name' in 14:1. The mark is symbolic of their selling out to the false, idolatrous system. The forehead symbolizes the mind and the hand, the act of trade. Thus, to receive the mark is to yield to the false system. This passage applies to any age in which Christians are drawn to false systems. There is thus no need to work out who 666 is, as it symbolizes false religion. Some who take this view may accept the *Nrwn Osr* idea mentioned above but see it as pointing to any future leader who is like him. Such people will come and go in history, and bad events will happen as Revelation predicts, but in the end, God will win.

One can see in these interpretations differing approaches. As noted above, many moderate futurists would hold that there may well be a future final empire with a despotic ruler with the same sort of mindset as Nero, Domitian, or other despots (cf. Matt 24:15; 2 Thess 2:3–10; 1 John 2:18). Christians will be forced to yield to that empire either through taking an actual mark or as is more likely, yielding to its idolatrous rule (taking 666 symbolically). However, idealist interpreters will resist associating every literal element of the vision with specific figures and particular events or situations.

Historical

The historicist solutions include that of Irenaeus, who believed the name to be *Lareinous* (Greek for "Latin"), and so this is the name of the last of Daniel's four kingdoms (the Roman Empire). Others with a historicist perspective accepted this as the Roman Catholic Church, i.e., the *Latin* (Roman) church patriarch. The beast is thus the Papacy. The mark of being Catholic is Latin worship. The mark on hands or foreheads may refer to slaves and soldiers wearing the name of their owner or Emperor on their hands or foreheads. The ban on buying and selling relates to banning commercial engagement with Protestants or heretics. Others who read it this way find the number appropriate for the Latin *Basileia* (kingdom), *apostaths* (apostate), the Hebrew for 'Roman,' the pope's title *Vicarius filii Dei* ("vicar of the Son of God"). Few would accept this view today.

Futurists

As with much popular Christianity, many *Futurists* see a worldwide empire with an associated cashless economy that requires a mark on the body for trade. Others take this non-literally, referring to pledging allegiance to the ruler, the beast. If so, to take the mark is to yield to his rule, and without doing so, one is shut out of the system. The number 666 has been variously interpreted. Some notice that six Roman numerals (I, V, X, L, C, D) add up to 666, suggesting a Roman antichrist. The word "beast" occurs thirty-six times in Revelation, which is six times six. Names have been associated with it, including on some popular websites concerning Donald Trump and Vladimir Putin. Another possibility is that the number six represents humankind, so 666 could symbolize humanity's rebellion against God.

Moderate futurists see the climax of history in Revelation. A ruthless empire will develop, led by a beastly leader. He will subjugate the world. There will be a horrific time of suffering. The mark is not necessarily literal but points to abandoning God and yielding to this ruler and the system. The end will come as Jesus returns. However, they will not speculate on this but watch current events carefully and judiciously.

Conclusion

While Revelation is a difficult book, apocalyptic in form and full of fascinating imagery, we must grapple with it. It forms a brilliant *inclusio* with Genesis, completing the story of God's creation, the fall of humanity, God's redemption through Israel and Jesus, the church's mission in the world, and the return of Christ and the new heavens and earth.

We must beware of reading it literally, as this assumes the writer wants us to do this. Instead, as Jacob wrestled with God (Gen 32), we must struggle to understand its rich symbolism. We must resist reading past and future specific history into it. Reading current events into it leads to misreading the signs of the times and falsely predicting the return of Christ. Yet, we must also avoid making it a book without meaning for the present and future. It does summon us to be faithful to the end, even prepared to die for our faith. It tells us that while we submit to the State (Rom 13; Tit 3:1; 1 Pet 2:13–18), there is a time to resist the Beast non-violently, refusing to join it in its corporate evil (Rev 13). We must not bear its marks and instead must be clothed with Christ.

Revelation also gives us great hope, for Jesus will win! He is at work in the world amidst the carnage of sin. He is bringing redemption. People from every nation will be among his people, joined together in worship of God. Praise him!

He will return. He will judge the world. Evil will be destroyed. Heaven and earth will be merged. God, his Son, and his people will be together forever. The world will be recreated. Then, as eternal beings, with our eternal God, we will get to participate in his subsequent works. What a fantastic thought and privilege! We should use our imaginations and let this vision motivate us to the end. Amen!

Works Referenced

Arndt, William, Frederick W. Danker, Walter Bauer, and F. Wilbur Gingrich. *A Greek-English Lexicon of the New Testament and Other Early Christian Literature*. Chicago: University of Chicago Press, 2000.

Barry, John D., David Bomar, Derek R. Brown, Rachel Klippenstein, Douglas Mangum, Carrie Sinclair Wolcott, Lazarus Wentz, Elliot Ritzema, and Wendy Widder, eds. *The Lexham Bible Dictionary*. Bellingham, WA: Lexham Press, 2016.

Bauckham, Richard J. "Gospels (Apocryphal)." Pages 286–91 in DJG.

————. *Jesus and the Eyewitnesses. The Gospels as Eyewitness Testimony*. Grand Rapids: Eerdmans, 2006.

————. *The Testimony of the Beloved Disciple: Narrative, History, and Theology in the Gospel of John*. Grand Rapids, MI: Baker Academic, 2007.

Berchman, Richard. "Pagan Philosophers on Judaism in Ancient Times." Pages 1038–1051 in *The Encyclopedia of Judaism*. Edited by Jacob Neusner, Alan J. Avery-Peck, and William Scott Green. Leiden; Boston; Köln: Brill, 2000.

Blomberg, C. L. "Form Criticism." Pages 243–49 in DJG.

Bonhoeffer, Dietrich. *The Cost of Discipleship*. Translated by R. H. Fuller and Irmgard Booth. London: SCM Press, 2001.

Burridge, R. A. "Biography, Ancient." Pages 167–70 in DNTB.

Corley, Bruce, Steve W. Lemke, and Grant I. Lovejoy. *Biblical Hermeneutics: A Comprehensive Introduction to Interpreting Scripture*. Second Edition. Nashville, TN.: Broadman & Holman, 2002.

Davids, Peter H. *The Letters of 2 Peter and Jude*, PNTC. Grand Rapids, MI: Eerdmans, 2006.

DeMoss, Matthew S. *Pocket Dictionary for the Study of New Testament Greek*. Downers Grove, IL: InterVarsity Press, 2001.

Dunn, James D. G. *The Epistles to the Colossians and to Philemon:*

A Commentary on the Greek Text, NIGTC. Grand Rapids, MI; Carlisle: Eerdmans; Paternoster Press, 1996.

Freedman, David Noel, Gary A. Herion, David F. Graf, John David Pleins and Astrid B. Beck, eds. *The Anchor Yale Bible Dictionary.* New York: Doubleday, 1992.

Gamble, Harry Y. "Canon: New Testament." Vol. 1 Pages 852–58 in AYBD.

Gregg, Steve. *Revelation, Four Views: A Parallel Commentary.* Nashville, TN: T. Nelson Publishers, 1997.

Hadjiantoniou, G. *Learning the Basics of New Testament Greek.* Chattanooga, TN: AMG Publishers, 1998.

Hansen, G. Walter. "Rhetorical Criticism." Pages 822–26 in DPL.

Hawthorne, Gerald F., Ralph P. Martin, and Daniel G. Reid, eds. *Dictionary of Paul and His Letters.* Downers Grove, IL: InterVarsity Press, 1993.

Hays, Richard B. *Echoes of Scripture in the Letters of Paul.* New Haven; London: Yale University Press, 1989.

Kennedy, Brendan. "Biblical Languages." LBD.

Keown, Mark J. *Discovering the New Testament: An Introduction to Its Background, Theology, and Themes: The Gospels & Acts.* Vol. I. Bellingham, WA: Lexham Press, 2018.

—————. *Discovering the New Testament: An Introduction to Its Background, Theology, and Themes: The Pauline Letters.* Vol. II. Bellingham, WA: Lexham Press, 2021.

—————. *Discovering the New Testament: An Introduction to Its Background, Theology, and Themes: General Letters & Revelation.* Vol. III. Bellingham, WA: Lexham Press, 2022.

—————. "The Consummation of the Kingdom." https://www.academia.edu/92023729/The_Consummation_of_the_Kingdom.

—————. "The Death of Christ." https://www.academia.edu/91884498/The_Death_of_Christ.

—————. "The Ethics of the Kingdom." https://www.academia.edu/41159580/THE_ETHICS_OF_THE_KINGDOM.

─────. "The Mission of God's People (the Gospels)." https://www.academia.edu/41159857/ THE_MISSION_OF_GODS_PEOPLE_THE_GOSPELS.

─────. *The New Testament A Taster*. Auckland, NZ: Morphe, 2020.

─────. "The Resurrection of Christ." https://www.academia.edu/92023663/ The_Resurrection_of_Jesus.

─────. "Who is Jesus?" https://www.academia.edu/91877704/ Who_Is_Jesus_Introduction.

Marshall I. Howard and Philip H. Towner. *A Critical and Exegetical Commentary on the Pastoral Epistles*, ICC. London; New York: T&T Clark International, 2004.

Metzger, Bruce Manning, United Bible Societies. *A Textual Commentary on the Greek New Testament, Second Edition a Companion Volume to the United Bible Societies' Greek New Testament (4th Rev. Ed.)*. London; New York: United Bible Societies, 1994.

Montanari, Franco. *The Brill Dictionary of Ancient Greek*. Leiden; Boston: Brill, 2015.

Moo, Douglas J. *The Letters to the Colossians and to Philemon*, PNTC. Grand Rapids, MI: Eerdmans, 2008.

Morris, Leon. *The Epistle to the Romans*. PNTC. Grand Rapids, MI; Eerdmans, 1988.

─────. *The Revelation of St. John*, TNTC. Grand Rapids: Eerdmans, 1969.

Mounce, Robert H. *The Book of Revelation*, NICNT. Grand Rapids, MI: Eerdmans, 1997.

Omanson, Roger L. and Bruce Manning Metzger, *A Textual Guide to the Greek New Testament: An Adaptation of Bruce M. Metzger's Textual Commentary for the Needs of Translators*. Stuttgart: Deutsche Bibelgesellschaft, 2006.

Osborne, Grant R. *Revelation*, BECNT. Grand Rapids, MI: Baker Academic, 2002.

Osburn, Carroll D. "Discourse Analysis and Jewish Apocalyptic in the Epistle of Jude." Pages 287–319 in *Linguistics and New Testament*

Interpretation: Essays on Discourse Analysis. Edited by David A. Black. Nashville: Broadman, 1992.

Patzia, A. G. & A. J. Petrotta. *Pocket Dictionary of Biblical Studies.* Downers Grove, IL: IVP, 2002.

Porter, Stanley E., and Craig A. Evans. *Dictionary of New Testament Background: A Compendium of Contemporary Biblical Scholarship.* Downers Grove, IL: InterVarsity Press, 2000.

––––. *Dictionary of New Testament Background: A Compendium of Contemporary Biblical Scholarship.* Downers Grove, IL: InterVarsity Press, 2000.

Snodgrass, K. R. "Parable," DJG 591–601.

Thielman, Frank. *Ephesians,* BECNT. Grand Rapids, MI: Baker Academic, 2010.

Watson, JoAnn Ford. "Thaddaeus." Page 435 Volume 6 in AYBD.

Witherington III, Ben. *The Letters to Philemon, the Colossians, and the Ephesians: A Socio-Rhetorical Commentary on the Captivity Epistles.* Grand Rapids, MI: Eerdmans, 2007.

See also

"Best-selling Book." *Guinness World Records.* https://www.guinnessworldrecords.com/world-records/best-selling-book-of-non-fiction.

"Biblical Language Center." https://www.biblicallanguagecenter.com/.

"Diatessaron." *Early Christian Writings.* http://www.earlychristianwritings.com/text/diatessaron.html.

"Lycus R. (Ionia) 22 – Λύκος," *Topos Text,* https://topostext.org/place/379291WLyc.

"New Testament Manuscripts and Why They're Important," *Logos.* https://www.logos.com/how-to/study-nt-mss.

"Paul's Journey to Rome." *Net Bible.* https://classic.net.bible.org/map.php?map=jp2.

"The Global Religious Landscape." Pew Research Center (2012). https://www.pewresearch.org/religion/2012/12/18/global-religious-landscape-exec/#:~:text=The%20demographic%20study%20%E2%80%93%20based%20on,the%20world%20as%20of%202010.

"The Seven Churches of Revelation." *Net Bible.* https://classic.net.bible.org/map.php?map=nt2.

www.ingramcontent.com/pod-product-compliance
Lightning Source LLC
Chambersburg PA
CBHW071951290426
44109CB00018B/1986